WITHDRAWN

SAMS Teach Yourself

Microsoft®
Access 2002
Programming

in 24 Hours

Paul Kimmel

 *201 West 103rd St., Indianapolis, Indiana, 46290 USA*

Sams Teach Yourself Microsoft Access 2002 Programming in 24 Hours

Copyright © 2002 by Sams Publishing

International Standard Book Number: 0-672-32098-3

Library of Congress Catalog Card Number: 00-109719

Printed in the United States of America

First Printing: July 2001

04   03   02   5   4   3   2

Trademarks

Warning and Disclaimer

EXECUTIVE EDITOR
Rosemarie Graham

ACQUISITIONS EDITOR
Angela Kozlowski

DEVELOPMENT EDITOR
Kevin Howard
Jason Merrill

MANAGING EDITOR
Charlotte Clapp

PROJECT EDITOR
Leah Kirkpatrick

COPY EDITOR
Bart Reed

INDEXER
Erika Millen

PROOFREADER
Juli Cook

TECHNICAL EDITOR
Jason Merrill

TEAM COORDINATOR
Lynne Williams

INTERIOR DESIGNER
Gary Adair

COVER DESIGNER
Aren Howell

PAGE LAYOUT
Stacey Richwine-DeRome

Contents at a Glance

Contents

PART VII Creating Access User Interfaces 347

Hour 19 Creating Custom Forms and Reports 349

Hour 20 Adding Data to Web Pages 379

About the Author

PAUL KIMMEL is the founder of Software Conceptions. Software Conceptions provides software development and consulting services to small, medium, and large companies worldwide. Paul has been developing business solutions in Microsoft Access for more than 10 years and is available for consulting and development projects (at pkimmel@softconcepts.com).

Paul is the author of several books on Visual Basic and Access programming, including the upcoming *Visual Basic.NET Unleashed*, and is the co-author of *Sams Microsoft Access 2002 Development Unleashed*. Paul is the weekly author of the free newsletter *Code Guru Visual Basic Tech Notes* from Internet.com. Paul resides in Okemos, Michigan with wife Lori and children Trevor, Douglas, Alex, and Noah, all accompanied by their assorted critters.

Dedication

This book is dedicated to my father, Gerald Kimmel. For all the things that embody the very important relationship between a father and son, I love you.

Pudge

Acknowledgments

I would like to thank Angela Kozlowski. I worked with Angela (at the time for Que) on one of my very first books, and working with her again on this project was a pleasure. Thank you for all your help, Angela. And thanks to all the fine people at Sams who continually help make rough text, code listings, and screenshots into a great finished product.

Thank you, the reader, for reading these acknowledgments. You help me honor the people who have helped me over a lifetime, and I appreciate it.

A special, long-overdue thank-you to all the teachers I have had (so far). (I apologize in advance if I have misspelled anyone's name or misrepresented the circumstances in which I have learned from you.) Thank you Mr. Keinitz and Mrs. Shaw at Washington Elementary in Owosso, Michigan. Thanks to Mr. Rice at Owosso Junior High. Mrs. Craddock for not failing me in Analytical Geometry in the 10th grade at Lansing's Sexton High School, even though I probably deserved it; adolescence made me really sleepy. Thanks to James Bond, the Driver's Education teacher at Sexton. Thanks to Dr. Baughman and Mrs. Montgomery, who team-taught English and History. It was Dr. Baughman's doctoral thesis that made me realize writing was quite attainable. Even though I got a well-deserved C and my grammatical skills are still somewhat lacking, I find reading historical biographies and poetry a pleasurable pastime. Dr. Baughman and Mrs. Montgomery taught at Jefferson Community College in Louisville, Kentucky. Thanks to Dr. Forsyth and Dr. Sticklen at Michigan State University. I would like to thank both Computer Science professors for the excellent learning experience and Dr. Forsyth for the encouraging words on more than one occasion. Thanks to Bill Zustiak for teaching me how to fly a Skyhawk, and Craig Fordem for the Roles, Spins, Hammerheads, and Immelman in the Extra 300L in Boulder City, Nevada at the Aerobatic Experience. The last, best teacher I have had is my wife, Lori. Lori has taught me many of life's lessons about love, patience, kindness, and compassion.

Special thanks to Michael Beitz from Germany. Michael found some technical errors in a couple of code listings in Chapter 22. Subsequently, the code was revised for this edition. Thanks, Michael.

Thanks to Stephen King—whom I don't know—for the surprisingly enjoyable *On Writing*, a nonfiction book about the subject of writing. I thoroughly enjoyed this book and was able to take away a couple of good writing tips that I believe will help make my writing a little more lucid.

Finally, my heartfelt appreciation to all the publishers, editors, book buyers, and readers who purchased or commented on the first edition of this book. Feel free to contact me at `pkimmel@softconcepts.com` or the publisher of your edition of *Teach Yourself Access 2002 Programming in 24 Hours* if you need assistance.

Bibliography

Fowler, Martin. *Refactoring: Improving the Design of Existing Code*. Addison-Wesley. Reading, MA, 2000.

Purdum, Jack. *C Programmer's Toolkit*. Que Corporation. Carmel, IN, 1989.

Tell Us What You Think!

As the reader of this book, *you* are our most important critic and commentator. We value your opinion and want to know what we're doing right, what we could do better, what areas you'd like to see us publish in, and any other words of wisdom you're willing to pass our way.

As an Executive Editor for Sams, I welcome your comments. You can fax, email, or write me directly to let me know what you did or didn't like about this book—as well as what we can do to make our books stronger.

Please note that I cannot help you with technical problems related to the topic of this book, and that due to the high volume of mail I receive, I might not be able to reply to every message.

When you write, please be sure to include this book's title and author as well as your name and phone or fax number. I will carefully review your comments and share them with the author and editors who worked on the book.

Fax: 317-581-4770

Email: feedback@samspublishing.com

Mail: Rosemarie Graham
         Sams
         201 West 103rd Street
         Indianapolis, IN 46290 USA

Introduction

This introduction is kept intentionally short. *Teach Yourself Access 2002 Programming in 24 Hours* is for the busy professional. I will just take a minute to tell you why you should buy this book.

This book was written specifically for those who know Access from the perspective of a power user. It was also written as a companion to *Sams Teach Yourself Access 2002 in 21 Days*. This means you will not learn about defining a database, normalization, and Access menus in this book. (The companion book will teach you that stuff.) This book is for the nonprogrammer. If you have a problem and need a solution that requires writing some code, defining a user interface, creating data-aware Web pages, or writing some SQL to solve a problem, this book is for you. (Note, however, that the coverage of SQL is limited to specific problems; the companion book covers SQL.)

Teach Yourself Access 2002 Programming in 24 Hours is not for beginning Access users, but it covers the most advanced topics in programming as you might encounter them when trying to solve a problem. You will find moderate coverage of theory and significant emphasis on problem solving.

This book is a revised addition of *Sams Teach Yourself Access 2000 Programming in 24 Hours*. If you purchased that book, you may find this one a useful 2nd edition. Because the Internet has taken on increasing importance in the last five years, I have expanded coverage of creating Data Access Pages and provided information about publishing those pages, including how to use the PivotTable for Web pages.

Happy reading. I hope you find the experience profitable and pleasurable. As always, you may contact me at pkimmel@softconcepts.com if you have any questions or suggestions.

PART I

Access Programming 101

Hour

Hour 1

What's New in Access 2002

Access 2002 programming is more exciting than ever. Access 2002 has incorporated advanced programming features that promote object-oriented programming. Usability features, such as side panes, enhanced editing and spell checking, menu and toolbar customizations, and speech command and control make using Access easier than ever. Online collaboration is added, via NetMeeting, to facilitate user and developer collaboration over the Internet. The more powerful ActiveX Data Objects (ADO) make it easier than ever to program databases in Access 2002. Access 2002 also enables you to write stored procedures, create database Web pages, and easily scale to Microsoft SQL Server with the Microsoft Access Project.

Collectively, these features will enable you to build database applications more easily, build Web-enabled solutions, scale to a client/server database platform (SQL Server), and write and share object-oriented code among Visual Basic and other VBA-enabled Windows Office 2002 applications.

In this hour, I will introduce these features and demonstrate how to use some of them. Features not explicitly demonstrated in this hour (because they require more space than this hour allows) will be clearly demonstrated in the rest of this book. In this hour, you will learn

- How to customize the enhanced IDE
- How to use the built-in spell checker
- How to configure and use Online Collaboration
- How to use the Data Page Wizard

New Side Panes for Easier Navigation

Access 2002 includes a Task (or Side) Pane View. If the side pane is not visible when you start Access, right-click over the toolbar and click Task Pane from the context menu. The task pane makes it easy to open existing databases and create new databases (from templates installed with Access or online at Microsoft). You can also create a Network Place. Network Places are folders which may reside on your local PC or somewhere else, accessible by a URL (uniform resource locator; for example, http://www.softconcepts.com.)

The Open File group of the task pane contains recently opened databases. The New File group offers quick choices for creating new databases. The Choose File option in the New from Existing File group displays the Explorer, allowing you to search for files. New from Template allows you to pick from various templates on your PC and at Microsoft's Web site. Add Network Place allows you to create a folder that resides at the other end of a URL.

If you don't want the task pane showing up at startup, you can simply uncheck the Show at Startup box.

Customizing Menus and Toolbars

Access 2002 enables you to personalize menus and toolbars. You can display a limited set of menus or toolbars or allow Access to automatically list them based on how frequently you use them. Toolbars can be moved, resized, inserted, or extracted from the menu bar, enabling you to position them where it is convenient for you to work with them. (For an example, see Hour 19, "Creating Custom Forms and Reports." The section "Adding a Menu Item to Access" demonstrates how to customize menu items for your applications.)

Another new feature is the capability to associate a hyperlink to a toolbar or menu, providing you with direct access to resources on the World Wide Web or an intranet.

Using the More Menu Item

Access 2002 only shows a limited subset of the menu items available. The More menu item displays the remaining menu items available for a particular menu (see Figure 1.1). When you select a menu item that isn't automatically displayed, that item is added to the list of items that are displayed without clicking the More menu item.

FIGURE 1.1

Use the More menu item (two chevrons adjacent to the mouse pointer) to display all the menu items on a particular menu.

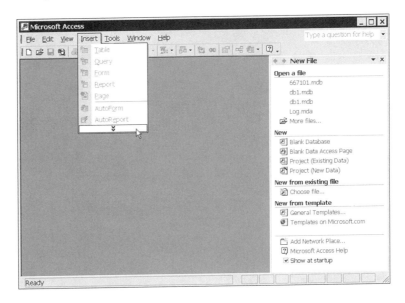

Hiding some of the menu items simplifies the appearance of menus, making them easier to use. This feature also adapts to accommodate your usage of the available feature set.

Personalizing Menus and Toolbars

The Move handle, shown in Figure 1.2 (adjacent to the resize mouse cursor), can be clicked and dragged to customize the organization of your menus and toolbars.

Both menus and toolbars can be anchored to the top of the main window or remain free floating. This feature allows you to personalize the Access 2002 interface to make it easier to work the way you want it to work. To unanchor a toolbar or menu, click the menu or toolbar's Move handle and drag it from the edge of the frame. To anchor a menu or toolbar, drag it to the edge of the window frame.

Many other menus and toolbars are available, as shown in Figure 1.3, that you can manually show and hide. However, these toolbars and menus are typically displayed in the context in which they are needed.

FIGURE 1.2

Use the Move handle to customize the position of menus and toolbars.

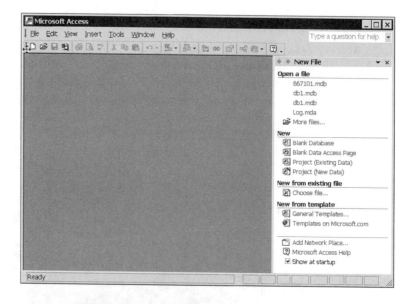

FIGURE 1.3

Right-clicking the main menu toolbar displays a pop-up menu that allows you to display the Customize dialog.

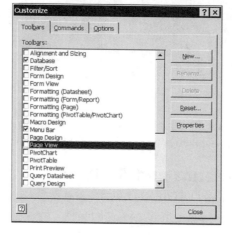

Click Tools, Customize to display the menu- and toolbar-customization dialog.

To display additional available menus, place your mouse cursor over any available menu or toolbar and click the right mouse button. From the pop-up menu, click the Customize menu item. On the Toolbars tab of the Customize dialog, place a check mark next to the toolbars you want displayed and uncheck the toolbars you want hidden.

Assigning Hyperlinks to Menus and Toolbars

You can assign a hyperlink to any menu item of a toolbar. There are several uses for this feature. You might associate HTML help documentation or tutorials to menu items, or you can add completely new toolbar buttons or menu items to your applications to include access to other resources in your programs.

To add a hyperlink to a menu item or toolbar, follow these steps:

1. Open the Tools, Customize dialog.

2. Move the mouse pointer over the toolbar or menu item to which you want to add a hyperlink. (If the menu item or toolbar is not visible, make it visible.)

3. With the Customize dialog open, right-click over the toolbar or menu item (not the Customize dialog) that you want to assign a hyperlink to and click the Assign Hyperlink: Open item on the pop-up menu.

4. In the Assign Hyperlink: Open dialog, shown in Figure 1.4, enter the URL of the hyperlink in the Type File or Web Page Name entry field.

FIGURE **1.4**

The Assign Hyperlink: Open dialog can be used to assign a hyperlink to a toolbar button or menu button.

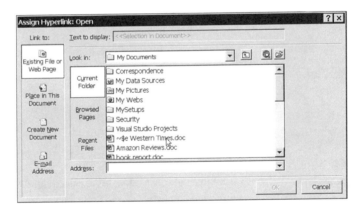

5. Click OK.

To remove the hyperlink, repeat the previous numbered steps, replacing step 3 by choosing Edit Hyperlink, Remove Link.

Spell-Checking Data

The Tools, Spelling menu item iterates through recordsets and finds words that are misspelled. To check spelling, click a table, query, or form and then click Tools, Spelling. Access will check the text in all the fields in the recordset, pausing on fields that have misspelled words. When Access encounters a word that it doesn't recognize, it displays the dialog shown in Figure 1.5, which enables you to modify the text. The options for checking spelling are described in Table 1.1.

FIGURE 1.5

The Spelling dialog allows you to specify how the spelling checker will handle misspelled data.

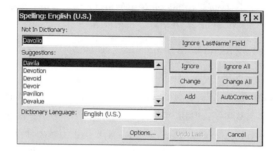

TABLE 1.1   Features for Checking Spelling in Access

Feature Name	Description
Ignore *fieldname* Field	Enables you to instruct the spelling checker to ignore specific fields, discontinuing checks in those fields
Ignore	Ignores this occurrence only
Ignore All	Ignores all occurrences of the current selection
Change	Changes the current occurrence of the word not in the dictionary to the word in the Change To field
Change All	Changes all occurrences of the word not in the dictionary to the selected word
Add	Adds the current word to the selected dictionary
Suggest	Suggests the most likely words
Options	Enables you to select a language, elect to ignore uppercase words and words with numbers, and moderate suggestion options
Undo Last	Undoes the most recent change
Cancel	Closes the Spelling dialog without making any changes

The spelling checker ignores spurious letters that it does not interpret as words. It limits the checking to contiguous letters that appear to be attempts at words. This useful feature is available at design time and runtime; it ensures that users who might not be especially good spellers are adding properly spelled text to the database.

As with all programs that check spelling, Access 2002 can be tripped up by *homophones* (words that sound the same, but are spelled differently and have different meanings). For example, if you wrote the word *too*, but meant *two*, Access won't catch the problem because the wrong word is, in fact, spelled correctly.

This is also true of words that don't sound the same, but are often confused with similar words—for example, *affect* versus *effect*, *disinterested* versus *uninterested*, *fewer* versus *less*, *then* versus *than*, and *worse* versus *worst*. In other words, spelling checkers are wonderful tools, but you can still end up with egg on your face if you aren't mindful of tricky language issues.

Editing Options

Access 2002 has added several editing features that will help you be more productive. The subsections that follow briefly describe some of the new features in Access 2002.

Multiple Undos and Redos

Access 2002 supports several levels of Undo or Redo operations. This feature allows you to roll forward or backward changes you might have made to objects in Design View or in other views, stored procedures, and functions.

Clippit Office Assistant

The Office Assistant Clippit has been placed in semi-retirement. By default, the Office Assistant is disabled. However, you can enable the Office Assistant if you like using it. Select Help, Show Office Assistant. You may also programmatically control the Office Assistant as demonstrated in Hour 24, "Managing Outlook Contact Information," in the section titled "Creating an Instance of Outlook."

Ask a Question

The Ask a Question combo box, shown in the top-right corner of Figure 1.1 (indicated by the text "Type a question for help"), allows you to quickly search for text-related help. Simply enter text in the combo box (containing the grayed text "Type a question for help") to quickly search for free-text information on Access.

Type **Clippit** in the Ask a Question box and you will get a drop-down list of links, including an option to hide or show the Office Assistant. Previously entered questions are stored in the combo box.

Expanded Clipboard Functionality

The Clipboard has been expanded to store up to 24 items in a circular list. When you copy more than 24 items to the Clipboard, the items are added to the top of the list so that the most recently clipped items are stored in the Clipboard.

 To quickly show the Office Clipboard, press Ctrl+C two times.

To show the Clipboard, select Edit, Office Clipboard. The Office Clipboard is displayed as a task pane on the right side of Access, by default.

Speech Command and Control

The Speech recognition tools allow you to use a headset and microphone to control your computer and Access. You can surf the Web as well as navigate around Access. After you install the Speech recognition tools, you can show the Speech recognition toolbar from the Tools menu.

This technology seems to work best if you use a headset and microphone and combine keyboard and mouse use with speech. When you install speech, you will be asked to read out loud about 10 minutes worth of text. This training session is designed to help the speech-recognition software work more efficiently with the way you speak.

It takes some practice to get very high quality text as the following sentences show: "This pair of was to cave in slowly using the speech software. The mistakes in this pair of our reflective of the approximately 85 percent accuracy level of Chino bowl after ten minutes of trading the speech software." Additional training may help you achieve higher levels of accuracy.

Collaborating Online

The Online Collaboration tool is cool! This is an offshoot of Net Messenger and NetMeeting products (which are free to download and use from the www.microsoft.com Web site). The Tools, Online Collaboration, Meet Now menu option allows you to place an Internet call, using your Internet connection, to other users of the NetMeeting service.

This is a relatively new service, so I can't tell you the full impact it will have on how you work and collaborate. I can tell you how I have used it. The service allows voice, audio, video, whiteboard, and desktop file-sharing capabilities. For example, you can make the

1

equivalent of a long-distance phone call through your PC's Internet connection. If your Internet connection is on a LAN, you don't need to use the phone company. If you have a video device connected to your PC, you can see the person to whom you are talking. (Look out Ma Bell and Baby Bells.)

Although the voice quality is not as good as phone technology, it is getting better. Also, you might have trouble getting through a proxy server, such as WinProxy. However, if you have a direct or dial-up connection to the Internet, things work pretty smoothly. The ultimate impact this will have on conferencing and remote collaboration is hard to predicate, but I can envision a scenario where the telephone providers are at a distinct disadvantage and their subscription rates fall off.

Setting Up NetMeeting

You will need a connection to the Internet or an IP address on an intranet to use NetMeeting. If you have an existing connection, click Tools, Online Collaboration, Meet Now to set up NetMeeting and start a meeting. Follow the instructions in the NetMeeting Wizard to get connected.

You will be prompted to select a Directory Service during NetMeeting setup. A *Directory Service* is a program that helps you locate and connect to other NetMeeting users.

So You're Connected. Now What?

NetMeeting is a program in its own right. When you have started a meeting, you select someone to connect to using a directory service (see Figure 1.6). If the name you are looking for doesn't appear in the selected directory service, choose another directory service from the Select a Directory combo box.

FIGURE 1.6

The Find Someone dialog uses a Directory Service— a program that finds other people and computers—to list the people who are online whom you can call.

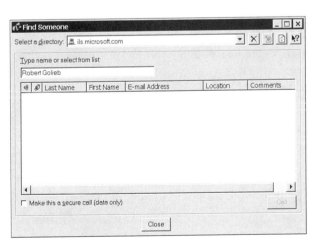

Having selected the person you want to call, click the Call button. NetMeeting will start, as shown in Figure 1.7, and you can begin communicating. The level of communication depends on the hardware you have. If you have a microphone and speakers, you can use the voice services. If you have a video device, you can see the other party. Of course, you can also chat, transfer files, use the whiteboard, and participate in sharing from the NetMeeting Tools menu.

FIGURE 1.7

The NetMeeting program shows who is participating in your meeting. The Tools menu allows you to share files, use a community whiteboard, transfer files, and initiate a chat session.

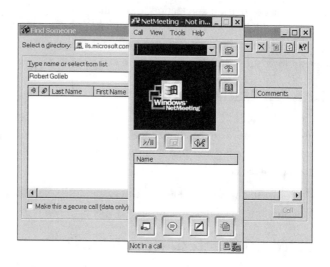

The Tools, Sharing menu allows you to share files on your desktop, including your Access database. This can be a useful aid in debugging database problems, directly helping your users, or getting help from other developers.

Network Places

Network places are folders at the other end of a network connection. This connection may be a local intranet or somewhere on the Internet. Information stored in a Network Place can be public or private, allowing you to more easily share work with others physically located somewhere else in the shrinking world.

Use the Add Network Place at the bottom of the task pane. To add a Network Place, complete the following steps:

1. Select File, New to display the task pane if it isn't already open.

2. Near the bottom, click Add Network Place.

1

3. Indicate the URL (http://www.*address*.com) of the Web address. (You will have to have permissions on that server and may need to log in with a username and password.)

4. Provide a folder name and complete the wizard. If you are running a Windows 2000 workstation, you can install Internet Information Services (IIS) and host an intranet site from your PC.

After you have created a network place, you can store Data Access Pages (stored as external Web pages, created using Access) in the folder at your network place. This capability makes it very easy to create a data-aware Web site with Access 2002. Read Hour 20, "Adding Data to Web Pages" for more information on Data Access Pages and intranets.

Remove Author Information

You may have many reasons for desiring anonymity when publishing databases and Data Access Pages (see Hour 20). Therefore, Access 2002 allows you to hide author information. To remove personal information, check Remove Personal Information from This File on the General tab of the Options dialog, which is opened by clicking Tools, Options.

Introducing ActiveX Data Objects

ADO (or *ActiveX Data Objects*) provides new database objects that make database programming easier than ever. ADO can be used in Access, Visual Basic, Web applications, and any other programming environment that can create a COM object. This means most, if not all, Windows programming languages can use the ADO object defined in Msado15.dll.

ADO.NET is the newest database protocol. ADO.NET is not currently available for Access. Microsoft may eventually incorporate Office into the .NET Framework, but Office XP is not currently part of .NET and therefore does not use ADO.NET.

You can find out more about .NET technologies at the Microsoft Web site.

ADO contains objects that enable you to create and maintain a data source. You will learn all about ADO in Hour 15, "Data Programming Made Easy with ADODB."

Introducing a New Object for Database Security— ADOX

The ActiveX Data Objects 2.1 for DDL and Security object (known as *ADOX*) supports database creation and security aspects of database programming. You will learn about using ADOX in various locations throughout this book, with special emphasis occurring in Hour 15.

Support for Stored Procedures

The ADOX object, defined in `Msadox.dll`, contains the `Procedure` object. The `Procedure` object supports writing SQL stored procedures and storing them with your database. You will learn how to create and use stored procedures in Hour 15 in the section titled "Stored Procedures." Hour 15 also contains examples of using other ADOX objects.

Programming Objects

Microsoft Access 2002 incorporates the Visual Basic for Applications (VBA) programming language. VBA, a close cousin to the Visual Basic language (pre–Visual Basic.NET) incorporates object-oriented idioms similar to those found in VB6. The main idiom in object-oriented programming is the *class*.

Visual Basic has been dramatically improved in version 7.0, which is part of the .NET Framework. The current release of Office does not use VB.NET, but it is likely that some level of compatibility will exist in the future.

A *class* is a user-defined type that facilitates an object-oriented programming style. Classes enable programmers to create modules that contain data and procedures within a single entity. Instances of classes, called *objects*, are the basic advantage of object-oriented programming. The advantage of object-oriented programming is that it allows us to abstract solutions at a higher level than the disassociated data and procedures of structured programming.

Without classes, creating and sharing graphical user interfaces and database objects, such as ActiveX Data Objects, would be much more difficult. You will learn all about object-oriented programming by using objects throughout this book. You will learn how to write classes in Hour 21, "Class Programming Basics," and Hour 22, "Adding Capabilities to Your Data Types."

Adding Data to Web Pages

Many recent revisions to programming languages revolve around adding features that facilitate Internet programming. A Web page is typically a text file that contains hypertext (HTML) or Active Server Pages (ASP) text. HTML and ASP files contain text that can be interpreted by a Web browser, such as Netscape Communicator or Internet Explorer. In that sense, HTML and ASP files contain code, and the browser is a kind of programming language interpreter.

Until recently, defining Web pages that contain data from a database was difficult. However, Data Access Pages in Access 2002 include wizards that automate the process of creating the necessary HTML to connect the data to the page. Office XP incorporates pivot tables and pivot charts—powerful tools that allow users to dynamically revise the presentation of the data.

Hour 20 will teach you how to create data-aware HTML pages that can be viewed in a browser over an intranet, an extranet, or the Internet.

NEW TERM An *intranet* is a private network that is based on the same technology as the Internet. Essentially, an intranet is a "private Internet" where the members are generally associated with a particular company or group and are physically connected to the network.

NEW TERM An *extranet* is a private network that can be extended to allow a specific subset of members to access the network. Whereas an intranet is designed only for the employees of a company or members of a group or community, an extranet uses Internet technology to provide access for a broader range of users, and access is restricted to authenticated users.

Access Projects

Microsoft Access 2002 allows you to define projects based on the Jet engine or Microsoft SQL Server 2000. In prior versions, you had to create an Access database that was contained in an MDB file. Access 2002 allows you to create a Microsoft Access Project file (a file with an .adp extension).

Access Project database files are designed for upsizing your Access databases to SQL Server 2000. This means you can use the Access interface you are used to, and you can use the SQL Server database engine instead of the Jet engine (Access's default database server).

You will need Microsoft SQL Server 2000 installed on your network or MSDE (Desktop SQL Server) installed on your PC to upsize your Access databases to SQL Server.

Summary

This hour covers many of the new features introduced in Access 2002. Being able to collaborate online, use ActiveX Data Objects, create data-aware Web pages with easy-to-use wizards, write object-oriented code, and upsize to the more powerful Microsoft SQL Server database makes Access 2002 a product worth owning and mastering.

Access 2002 can help you automate your day-to-day business tasks with a minimum of fuss, and it can also help you create powerful client/server and object-oriented solutions that you can provide to your users with a Windows graphical user interface or a Web-based interface.

The rest of this book will teach you how to program in Access 2002. You will learn how to write everything from the most basic and essential kinds of code to advanced code that incorporates powerful object-oriented idioms. All these lessons will help you rapidly build business solutions for Windows or the world beyond. To begin employing some of the new features introduced in this hour, complete the "Q&A" and "Workshop" sections.

Q&A

Q Should I spend a lot of time worrying about the layout and customization of menus and toolbars?

A That depends on your tastes. Personally, I hardly ever modify the standard menu and toolbar layout unless it is related to helping me solve a problem, such as adding a macro that speeds up a repetitive task.

Q Do I have to have an Internet connection to use the Online Collaboration feature?

A No. You can use Online collaboration over your local area network. All you really need is the IP address of the person you want to call or the means to find that person in a Directory Server.

Q Am I required to pay extra for NetMeeting?

A No. NetMeeting comes with Access 2002 and is accessible through all the Office XP desktop applications. (Even if you don't have NetMeeting, it is available free online from Microsoft's Web site.) You must be connected to an Internet service provider, such as MSN or AOL, or participate in an intranet.

Q Can I use all the features of Access 2002 using the old MDB databases?

A You can use almost all of them. You certainly have all those features available in previous versions of Access as well as many new ones, including the class idiom and procedures. However, some features are specifically attributable to the database engine rather than Access, and the Microsoft SQL Server database engine is much more powerful than the older Jet engine (the original Access database engine).

Workshop

The Workshop includes quiz questions designed to help you test your understanding of the material covered and exercises to help put what you've learned into practice. You will find the answers to the quiz and exercises in Appendix A, "Answers."

Quiz

1. What action does the More menu item perform?

2. When you assign a hyperlink to an existing toolbar button or menu item, it circumvents the previously defined behavior for that button. True or false?

3. The spelling checker will check spelling in SQL text and simple text data, such as abbreviations and non-words. True or false?

4. What is the name of the object that contains `Procedure` objects used for creating stored procedures?

5. Access 2002 contains wizards that will generate data-aware Web pages. True or false?

Exercises

1. Open the Online Meeting toolbar and anchor it to the top of the Access application?

2. Add a new menu item to the main menu.

3. Rename the menu, using the new name Contacts.

4. Add a command item containing a hyperlink to the publisher of this book (`http://www.samspublishing.com`).

5. Establish a NetMeeting connection with another user on the Internet or your intranet.

HOUR 2

Exploring VBA

Baking soda, flour, salt, sugar, water, eggs, and milk are essential ingredients in cooking a lot of basic kinds of foods, such as bread. In this hour, you are the baker. I will teach you how to combine the essential ingredients in every program. Whether you are solving basic automation problems, such as importing your essential contact information into a database, or managing employee pensions and benefits, you can do it with Access. Every time you work with Access, you will use skills learned in this chapter.

There are five basic ingredients to every Access program. You will learn the basic syntax of Access VBA, the keywords and operators that comprise Access, how to declare variables, how to write functions and subroutines, and how to create user-defined types.

In this hour, you will learn

- About the syntax of Access VBA
- How to use operators
- How to declare variables for storing your program's data
- How to write basic statements

Understanding How Access VBA Works

Access VBA is a programming language. It is basically a language, much like any other. That's a plus because you already know at least one language—probably English. Because Access VBA is a language, it has basic rules, as does any language. These rules are referred to as the *grammar* or *syntax*. You might be familiar with the word *grammar*, but programmers generally say *syntax*, so I will use syntax in this text.

NEW TERM *Syntax* is the set of rules that governs the structure of a programming language.

Access VBA contains several categories of users. Programming languages are employed by humans first, computers second, and then by humans, computers, or both.

First, a person writes a computer program in a programming language. The programming language is usually something like a pseudo-English language that has its own syntax. (There are exceptions, such as machine language and assembler. Although programmers still program in these languages, they are more difficult than high-level languages such as VBA.)

The text you write in a programming language is generically referred to as *code*. After the code is written, Access uses the syntax rules to convert the code into something the computer can use—a machine-readable version. That's why I refer to the computer as the second category of user of your code.

The final users of code can be persons, computers, or a combination of both, depending on the intended purpose of the code. The Windows 98 operating system is comprised of programs used by your computer and by you. For example, I have written Access programs that download and read commission statements from the National Securities Clearing Corporation. The whole process is automated. Windows NT has a Task Scheduler program that actually runs the Access code for commission statements; therefore, the user of the code is the computer that runs the task.

Access VBA already knows how to read code. If you conform to the syntax rules, Access will understand what you mean. There are several things you must learn to convey your meaning to Access. The rest of this chapter will teach you the basic, essential building blocks of writing Access code.

Learning Access VBA Keywords

Access already knows several keywords, but it doesn't have a very big vocabulary. If you compare Access's vocabulary to a person's vocabulary, Access is like a five-year-old child in terms of word recognition. The good news is that you won't have to learn a lot of words to communicate with Access. The bad news is that the combinations of these words are limitless, and programmers use language features to extend Access's vocabulary.

NEW TERM   A *keyword* is a word that is in the Access vocabulary—that is, a word Access recognizes that has some capability associated with it.

The best source for all the keywords Access understands is the online Help reference. I include Table 2.1 so that you can see examples of some of the most common keywords.

TABLE 2.1   VBA Keywords and Definitions

Keyword	Description
As	Used between variable names and data types in variable and argument declarations.
Binary	Used to indicate a string comparison type in Option Compare and a file access type when used with the Open Statement.
ByRef	Used to indicate that variables are passed to procedures by reference.
ByVal	Used to indicate that variables are passed to procedures by value.
Call	Precedes a subroutine call.
Dim	Used to allocate memory for a variable.
Do	Used with While and Loop for iterating.
Empty	Used to indicate an uninitialized variant type.
End	Halts execution of your program.
Else	Used to provide an alternate default condition to an if condition.
Error	Establishes error trapping. It's also a function that returns the error message of an error number and simulates an error condition.
Exit	Used with Exit For, Exit Sub, Exit Function, and so on, to immediately exit the current scope.
False	Has a value equal to 0. Used for Boolean test conditions.
For	Used with next for looping.
Function	Used to declare or define a function.
Get	Used in a Get statement to read from a disk file or the read accessor of a property statement.
If	Used with End If and optionally else for testing values for a Boolean result.
Let	Prefixes a variable assignment or the write accessor of a property statement.
Loop	Last line of a loop statement; causes code to continue until test condition fails.
Me	A variable reference to the object. It's equivalent to C++'s this and Object Pascal's Self.

TABLE 2.1 continued

Keyword	Description
Next	Last line of a For loop; continues until For test condition fails.
ReDim	Used to reallocate memory for arrays.
Set	Used to assign an object instance to a variable.
Sub	Used to declare or define a subroutine.
Step	Indicates an increment value in For Next and For Each statements.
Stop	Pauses execution during testing. (You can resume after Stop.)
Then	Used in an If Boolean Test Then statement.
True	Has a value equal to -1. Used for Boolean test conditions.
Type	Used to define a new type comprised of one or more subtypes.
While	Part of a loop statement; precedes the loop test condition.

When you type a keyword in an Access module, Access changes the text color to blue. The default for incomplete text is red, and the default for non-keywords is black.

Although Table 2.1 isn't exhaustive (refer to the Keywords topic in the Visual Basic Language Reference for all keywords), it does contain most of the keywords. You will need a very limited subset of these words to perform most tasks. If you wish, you can copy the keywords from Table 2.1 to a list and pin them up next to your computer. However, after you have completed a few hours in this book, you will be surprised how easy it is to memorize the most frequently needed words just by using them. Throughout this book, you are encouraged to acquire extemporaneous knowledge of Access by using it rather than by rote.

By themselves, keywords aren't very useful. You need to use them in context. In other words, you need to read the rest of the chapter.

Access Operators and Operands

Keywords comprise only part of the picture. Another part involves operators and their operands. An operator usually takes the form of a single keyboard character. For example, + is the symbol for the operator for addition. It is also referred to as the *addition operator*. Table 2.2 contains a list of the operators that Access can understand.

NEW TERM An *operator* is a symbol that is used to perform a single task. For example, the multiplication operator (*) is used to perform multiplication.

TABLE 2.2 Operator Symbols

Symbol	Name	Description
#	Pound	Used for conditional compiler directives.
$	Dollar	Used in functions to signify that the function returns a string.
&	Ampersand	String concatenation.
*	Multiplication	Multiplication operator.
( )	Parentheses	Arithmetic grouping or array operators.
-	Subtraction	Subtraction operator.
+	Addition	Addition operator.
\	Division	Integer division.
/	Division	Floating-point division.
'	Single quote	Comment operator.
"	Double quote	Used in pairs to signify a string of text.
=	Assignment	Used to indicate assignment of right side value to left hand variable or tests for equivalency, depending on context.
.	Dot operator	Used to access members of types and objects.
<	Less than	A comparison operator that tests whether the left side is less than the right side.
<=	Less than or equal to	A comparison operator that tests whether the left side is less than or equal to the right side.
>	Greater than	A comparison operator that tests whether the left side is greater than the right side.
>=	Greater than or equal to	A comparison operator that testswhether the left side is greater than or equal to the right side.
=	Equal	Tests for equivalency.
<>	Not equal	Tests for unequivalency.

Every operator must be used in conjunction with one or more operands. The number of operands an operator takes is referred to as the *operand count*. Most operators require two operands: a left operand and a right operand. There are some unary operators, however, that take one operand. Most operators are binary—that is, they require two operands. Access has no ternary operators (operators that require three operands), although the C++ programming language does.

> The equals operator is a perfect example of something that has contextual meaning. In some instances the equals operator (=) means assign-to and others it presents an equivalency test. Generally, if = appears in where a test is expected than = tests for equivalency, for example, as might occur in a Do While statement. However, if the left-most token is a variable then = generally means assign-to, that is, assign the right-hand side value to the left-hand side variable.

NEW TERM   An *operand* is what an operator performs its operation on. In arithmetic, 5 + 3 contains the operands 5 and 3 and the operator +. The addition operator adds 5 and 3.

The Not operator is an example of an operator that takes one operand. An operator that takes one operand is called a *unary operator*. The integer division operator (represented by \) requires two operands. An operator that takes two operands is called a *binary operator*. By the way, the forward slash (/) is the floating-point division operator.

The benefit to using Access operators is that you already learned many of the rules that apply to operators in grammar school arithmetic. Arithmetic operations work as you would expect. If you know how to perform arithmetic operations on a calculator, you have already mastered most operators.

Data: What a Program Knows

I like the analogy that keywords and operators are the equivalent of atoms in the physical world. Keywords and operators are the smallest pieces of code. Add data to the mix, and you can write statements. Statements are the equivalent of English sentences and are analogous to molecules, which are made up of atoms.

NEW TERM   A *statement* is the equivalent of a sentence in a spoken language. Spoken languages can have simple statements, such as "I want some," or more complex statements, such as this sentence. VBA statements can be short and simple or long and complicated as well.

A program's data is stored in computer memory in variables. Variables are named chunks of memory that have data types. The type of the data defines the kind of information the data can store and the variable's range of values. To write a statement, you need, at a minimum, a variable (data), an operator, and a value. Before we practice writing statements, you must understand how data is represented.

Table 2.3 contains the data types Access recognizes.

TABLE 2.3 VBA Data Types

Name	Kind	Values
Byte	1 byte	0 to 255
Boolean	2 bytes	True or False
Currency	2 bytes	-922,337,203,685,477.5808 to 922,337,203,685,477.5807
Date	8 bytes	January 1, 100 to December 31, 9999
Decimal	12 bytes	decimal 12 bytes +/-79,228,162,514,264,337,593,543,950,335. With a 28 decimal places, the largest value is +/- 7.9228162514264337593543950335
Double	8 bytes	-1.79769313486231E308 to -4.94065645841247E-324 for negative values and from 4.94065645841247E-324 to 1.79769313486232E308 for positive values
Integer	2 bytes	–32,768 to 32,767
Long	4 bytes	– -2,147,483,648 to 2,147,483,647
Object	4 bytes	Any object reference
Single	4 bytes	-3.402823E38 to -1.401298E-45 for negative values and 1.401298E-45 to 3.402823E38 for positive values
String	10 bytes	0 to approximately 2 billion characters for variable-length strings and 64,000 characters for fixed-length strings
Type	N/A	Creates user-defined types
Variant	16 bytes	Any double or string value

When you want to store some data in your program, you declare the name of the variable to Access. You declare a variable in a very specific way. The following is a syntax example of declaring a variable:

```
Dim VarName As DataType
```

You declare a variable with the keyword Dim (refer to Table 2.1). Follow the keyword Dim by a name for your variable. This can be anything beginning with an alphabetic character. Separate the name for your variable with a data type chosen from Table 2.3. The name is best made up of something meaningful to you; I would recommend whole words. The data type should be chosen for its appropriateness.

Let's practice declaring some variables. For a variable to store a person's name in memory, I would use

```
Dim Name As String
```

For someone's birth date, I would use

```
Dim BirthDate As Date
```

Practice by thinking of some data that you commonly encounter and write the declaration for it on a piece of paper. If you can do this, you have all the basic ingredients for writing variable declaration statements.

Putting It All Together

The statement is the smallest piece of code that Access can understand and use to solve a problem. In the last section, the declarations of variables are examples of declarative statements.

By using the keyword `Dim` to declare a variable, you already have some practice writing statements. Although variables, by themselves, do not solve problems, they are essential pieces to writing solutions.

These are actually examples of valid code statements in Access.

Arithmetic Operators

Arithmetic statements can be used to perform simple as well as complex calculations. Listing 2.1 provides examples of addition, subtraction, assignment, division, and multiplication statements.

LISTING 2.1   Arithmetic Statements with Variables, Operators, and Operands

```
1: Dim A As Integer
2: A = 0
3: A = 5 + 3
4: A = 6 \ 2
5: A = 5 - 3
6: A = 16 * 16
```

Line 1 declares an integer, A. Line 2 demonstrates the assignment (or *equals*) operator. The value on the right side of the assignment operator is 0. The left side of the operator is the variable A, which is assigned the value 0. In the assignment, the operand on the left is assigned the value on the right. The left side is referred to as the *lvalue*, and the right side is referred to as the *rvalue*. In assignment operations, the rvalue can be a constant (such as 5), another variable, or the result of an operation. Line 3 demonstrates addition and assignment. Access performs the arithmetic operation (5 + 3) first and assigns the result to the assignment lvalue A. Therefore, after line 3, A has a value of 8. Line 4 results in A being equal to 3. Line 5 results in A having a value of 2, and line 6 leaves A with a value of 256.

Listing 2.1 demonstrates the fundamentals of arithmetic operations. Although these examples won't be especially useful in a program, they do demonstrate proper usage. You can daisy-chain operations together. For example, A = 5 * 3 + 6 - 7 is a valid statement. It is best, however, to keep operations simple.

If you have many values or variables in an arithmetic statement, I would suggest using the parentheses operators to clarify your meaning. For example, A = 5 * 3 + 6 - 7 is really A = (5 * 3) + 6 - 7.

Arithmetic operators have the same precedence in Access as they have in mathematics. Multiplication and division are performed before addition and subtraction.

Comparison Operators

The comparison operators (<, <=, >, >=, =, <>) are listed in Table 2.2. These operators are binary operators. Each of the comparison operators has an lvalue and an rvalue. The result of the comparison is a Boolean value—either True or False.

NEW TERM A *Boolean* variable is one that can have a value of True or False. George Boole is the person credited with founding the calculus of logic, referred to as *Boolean logic*. Boolean logic determines how combinations of true and false values can be arithmetically evaluated.

Listing 2.2 demonstrates comparison operators by assigning the result of a comparison to a Boolean variable.

LISTING 2.2 Comparison Test Examples

```
1: Dim Result As Boolean
2: Result = 5 > 4
3: Result = 6 = 7
4: Result = 4 <= 7
```

Some parts of Access are contextually dependent. In Listing 2.2, line 3 demonstrates the = operator used for equivalency testing (6 = 7) as well as the assignment of that result to a variable. It may take some getting used to.

Line 1 declares a Boolean variable. Line 2 performs a test of 5 greater than 4. This test evaluates to False. Line 3 tests 6 and 7 for equivalency, assigning the value False to the result. Line 4 tests whether 4 is less than or equal to 7. It is, so the result in line 4 is True.

Logical Operators

The logical operators are used to perform Boolean calculations. They are listed in Table 2.4. Boolean operations can be as simple or as complex as you like. Look at Listing 2.3 for some examples.

TABLE 2.4   Boolean Operator Tokens

Tokens	Description
And	If both operands for this binary operator are True, the evaluation is True. Otherwise, the result is False.
Eqv	Bitwise equivalency test.
Imp	Used to test logical implications.
Not	A unary operator that negates the rvalue (that is, Not True is False, and Not False is True).
Or	A binary operator evaluating to True if either side of the operator is True.
Xor	A binary operator that results to True if the lvalue and rvalue are different.

LISTING 2.3   Boolean Statements

```
1: Sub TestLogicalOperators()
2:    Dim Test As Boolean
3:    Test = True And False
4:    Debug.Print "Test = True And False is " & Test
5:    Test = False Or False
6:    Debug.Print "Test = False Or False is " & Test
7:    Test = Not (5 > 4)
8:    Debug.Print "Test = Not(5>4) is " & Test
9:    Test = (((3.146 > 3.1459) And (7 <= (6 + 5))) Or True)
10:   Debug.Print _
11:      "Test = (((3.146 > 3.1459) And (7 <= (6 + 5))) Or True) is " & Test
12:   Test = False Imp True
13:   Debug.Print "Test = False Imp True is " & Test
14:   Test = 13 Eqv 14
15:   Debug.Print "Test = 13 Eqv 14 is " & Test
16: End Sub
```

Here's the output from Listing 2.3:

```
Test = True And False Is False
Test = False Or False Is False
Test = Not (5 > 4) Is False
Test = (((3.146 > 3.1459) And (7 <= (6 + 5))) Or True) Is True
Test = False Imp True Is True
Test = 13 Eqv 14 Is True
```

The Debug.Print statement sends the output to the Immediate window while running in the Visual Basic Editor. The output is straightforward, except for the equivalency (Eqv) test. The Eqv operator performs a bitwise test. Because 13 and 14 have some bits in common, the result is non-zero. A non-zero Boolean is treated as a True result; hence, the output result is True.

> Keep your logical tests simple by breaking up the testing of values. A good strategy is to use a single test per line of code. Logical tests can quickly become a snarled mess of code otherwise.

The results of logical tests are condensed into truth tables in the Access Help. You can use these truth tables to help you evaluate your logical statements. Also, courses in mathematics are available that teach the calculus of logic. I took a course titled "Discrete Mathematics" at Michigan State University. I would recommend that you keep your comparisons to one per line or use parentheses to clarify your meaning.

String Concatenation Operators

String manipulation is one of the most common kinds of statements. String is a data type represented by a contiguous length of alphanumeric characters. String concatenation is a means to append strings together.

There are two string concatenation operators: the plus (+) and the ampersand (&) characters. Both operators are binary operators that append the rvalue to the lvalue, resulting in one string. Consider the code in Listing 2.4.

LISTING 2.4   String Concatenation

```
1: Dim Greetings As String
2: Greetings = "Hello" + " World!"
3: Greetings = "Hello" & " World!"
```

Line 1 declares a variable named Greetings as a String. Lines 2 and 3 assign the concatenated values Hello and World! together, resulting in the single phrase Hello World! being assigned to Greetings. In this respect, the + and & concatenation operators are identical.

However, + and & can differ. For example, the & operator will concatenate any native data type to a string. Hence, concatenating "My age is" to the number 5 results in the string "My age is 5". The & string concatenation operator performs an implicit type conversion from any native data type to String. Consider the code in Listing 2.5.

NEW TERM   A *native* data type is a type that is defined as part of Access VBA.

LISTING 2.5   Using the & Concatenation Operator

```
1: Dim MyAgeString As String
2: MyAgeString = "My age is " & 5
3: MsgBox MyAgeString
4: MyAgeString = "My age is " + Str(5)
5: MsgBox MyAgeString
```

Line 2 is equivalent to line 4. In both instances, MyAgeString is assigned the string "My age is 5". The ampersand eliminates the need for using the built-in function Str(). (Read more about functions in Hour 8, "Solving Problems a Piece at a Time.") In essence, the ampersand has the built-in capability to perform implicit data type conversion.

Prelude to Advanced Topics

Keywords, operators, and variables are necessary in all programs as very essential building blocks. There are several other essential building blocks derived from these items, including functions and subroutines, user-defined data types, existing objects, and user-defined classes.

In Hour 8, you will learn how to write subroutines and functions. In Hour 10, "Employing Access Predefined Solutions," you will learn about the extensive library of functions available from Microsoft that ship with Access and how to use these functions. Hour 11, "Making the Complex Simple: Creating Your Own Data Types," teaches you how to define user types. Also, Hour 21, "Class Programming Basics," begins the lessons on object-oriented programming.

After you learn to write subroutines and functions, you will be able to solve business problems and program successfully in Access VBA. In order to leverage the most powerful aspects of Access programming, however, you must learn about object-oriented programming. Object-oriented programming includes concepts such as class, object, and component.

Summary

Problems can be divided into three levels of complexity: the statement, the algorithm, and the program. In this hour, you learned about the code used to write statements. Statements use keywords, variables, and operators. All programs are built from statements.

In this hour, you learned how to use operators, including how to leverage what you already know about arithmetic operators to write equations. You learned about the Access VBA keywords, and you learned how to declare and initialize variables.

A *variable* is a named piece of memory of a certain data type. You choose the data type based on the kind of information your program will need to use and store. The most commonly used data types are `String` and `Integer`. These are simple concatenations of alphanumeric characters and numbers.

It is essential that you learn to write functions and subroutines before you can begin solving real problems.

Q&A

Q I want to declare a variable that can store decimal places. How do I do that?

A Fortunately, all variables are declared using the `Dim` keyword as described in the section "Data: What a Program Knows." In this case, you write a statement starting with `Dim`, followed by a name for your variable, the `As` keyword, and the data type `Double`.

Q How do I convert a string value, such as `"02/12/1966"`, to a date value?

A Access VBA has built-in functions for many basic kinds of data conversions. The `Format` function was defined for that purpose. The `CDate` function performs this task for you. The code will look like this: `CDate("02/12/1966")`.

Q How do I initialize the current date and time?

A Access VBA has functions that return the system date and time. These are `Date` and `Time`, respectively.

Q What is a good way to learn all these keywords and operators?

A Remember, you already know many of them. If you have used a calculator, you know how to use many operators. Use the Access Help system to find specific examples and descriptions of those items with which you are unfamiliar. Practice makes perfect.

Workshop

The Workshop includes quiz questions designed to help you test your understanding of the material covered and exercises to help put what you've learned into practice. You will find the answers to the quiz and exercises in Appendix A, "Answers."

Quiz

1. What is the best data type to represent data with decimal points?
2. What is the data type of variables you need to use for the floating-point division operator?
3. What is the difference between the + and the & string concatenation operators?
4. What is the difference between declaring and initializing a variable?
5. What keyword is used to declare and initialize constants?

Exercises

1. Write the statements that define a date variable and initialize it to today's date.
2. Write a statement that calculates the sum of a number and the number multiplied by a percentage.
3. Write a statement that concatenates data into a string and performs implicit type conversion between two or more data types.

Hour 3

Storing Your Program's Data

All programs use data. Access is a kind of program that uses two types of data: permanent and temporary. Permanent data can be stored in a database; this type of data is remembered even when Access is not running in memory. Temporary data, on the other hand, is used by your program in memory but is not kept in memory when your Access program is not running.

Permanent memory involves the use of magnetic media, such as a floppy or hard disk drive, a CD-ROM drive, or a tape drive. Temporary memory is the memory used in integrated semiconductor computer chips, called Random Access Memory, or RAM.

In this hour, you will learn how to store data temporarily in RAM. The temporary RAM memory is where data manipulation occurs. You might store some kinds of data permanently, but no usable data will exist on your hard disks or tapes unless it is used in RAM memory.

Your computer and the Windows operating system handle much of the hard part of using RAM. You must, however, take some specific steps to use data in your programs, and you'll learn about these steps in this hour.

In this hour, you will learn

- How to use the essential data-declaration statements
- How to use and evaluate data with code
- How to use Access pop-up hints
- How to try code in the Immediate window
- How to use the Watches window
- How to use the call stack

How Memory Is Used

Permanent memory and temporary memory are both important to Access programmers. Database files are stored on your hard drive when your Access programs aren't running, and they are copied to RAM when you need to use them in your programs.

Hard disk drives use magnetism to encode data. RAM uses microswitches. Fortunately for us, the computer handles magnetizing hard drives and electrifying semiconductor switches. The computer also handles the accessing of disk drives and semiconductor memory. The operating system gets the data from RAM and disk drives. The workhorse behind these operations is the microprocessor. If you have an Intel Pentium 800, for example, that big semiconductor controls the movement of data in and out of RAM.

The electrical wire along which information travels is referred to as a *bus*. The micro-processor's address and data bus store the information of where data resides in memory. The piece of the puzzle I haven't yet discussed is the bridge between the memory address of data and how you refer to it.

A microprocessor needs some specific instructions and an address to use computer data internally. The missing piece includes the code you write and the VBA compiler. When you write code, you use the Visual Basic for Applications (VBA) language. Access has a compiler that converts what you write into addresses the computer can use.

 A *compiler* is a program that converts text written in a programming language to machine-readable code that the computer can use.

A compiler is the necessary bridge between the text you write in a programming language and memory, which is what the computer needs to carry out your instructions. Memory is where your program does its work. When you declare a variable in your Access program, the compiler assigns an address to that variable.

Declaring Variables

To declare a variable means to write a line of code that contains a name and a data type. In Hour 2, "Exploring VBA," you learned how to use Dim statement variable declarations, but there are a few other declarations you need to learn. As a refresher, the Dim variable declaration takes the following form:

```
Dim VariableName As DataType
```

VariableName is the meaningful name you use to refer to the data in your code, and DataType is the actual type of data you store in that variable.

You already know about the Dim variable declaration, so you'll focus most of your energies on the new declaration types in the next section.

The four basic types of declarations are Dim, ReDim, Const, and Global. The following subsections describe each type, in turn, and offer examples so that you can practice declaring variables.

Dim Variables

In Hour 2, you learned that the Dim keyword is the most basic kind of variable declaration. By using Dim, you are instructing the compiler to assign memory to the name in the Dim statement.

Currently, the memory size of an Integer type is 16 bits, or 2 bytes, of memory. This number of bits means you can store about 4 billion different values in an Integer.

There are 8 bits in a byte of memory. Therefore, a 2-byte data type contains 16 bits. The mathematics of permutations says that you can raise 2 to the power of the number of elements in a set, in this case 16, thus yielding the number of combinations. The calculation is $2^{16} = 65536$. Accounting for both positive and negative numbers, a 16-bit integer data type can store values between -32768 and +32767. The easiest way to cope with data type limitation is to use the Access Help file.

Remember these three data types when getting started: Use String for text, Integer for numbers without decimals, and Double for numbers with decimal places.

Although it isn't important to know how much memory is assigned to variables, it is important to know the data types available for variables and what values are allowable for these data types. This is a job best left to the Access Help file.

The three most commonly used data types are String, Integer, and Double. The String type is used for text. The Integer type is used for numbers from values ranging from positive 32,767 to negative 32,767, and the Double type is used for very small or very large, positive and negative numbers with decimal places.

ReDim Variables

The ReDim declaration type is used for arrays of data. An array of data is data that is contiguously stored in memory and accessed by an index. Arrays are used when you have more than one value of a similar type. For example, if you want a variable that contains 10 social security numbers, you might use an array of the String type. The following example demonstrates the syntax for ReDim:

```
ReDim ArrayVariableName(NumberOfElements) As DataType
```

You place the ReDim keyword first, followed by the name of the array, followed by the number of elements in parentheses. At the end of the line is the now familiar As keyword and the data type. The next line of code is an actual example of an array declaration using ReDim.

```
ReDim SSN(5) As String
```

This code fragment is interpreted as a variable array of five strings whose size can be changed. ReDim is used only with arrays. When you use ReDim to declare an array, you are indicating to Access that you might change the number of elements that the array can store.

You can use Dim to declare an array, but you can't change the number of elements after you declare an array with Dim. ReDim enables you to enlarge or shrink the array as needed.

Arrays are useful when you want to store more than one of a similar kind of data in memory. To use an array, you need to know ReDim. Hour 12, "Managing Varying Amounts of Data," covers arrays in detail.

Const Variables

Use Dim when you want to declare a variable whose value can be changed by the program. Use Const when you mean exactly the opposite—that is, the value of the variable that can never be changed.

There are perfect examples of constant values in the real world. The value for pi, for example, is approximately 3.1459. If you were using pi in an equation, you might want to declare it using `Const`. Here's the syntax for `Const`:

```
Const ConstName = Value
```

The `Const` keyword is followed by the name of the constant. You then insert the equals operator and a value of the appropriate data type. The compiler determines the data type automatically by the value you assign the constant. Therefore, you don't need to indicate the data type literally. To declare `PI` using `Const`, you would write the following:

```
Const PI = 3.1459
```

A popular practice among programmers is to name constants in all capital letters. Access doesn't require this, but it's a nice convention. If you adopt a convention, use it consistently. Your code will appear more professional and be easier for others to follow.

In programming, an unexpected change in the value of a variable is a common cause of problems. A constant can never be changed accidentally by you or any other programmer. Constants are reliable values. Use them as much as possible. When you have been programming for awhile, you will learn to appreciate reliability.

Global Variables

`Global` variables are defined using the `Global` keyword as the first word in the declaration. A `Global` variable is a variable that can be used from anywhere in your program. Here's the syntax for a `Global` variable:

```
Global GlobalVarName As DataType
```

Replace `GlobalVarName` with the name for your variable and replace `DataType` with the type of the `Global` data. The value of a `Global` variable can be changed from anywhere in your program. For this reason, you should limit the number of `Global` variables you use.

If you think about it for a moment, limiting the number of `Global` variables makes sense. When you write code, you make assumptions about the value of variables as you use them. If you are using a `Global` variable, the value can be modified by another block of code. The end result is that assumptions you make when writing your code can be invalidated by another fragment of code modifying the `Global` variable. Maintaining control over your data in a program is critical to reducing the number of potential defects that can be induced.

Data Assignment and Evaluation

A variable is used as the left or right operand in a statement and as a parameter to a function or subroutine. When a variable is on the left side of an operator, it is the left operand. When a variable is on the right side of an operator, it is the right operand.

NEW TERM A *function* is a block of code comprised of one or more statements referred to by name. A function has a return data type, indicating the type of the value you wish to return from the function.

NEW TERM A *subroutine* is a block of code comprised of one or more statements referred to by a name in your program. A subroutine does not have a return data type.

NEW TERM A *parameter*, also called an *argument*, is a variable that is passed to a function or subroutine to be evaluated or modified by the lines of code in the function or subroutine.

When the operator is an equals operator (=), the variable on the left side is being assigned the value on the right side of the equals operator. Listing 3.1 contains five statements that demonstrate declaration assignment and evaluation.

LISTING 3.1   Variable Assignment and Evaluation

```
1: Dim Circumference As Double
2: Dim Radius As Double
3: Const PI = 3.14159
4: Radius = 10
5: Circumference = PI * Radius ^ 2
```

> A line of code can be counted literally as one line of text, but one statement may contain more than one line of text.

Line 1 declares the variable Circumference as Double. Line 2 declares the variable Radius as Double. Line 3 defines a constant value for PI. Line 4 assigns the value 10 to Radius. In line 5, Circumference is being assigned the value of PI * Radius squared. (The caret (^) is the square operator.)

> If you want to define multiple variables of the same type, you can do so on one line by comma-delimiting the variable name. Here's an example:
>
> Dim Circumference, Radius As Double

However, the preceding type of declaration is commonly mistaken to mean that all variables in the comma-delimited list are the same data type. For example, in the preceding fragment it is commonly and mistakenly assumed that `Circumference` and `Radius` are both `Double`. In fact, `Radius` is a `Double` type and `Circumference` is a `Variant` type. When a data type is not clearly indicated, the type of the data will default to a Variant type.

When you declare a `Const` value, you refer to the assignment of an initial value to `Const` as an *initialization*.

Many of these terms can be a little confusing, but they evolved to help programmers clearly and concisely articulate meaning. Although you do not have to master all terminology, it is beneficial to use the appropriate terms when communicating with other programmers.

In Listing 3.1 (lines 3, 4, and 5), the constant `PI`, the variable `Radius`, and the variable `Circumference` are all being assigned to. In line 5, `PI`, `Radius`, and the literal 2 are all part of an evaluation.

Be Explicit

Your code communicates your meaning by the way in which you use variables. Here are two things you should keep in mind when writing your code:

- You should not declare `Variant` data types.
- You should not implicitly declare variables.

These points are discussed in detail in the following subsections.

`Variant` Data Types

`Variant` data types were introduced in Hour 2. A `Variant` data type is a generic data type that incurs a lot of overhead. When a Variant is used, the compiler adds code at runtime to determine the actual data type. Microsoft uses Variant variables in existing code, and Variants are necessary for COM objects. However, it is generally preferable to use the exact data type you need for your variables. This conveys your meaning more precisely and ensures your variables contain the appropriate type and range of values.

NEW TERM *COM* (or Common Object Model) is a standard for writing compound data types that can be packaged as separate chunks of executable code. Often COM objects are referred to as *components*.

Implicit Variable Declaration

Access lets you implicitly declare a variable, which means that you simply introduce the variable at the point of use. Listing 3.2 is a revision of Listing 3.1. All the variables in this listing are implicitly defined.

LISTING 3.2   Implicit Variable Usage

```
1: Const PI = 3.14159
2: Radius = 10
3: Circumference = PI * Radius ^ 2
```

Notice that there are no variable declaration statements. `Radius` in lines 2 and 3 and `Circumference` in line 3 are simply introduced at their point of first use. At first glance, this might seem slick, but after a few hundred lines of code, it can cause confusion. You should be aware of this practice but avoid its use.

As a rule, you should write the statement `Option Explicit` as the first line of code in a module. This prevents you or anyone else from inadvertently introducing implicit variables in your code.

 NEW TERM   A *module* is a file that contains Access code.

When you have `Option Explicit` in your module, Access displays the error message shown in Figure 3.1 if you try to run your code with an implicit variable.

FIGURE 3.1

Variable not defined *error caused by implicit declaration.*

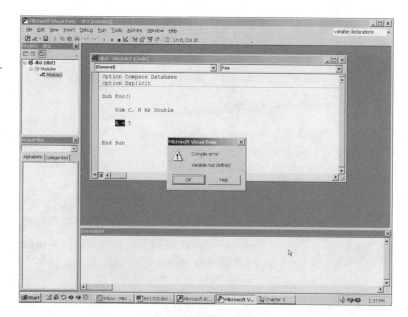

It is easy to keep track of implicit variables when you write a few lines of code. However, any useful code has a tendency to grow and evolve over time. If your program contains enough code, it is important to have as many aids to understanding your code as possible. Explicit variable declaration is the preferred way to go.

Using Pop-up Hints

You now know how to declare variables and write statements. Before you proceed to more complex subjects, let's take a look at how Access helps you manage your variables.

The Access Integrated Development Environment (or IDE) has a built-in mechanism called the *pop-up hint*. A pop-up hint is a little message box that automatically pops up when your mouse pointer hovers over one of your variables. This works only in debug mode. Let me take a moment to explain.

Code is written in a module file. *Module* is Access's term for a file that contains programming language text. Almost all code, except for statements such as `Option Explicit`, is written in subroutines or functions. (I will explain functions and subroutines in Hour 8, "Solving Problems a Piece at a Time." For now, I will provide an example that you can copy directly.) After you have at least one function or subroutine, you can test your code line by line.

Setting Up Test Code

Debugging mode refers to running your code while you are looking at the lines of code. This is accomplished in the Microsoft Visual Basic editor. Because Visual Basic for Applications (VBA) is used in desktop tools besides Access, such as Excel, Microsoft reuses the same Visual Basic editor for code (see Figure 3.2). This is a lot of information, but a couple of examples will help you.

Follow these steps for a demonstration:

1. Open Access 2002.
2. In the New side pane, select Blank Database or click File, New from the menu.
3. In the File New Database dialog use the default database name and click the Create button. (Or, you can give the database a name that is meaningful to you as I did with the ISBN, chapter scheme shown in Figure 3.2.)
4. In the Database dialog, select Modules in the Objects group on the left and click New. This will invoke the Visual Basic editor and create a new module (refer to Figure 3.2).

You are now ready to proceed. If you completed steps 1 through 4, you are looking at the Microsoft Visual Basic editor with a module named Module1 on your desktop. This is where you write your code. For now, just add the code in Listing 3.3. (This is basically the code from Listing 3.1 with a subroutine wrapped around it.)

3

FIGURE 3.2

Access shares the Microsoft Visual Basic editor for editing VBA code (Note: I named my database 661703.mdb to coin-cide with the ISBN and chapter number. By default your database will be db1.mdb or something similar. Name the database something that makes sense to you.)

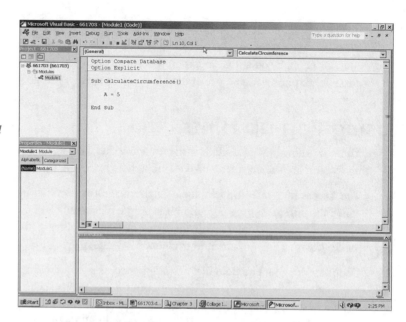

LISTING 3.3   A Subroutine with the Code from Listing 3.1

```
 1:  Sub CalculateCircumference()
 2:    Dim Circumference As Double, Radius As Double
 3:    Const PI = 3.14159
 4:    Radius = 10
 5:    Circumference = PI * Radius ^ 2
 6:  End Sub
 7:
 8:  Sub CallCalculate()
 9:    Call CalculateCircumference
10:  End Sub
```

For now, if you want to try the example, just focus on the code on lines 2 through 5 but copy, excluding the line numbers, all six lines verbatim. I will be referring to this code throughout the chapter to demonstrate how Access provides you with helpful tools for writing code. Lines 8 through 10 are used to test the CalculateCircumference subroutine. Lines 8 through 10 are used to demonstrate how the Call Stack works in the section Employing the Call Stack at the end of this chapter.

Debugging and Using Pop-up Hints

You can debug code by clicking the code you want to test and pressing the F8 key. (Carefully follow the steps in the previous section "Setting Up Test Code.") The first line of code to be executed is line 1. This is indicated by line 1 being highlighted in yellow in the editor.

Every time you press F8, the debugger advances the program to the next line of code. Press F8 two more times until the line containing the code in line 5 is highlighted. This represents the location of the debugger in your program and the next line of code that will be run.

You now have some values for PI and Radius because those lines of code have been executed. You can inspect the values of PI and Radius using pop-up hints. To see the value of the Radius variable move the mouse over line 4 containing the assignment to Radius as shown in Figure 3.3.

FIGURE 3.3

A pop-up hint showing the value assigned to the Radius variable.

Pop-up hints are useful for quickly scanning the values of your variables while testing your code.

Using the Locals Window

The term *local* refers to variables defined in subroutines and functions. Locals in Listing 3.3 are Radius, Circumference, and PI. The Locals window is opened in the Editor by clicking the View, Locals Window menu item. Figure 3.4 shows the local variables for the code in Listing 3.3.

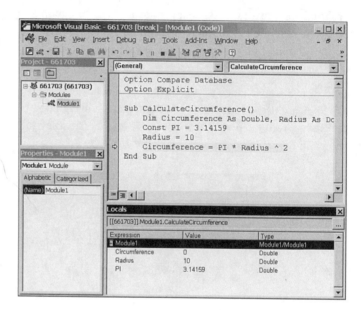

The term *variable* is used loosely to mean local data names that are both variable and constant.

The Locals window is useful because it shows you at a glance all the variables defined in a subroutine or function. More important, it enables you to look at all the values and sub-values of user-defined types. A *user-defined type* is a type that contains one or more sub-types. You will learn more about user-defined types in Hour 11, "Making the Complex Simple: Creating Your Own Data Types."

Using the Watches Window

The Watches window is similar to the Locals window in that it enables you to see at a glance one or more simple or user-defined types.

The Watches window, shown in Figure 3.5, looks similar to the Locals window, but you add only those variables you want to examine in the Watches window. The variables you add can be local to the subroutine or function, but they also can be variables outside of the subroutine or function.

FIGURE 3.5

The Watches window enables you to add variables, as well as expressions, to examine.

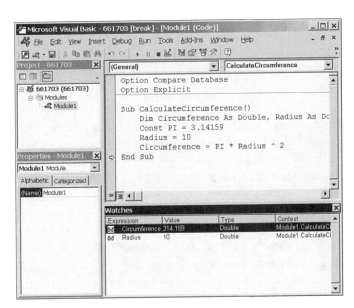

The Watches window has four columns. The Expression column contains a variable or an evaluation using an operator, and the Value column contains the value of the expression. The Type column contains the data type of the expression. This is the data type of the variable or a Boolean, if the expression uses an operator. The Context column is the module name and procedure name connected by a dot operator (represented by a period). For this example, I use the default module name, Module1, and I name the subroutine CalculateCircumference. Therefore, the Context column of the Watches window contains Module1.CalculateCircumference.

Adding a Watch Item

The most important difference between the Watches and Locals windows is that Watches enables you to define expressions that appear in the window. I will use Figure 3.6 as a point of reference to describe the benefits of the Watches window. Variables to watch are added in the Add Watch dialog shown in Figure 3.6.

FIGURE 3.6

Adding a variable watch.

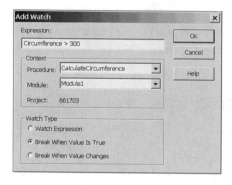

You add a watch by selecting the Debug, Add Watch menu item. Watches are most useful when the code is running, but you can prepare them before you run your code. Referring to the Add Watch dialog in Figure 3.6, you add a watch by placing an expression in the Expression text box. An expression can be just a variable name, or you can use an operator expression, such as Circumference > 300. The context can be set manually; by default, the Watches window uses the current context. *Context* refers to where the debugger is currently stopped, indicated by the yellow-highlighted line of code. The Procedure text box specifies the function or subroutine. The Module text box specifies the current module, by default; however, keep mind that your program can have more than one module. The key part of the Add Watch dialog is the Watch Type area (refer to Figure 3.6).

The Watch Type area enables you to instruct the editor under what condition, relative to the watch expression, the debugger should stop. In Figure 3.6, I selected the Break When Value Is True watch type. Therefore, when Circumference is greater than 300, represented by the expression Circumference > 300, the debugger stops.

If you are using the F8 key to step through the code, your program executes only one line at a time. However, if you want to stop the program only if the expression is True, you can press the F5 key.

Editing Watches

The Edit Watch dialog is the same as the Add Watch dialog. The only difference is that when you open the Edit Watch dialog, it contains the currently selected expression in the Watches window. To edit a watch, perform the following steps:

1. Click the watch value you want to edit in the Watch window.
2. Click the Debug menu.
3. Click Edit Watch.

The Edit Watch dialog should open with the expression you selected in the Watches window. The Edit Watch dialog is similar to the add Watch dialog; the caption of the Edit Watch window is "Edit Watch" and the Edit Watch window contains an additional Delete button, to allow you to remove the watch.

Using Quick Watches

You can use a *quick watch* when you want to take a quick peek at the value of a variable or an expression already defined in your code. For example, you could perform a quick watch on the expression `Radius ^ 2` to evaluate only that part of the expression. Follow these steps to complete a quick watch:

1. While your program is in debug mode and paused, highlight the expression you want to evaluate.

2. Click the Debug menu.

3. Click the Quick Watch menu item.

If you perform the preceding steps over `Radius ^ 2`, you will see a Quick Watch dialog similar to the one shown in Figure 3.7.

FIGURE 3.7

Use the Quick Watch dialog to evaluate variables and sub-expressions quickly.

As you may recall from Listing 3.3, `Radius` was assigned the value `10`. The square of 10 is, of course, 100. The watch and quick watch are useful tools for testing your programming and learning to use different kinds of data.

Running Code in the Immediate Window

The Immediate window is one of my favorite tools. The Immediate window lets you try code outside of your program. You can test very simple or very complex code in the Immediate window. To open the Immediate window, click the View, Immediate Window menu item in the editor.

The Immediate window takes some getting used to because there are few limitations on the code you can write and test in the Immediate window (see Figure 3.8).

FIGURE 3.8

The Immediate window used to print the value of the constant PI.

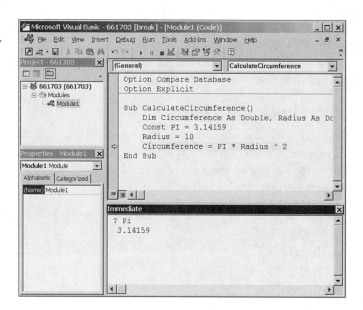

To run code in the Immediate window, open the Immediate window, type code in the window, and press the Enter key. Try these steps to print the value of the constant PI from Listing 3.3:

1. Step through the code in Listing 3.3 until you get to line 5.

2. Click View, Immediate Window to open the Immediate window.

3. Click the Immediate window to select it.

4. Type ? PI in the Immediate window. (? is the abbreviated version of the print command; ? is a remnant from older versions of Basic. If you type ? in your code the Visual Basic Editor will expand ? to Print. For example, Debug.? Pi is converted to Debug.Print Pi.)

5. Press Enter.

The value assigned to PI, 3.14159, is shown in Figure 3.8. Listing 3.4 demonstrates that you can write complex code in the Immediate window.

LISTING 3.4   Immediate Code That Opens and Reads a Text File from Your Computer

```
1: open "c:\winnt\win.ini" for input as #1
2: line input #1, s
3: print s
4: close #1
```

Line 1 opens the file `c:\winnt\win.ini`, which is on every Windows computer. Line 2 uses the `Line Input` command to read the first line of text from the opened file referred to by the handle #1. Line 3 prints the value read into the implicit variable. The output from line 3 on my PC running Windows 2000 is

```
; for 16-bit app support
```

Line 4 closes the file. The Immediate window is a great place to test your code ideas before implementing them in your program.

Employing the Call Stack

The word *call* originates from the assembly language instruction of the same name. VBA still allows you to type `Call` before the name of the procedure. In a very technical sense, a call instruction indicates to the computer that the Code Segment and Instruction Pointer registers in the CPU need to begin processing the instructions at the address indicated by the CS:IP address (this is a 16-bit address, but essentially the same thing occurs in 32-bit Windows, too). A stack frame is created for allocating local variables, the current CS:IP address is stored on the stack, and local variables are allocated just after the call cs:ip instruction occurs. This is nuts and bolts assembler stuff.

For our purposes, *call* means the same thing, but we understand it simply to mean "go and execute the procedure named in the code." Because the call is indicated by name (and address), the debugger can examine the call stack to look at all the locations in which a procedure was called. This list of calls is referred to as the *call stack*. In the Visual Basic editor, you can view the call stack, as shown in Figure 3.9.

FIGURE 3.9

The Call Stack dialog showing the most recent procedure called, followed by the next most recent. It enables you to follow the actual operation of your program.

Why would you want to use a call stack? The answer is, if you run into trouble, it is often helpful to be able to deduce exactly the flow of control your program is following to determine where an error has occurred. From Figure 3.9, you can see that procedures are listed from most recent to least recent. Like Hansel and Gretel with their breadcrumbs, you can backtrack to figure out where your program went awry.

To backtrack to any location in your code, simply double-click an item in the Call Stack dialog, and the editor will reposition the cursor to the location in your code where the branch occurred (that is, where the call occurred).

Summary

By now, you have mastered using variables. All that is left to do is to gain a diversity of experience with the techniques learned in this hour. You learned how to declare a variety of variable types. By practicing with different variable types and assigning data to those variables, you will perfect the capability to use the most integral part of all programs— data.

You also learned how to use the Popup Hints, the Locals and Watches windows, and the Immediate window. These debugging tools are useful in testing and perfecting your programs at the data and expression levels. You will see these again in later chapters.

Q&A

Q Can I declare more than one variable in a declaration statement?

A Yes. However, keep in mind that nonspecific comma-delimited variables will be `Variant` types.

Q Can I declare constants in one place and use them in more than one place?

A Yes. Constants are declared at the top of the module, just as `Global` variables are. Effectively, a constant declared outside of a function or subroutine is `Global`. These are the safest kind of `Global` variables because their values are unchangeable.

Q Can I experiment with different implementations of the same solution without writing different functions and subroutines?

A Yes. This is one possible use for the Immediate window.

Workshop

The Workshop includes quiz questions designed to help you test your understanding of the material covered and exercises to help put what you've learned to practice. You will find the answers to the quiz and exercises in Appendix A, "Answers."

Quiz

1. What are the differences between an explicit and an implicit variable declaration?

2. How do you enforce explicit variable declarations?

3. What is the `ReDim` declaration type used for?

4. Where are global variables defined?

5. What kinds of data can be assigned to `Variant` variables? Should `Variant` variables be commonly used?

Exercises

1. Write a constant definition for `PI` outside of the `CalculateCircumference` subroutine from Listing 3.3.

2. Modify the code in Listing 3.3 to use the new constant `PI`.

3. Write the statement that declares a dynamic array of 10 `Double` precision numbers.

3

HOUR 4

Controlling Program Flow and Performing Calculations

Thus far, you have learned about operators, keywords, variables, and statements. This hour teaches you about specific kinds of statements—equations. For our purposes, an *equation* is a statement that contains an operator and variable operands.

Almost every kind of statement, in every program you will write, will use one or more of the operators in this hour. Operators enable you to control program flow, perform arithmetic calculations, and concatenate and format text data.

In this hour, you will learn

- About operator count
- How to write common kinds of equations
- How to perform data comparisons
- How to use truth tables to manage data

What Goes into an Equation

An *equation* is a statement that contains an operator. You will write logical, arithmetic, comparison, and concatenating equations in most all your programs. In this hour, you will learn all about the operators that go into these equations. First, however, you will learn about the operands that comprise the data you will use.

As you might recall from Hour 2, "Exploring VBA," in the section titled "Access Operators and Operands," an *operand* is the data that an operator uses in an equation. As an example, recall that the addition operator (+) requires two operands. The addition operator has a lhs (left-hand-side) operand and a rhs (right-hand-side) operand. In the equation 2 + 3, the lhs operand is 2 and the rhs operand is 3.

| NEW TERM | *Equations* are statements that use arithmetic, logical, concatenating, or comparison operators. |

In this section, you will learn about all the different kinds of operands used in equations.

Equation Data

Every equation has at least one operand. An operand can be one of several kinds of data. An operand can be a literal value, a variable, a constant, a global value, or the result of a function.

Additionally, every data type can be used as an operand for at least one operator or another. The controlling factor for data in equations is the suitability of the type of the data to the type of the operator. I will talk about that later in the hour.

For now, let's look at the different operand types. Remember as you read that an operand can be any data type as long as the operator accepts data of that type.

Literal Values

A literal value is a value that is not represented by a named variable or constant. Examples of literal values are shown in Listing 4.1.

LISTING 4.1   Examples of Literal Values

```
1: 13
2: "http://www.softconcepts.com"
3: "(555) 123-4567"
4: 10#
5: "A"
6: 3.14159
7: False
```

A *literal* is a value that stands for itself as opposed to representing some other value. For example, #13 is the literal value for a carriage return and vbCrLf is a constant representing the carriage return and line feed pair of characters, not a literal.

In line 1, the number 5 is clearly the value 5. You can use literal values of any data type, as long as that type suits the operator. Line 4 is a little unusual. The pound (#) symbol after the number 10 tells the Access compiler to treat the value 10 as a Double precision type instead of an Integer type.

Variables

The variable is our familiar friend from Hour 3, "Storing Your Program's Data." A *variable* is a name that represents a value and a type. Some operators will be particular about the type of the data with which you use them. The compiler will inform you when you use data that doesn't match the operator in an equation. Access will display runtime error 13, Type Mismatch, as shown in Figure 4.1.

FIGURE 4.1

The Type Mismatch *error is displayed by Access when operand types don't match operator types.*

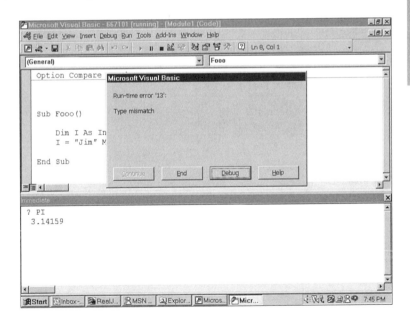

Use variable data when you anticipate that you might modify the value of your data. Use constants when you want to make sure the values will not be changed.

Constants

A *constant* is a name for a value. Constants are immutable; that is, they cannot be changed accidentally or otherwise. Use a constant when you want to ensure the integrity of a value is referred to by name.

A constant of an appropriate type can be used as an operand for any operator, except as the left side of the assignment operator. You cannot assign a value to a constant after the initial value is set. A constant (Const) is initialized at the point where it is introduced in code, as in the following example:

```
Const MyConst = 5
```

The data type of the constant is implicit. The compiler will automatically determine the data type when you initialize the constant. In the line Const MyConst = 5, the data type will be an Integer type.

Globals

Defining a variable as Global has more to do with the scope of the variable than it does with the type. A Global variable can be any type. Global data can be constant or variable. That means a Global variable can be used just as any other variable. Defining data as Global simply increases the number of places in your code it can be used. Listing 4.2 demonstrates how to define global data.

LISTING 4.2   Global Definitions

```
1: Global Const FILE_NAME = "Module1.bas"
2: Global MyInteger As Integer
```

NEW TERM   *Scope* has to do with accessibility. Data that has global scope can be used from anywhere in your program. Data that does not have global scope (that is, it has local scope) can only be used within the scope in which it is defined. Scope is created by many different kinds of code; therefore, I will postpone the discussion on scope until later. I will talk more about scope in Hour 8, "Solving Problems a Piece at a Time."

Line 1 defines a global constant, FILE_NAME. Notice that the only difference between a global constant and non-global constant is that the first word is Global. Line 2 defines a Global variable, MyInteger. The value of FILE_NAME cannot be changed; the value of MyInteger can be modified in your code.

Function Results

You also will see the name of functions used as operands in equations. A *function* is a collection of one or more statements that can be referred to by name and return a result value. Hour 8 covers functions. For now, Listing 4.3 demonstrates how a function name might appear in an equation.

LISTING 4.3   Using Function Names As Operands

```
1: Function GetUserName() As String
2:  GetUserName = InputBox("Enter user name:", "User Name", "Paul Kimmel")
3: End Function

4: Sub Main()
5:   Dim Greeting As String
6:   Greeting = "Hello " + GetUserName
7:   MsgBox Greeting
8: End Sub
```

Lines 1, 2, and 3 define a function that returns a username as a string. Line 4 declares a variable named `Greeting`. Line 5 assigns the concatenated strings `"Hello, "` and the result of the `GetUserName` function to the variable `Greeting`. Line 6 uses the VBA predefined subroutine `MsgBox` to display a message box. (Read the section "Concatenate It" for more on string concatenation, as shown in line 5.)

Rules of the Road

You now know that many different data types and definition types can be used in equations. Learning the appropriate data types and the appropriate number of operands for data will take you a long way on your journey of mastering Access 2002 programming. However, there are some rules of the road that will help keep you on the blacktop.

The first rule is to prefer constant, named variables instead of literal values. If you define a constant and use it in many places, you only have to make one change if you initialize the constant to a new value. If you use a literal, you will have to change the literal everywhere it occurs.

A good second rule of the road is to avoid global values. Global data will lead to confusion and trouble. You and I are good at tracking very small bits of information at a time. If you define your variables when and where you need them, context will make their meanings clear for you and other readers—both now and in the future. It also is easier to avoid accidental misuse of data if the data isn't global.

Finally, consider breaking up long statements that are comprised of many predicates into several, single predicate statements. Long equations might seem cool, but they are harder to debug, harder to write correctly the first time, and often lead to confusion about their intended meanings.

Understanding Operator Count

Programming languages commonly use three kinds of operators: unary, binary, and ternary. These names refer to the operand count. A unary operator takes one operand: a rhs operand. The binary operator takes two operands: lhs and rhs operators. A ternary operator takes three arguments. The only ternary operator I am aware of is the C/C++ ?: operator. Because Access isn't C or C++, you won't have to worry about ternary operators.

There are only two unary operators in Access—the Not operator and the AddressOf operator. Both Not and AddressOf take one lhs operand. In Access, all other operators are binary. This means they are of the form

```
lhs-operand binary-operator rhs-operand
```

You simply replace *lhs-operand* with a data value and *lhs-operand* with a data value. You also replace *binary-operator* with any one of the operators (except Not and AddressOf).

Here is the form for unary operators:

```
unary-operator lhs-operand
```

Replace *unary-operator* with either Not or AddressOf and replace *lhs-operand* with an appropriate data value. The Not operator is discussed in the section "The Truth of Logical Operators," and the AddressOf operator is discussed in the section "Special Operators." Keep reading for practical examples of equations.

Using Arithmetic Operators

I refer to the arithmetic operators as the *calculator operators*. You learned how to use these operators way back in the second grade. (Can you remember your second grade teacher's name?) The arithmetic operators are all binary operators. I won't spend much time here because you already know how to perform these operations. I will just cover the operator symbols and a few arithmetic operators you might have forgotten. Table 4.1 contains the symbols, names, and descriptions of the arithmetic operators.

TABLE 4.1   Arithmetic Operators

Symbol	Name	Description
^	Exponent	Used as in X ^ Y. Raises X to Y power.
*	Multiplication	X * Y.
/	Floating-point division	X / Y returns a floating-point value.
\	Integer division	X \ Y returns an integer.

TABLE 4.1 continued

Symbol	Name	Description
Mod	Modulo	The remainder operator returns the remainder of a division operation only (for example, 5 Mod 3 = 2).
+	Addition operator	Numeric addition (for example, X + Y).
-	Subtraction operator	Numeric subtraction (for example, X-Y).

The forward slash symbol (/) is the floating-point division operator. The lhs and rhs operands can be any numeric value. The result is a floating-point number (that is, a decimal number). For example, 5 / 3 = 1.666. However, if you perform the same calculation with the integer division operator—the backward slash (\)—then 5 \ 3 = 1. Use the division operator that suits your purposes.

You are probably familiar with the exponent operator (^), even though it is not used in everyday arithmetic. The exponent operator is useful for squaring and cubing numbers. Exponential math can be useful in business computing.

The last operator, one that might be the most unfamiliar to you, is the modulo operator: Mod. Modulo (or *remainder*) arithmetic is useful in performing circular arithmetic—checking whether a number is evenly divisible by another number—and it is also used in a whole system of mathematics, called Rings. To see whether a number is evenly divisible, use this equation: X Mod Y = 0.

Performing Comparisons

Comparison operators enable you to test the relative value of a lhs-operand to a rhs-operand. The result of a comparison is a Boolean value. Table 4.2 describes the comparison operators.

TABLE 4.2 Comparison Operators

Operator/(Name)	True	False	Null
< (less than)	lhs < rhs	lhs >= rhs	lhs or rhs = Null
<= (less than or equal to)	lhs <= rhs	lhs > rhs	lhs or rhs = Null
> (greater than)	lhs > rhs	lhs <= rhs	lhs or rhs = Null
>= (greater than or equal to)	lhs >= rhs	lhs < rhs	lhs or rhs = Null
= (equal to)	lhs = rhs	lhs <> rhs	lhs or rhs = Null
<> (not equal to)	lhs <> rhs	lhs = rhs	lhs or rhs = Null

4

If you read the name of the comparison operation starting with the left-side operand, followed by the operator and the right-side operand, the Boolean result is readily apparent. Consider the following example:

```
5 > 6
```

The line of code is read as "Five is greater than six." Five is not greater than six; therefore, the Boolean result is False. If you have a hard time remembering the names of the symbols, make a cheat sheet and post it next to your computer. A good trick is to think of the symbol < or > as an arrow, and the small (pointed) end points to the value that must be smaller for the result to be true. Listing 4.4 contains several statements with literal operands that demonstrate how to use the operators. The code analysis that follows states how you read each statement.

LISTING 4.4   Using Comparison Operators

```
1: Sub TestComparisonOperators()
2:    Dim Result As Boolean
3:    Result = (6 > 5)
4:    Result = (6 >= 5)
5:    Result = ("Hello" < "World")
6:    Result = ("Hello" <= "World")
7:    Result = (True = False)
8:    Result = (False <> False)
9: End Sub
```

Line 1 declares a Boolean variable to which you can assign the result of each comparison. (In general, you will use comparisons in conditional statements. You will learn how to write conditional code in Hour 5, "Learning to Write Conditional Code.") In line 2 and every subsequent line, I used the parentheses for clarity; they aren't necessary, but they do make the meaning clear. In line 2, Result will be True because 6 is greater than 5. In line 3, Result is also True because 6 is greater than or equal to 5. In line 4, Result is True because "Hello" is less than "World". In line 5, Result is True again because "Hello" is less than or equal to "World". Line 6 compares to literal Boolean values. In line 6, Result is False because True is not equal to False. In line 7, Result is False, too, because the statement False is not equal to False is False.

Listing 4.4 demonstrates another implied set of facts. Comparisons are not limited to integer values. You can evaluate Boolean values, integers, floating-point numbers, and strings. String comparisons in Access are not case sensitive. The alphabetic characters are compared as ordinal values relative to their position in the alphabet, regardless of case. Therefore, "hello", "HELLO", and any combination of upper- and lowercase letters have the same value for comparison purposes.

The Truth of Logical Operators

Logical operators can be a little harder to use. If you have never taken any math logic classes, understanding logical operators might take a little practice. The operators in Table 4.3 are called Boolean or logic operators.

TABLE 4.3 Boolean or Logic Operators

Operator	Name	Description
And	And operator	Logical conjunction
Eqv	Equivalence	Logical equivalence
Imp	Implication	Logical implication
Not	Not operator	Logical negation
Or	Or operator	Logical disjunction
Xor	Not Or operator	Logical exclusion

You might have already had some experience with logic operators and not know it. The last sentence is a logic statement. The first proposition is "You might have already had some experience with logic operators," and the second proposition is "know it." The two logic operators used are "and" between the two propositions and "not," which negates the second proposition.

And-logic statements are true only when both propositions are true. Or-logic statements are false only when both propositions are false. Not-logic statements negate any proposition. Truth tables were developed because stating the result of logic tests sounds a little like talking in circles (see Table 4.4).

TABLE 4.4 Boolean Logic Truth Tables

Values	And	Eqv	Imp	Or	Xor
FF	False	True	True	False	False
FT	False	False	True	True	True
TF	False	False	False	True	True
TT	True	True	True	True	False

NEW TERM A *truth table* is used to condense the evaluation of values and operators into tabular format, where the intersection of an item in the left column with an item in the first row yields the result. You read the truth table by using the first letter (T = True and F = False) as the left operand, paired with the operator in a column, followed by the

4

second character. For example, the intersection of FF and Or is read as False Or False, and the intersection of FF and the Or column is False.

In Table 4.4, in the Values column, F represents False and T represents True. The table is read by matching a value in the left column with an operator in the first row. FF in the first column matched with And in the first row is the result of False And False. The result is False. If the logical operators are unclear to you, copy the truth table onto a piece of paper and paste it near your computer.

Notice that the Not operator was not listed in Table 4.4. The Not operator has its own truth table because it is the only unary operator (see Table 4.5).

TABLE 4.5   Logical Negation

Value	Not
False	True
True	False

The negation of anything is the equivalent of asking for the opposite.

Logic operators have two uses. The first use is in logic statement testing. Listing 4.5 demonstrates logic statements using the operators in Tables 4.4 and 4.5.

LISTING 4.5   Boolean Logic Operations

```
1: Dim Result As Boolean
2: Result = True Or False
3: Result = True And True
4: Result = False Xor True
5: Result = False Imp False
6: Result = True Eqv False
7: Result = Not True
```

Line 1 declares a variable named Result to which you assign the result of the statements in lines 2 through 7. Line 2 evaluates to True. Line 3 evaluates to True as well. Line 4 evaluates to True because the result of Not-Or is True when the operands are different. From the truth table shown in Table 4.4, you know that if both operands (in line 5) are false, the result of the implication is true. In line 6, True is not equivalent to False; therefore, the result in line 6 is False. Line 7 evaluates to the opposite of True, which is False.

And

The logical And operator is a commonly used conjunction in the English language. Remember that in an And statement, the result is true only when both propositions are true. The operands for the binary operator And can be simple variables that have relative True or False values or can be expressions themselves. Listing 4.6 demonstrates some additional examples of using And.

LISTING 4.6   Logical *And*

```
1: Dim Result As Boolean
2: Result = False And False
3: Result = (6 > 5) And (7 = 7)
```

Line 2 represents any variables or statements that evaluate to False. `False And False` equals `False`. Line 3 demonstrates each operand as a logic statement. Although all operators have a precedence defined by the Access language (which I will discuss in the section titled "Who Has Precedence Here?"), it is easy to use parentheses for clarity. In line 3, 6 > 5 evaluates to True. Then, 7 = 7 evaluates to True. Finally, in line 3, each of the parenthetical results is used to evaluate the And operation. The result of the test in line 3 is True.

Eqv

You might ask yourself why there is an equivalence operator when there is the equals operator (=). On the surface, both Eqv and = yield the same result in a Boolean operation. The difference is that Eqv can also perform a bitwise operation. Consider the code in Listing 4.7.

NEW TERM	A *bitwise* operation is an operation that combines the bits of two operands, yielding a new value rather than a Boolean True or False.

LISTING 4.7   Comparing the = Operator to the *Eqv* Operator

```
1: Dim I As Integer
2: Dim B As Boolean
3: B = (5 = 7)
4: I = (5 Eqv 7)
```

The result of a comparison with = on two integers is a Boolean value. The result of the comparison of two integers using Eqv is an integer. Line 3 results in the Boolean value False. Line 4 results in I having the value -3.

When performing a Boolean comparison, remember that the equals operator and the equivalence operator perform identically. When performing tests on integer values, the equals operator still performs a logical test, but the equivalence operator performs a bit-wise arithmetic operation. Read the section, "Bitwise Operations," later in this hour, for more information on operations on bits.

Imp

The implication operator is used for logical implication statements. Implication is a study of math logic that describes the truthfulness of propositions. If I say, "When Charlie wears his red hat, he is in a grumpy mood," Charlie's wearing his red hat implies that Charlie is grumpy. If Charlie isn't wearing his red hat, by implication Charlie might not be grumpy. Unfortunately, Charlie might also be grumpy but has merely lost his red hat.

The only time an implication is false is when rhs proposition is false. Unless implication is easy for you, I would suggest using the truth table (Table 4.4) if you are going to use implication.

Or

The Or operator, like And, is relatively easy to understand because you and I use it in speech every day. You will find that Or and And are the most frequently used logical operators.

Like all the logical operators in this section, Or also performs bitwise operations on inte-gral values. Read "Bitwise Operations," later this hour, for more details.

Xor

The Xor operator is sometimes referred to as the Not-Or operator. However, this is a mis-nomer. If you think of the logical exclusion operator as Not-Or, you might calculate the Or value and then negate the result. This will yield an incorrect result. Logical exclusion means if one proposition evaluates to True, the other must evaluate to False for the statement to evaluate to True. That is, when the operands are different, the result is True.

Not

The logical negation operator is the only unary operator of the logical operators. In fact, Access has only one other unary operator—the AddressOf operator. Use Not when you want the opposite value.

Bitwise Operations

Bitwise operations are arithmetic operations performed by comparing bits. You might recall that a byte is roughly equivalent to one character. A byte is made up of bits and has the binary value of 0 or 1. A byte is comprised of eight bits.

When you use the operators in this section and assign the result to a numeric variable, the compiler will perform bit arithmetic. To understand bitwise operations, you have to convert a value into the equivalent bit value and compare the bits of each number at the same position.

Computers use binary numbers because computer memory is comprised of semiconductors that have millions of microswitches that can have two states: on and off. Plus, binary evaluations are faster than decimal evaluations.

It is important to remember that binary numbers are base 2 numbers, and for the most part, you and I work in the world of base 10 numbers (or decimal numbers). The number system determines the actual number of unique symbols used to represent a value. Therefore, base 2 uses the numbers 0 and 1, and base 10 uses the digits 0 through 9.

Each position in a number system is evaluated by multiplying the digit by the base raised to the power of the base. The first position is 0, the second is 1, and so on. Hence, in decimal, 13 is

```
(1 * 10¹) + (3 * 10⁰) = (1 * 10) + (3 * 1) = 10 + 3 = 13
```

The value 13 in base 2 looks like this:

```
1101
```

This is read as "one-one-zero-one," which is

```
(1 * 2³) + (1 * 2²) + (0 * 2¹) + (1 * 2⁰) = (1 * 8) + (1 * 4) +
```

```
➥(0 * 2) + (1 * 1) = 8 + 4 + 0 + 1 = 13
```

The general equation is

```
(digit * baseʳᵃᵈⁱˣ + … + digit * base⁰)
```

where digit is a symbol representing a value in the number system, base is the number system, and radix is the index position of the number from the right-most position. Remember to begin counting at zero from the right.

To perform bitwise calculations, you first convert the number to bits and then compare each digit at the same radix from the right. The Windows Calculator in scientific mode can be used to perform the conversion from decimal to binary. Listing 4.8 contains a brief example.

LISTING 4.8   Bitwise *And* Comparison of Two Integers

```
Dim R As Integer
R = 5 And 4
MsgBox R
```

 Bitwise operations only use the integer value of numbers.

Converting 5 to binary yields 0101, and 4 becomes 0100. The bitwise And in line 2 results in R having the value 4. Bitwise And returns 1 bit at the radix, where both values are 1. The bit 1 is equivalent to True, and the bit 0 is equivalent to False.

Concatenate It

The two concatenation operators are two of the most commonly used operators. The & and + operators, described in Table 4.6, both perform string concatenation. String concatenation is defined as appending two strings together to make one string.

TABLE 4.6   Concatenation Operators

Symbol	Name	Description
+	+ operator	String concatenation
&	& operator	Unambiguous concatenation and implicit conversion

If you use the + operator, it might not be clear to your reader whether you mean to perform arithmetic or string concatenation. However, the & operator is clear and unambiguous. The & operator only performs string concatenation. Listing 4.9 demonstrates both operators.

LISTING 4.9   String Concatenation

```
Dim Greeting As String
Greeting = "Hello, " + "World!"
Greeting = "Hello, " & "World!"
Greeting = "I am " + 5 + " years old"
Greeting = "I am " & 5 & " years old"
```

> The & operator will concatenate strings and perform an implicit type conversion of non-String values.

In Listing 4.9, lines 2 and 3 demonstrate that the + operator and the & operator work identically when strings are used. However, line 4 will display the Type Mismatch error, shown earlier in Figure 4.1. Line 5, which uses the & operator, performs an implicit type conversion of 5 to the string "5" and works successfully. Use the & operator consistently for string concatenation.

Who Has Precedence Here?

Operators have precedence. Operator *precedence* means that some operations will be performed before other operations; for example, multiplication and division are performed before addition and subtraction. That is, multiplication and division operations precede addition and subtraction; they have precedence.

The Access compiler does not rely on you to indicate the order in which you want operations evaluated. Their precedence is defined as part of the programming language. Table 4.7 depicts operator precedence. In general, arithmetic operations are performed before comparison operations, which in turn are performed before logical operations, which are performed last.

TABLE 4.7　Operator Precedence

Arithmetic	Comparison	Logical
^	=	Not
-	<>	And
*, /	<	Or
\	>	Xor
Mod	<=	Eqv
+, -	>=	Imp

Read the table from the top left, column by column, working to the bottom right. All arithmetic operators have precedence over comparison and logical operators. In the arithmetic column, exponentiation has the highest precedence. String concatenation, although not an arithmetic operation, has the lowest precedence. It is, however, performed before comparisons and logical operations.

Memorizing this table presents quite a challenge. You will get more mileage out of your time if you remember to group items parenthetically to clarify your meaning. Additionally, break statements with multiple operations into several single-operation statements, writing the equations in the order you want them performed. This way, you won't have to remember precedence.

Special Operators

There are three more operators you will find useful in later chapters. The three operators are the binary Is and Like operators and the unary AddressOf operator. Table 4.8 describes each operator.

TABLE 4.8   Special Operators

Name	Syntax	Description
Is	object1 Is object2	Checks to see if two object variables refer to the same object
Like	result = string-Like pattern	Checks to see if a string matches a pattern
AddressOf	AddressOf procedurename	Returns the location in memory of the procedure as a number

Using the Is Operator

The Is operator is used to see if two object references point to the same object. An object is a user-defined data type that contains data and methods. You will learn about objects in Hour 21, "Class Programming Basics."

Pattern Matching with Like

The Like operator returns a Boolean result that indicates whether the lhs string is like the rhs pattern. Patterns can be literal alphanumeric characters or pattern characters. For example, ? represents a single character, * (asterisk) represents zero to many characters, # represents any numeric character. The rhs value can be a set of characters to compare to, contained in a set expressed by the set operator [] (see line 7 of Listing 4.10). Listing 4.10 contains some examples of pattern matching.

LISTING 4.10   Pattern Matching with *Like*

```
1: Dim Result As Boolean
2: Dim ZipCode as String
3: ZipCode = "48864"
```

LISTING 4.10   Continued

```
4: Result = ZipCode Like "488##"
5: Result = "Robertson" Like "Robert*"
6: Result = "(555) 555-1212" Like "(555) 555-####"
7: Dim CustomerName As String
8: CustomerName = "Jones"
9: Result = CustomerName Like "[!K-Z]*"
```

In Listing 4.10, line 4 checks to see if ZipCode has the prefix "488". Line 5 compares "Robertson" to the pattern "Robert*", which results in True. Use code such as that in line 5 to find variations of a name, such as Roberts, Robert, Robertson, and Robertsen. Line 6 performs pattern matching, finding numbers in area code 555 with a 555 prefix. All phone numbers from (555) 555-0000 to (555) 555-9999 would return a True value. Line 9 effectively returns True for any strings starting with the letters A through J. The ! means to negate the set; the operation is read as CustomerName Like the set not containing K through Z.

AddressOf Operations

The Windows Application Programming Interface (Windows API) has some special functions that use callbacks. A *callback* is a variable that contains the address of a subroutine or function. Because all variables and procedures are converted to addresses by the Access compiler, having an address of a procedure enables the code to call that procedure. There are times when Windows API procedures must be able to call user-defined procedures.

I want you to be aware of the AddressOf operator, but 99.9 percent of your code will never use this. There are advanced Windows API programming books you can buy from Sams, such as *Peter Norton's Complete Guide to Windows 98, Second Edition*, that cover API programming and will show you how to use the AddressOf operator.

Summary

In this hour, you learned about every operator in Access programming. Almost every statement you write will use the operators described in this hour. You learned that operator count, data types, and precedence all play a role in writing equations.

Comparison and logical operators are used to control program flow. Arithmetic and logical operators are used to calculate results. You will see these operators used again and again throughout the remaining 20 hours, so you will acquire a lot of experience before we are through.

In the next hour, the logical and comparison operators are used in conjunction with flow-control statements. Routing the program flow is one of the most important aspects in deriving solutions. Hour 5 and the following hours build on the material covered thus far.

Q&A

Q How do I format several different variables of different types into a single string statement?

A Use a `String` variable and the & operator to implicitly convert data types.

Q How can I convert integer values to binary numbers?

A Use the Windows Calculator in scientific mode.

Q How can I simplify a complex equation?

A Use parenthetical groupings or break the equation into several intermediate equations.

Workshop

The Workshop includes quiz questions designed to help you test your understanding of the material covered and exercises to help put what you've learned to practice. You will find the answers to the quiz and exercises in Appendix A, "Answers."

Quiz

1. What is one use of the + operator?
2. What are the four groups of operators?
3. What is the precedence order of operators?
4. How do you redefine the natural precedence of operators?
5. What group of operators has the highest precedence?

Exercises

1. Using the sample function `CalculateCircumference` from Hour 3, write a function that demonstrates all the possible tests of `True` and `False` with the `And` operator.
2. In the Microsoft Visual Basic editor, use the Immediate window to evaluate the bitwise `Or` of the following number pairs: 2 or 3; 4 or 5; 6 or 7.
3. Use the Immediate window to calculate the remainder of the preceding number pairs.

Part II
Writing Code to Manage Your Access Data

Hour

Hour 5

Learning to Write Conditional Code

Conditional code is the traffic cop of computer programs. Individual lines of code solve singular problems. A single statement can perform a calculation, store a customer's name, or read an HTML file from the Internet. It is the orchestration of the individual statements that solve a complete, practical problem.

I like the traffic cop metaphor, but many metaphors work. You might prefer the orchestra conductor, air-traffic controller, or bus driver. All these concepts depict what conditional code does. Conditional code helps the program change course at an appropriate time so that the computer executes your lines of code in the right order.

You might ask, at this point, how there can be more than one right order. There is more than one right order because programs work with data, and what is appropriate for one piece of data may not be appropriate for another. A useful example is the income tax. Different levels of income are taxed differently; therefore, you need a different tax rate to calculate different income taxes.

This hour teaches you how to organize your lines of code. In this hour, you will learn

- How to write conditional code
- How to use the Select Case construct to avoid messy, nested code
- How to effectively test multiple code paths
- How to use collections of data

A Programmer's Traffic Cop

I use policeman metaphors because I am comfortable with them. I was a military policeman in the army 15 years ago. I have found that it is useful to think of the means to give you more control over your code in terms of an authority figure.

The most common construct in Access programming is the If…Then…End If statement. For the remainder of this section, I will refer to this construct as an If statement. The If statement can be used most easily in the following manner:

```
If ( conditional-test ) Then
One or more statements
End If
```

 A *construct* is a concept. You can say that the If statement is a construct because it typifies the concept of conditional code.

The unitalicized words in the If statement are keywords. Therefore, you may place any code between the first line and the last line of code, containing End If. In this sample syntax, *conditional-test* is the most important part of the construct. The test can be any code that evaluates to a Boolean result—True or False—or an integer value. If the test is for an integer, zero is False and nonzero is treated as True. Literally, a conditional test can be code that uses logical or comparison operators (discussed in the last hour) or a function that returns a Boolean type. (Read Hour 8, "Solving Problems a Piece at a Time," for more on functions.)

The usefulness of the If statement is that the code between the line containing If and Then and the line containing End If is only run if the test passes. The test can be a comparison or logical equation that evaluates to True or the negation of a False test. Listing 5.1 contains many examples you can use to learn the If statement. (You also can test conditional code in the Immediate window of the editor.)

LISTING 5.1   Using the If…Then…End If Construct

```
1: Sub DemoIfConditions()
2:     Const PROMPT = "Enter taxable income:"
3:     Const TITLE = "Taxable Income"
```

LISTING 5.1   continued

```
4:      Const HIGH_TAX_RATE = "You will be taxed at a high rate"
5:
6:      Dim TaxableIncome As Double
7:
8:      TaxableIncome = Val(InputBox(PROMPT, TITLE, "40000"))
9:
10:     If (TaxableIncome > 40000) Then
11:        MsgBox HIGH_TAX_RATE
12:     End If
13:
14:     Const PROMPT_1 = "Enter user name:"
15:     Const TITLE_1 = "User Name"
16:     Const WELCOME_ADMIN_USER = "Granted admin privileges"
17:     Dim UserName As String
18:     UserName = "guest"
19:     UserName = InputBox(PROMPT_1, TITLE_1, UserName)
20:     If (UserName = "Admin") Then
21:         MsgBox WELCOME_ADMIN_USER
22:     End If
23: End Sub
```

Remember that you can test the previous code by typing it into the Microsoft Visual Basic editor and pressing the F8 key repeatedly to step through the code.

The first thing you might notice about Listing 5.1 is that the code you are now writing is beginning to look like a program and is more complex. I will break this listing down one line at a time. Line 1 and line 23 define the beginning and ending of a subroutine named DemoIfConditions. Lines 2, 3, and 4 define constant-named values containing three strings. The first one, in line 2, is named PROMPT and is equal to "Enter taxable income". Line 6 declares a variable named TaxableIncome as Double. The Double type is a floating decimal point number. Line 8 uses two functions. The code in line 8 will run from right to left, working from inner code to outer code; therefore, the function InputBox is run first. (For now, take this on faith, but you can look up the function InputBox in the editor's Help system if you want a lot of detail.) The InputBox function produces the dialog shown in Figure 5.1.

The InputBox function returns the string data entered by the user in the dialog shown in Figure 5.1. The outer function, Val, is executed after the InputBox function. (Again, look up Val in the Help system of the Microsoft Visual Basic editor, the code editor for

5

Access, if you want a lot of detail on the Val function.) The Val function converts string data containing a number into a Double type. Because InputBox returns a string and TaxableIncome is a Double, Val is perfect for our needs on line 8 of Listing 5.1. Lines 10 through 12 contain an example of conditional greater-than testing of TaxableIncome.

FIGURE 5.1

The InputBox function displays the simple user-input dialog shown.

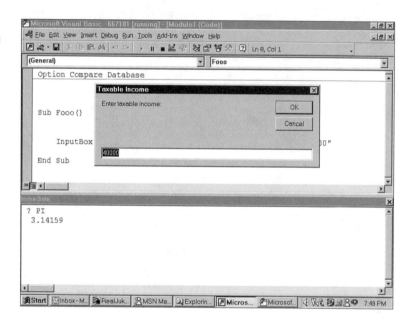

Lines 14 through 16 declare three more string constants for use with the InputBox function in line 19. Lines 17 and 18 declare and initialize a variable named UserName with the value "guest". Lines 20 through 22 contain an If statement that compares UserName to the literal string "Admin".

As you can see from the listing, you can perform numeric tests and string tests with If statements. Remember when you write conditional code to ensure that you test the code when the If statement is True and when it is False.

Using Else

The Else keyword is used to break an If statement into two blocks of code. The top half is run when the conditional test is True, and the second half is run when the conditional test is False. The following syntax example depicts the correct placement of the Else keyword:

▲ SYNTAX

```
If ( conditional-test ) Then
    ' code executed when the conditional test is True
Else
    ' code executed when the conditional test is False
End If
```

Notice that the Else keyword is on a line by itself and splits the If statement into two halves. You can put as much code in either half as you need. Remember that the code above the Else keyword executes when *conditional-test* evaluates to True, and the code beneath Else and above End If executes when *conditional-test* evaluates to False.

Use Else when you have definitive code that should be run when the conditional test is False. The Else clause is optional. Remember to devise a test to ensure that you know what your program does when the True part, the False part, or none of the If statement code is executed.

Nesting Conditional Statements

You can do several things with an If statement. For instance, you might add additional If statements inside of other If statements, above or below the Else keyword. If statements containing additional If statements are referred to as *nested* If statements. On the surface, this might seem like a pretty neat thing, but I encourage you not to do it. To help you recognize nested If statements when you see them, Listing 5.2 contains an example.

LISTING 5.2   An Example of Nested If Statements

```
1:  Sub NestedIfConditions()
2:
3:     Const PROMPT = "Enter user name:"
4:     Const TITLE = "User Name"
5:     Dim UserName As String
6:     UserName = InputBox(PROMPT, TITLE, UserName)
7:
8:     If (UserName = "Admin") Then
9:       ' Some code here
10:    Else
11:      If (UserName = "guest") Then
12:        ' Some code here
13:      Else
14:        If (UserName = "pkimmel") Then
15:          ' Some additional code here
16:        End If
17:      End If
18:    End If
19: End Sub
```

5

The 17 lines of code simulate multiple nested `If` statements that evaluate `UserName`. Although this code is not complex, it doesn't take long for nested `If` statements to become a viper's nest of snarled, writhing code. I was intentionally meticulous in using tabs and whitespace to line up my `If` blocks of code. Generally, this kind of code becomes difficult to read and maintain and should be avoided at all costs.

Nested `If` statements produce long, difficult-to-read code. Avoid nested `If` statements as much as possible. You will learn about a construct known as a Select `Case` statement shortly. The Select `Case` statement helps you avoid multiple `If` and nested `If` statements.

Housekeeping

The code in Listing 5.2 is contrived, but it is the neatest code containing nested `If` statements that you are likely to see. It is too easy to lose track of `If` conditional statements that are nested too deeply.

Fortunately, there is a way to avoid writing convoluted nested code. The first step is to decide that you want to avoid nested `If` statements. The second step is to practice a style of writing code that avoids them.

In upcoming sections, you will learn about the Select `Case` construct and a couple of functions that can help you avoid nested `If` statements. You'll also learn a technique for breaking apart the code that is not conditional—the part that is between the `If` and `Else` and the `Else` and `End If`—into separate functions that name what the code does. However, you need to complete Hour 8 before you are thoroughly familiar with functions.

Listing 5.2 demonstrates what partitioning code is like. Everywhere there is a comment (a line of text preceded by an apostrophe [']) in Listing 5.2, you place a well-named function. (Read Hour 8 for more about functions.)

Tidying Up Nested Conditional Statements

When you have more than one `If` and `Else` in any one place in your code, consider replacing the `If` statements with the `Select Case` statement. (From now on, I will refer to the `Select Case` statement as the `Select` statement.) The `Select` statement has the following syntax.

▼ SYNTAX

```
Select Case Value
Case test-value-1
    ' code for case 1
Case test-value-n
    ' code for case 2
[Case Else]
    ' optional Case Else code
End Select
```

▲

The Select statement has a first line containing the keywords Select Case followed by a value that can be a variable of any simple data type, such as String, Integer, or Double. The last line of the Select statement contains End Select. You may have one or more cases in between the first and last lines. To add a case, simply place a literal or constant value of the same type as the data in the Select Case line of code. Immediately after the line containing the keyword Case and the test value, write the code that you want executed for that case. A Select statement with one Case value is exactly the same as an If statement. At the end of your Select statement, you can place the optional Case Else clause. I would recommend using the Case Else clause because it is designed to handle any values that you don't specifically handle.

Listing 5.3 demonstrates how to clean up the code in Listing 5.2 quickly and easily. Listing 5.3 replaces multiple If statements with a nice blocked Select statement.

LISTING 5.3 Replacing Multiple If Statements with One Select Statement

```
1:  Sub CaseStatement()
2:     Const PROMPT_1 = "Enter user name:"
3:     Const TITLE_1 = "User Name"
4:     Const WELCOME_ADMIN_USER = "Granted admin privileges"
5:     Const WELCOME_GUEST_USER = "Granted guest privileges"
6:     Const WELCOME_SUPERUSER = "Granted superuser privileges"
7:     Const BAD_USER = "You're not getting in here!"

8:     Dim UserName As String
9:     UserName = "guest"
10:    UserName = InputBox(PROMPT_1, TITLE_1, UserName)
11:    UserName = UCase(UserName)
12:    Select Case UserName
13:      Case "ADMIN"
14:        MsgBox WELCOME_ADMIN_USER
15:      Case "GUEST"
16:        MsgBox WELCOME_GUEST_USER
17:      Case "pkimmel"
18:        MsgBox WELCOME_SUPERUSER
19:      Case Else
20:        MsgBox BAD_USER, vbExclamation
21:    End Select
22: End Sub
```

Lines 2 through 7 define various constant values used throughout the code. Line 8 declares a string variable named UserName. Line 9 initializes UserName to "guest". I recommend initializing all your variables immediately after declaring them. Line 10 displays the InputBox dialog. Line 11 calls the UCase function, defined by the Access developers for your use, to convert the string to all uppercase letters, thus enabling you to perform only uppercase comparisons. After line 11, UserName will be in all uppercase letters. Line 12 starts the Select statement using the username as the value the code will try to match. The compiler will perform every Case test, starting with the first one, until it performs all tests, executes the code in the Case Else statement, or runs out of code. If UserName equals "ADMIN" in line 13, the MsgBox function is called with the WELCOME_ADMIN_USER string. If UserName is equal to "GUEST", the appropriate message is displayed. If UserName isn't "ADMIN", "GUEST", or "pkimmel", the Case Else code is executed, displaying the message box shown in Figure 5.2.

FIGURE 5.2

The MsgBox function called with a message parameter and the vbExclamation argument that displays the yellow exclamation icon.

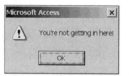

Access has a vast library of predefined functions that you can learn to use. Many of these functions, such as MsgBox, contain many optional parameters. If you examine Listing 5.3, you will notice that I used MsgBox twice with only one argument, and the last time, on line 18, I passed two arguments. The second argument is the predefined constant vbExclamation. To learn how to use Access predefined functions, you must explore the integrated Help files. There are more predefined functions than I could cover in a thousand pages, and it is impossible to memorize them all. Therefore, I encourage you to make frequent use of the Help files.

Want to Go for a Spin?

The While Wend statement is a loop-control construct. The While Wend construct enables you to write code that loops over the same code until the While test fails. The While Wend construct has the following syntax:

```
While( conditional-test )
    ' any amount of code here
Wend
```

The first line of a While loop uses the keyword While and any logical, integral value or comparison statement that can be treated like a Boolean True or False.

If the While test fails, the code isn't run at all. Use the While Wend statement when you want to run the same code—the code between While and Wend—zero or more times. Listing 5.4 contains a code fragment that demonstrates using the While Wend statement.

Conditional tests, such as those needed for the While Wend statement, can be comprised of equations that evaluate to an integer, too. For example, 1 = 1 would compile and work. If you use an equation that evaluates to an integer, zero is treated as False and nonzero values are treated as True evaluations.

LISTING 5.4   Using While Wend Loops to Execute the Same Code Zero or More Times

```
1: Sub WhileWendDemo()
2:     Dim User As String
3:     User = InputBox("Add user:", "Add System Users", User)
4:     While (Len(User) > 0)
5:         MsgBox "Adding user " & User, vbInformation
6:         User = InputBox("Add user:", "Add System Users", User)
7:     Wend
8: End Sub
```

Listing 5.4 demonstrates a loop that accepts all user input, as long as the user doesn't click Cancel or enter a zero-length string. Lines 1 and 8 define the boundaries of the test subroutine. Line 2 declares a variable named User as a string. Line 3 uses the now familiar InputBox function to elicit input from the user. The test in the While loop, in line 4, is Len(User) > 0. Line 5 simulates some processing of the user information; in this instance, the code shows a message box with the response to the input box. Line 6 repeats the request for user input. Line 7 tells the compiler to go back to line 4 and start over. If a user clicks the Cancel button or an empty value is entered, the loop terminates and code execution continues on line 8. Until the loop condition fails in line 4, this code repeats itself.

Always remember to test your conditional code when the condition passes and when it fails.

You also can write an equation that results in an infinite loop. The While test is usually the loop control condition, but if you write a test such as (1 = 1), the condition will always be True. An *infinite loop* is a loop that has a nondeterminant test condition; branching outside of the loop must occur at some other point within the loop. The following code fragment demonstrates an infinite (or *nonterminating*) loop:

 If you try the InfiniteLoop example you can press the Ctrl+Break keys to stop running the code. In Access, Ctrl+Break can be used if your code ever seems to inadvertently get stuck in an infinite process.

```
Sub InfiniteLoop()
  While (1)
    MsgBox "This never ends"
  Wend
End Sub
```

Read the upcoming section "Short-circuiting Code" for more information.

Take It Once Around the Block

A Do Loop statement has two forms. One form uses a conditional test at the start of the loop, and the other uses a conditional test at the end of the loop. The first general form of Do Loop is as follows:

```
Do [{While | Until} condition ]
    ' any number of lines of code
Loop
```

In the preceding form of Do Loop, the test is at the top of the loop, and Do Loop works much like a While Wend loop. If you use While, it is exactly like a While Wend loop. If you use Until, you have to invert the test. A greater-than test in a Do While loop is inverted to a less-than or equal-to test when using Until.

In the While Wend loop in Listing 5.4, I used Len(User) > 0 to terminate the loop. If this were written using Until, the test would become Len(User) = 0 in order to terminate under the same condition (an empty user entry from the user).

When the test is at the beginning of Do Loop, it might not be executed even once. If you place the test at the end of Do Loop, the code in the loop is executed at least once every time. The syntax for a post testing Do Loop is

```
Do
' any number of lines of code
Loop [{While | Until} condition ]
```

You can use either `While` or `Until` at the end of the `Do Loop` statement. If you use the `Until` test, remember to invert the test. Whether you use `While` or `Until` depends on the way you choose to think about your loop-termination condition.

As with the `While Wend` loop, the conditional code can be an integer value instead of a Boolean value. However, if you use an integral result, remember zero will be treated as `False`, and nonzero will be treated as `True`. The code in Listing 5.5 modifies Listing 5.4, resulting in code that performs roughly the same task.

LISTING 5.5   Demonstrating the `Do Loop` Statement

```
1: Sub AddUsers()
2:    Dim User
3:    Do
4:        User = InputBox("Add user:", "Add System Users", User)
5:        MsgBox "Adding user " & User, vbInformation
6:    Loop Until (Len(User) = 0)
7: End Sub
```

There are some subtle differences between the code in Listing 5.4 and Listing 5.5. First, note that I only called the `InputBox` function once in Listing 5.5. The problem with Listing 5.5 is that some additional code is necessary to make sure an empty user is not processed on line 5. Notice that the test from line 4 of Listing 5.4 is inverted on line 6 of Listing 5.5. When you use `While`, you are writing a continuance test. When you use `Until`, you are writing a discontinuance test.

Forgetting to invert the condition tests when converting code from `While` to `Until` is a common mistake. Listing 5.6 demonstrates a slight modification to the `Do Loop` statement that accounts for the input being invalid.

LISTING 5.6   Modified `Do Loop` to Check for Invalid Input

```
1: Sub DoLoopDemo()
2:    Dim User
3:    Do
4:        User = InputBox("Add user:", "Add System Users", User)
5:        If( Len(User) > 0) Then
6:            MsgBox "Adding user " & User, vbInformation
7:        End If
8:    Loop Until (Len(User) = 0)
9: End Sub
```

Adding the modification of the internal `If` statement effectively makes the code much safer because empty users won't get processed. However, it also makes the code in Listing 5.6 identical to the code in Listing 5.4 for all intents and purposes.

5

Iterating Through Data

Thus far, you have learned how to write If, While Wend, and Do Loop statements. The latter two constructs have a terminating condition determined by evaluating some code. However, there are instances when you know exactly how many times you need to iterate through the same code. Often you know the number of iterations needed when you have an array or a collection.

NEW TERM An *array* is a contiguous block of memory referred to by name, whose elements you can access with the array name and an index.

NEW TERM A *collection* is a user-defined data type. The users who defined the collection are the programmers who wrote Access. A collection is similar to an array, but it has some capabilities beyond simply storing indexed data. Hour 6, "Managing Your Database," covers collections in more detail.

The For Next loop construct is available when you know or can derive the number of times you want the same block of code to execute. The For Next construct, in its simplest form, has the following syntax:

```
For Index = low-bound To high-bound
    ' any number of lines of code
Next [Index]
```

The first line requires For, the equals symbol, and To. The first line of code means "Increment *Index* starting with the *low-bound* value, execute the code in between the first and last line, and increment and repeat until *Index* exceeds the *high-bound* value." The *Index* value can be an integer-named variable. The variable I is commonly used and quite acceptable. The *low-bound* and *high-bound* values may be literal values, constants, or the return values of functions. (Refer to the section "Ubound and Lbound" for more details on using bound functions.) The last line of code uses the keyword Next and the named index variable. Although it is not required to use the *Index* variable with the last line of a For Next statement, it is a good idea to do so because For Next loops can be nested. It is easier to match up the For and Next statements if you include the *Index* variable.

The code in between the For and Next statements can be as simple or as complex as you require. A good rule of thumb is that if you need more than a few lines of code, make the code a function, and call the function from within the loop. (Hour 8 teaches you how to write functions.) Listing 5.7 demonstrates a For Next statement, modifying the code from Listing 5.6.

LISTING 5.7 Using a For Next Statement

```
1: Sub AddUsers()
2:   Dim Users(10) As String
3:   Dim I As Integer
4:   For I = 1 to 10
5:     Users(I) = InputBox("Enter user name", "User Name")
6:   Next I
7: End Sub
```

A good convention to follow is to use a plural variable name for arrays and collections, as I did on line 2 of Listing 5.7.

AddUsers now requests exactly 10 usernames. Line 2 defines an array of 10 strings referred to by the name Users. Line 3 declares an index variable named I. Lines 4 and 6 define the boundaries of the For Next loop, and line 5 repeats the request for input, placing each value in the indexed position referenced by the I variable. The Locals window in Figure 5.3 depicts how an array looks in memory.

FIGURE 5.3

Contiguous, indexed memory in an array displayed in the Locals window in the editor.

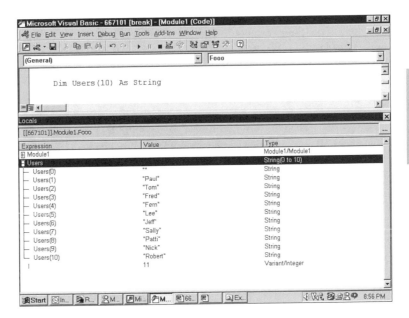

Iterating Forward and Backward

You can write code that iterates forward and backward with a For Next loop. The keyword Step is added to the For part of the statement, along with a positive or negative number, depending on which way you want the For statement to count. Here's the syntax:

```
For Index = low-bound To high-bound  Step step-value
    ' any number of lines of code
Next [Index]
```

The syntax between a For Next statement and For Next with a Step differs only by the Step keyword and step value. Note that I added the keyword Step and step-value at the end of the For part of the For Next statement. If you place the highbound value (that is, the higher number) first and the lowbound value last, you must use Step with a negative number; otherwise, the For Next statement won't execute. You may use a positive or negative Step value and any suitable value; for example, 1 or –1, 2 or –2, or whatever. Listing 5.8 demonstrates a negative Step value.

LISTING 5.8   A Demonstration of How to Add Items to the Users String from 10 Down to 1

```
1: Sub AddUsers()
2:    Dim Users(10) As String
3:    Dim I as Integer
4:    For I = 10 to 1 Step -1
5:       Users(I) = InputBox("Enter user name", "User Name")
6:    Next I
7: End Sub
```

The only change from Listing 5.7 to Listing 5.8 is line 4. Line 4 in Listing 5.8 indexes from 10 to 1. The first element added to the Users array is item 10.

Ubound and Lbound

Many times you will be able to derive the number of elements in an array or a collection, but you will not know the number when you write the code. In reality, it is unlikely, for instance, that you will know that there are 10 elements in any given array.

Because it is better to write flexible code, the creators of Access provide you with the Ubound and Lbound functions. Ubound returns the highest indexed element of an array, and the Lbound function returns the lowest indexed element of an array.

Once again, you can modify Listing 5.8 to make it generally useful. Listing 5.9 demonstrates using Ubound and Lbound.

LISTING 5.9   Using the Lbound and Ubound Functions

```
1: Sub AddUsers()
2:   Dim Users(10) As String
3:   Dim I As Integer
4:   For I = UBound(Users) to LBound(Users) Step -1
5:     Users(I) = InputBox("Enter user name", "User Name" )
6:   Next I
7: End Sub
```

Note that the only change from the previous listing involves replacing the literal values 10 and 1 with the UBound and LBound functions and passing the array name Users as an argument to these two functions. By examining the modification in line 4, you can derive the general syntax of UBound and LBound, which is as follows:

```
Ubound(array-variable)
```

This syntax applies to Lbound as well as Ubound. Ubound and Lbound return an integer value. Replace *array-variable* with the name of an actual array, and—presto—you have code that you only have to write once.

In general, you want to avoid lacing code with literal values. Professional programmers call literal numbers *magic numbers*. A magic number is a literal number whose meaning is ambiguous. If you want to use a constant value instead of Ubound or Lbound, declare a constant, give the constant a good name, and initialize it to the value you want to use. Place the constant where you would have placed the literal.

Iterating Collections of Data

The For Each construct was devised specifically for use with arrays and collections. You will learn about collections in the next hour, but for now you can learn how to use For Each with an array. The application of For Each is the same whether you are using an array or a collection. Here's the syntax:

```
Dim Element As Variant

For Each Element In ArrayName
    ' process element
Next element
```

I showed the declaration of the *element* variable because the For Each loop requires you to use a Variant data type for the referenced item. The For Each statement assigns each element in an array (or collection) to the variable referred to by *Element*. Between the For Each and the Next statements, write any code you want, referring to the *Element* variable as if it were a variable of the data type contained in the array. The last line, Next *element*, tells the compiler to assign the value of the next contiguous element to the variable. The code in Listing 5.10 demonstrates using the For Each construct to display the strings in a String array.

LISTING 5.10   Using For Each to Access Array Elements

```
 1: Sub ShowUsers()
 2:     Dim Users(2) As String
 3:     Users(0) = "Paul"
 4:     Users(1) = "Tom"
 5:     Users(2) = "Fred"
 6:     Dim User As Variant
 7:     For Each User In Users
 8:         MsgBox User
 9:     Next User
10: End Sub
```

> By default, arrays in Access are "zero based." Therefore, an array with a value of *n* in parentheses actually has *n+1-indexed* elements. To specifically indicate whether arrays start at 0 or 1, use the
>
> Option Base *n*
>
> statement at the beginning of your module, where *n* is the number 0 or 1.

Lines 2 through 5 declare and initialize the elements of a string array to some literal name values. In line 6, User is declared as a Variant type because VBA requires the Variant data type as the recipient of each element in the For Each statement. Lines 7 through 9 iterate through each of the elements in Users and assigns the *nth* element (not the *nth* index, as with a regular For Next statement) to the Variant type User. Finally, User is displayed with the MsgBox subroutine.

Short-circuiting Code

Sometimes you might need more than one exit point for your loop constructs. This can occur if you cannot think of a conditional test that will allow the loop to terminate or if there is more than one condition that can cause a loop to terminate. The Exit keyword was devised to enable you to short-circuit a loop if you want to or need to. The following two forms of the Exit statement apply to loops:

Exit For

Exit Do

You use the `Exit For` form with the `For Next` loop and the `Exit Do` form with `Do Loop`. You might prefer `Do Loop` to the `While Wend` loop because there is no short-circuit `Exit` for `While Wend` loops, and it is a desirable attribute of code to be consistent.

Listing 5.7 includes an `If` test inside of the `Do Loop` statement. (Take a quick glance at Listing 5.7 to refresh your memory.) Adding the `If` test is prudent because it precludes processing bad user data, but it is inefficient. Listing 5.7 can be improved with `Exit Do` (the modifications are shown in Listing 5.11).

LISTING 5.11   Short-circuiting to Avoid Repeating a Test

```
1: Sub AddUsers()
2:   Dim User As String
3:   Do
4:     User = InputBox("Add user:", "Add System Users", User)
5:     If( Len(User) = 0) Then Exit Do
6:     MsgBox "Adding user " & User, vbInformation
7:   Loop Until (Len(User) = 0)8: End Sub
```

In line 5, the `Exit Do` clause was added. If the user enters an empty username or clicks Cancel in the input box, the code exits at line 5. As an added benefit, the code is reduced by one additional line, and the `Len(User)` test won't be repeated, thus making the code more efficient.

> I came across a study in 1995 that priced lines of code at about $5 to $8 per line per year. That number has probably gone up considerably in the last four years. Any reduction in the number of code lines that you can accomplish easily will pay off in a reduction of uncompensated overtime.

5

Using the `Switch` Function

The `Switch` function takes a comma-delimited list of test and result pairs. The `Switch` function compares the value of the left side of the test and returns the value paired with it. Listing 5.12 demonstrates this.

LISTING 5.12   The `Switch` Function Uses Test and Result Pairs

```
1: Sub DemoSwitch()
2:   Dim ProductName As String: Dim MatchUp As Variant
3:   ProductName = InputBox( _
4:     "Enter tool name (e.g. Access, Visual Basic, Delphi)", _
```

LISTING 5.12   continued

```
5:     "Match tool to Programming Language")
6:   MatchUp = Switch(ProductName = "Access", "VBA (Visual Basic for
➥Applications)", _
7:     ProductName = "Visual Basic", "Visual Basic", _
8:     ProductName = "Delphi", "Object Pascal", Len(ProductName) >= 0, "<Not
➥Found>")
9:   MsgBox MatchUp
10: End Sub
```

In the listing, the user enters a value assigned to the variable ProductName, which is passed as the test half of the test and value pairs. Three tests are passed to the Switch function: ProductName = "Access", ProductName = "Visual Basic", and ProductName = "Delphi". If ProductName contains any of the test values, the value pair immediately after the test is returned by the Switch function. For example, if you enter "Access" in the input box, "VBA" is returned by the Switch function. Switch returns a Variant data type, thus allowing you to use a wide variety of test and value pairs.

Summary

This hour introduces many constructs related to looping through data. The If statement enables you to conditionally change the path your code executes. While, Do, and For loops enable you to repeat the same block of code as many times as you need to process small or large collections of data. Remember to devise tests that exercise your code when the loops are entered and when they are not.

Several new concepts were introduced in an effort to provide you with examples that are more concrete. I discussed infinite loops and short-circuiting loops and introduced arrays, collections, and VBA functions. Mastery will come as you proceed through the book and practice the concepts you have learned. The Workshop that follows provides you with ample opportunity to master the concepts in this hour.

Q&A

Q **When would I consider using a nested For Next loop?**

A Nested For loops are excellent when you need to manage two indexed elements at the same time, as you must when working with many sorting algorithms or when you are working with a multidimensional array.

Q **Should I use the While Wend construct or the Do While loop?**

A While Wend exists for backward compatibility. It is preferable to use the Do While loop consistently.

Q How do I find other useful functions?

A The Help files contain many good examples, but it is sometimes difficult to find just what you are looking for. The best way to learn of the existence of Access pre-defined functions is to read a lot of code.

Q Which is better—a collection or an array?

A Both collections and arrays are useful. In new code, however, you will want to use collections. Hour 6 introduces this powerful class.

Workshop

The Workshop includes quiz questions designed to help you test your understanding of the material covered and exercises to help put what you've learned to practice. You will find the answers to the quiz and exercises in Appendix A, "Answers."

Quiz

1. How would you define a loop to iterate through an array of 10 integers?

2. If you wanted code in a loop to execute at least one time, which looping mechanism would you use?

3. How might you ensure that code in an If statement works correctly?

4. What is the Exit For statement used for?

5. What is a loop short circuit? Under what circumstances might you use one?

Exercises

1. Use the Microsoft Visual Basic Help system to look up the Switch function. Define a Switch statement to return a first name given a last name.

2. Use the Help system to look up the Iff function. Write a statement that demonstrates the use of the Iff function.

3. Declare a collection object (you can write the code in the sample Fooo subroutine) and use the For Each construct to display each element of the collection in a message box.

5

HOUR 6

Managing Your Database

Congratulations. You have successfully completed five hours and read approximately 100 pages of text. This hour is a milestone. In one more hour, you will be able to apply what you have learned to manage databases, tables, columns, and fields of data.

Thus far, you have been working with generic code that could be used in many kinds of applications. In this hour, you will use much of the experience you have garnered to manage data in an Access table that you will create.

You will see two kinds of code in this hour. I will introduce code that I want you to learn, and I will also provide code that you can literally copy to provide you with a framework in which to learn. I will distinguish between the supporting cast of framework code and the code I would like you to master in this hour, on a case-by-case basis. Supporting-cast code will be covered in later hours.

In this hour, I will place the mechanics of writing code squarely in a database context. In this hour, you will learn

- About Access 2000 compatibility
- How to create a table dynamically
- How to add data to a database with code
- How to manage column and field data with loops and conditional code
- How to perform dynamic searches with queries and code

Access 2002 Is Backward Compatible with Access 2000

Access 2002 and Access 2000 use compatible file formats. Access 2002 can read and modify Access 2000 databases, and you can convert back and forth between the Access 2002 and Access 2000 formats.

If all users are using Access 2002, you may want to convert your files to the Access 2002 format. Read the next subsection for a brief overview of the new Access 2002 file format.

New File Format Provides Better Performance

Converting your databases to the Access 2002 format will allow you to take advantage of future changes to Access. Access 2002 offers an improved file format, and you can save Access 2002 databases to MDE or ADE files.

MDE Database File Extension

You have two options for adding security to your Access database: You can password-protect your database from the Tools, Database Utilities menu, or you can use the Tools, Database Utilities, Make MDE File menu.

Saving the database as an MDE file prevents users from viewing, modifying, or creating forms, reports, and modules. Furthermore, users cannot add, delete, or change references by code to other ActiveX libraries, and users cannot change code.

ADE Database File Extension

When you create an Access project using SQL Server instead of the Jet engine, you will create an ADP project (as opposed to an MDB database). You can add extra security to your Access and SQL Server project and code by converting an ADP database into an ADE database. The conversion is performed from the Tools, Database Utilities menu, but this is only available when you are working in an ADP project.

You will need SQL Server 6.5 Service Pack 5 or greater to create an Access ADP project and use SQL Server for data storage.

Improved Compact and Repair Feature

Access 2002 offers an improved Compact and Repair feature. The improvements help ensure that broken forms and reports are more frequently recovered.

Compacting and repairing an Access database will remove NTFS file permissions if the database is located on a drive that uses NT file permissions.

Creating a Database

You will need a database to work with to learn higher-level skills. As a refresher, I will walk you through building a database and a table. I will use the database you build throughout the rest of this hour.

After you have built the database and the table manually, I will show you how you can dynamically create the same table (or any table) with code. Access is all about database programming. Let's get started.

Defining the Database

Access 2000 is primarily a database tool. What it has in common with the Microsoft Office XP Suite is Visual Basic for Applications (VBA). VBA is the programming language you have been using. VBA in Access differs from VBA in other Microsoft tools, such as Excel, only in its application. In Access you are likely to use VBA to manage database data, and in Excel you'll use VBA to manage spreadsheets.

The discussion in this hour refers to a database with one table: CONTACTS. Before building the table, you will need to create a new database. If you need a refresher on creating a new database, read the following steps; otherwise, skip to the next section.

To create a database file, complete these steps:

1. Run Access 2002.
2. In the New side pane on the right, click Blank Database (see Figure 6.1).
3. Save the database file as `contacts.mdb`.

When you have successfully created the database, your screen should look similar to what's shown in Figure 6.2.

6

FIGURE 6.1

Create a blank data-base using the New side pane.

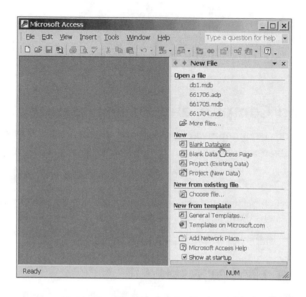

FIGURE 6.2

The contacts demo database.

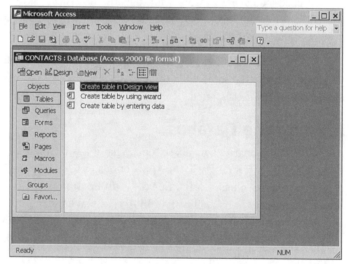

Creating a Table with Access 2002

The next step is to create the CONTACTS table using Access. If you have read *Sams Teach Yourself Microsoft Access 2002 in 21 Days* (the companion to this book) or a similar book, you are already familiar with the Access 2002 database development environment.

I will describe the steps for creating the CONTACTS table as a refresher. The CONTACTS table contains the field definitions shown in Listing 6.1.

LISTING 6.1   The CONTACTS Table's Definition

```
ID, AutoNumber, Primary Key
FIRST_NAME, Text, 20
LAST_NAME, Text, 20
PHONE_NUMBER, Text, 36
EMAIL, Text, 50
WWW, Text, 50
```

If you want to build the table and skip to the next section, feel free.

The numbered steps that follow assume you have created the `contacts.mdb` database and that this database is open. (If you haven't already done so, read the earlier section in this hour "Defining the Database.") To create the CONTACTS table, follow these steps:

1. With the `contacts.mdb` database open, click the Table button in the Objects view (see Figure 6.3).

FIGURE 6.3

Clicking the Tables button in the Objects view.

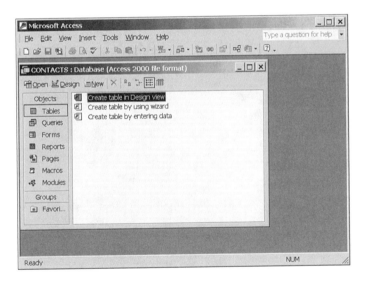

2. Click the New button (also shown in Figure 6.3).
3. In the New Table dialog, click Design View and then click OK.
4. In the Table Design view, complete the design by adding the fields described in Listing 6.1, using Figure 6.4 as a visual guide.
5. Right-click adjacent and to the left of the ID field definition and select the Primary Key menu item to make ID the primary key (see Figure 6.5).

6

FIGURE **6.4**

Define the CONTACTS table in the Table Design view.

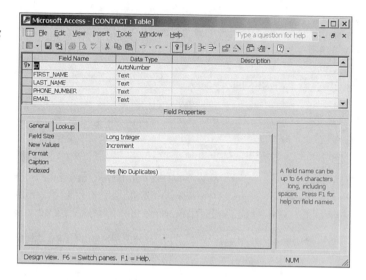

FIGURE **6.5**

Use the shortcut menu in the Table Design view to make the ID field the primary key.

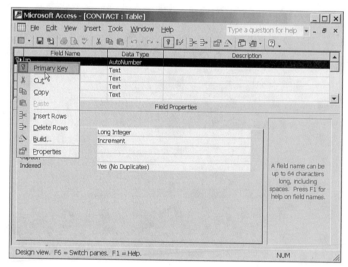

You will be using this table during the rest of this hour. The capability to create tables such as CONTACTS on-the-fly is important. The first thing I will teach you is how to write code to create tables programmatically. Creating tables while your program is running can be a useful skill in your programming repertoire. Before I demonstrate the code version of creating the CONTACTS table, let's review how to create a module in which to place your code.

Creating a Module in the Contacts Database

All the VBA you write is written in a module. A *module* is a VBA source file that is stored inside the Access database. Your database program can have as many modules as you need. When you create a module, it is opened in the Microsoft Visual Basic editor.

I will be referring to a module named *Main* in the rest of this hour. To create the Main module, follow these steps:

1. Click the Modules button in the Objects view (refer to Figure 6.3).

2. Click the New button (refer to Figure 6.3). This step will open the Microsoft Visual Basic editor (referred to after this as the *editor*).

3. In the editor, click File, Save CONTACTS. The Save As dialog will be displayed with the default name Module1.

4. Type **Main** for the Module Name value and click OK.

In the Main module, you will write all the code for the examples in this hour. Follow steps 1 through 4 every time you want to create a new module. To edit an existing module, you can simply double-click an existing module name in the database in Access.

Creating a Table with Code

There are many ways to create tables and queries in Access. From the previous section, you know that you can use the Access development environment's Design view to create a table. You can use CREATE TABLE SQL code to create a table and many other forms as well.

It is sometimes useful in database applications to create tables on-the-fly. For example, you might create a table when your application is running to act as a backup table. Listing 6.2 demonstrates a straightforward means of programmatically creating a table with Access code.

LISTING 6.2   Using the ADOX Object to Create a Table with Code

```
1:   Sub CreateTable()
2:     Const DatabasePath =
3:       "C:\Books\Sams\Teach Yourself Access 2002 Programming in " + _
4:       "24 Hours\Chapter 6\CONTACTS.mdb"
5:     Const ProviderStr = _
6:       "Provider=Microsoft.Jet.OLEDB.4.0;Data Source=" + DatabasePath
7:     Dim Table As New Table
8:     Dim Catalog As New ADOX.Catalog
9:     Dim Key As New ADOX.Key
10:    Catalog.ActiveConnection = ProviderStr
```

6

LISTING 6.2   continued

```
11:    Table.Name = "CONTACTS"
12:    Table.ParentCatalog = Catalog
13:    Table.Columns.Append "ID", adInteger
14:    Table.Columns("ID").Properties("AutoIncrement") = True
15:    Table.Columns.Append "FIRST_NAME", adVarWChar, 20
16:    Table.Columns.Append "LAST_NAME", adVarWChar, 20
17:    Table.Columns.Append "PHONE_NUMBER", adVarWChar, 36
18:    Table.Columns.Append "EMAIL", adVarWChar, 50
19:    Table.Columns.Append "WWW", adVarWChar, 50
20:    Catalog.Tables.Append Table
21:    Key.Name = "ID"
22:    Key.Type = adKeyPrimary
23:    Key.Columns.Append "ID"
24:    Catalog.Tables("CONTACTS").Keys.Append Key, kyPrimary
25:    Set Catalog.ActiveConnection = Nothing
26: End Sub
```

Listing 6.2 is one of those instances where it is not essential to understand every detail of the code. There are many levels of complexity here. To begin, Listing 6.2 defines a subroutine named CreateTable. Lines 7 through 9 declare Table, Catalog, and Key variables. The use of the keyword New can be copied verbatim. Special data types called *classes* require this additional keyword. Hour 21, "Class Programming Basics," explains the contexts in which you have to use the New keyword. ADOX is an ActiveX object defined by Microsoft programmers. Again, the code on lines 5 through 9, covering ADOX can be used verbatim; therefore, I will defer talking in depth about ADOX. However, you can look up ADOX in the Access Help file or wait until you get to Hour 21. You must include a reference to the ActiveX library that introduces ADOX to use it. The steps for adding a reference in Access are as follows:

1. Open the Contacts database.

2. Click the Modules button in the database's Objects view.

3. Double-click the Main module, opening the editor.

4. Select the Tools, References menu item.

5. In the Available References list in the References dialog, select the latest version of ADOX (because I have Visual Basic.Net installed I selected Microsoft ADO Ext. 2.6 for DDL and Security) by selecting the check box (see Figure 6.6).

6. Click OK.

Steps 1 through 6 make ADOX available to your code. Line 5 contains the information that enables your program to connect to the contacts.mdb database. Copy the complete reference exactly, except set the DatabasePath to the location of the database on your PC.

FIGURE 6.6

Adding a reference to the ADOX ActiveX object in Access.

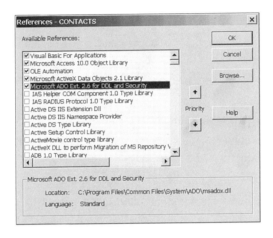

Ah-ha! I've Found It!

In the third century B.C., the king of Syracuse suspected that a gold crown commissioned by him was not pure gold. The king asked Archimedes (the father of geometry) if he could determine the truth of the matter. Archimedes wanted to determine the truth without damaging the crown. He thought about it for several days. Then one day, while in a public bathhouse, Archimedes noticed that when he settled into the bath, the water level rose. Archimedes jumped out of the bath stark naked and ran through the streets of Syracuse shouting, "Eureka! Eureka!" (I have found it!)

Archimedes had stumbled upon the solution, now known as Archimedes' Principle. It states that a body immersed in fluid is buoyed by a force that is equal to the weight of the fluid displaced. By comparing the displacement of a known quantity of pure gold to that of the suspect crown, Archimedes could demonstrate that the crown was not made of pure gold.

Grady Booch, chief scientist at Rational Corporation and Editor-in-Chief of object-oriented programming for Addison-Wesley, refers to these kinds of occurrences of understanding as a series of "ah-ha's!" Presentation and confusion followed by an instance of comprehension has been a valid modality of learning since at least the third century B.C. in Syracuse.

You do not have to understand all of Listing 6.2, but greater understanding will come as I reveal more information in this hour and the hours that follow.

6

In Listing 6.2, lines 13 through 19 define the columns that you created in the last section. Line 14 demonstrates how you define the AutoIncrement field. Line 20 adds the table to the catalog. A *catalog* refers to tables, views, users, and groups. Lines 21 through 24 demonstrate how you can define a primary key and add the key to the CONTACTS table. Line 25 closes the connection to the catalog.

Although the code in Listing 6.2 introduces many advanced techniques, think of it as a first look. For now, if you want to create a new table you can experiment with the code in Listing 6.2 to get you started. To create another table, do perform the following steps and run the code again:

1. Substitute the new table name for "CONTACTS" in line 11.
2. Substitute the column names and types for the new column names and types in lines 13 through 19.
3. Substitute a new key name for "ID" in lines 21 and 23.
4. Substitute the new table name for "CONTACTS" in lines 11 and 24.

Running the code with the substitutions described in the preceding list creates a new table. For now, it is enough to identify those aspects of the code you understand. Visually inspect the code, making sure you understand where variable declarations occur and where operators and operations occur. The code in Listing 6.2 is the kind of code you will be able to write proficiently by the end of Hour 24, "Managing Outlook Contact Information."

Managing a Table with Code

You know from experience that a table contains columns and fields. Tables provide one way to store (or *persist*) data between the times a program is running and the times it is not.

There are several terms you must know for you and I to understand each other. Some of them you might know, and some you might have forgotten. I will introduce the terms needed to discuss table management, and then you will learn how to write code to manage a database table. If you are completely comfortable with database vernacular, skip over the next section, "Database Terms Refresher Course." If you come across a database term you have forgotten, however, you can always return that section.

Database Terms Refresher Course

You need to complete several tasks to use a table in a database. For example, you have to connect to the database. Also, your code will have to open the table, manipulate the data in the table, and close the table. Your code will have to manage fields and columns in order to perform specific tasks. After you have written all of the code necessary to perform all these tasks, you have to perform cleanup. There are specific entities that are responsible for managing every aspect of database programming. In this section we will cover the names and responsibilities of the entities that support database programming.

The Catalog

Catalog refers to an Access database file. A catalog contains the references to tables, users, views, and groups.

The Connection

Connection refers to the link between your code and the database file. You must define the connection, which includes the location of the file. A connection tells Access which database you want to refer to with your code. The most important piece of a connection is the location of the database.

The Recordset

Recordset is the generic term for a variable that refers to a table, query, or view. You need a recordset to get at the rows of data. An Access recordset is equivalent to a cursor in Oracle, DB2, or Microsoft SQL Server.

Rows, Columns, and Fields

Mentally you can envision a recordset as being similar to one spreadsheet page. A *row* is all the data across one horizontal axis. Although a recordset is not exactly like a spreadsheet, the row analogy is close enough. A *column* is all the data up and down the vertical axis. The intersection of one row and one column is referred to as a *field*. (In a spreadsheet, a field is equivalent to a *cell*.) If you open a table in Access, you can see similarities between the way table data is shown and the way spreadsheet data is displayed.

Accessing Table Information

Thus far, you have created the CONTACTS table with the Access interface and with code. However, the table currently has no data. Before you put data in the CONTACTS table, let's examine how you can perform the tasks of opening and closing a database connection and a recordset.

You need to know how to connect to the database and open and close a recordset. These are the essential tasks that must be performed before any other recordset activity can occur. Listing 6.3 demonstrates opening and closing a recordset by opening the CONTACTS table and displaying all its fields.

LISTING 6.3 Code to Open CONTACTS and Display the Field Names and Descriptions

```
 1:  Sub DisplayFields()
 2:    Const DatabasePath = _
 3:      "C:\Books\Sams\Teach Yourself Access 2002 Programming " +
 4:      "in 24 Hours\Chapter 6\CONTACTS.mdb"
 5:    Const ProviderStr = _
 6:      "Provider=Microsoft.Jet.OLEDB.4.0;Data Source=" + DatabasePath
 7:
 8:    Dim Connection As New ADODB.Connection
 9:    Dim Catalog As New ADOX.Catalog
10:    Dim RecordSet As New ADODB.RecordSet
11:    Dim Field As Field
12:    Connection.Open ProviderStr
13:    Set Catalog.ActiveConnection = Connection
14:    RecordSet.Open "CONTACTS", Catalog.ActiveConnection, adOpenKeyset
15:    RecordSet.Fields.Refresh
16;    For Each Field In RecordSet.Fields
17:      Debug.Print Field.Name & ", " & Field.Type & ", " & Field.ActualSize
18:    Next
19:    RecordSet.Close
20:    Set RecordSet = Nothing
21:    Set Catalog = Nothing
22:    Connection.Close
23:    Set Connection = Nothing
24: End Sub
```

Note that I used an appropriate name for the subroutine. Because the subroutine displays the field information, I named it DisplayFields (line 1). Lines 2 through 6 define the constant provider and database path information. Remember to substitute the actual path of your copy of the database for the constant DatabasePath. Lines 8 through 11 declare variables of types defined by Microsoft programmers in the ADODB and ADOX libraries. These types are Connection, Catalog, Recordset, and Field. (You can learn more about these types later in this book and in the Access Help files.)

Line 12 opens the connection. You can use the code verbatim, except you must replace the data source part with the file location of your CONTACTS database. Line 13 can be copied exactly for this table or any other. Line 14 opens the table. You can use the code in line 14 for other tables by replacing "CONTACTS" with the other table name. By calling Refresh in line 15, Access makes sure to get the current data. (Remember, other programmers might be updating the table in a real program.)

Listing 6.3, lines 16 through 18, demonstrates a real use of the For Each loop, introduced in Hour 5, "Learning to Write Conditional Code." Line 17 prints the field name, the field type (the field type is printed as an integer), and the actual size of the field. Go to the Immediate window in the editor to view the output from line 17. See Figure 6.7 for an example of the output from Listing 6.3. The remaining lines of code—lines 19 through 24—perform cleanup. The recordset and connection are each closed before the memory for the variables is returned to the general memory pool by setting these variables to the defined word `Nothing`. (Refer to the Access Help system for more information on `Nothing`.)

FIGURE 6.7

A list of the field names, types, and sizes from a recordset's `Fields` *collection.*

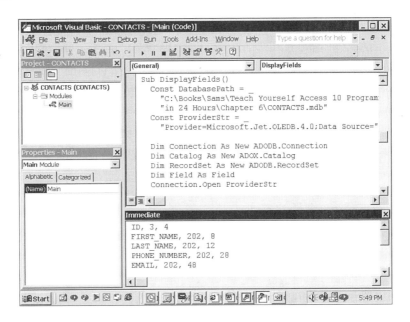

> You might have to enter a single row of data to the CONTACTS table for the code in Listing 6.3 to work correctly. Essentially, the code prints the table schema to the Immediate window and should not need any data; however, Access 2002, Beta 2 required me to enter a row of data.

Every time you write code to manage data, you are performing some or all the tasks in Listing 6.3. The timing, location, and frequency with which each of these activities occurs depend on many factors. For example, although you might have to open and close a table each time you use it, you will likely need to connect to the database only at the start of your program.

The next section demonstrates how you can easily enter data into the CONTACTS table with code.

Iteratively Inputting User Data

Iteratively inputting data implies the use of a loop. This section demonstrates how to get data into your database using a For Next loop. I will use a simple interface to facilitate data entry. Hour 19, "Creating Custom Forms," shows you how to create graphical user interfaces for your code.

From Listing 6.3, you learned how to connect to the CONTACTS table, open the table, and visit each field. To enter data, you will add code to insert a row, save user input to each field, and save the data. Listing 6.4 demonstrates a modification to DisplayFields, called InputData, that shows you how to get data into the CONTACTS table with code.

LISTING 6.4   Using a Simple Interface to Add Contact Data

```
1:  Sub InputData()
2:    Const DatabasePath = _
3:      "C:\Books\Sams\Teach Yourself Access 2000 Programming " + _
4:      "in 24 Hours 2nd Ed\Chapter 6\CONTACTS.mdb"
5:    Const ProviderStr = _
6:      "Provider=Microsoft.Jet.OLEDB.4.0;Data Source=" + DatabasePath
7:
8:    Dim Connection As New ADODB.Connection
9:    Dim Catalog As New ADOX.Catalog
10:   Dim RecordSet As New ADODB.RecordSet
11:   Dim Field As Field
12:
13:   Connection.Open ProviderStr
14:   Set Catalog.ActiveConnection = Connection
15:   RecordSet.Open "CONTACTS", Catalog.ActiveConnection, _
16:     adOpenDynamic, adLockOptimistic
17:   RecordSet.Fields.Refresh
18:
19:   Dim Temp As String
20:   Do While (1)
21:     RecordSet.AddNew
22:     For Each Field In RecordSet.Fields
23:       If (Field.Name <> "ID") Then
24:         Temp = InputBox("Enter value for " & Field.Name & _
25:           " (Q=Quit):", Field.Name)
26:         If (Temp = "Q") Then Exit For
27:         Field.Value = Temp
28:       End If
29:     Next
30:
31:     If (Temp = "Q") Then
32:       Exit Do
33;     Else
34:       RecordSet.Update
35:     End If
```

LISTING 6.4   continued

```
36:    Loop
37:
38:    Set RecordSet = Nothing
39:    Set Catalog = Nothing
40:    Connection.Close
41:    Set Connection = Nothing
42: End Sub
```

> The way Listing 6.4 is implemented pressing the OK button indicates that you want to save the value entered to the field name. Pressing Cancel will cause an empty string to be stored in the field. Enter "Q" to exit the loop and end data entry.

A lot of the code in Listing 6.4 you have seen twice now. Lines 1 through 12 establish a database connection and open the CONTACTS table. The crux of this code is contained in the Do While loop (starting on line 20 and ending on line 36) and the nested For Next loop (starting on line 22 and ending on line 29).

The Do While instance on line 20 creates an infinite loop. The value 1 will always evaluate as equivalent to True. An infinite loop is a good technique if you want to define an alternate exit point for the loop. The exit test for the inner For loop and the outer While loop occurs on lines 26 and 31, represented by the If (Temp = "Q") Then test. The outer Do While loop controls inserting a new record and updating the record on lines 21 and 34, respectively. The inner For Next loop controls iterating over each field in the new row, one field at a time. Line 18 uses the familiar InputBox function to display the current field name and accept the user input. Part of the prompt for the input is the field name and the reminder to enter "Q" to quit inputting data.

At the end of the InputData subroutine, the recordset, the catalog (the database), and the connection to the database are closed in reverse order, and their variables are deinitialized.

The code in Listing 6.4 is similar in kind to using any recordset, whether you want to input data, format fields, or perform calculations. Opening and closing tables and iterating through data are tasks you will perform over and over.

Using Conditional Code to Find Data

Iterative loops also can be used to perform tasks such as finding data. In the last section, the If (Temp = "Q") Then test was used to terminate input. With a few modest modifications, InputData can be converted to the FindData subroutine in Listing 6.5.

LISTING 6.5   Using Loops and Conditional Tests to Find Any Data

```
 1:  Sub FindData()
 2:     Dim Connection As New ADODB.Connection
 3:     Dim Catalog As New ADOX.Catalog
 4:     Dim RecordSet As New ADODB.RecordSet
 5:     Dim Field As Field
 6:     Const DatabasePath = _
 7:        "C:\Books\Sams\Teach Yourself Access 2002 Programming in" & _
 8:        "24 Hours \Chapter 6\CONTACTS.mdb"
 9:
10:     Connection.Open "Provider=Microsoft.Jet.OLEDB.4.0;" & _
11:        "Data Source=" & DatabasePath
12:
13:     Set Catalog.ActiveConnection = Connection
14:     RecordSet.Open "CONTACTS", Catalog.ActiveConnection,
➥adOpenDynamic, adLockOptimistic
15:     RecordSet.Fields.Refresh
16:
17:     Dim Temp As String
18:     RecordSet.MoveFirst
19:     Do While (RecordSet.EOF = False)
20:
21:        Temp = InputBox("Enter data to find: (Q=Quit)", "Data Finder")
22:        If (Temp = "Q") Then Exit Do
23:        For Each Field In RecordSet.Fields
24:          If (Field.Value Like Temp) Then
25:            MsgBox "Found: " & Field.Value & " in " & RecordSet("ID").Value
26:            Exit For
27:          End If
28:        Next
29:
30:        RecordSet.MoveNext
31:     Loop
32:
33:     RecordSet.Close
34:     Set RecordSet = Nothing
35:     Set Catalog = Nothing
36:     Connection.Close
37:     Set Connection = Nothing
38:  End Sub
```

Listings 6.4 and 6.5 are almost identical. The biggest changes occur in the Do While loop between lines 19 and 31. Here, While test checks for the EOF (end of file, or the last record in the table). Before the test begins, be sure that you are looking at the first record on line 18. Again "Q" input is used to terminate the loop; therefore, Do While has two exit points: EOF and user input of "Q". In line 24, I use an If Then conditional test to compare data in every single field to the user input value. If you recall from Hour 5, the Like condition allows for some very intricate pattern matching.

I call this kind of searching a blind search. Imagine that you have a piece of information, such as a fragment of a number. You might not know whether it is an account number, social security number, license plate number, address, or phone number. A blind search is useful when you don't know what the data is, but you want to narrow down the search. The search in Listing 6.5 would be much faster if you knew the field to which the value related.

Variations of the code in Listing 6.5 can enable the user to enter field names dynamically in a `FieldName` = `Value` format or use a query (SQL) for the recordset, thus resulting in very fast searches.

Summary

This hour reinforces using loops and conditional statements in the context of the database problems you encounter on a regular basis. You also were introduced to catalogs, recordsets, connections, and fields. *Catalog* refers to Access database tables, views, users, and groups. *Recordset* is the generic term for a table, query, or view. *Connection* refers to a reference to the physical database file, and, finally, *field* refers to a single piece of data.

I will be covering the different objects that facilitate database programming in the following hours. Complete the "Workshop" section to reinforce this hour's learning experience.

Q&A

Q Do I have to learn about ActiveX Data Objects (ADO) to program a database?

A No. There are other ways to manage data. ADO happens to be one of the newest and most powerful toolsets for managing data.

Q What other ways can I manage data?

A You can use the Access interface and manage data directly. You can also successfully manage data with macros, the `DoCmd` object (see the Access Help file for more information), and older protocols such as Direct Access Objects (DAO) and Remote Data Objects (RDO). Microsoft encourages you to use ADO.

Q Do I have to open and close a recordset every time I want to manage data?

A At some point. You can, however, open the recordset one time and use it many times before closing the recordset.

Q How do you recommend I go about learning all this information—for example, everything related to fields?

A I would suggest you inquire about new information as you need it. In general terms, if you can name what it is you want your code to accomplish, you might be

6

able to find existing solutions in the Help files. Remember to use peers and online user groups as effective means of acquiring knowledge.

Finally, contact the publisher of this book or visit the Web site and inquire about related topics. If you are really in a jam, send me an e-mail at pkimmel@softconcepts.com. I try to respond to as many inquiries as I can.

Workshop

The Workshop includes quiz questions designed to help you test your understanding of the material covered and exercises to help put what you've learned to practice. You will find the answers to the quiz and exercises in Appendix A, "Answers."

Quiz

1. What besides a table can be used as a recordset?
2. How do you create a new module in Access?
3. What are the steps for testing your code in a module?
4. What does a catalog refer to?
5. How can you position a recordset to the first record?
6. What kind of loop would you use to iterate through a defined number of items?

Exercises

1. Modify the CreateTable code in Listing 6.2 to add address information to the CONTACTS table. Include the street address, city, state, and ZIP Code.
2. Define a query that displays all the columns in the CONTACTS table, ordered by the ZIP Code.
3. Using Listing 6.5 as an example, use the query in exercise 2 to find a row by last name and ZIP Code.

HOUR 7

Using Advanced Data Types to Manage Data

Hour 6, "Managing Your Database," demonstrates loops and conditional statements in context. The context I am referring to in this hour is that of the ActiveX Data Objects (ADO) protocol.

During the last five years or so, Microsoft has developed several protocols based on object linking and embedding (OLE). Originally, dynamic data exchange (DDE) was defined to describe how compiled code could be reused. Think of DDE as one of the early black box standards for reusable code. After DDE, Microsoft provided us with what's referred to as *OLE* (pronounced "oh-lay"). About 1996, Microsoft revised parts of OLE and renamed OLE as *ActiveX*.

All these protocols provide the means by which programmers can use and share compiled code. The earliest reuse protocol was the dynamic link library (DLL), still widely in use today. (Just look in your `C:\Windows\` or `C:\Winnt` directory for files with the `.dll` extension. I am running Windows 2000, which returned a total of 3,120 DLLs on my PC.)

To simplify database access, Microsoft developed specific protocols for database access on top of ActiveX. Microsoft originally created Remote Data Objects (RDO), followed by Direct Access Objects (DAO) and the current protocol ActiveX Data Objects (ADO), as protocols for facilitating database access. (Open Database Connectivity, or *ODBC*, is another protocol.) *ActiveX* is a generic term for compiled code reuse; however, RDO, DAO, and ADO are specific protocols designed to facilitate database code reuse.

You could choke on the acronyms alone. If this is your first foray into programming, you are lucky. You can start by learning ADO and, for the most part, stay away from the others. I started programming before DLLs and have had to suffer through LIB, DLL, DDE, OLE, ODBC, RDO, DAO, and ADO (and the .NET Framework introduces ADO.NET).

The .NET Framework, which includes the Common Language Runtime (CLR) and other technologies, is Microsoft's initiative to address Internet development. At the present time, Microsoft has indicated that Microsoft Office will not support .NET. The effect for the next version of Microsoft Office is that VBA is not supported in the Visual Basic.NET programming language, and you will not have to worry about ADO+. For now, Microsoft Office VBA and the Visual Basic programming language are on divergent paths.

I am not sure why there are so many protocols, but one of the end results is that performing tasks such as reusing compiled code and managing data has become progressively easier.

Be prepared to encounter Access code in the Help files and code written by other developers who use any one of the protocols mentioned. However, you and I are on a direct route to solving problems, so you can stick with the latest and greatest protocol—ADO. Except for a brief introductory section that compares DAO to ADO, I will be using ADO in the code examples in this hour and the remaining hours.

In Hour 6, I asked you to take some aspects of the sample code on faith. This was done deliberately to limit focus to the hour's allocated subject. In this hour, I will offer descriptions for the ActiveX Data Objects introduced in the preceding hour. In this hour, you will learn

- An introduction to OLE Automation services and a comparison of DAO and ADO
- ADODB and ADOX data-management capabilities
- Examples of code that will help you manage and understand ActiveX Data Objects

Understanding OLE Automation

OLE Automation (or *automation* for short) is the name of a standard for sharing compiled code. A program that supports automation is a program that has a minimum amount of precisely defined procedures and data exposed to other programs. Such programs are called *automation servers*. A program that uses an automation server is called a *client*.

A client can run an automation server and can use any of the services the server provides in a manner that suits the client. An automation server can contain many services, and the client can use some or all of them in different combinations. Access is an automation server. This means that other programs can use Access to perform tasks.

Access provides an interface that other programs, such as Excel, Visual Basic, and even Borland's Delphi programming language, can use to perform database and other programming tasks.

NEW TERM An *interface* is a generic term meaning the capabilities and data other code can use.

The Access interface is vast indeed. You will come across code that uses `Application`, `DoCmd`, and `CurrentDB`, which are examples of objects that are pre-created and available for programmers to employ to solve problems. Each of these three Access objects has their own methods and properties. The good news is that you do not have to learn them before you begin programming. The bad news is that they all exist, and you will have to investigate them to determine whether they can help you solve a problem versus your writing new code.

Welcome to the World of Objects

The term *interface* implies the term *object*. An object is a special kind of data type. Thus far, you have declared variables that store just one piece of information. In the preceding hour, you were introduced to ADODB, which is an object.

An object is a special data type because it contains more than one piece of information. An object can contain data and methods. A *method* is a generic reference to functions and subroutines (which you will learn how to create in Hour 8, "Solving Problems a Piece at a Time").

NEW TERM An *object* is an instance of a compound data type containing information and capabilities.

Let's take a moment to compare different kinds of code. You know about variables. Your age is a single piece of data, and, therefore, can be captured in a variable. Something you

7

might do is a capability; capabilities are represented by subroutines or functions. An instance of a type that contains subroutines, functions, and data is called an *object*. An object describing you would contain data representing your physical attributes as well as functions and subroutines describing things you can do.

You will learn more about objects in later hours.

Useful Objects

Several useful objects can make your job a lot easier. Three of these in Access are the `Application`, `DoCmd`, and `CurrentDB` objects. Each of these objects contains a tremendous number of capabilities that you can use in your programs.

The `Application` object refers to the current Access program itself. The `Application` object provides many services you can use to manage Access.

The `DoCmd` object contains capabilities that enable you to select and manage tables, queries, and views, as well as load spreadsheets, copy databases, and import text.

Access is a database-development tool. The `CurrentDB` object references the database part of the opened database file in the current running Access session.

These three objects are complex enough to warrant their own book. I will be using aspects of `Application`, `DoCmd`, and `CurrentDB` at various points in this book. For more information and examples of how to use these objects, search in the Access Help file.

Comparing ADO to DAO

The ADO and DAO objects are particularly useful. They both provide similar services, enabling you to easily manage every aspect of your database. This hour introduces useful aspects of ADO, and Hour 15, "Data Programming Made Easy with ADODB," provides you with ample opportunity to perfect your technique.

DAO was yesterday's database standard. Although you may find examples of VBA code using DAO, DAO is probably going the way of the dinosaur, and I encourage you to use ADO in new development. ADO provides you with more powerful capabilities and results in shorter, simpler code. Listing 7.1 and 7.2 demonstrate two examples of code that both perform the same task; you can see a measurable difference in the required amount of code. Listing 7.1 contains the longer DAO code, and Listing 7.2 contains the shorter ADO code.

Listing 7.1 requires that you include the Microsoft DAO 3.6 Object Library (DAO). Listing 7.2 requires that you include the Microsoft ActiveX Data Objects 2.6 Library (ADO). To add the reference libraries, open the Microsoft Visual Basic editor from Access and select Tools, References. (The reference libraries are in alphabetic order.)

LISTING 7.1 DAO Code to Add a Row to a Library Table

```
 1:  Sub DAOAddRow()
 2:
 3:     Const TITLE = "Sams Teach Yourself Access 2002 " + _
 4:        "Programming in 24 Hours"

 5:     Dim DB As Database
 6:     Dim Rs As DAO.Recordset
 7:     Set DB = CurrentDb()
 8:     Set Rs = DB.OpenRecordset("LIBRARY")
 9:
10:     Rs.AddNew
11:
12:     Rs("TITLE").Value = TITLE
13:     Rs("AUTHOR").Value = "Paul Kimmel"
14:     Rs("ISBN").Value = "0-672-32098-3"
15:     Rs("PAGECOUNT").Value = 400
16:     Rs("PUBLISHER").Value = "Sams"
17:     Rs("PUBLICATIONDATE").Value = Date
18:
19:     Rs.Update
20:
21:     Rs.Close
22:     Set Rs = Nothing
23:     Set DB = Nothing
24: End Sub
```

LISTING 7.2 ADO Code to Add a Row to a Library Table

```
 1:  Sub ADOAddRow()
 2:     Const Title = "Sams Teach Yourself Access 2002 " + _
 3:        "Programming in 24 Hours"
 4:
 5:     Dim Rs As New ADODB.Recordset
 6:     Rs.Open "LIBRARY", CurrentProject.Connection, adOpenKeyset, _
 7:        adLockOptimistic
 8:     Rs.AddNew
 9:
10:     Rs("TITLE").Value = Title
11:     Rs("AUTHOR").Value = "Paul Kimmel"
12:     Rs("ISBN").Value = "0672316617"
13:     Rs("PAGECOUNT").Value = 400
14:     Rs("PUBLISHER").Value = "Sams"
15:     Rs("PUBLICATIONDATE").Value = Date
16:
17:     Rs.Update
18:     Rs.Close
19:     Set Rs = Nothing
20: End Sub
```

7

ANALYSIS   Comparing Listing 7.1 (DAO) to 7.2 (ADO), you can see that ADO is a moder-
ately more concise implementation. ADO requires the Recordset declaration
only, whereas the DAO declaration requires the Database object in addition to
Recordset. When lines of code are complex, that complexity translates to lost time, and
consequently lost money. DAO has been deprecated in favor of ADO; the ADO code is
preferable for new applications.

Both DAO and ADO will work in new development, and you are likely to encounter both
in existing development. In this book, I will use ADO.

Using the ADODB Object

The ADODB object is a COM object. That means you can use ADODB with any programming tool that supports creating instances of COM objects, including any program
capable of running VBA code (such as Excel, Word, Access, Visual Basic, and even other
non-Microsoft development tools, such as Borland's Delphi). Listing 7.3 contains a fragment from Delphi that uses the ADODB automation server.

LISTING 7.3   ADODB Server Used in Borland's Delphi

```
1:   procedure TForm1.Button1Click(Sender: TObject);
2:   const
3:    sTitle = 'Sams Teach Yourself Access 2002 ' +
4:             'Programming in 24 Hours';
5:
6:    sProvider = 'Provider=Microsoft.Jet.OLEDB.4.0;';
7:    sDataSource = 'Data Source=661707.mdb';
8:   var
9:     Recordset : Variant;
10:   Connection : Variant;
11:  begin
12:
13:   RecordSet := CreateOLEObject('ADODB.RecordSet');
14:   Connection := CreateOleObject('ADODB.Connection');
15:   Connection.Open( sProvider + sDataSource );
16:   RecordSet.Open( 'LIBRARY', Connection, 1, 3 );
17:   RecordSet.AddNew;
18:   RecordSet.Fields.Item('TITLE').Value := sTitle;
19:   RecordSet.Fields.Item('AUTHOR').Value := 'Paul Kimmel';
20:   RecordSet.Fields.Item('ISBN').Value := '0672316617';
21:   RecordSet.Fields.Item('PAGECOUNT').Value := 400;
22:   RecordSet.Fields.Item('PUBLISHER').Value := 'Sams';
23:   Recordset.Fields.Item('PUBLICATIONDATE').Value := Date;
24:
25:   RecordSet.Update;
26:   RecordSet.Close;
27:
```

LISTING 7.3   continued

```
28:   RecordSet := varNull;
29:   Connection := varNull;
30:
31: end;
```

ANALYSIS   Even though you may have never seen Object Pascal code, you can easily identify many of the same aspects in Listing 7.3 that appear in Listings 7.1 and 7.2. The code in Listing 7.3 inserts a row into the LIBRARY table, similar to the prior two listings. The Object Pascal code, however, uses a more verbose form of field access:

```
Recordset.Fields.Item(fieldname)
```

The code in Listing 7.3 displays the data in the field in the second column of the LIBRARY table.

> Delphi is the programming environment for Object Pascal just as Access is the programming environment for VBA.

Although Borland's Delphi provides many database services for developers, the simple fact that a few lines of code enable you to use the ADODB object is powerful stuff. Let's take a closer look at some of the ADODB services you have seen used.

Using a Connection

A *connection* is the information that tells Access how to read a database. There are many database vendors and database types, including SQL Server, Sybase, Oracle, Interbase, Informix, and UDB. Your Access programs can read data from any of these databases, and the connection makes this possible. If you want to refer only to the recordsets within the database in which you are currently writing code, you can use `CurrentProject.Connection`, as demonstrated in line 3 of Listing 7.2.

To open a new connection, you must first declare a `Connection` object. The syntax for declaring a `Connection` is

```
Dim ConnectionName As New ADODB.Connection
```

> When you type **ADODB** in the code editor, a list of object properties should pop up after you type the period. If the properties list doesn't display a list of properties, you may not have the Microsoft ActiveX Data Objects 2.6 Library (that is, the ADODB library) checked in the Tools, References dialog.

As does any other variable, the declaration statement begins with the keyword Dim. Supply a variable name for *ConnectionName*, followed by As and New, both Access keywords. Prefix Connection with ADODB. The ADODB prefix on Connection is necessary because there are other Connection types—for example, the one defined in DAO automation servers.

After you have declared a Connection variable, you open the connection.

Opening a Connection

Before you can open a connection, you must have a connection string. The connection string can contain the user id and password, or the user id and password can be passed to the Open method if the database is password protected. User id and password are optional parameters.

The connection string contains the provider and datasource information. Datasource information represents the physical location of your database; provider information represents the libraries that are used to allow you to access a particular manufacturer's database. Provider information varies among database vendors. Check your database vendor's documentation for provider information. Here's an example of a provider string for the newest version of the Jet database engine (an Access 2002 database):

```
"Provider=Microsoft.Jet.OLEDB.4.0;Data Source=databasepath"
```

The syntax example is exact, except for *databasepath*. You must provide an actual location for your database. The connection string can open an Access connection even if you have not specified a user ID and password and you use the default options.

The user ID and password are both string values. The options parameter for Open is an enumerated value. The possible options values are adConnectUnspecified and asAsyncConnect. (Search the Help files for more information about connections.)

Closing a Connection

Remember to close any declared and opened connections when you are finished with them. Listing 7.4 demonstrates how to declare, open, and close a connection with Access code.

LISTING 7.4 Using an ADODB Connection

```
1:  Sub OpenConnection()
2:      Const Provider = "Provider=Microsoft.Jet.OLEDB.4.0;"
3:      Const DataSource = _
4:      "Data Source=C:\Books\Sams\Teach Yourself Access 2002 " & _
5:      "Programming in 24 Hours\" & _
```

LISTING 7.4   continued

```
5:        "Chapter 7\db1.mdb"
6:
7:    Dim Connection As New ADODB.Connection
8:    Connection.Open Provider + DataSource
9:    Connection.Close
10: End Sub
```

> The ampersand and underscore pair (& _) at the end of line 4 and 5 of
> Listing 7.4 demonstrates how to use string concatenation and continuation
> (represented by the underscore) to continue a string on several lines.

ANALYSIS Lines 2 through 5 define the provider and data source information. Line 7 declares the `Connection` object, and lines 8 and 9 demonstrate opening and closing a connection. You place the code to use the connection between lines 8 and 9.

Using a Recordset

After you have a valid `Connection` variable and open the connection, you can open a recordset. A recordset contains data and may be a table, query, view, or stored procedure. An open recordset refers to exactly one row of data at a time. A recordset is the most common variable type you will use to manage data.

> All the disparate types used to connect to a database and manage data
> were not created to confuse you. They were actually created to compart-
> mentalize responsibility. Database management is complicated stuff. Having
> objects such as `Connection` and `Recordset` objects makes it much easier to
> program databases. One huge control would be confusing and take too
> many system resources. The capability to delegate responsibility is one of
> the fundamental benefits of object-oriented programming.

Valid operations on recordsets include opening and closing, adding, removing, and updating data, and iterating over rows. Recordset data is managed via the `Fields` object. When you write `Recordset("fieldname")`, the recordset is implicitly accessing `Recordset.Fields` and returning a field object. The implicit behavior is exhibited in the code in Listings 7.1 and 7.2 and represented in the expanded Object Pascal version in Listing 7.3.

7

Opening a Recordset

A recordset must be opened before you can use the data in the recordset. To open a recordset, you must declare a `Recordset` variable and then write a statement such as this:

```
Recordsetname.Open Recordset, Connection, CursorType, LockType, Options
```

Here, *recordsetname* should be a declared `ADODB.RecordSet` object (demonstrated on line 5 of Listing 7.2). The *Recordset* information can be a table name (see line 6 of Listing 7.2) or a string containing SQL code. The *Connection* information can be `CurrentProject.Connection`, if you want to use the database you are working in or another valid connection (refer to "Using a Connection," earlier in this hour).

CursorType and *LockType* are among the several valid `CursorTypeEnum` and `LockTypeEnum` values defined in the Access Help file. Search on `CursorType` and `LockType` for all the possible values for *CursorType* and *LockType*. Line 3 of Listing 7.2 uses the `adOpenKeyset` cursor type and the `adLockOptimistic` lock type.

Closing a Recordset

Closing a recordset is done when you are finished with the recordset. It is best to open and close a recordset as the first and last things you do. This will reduce the likelihood that you accidentally leave a recordset open. Line 18 of Listing 7.2 demonstrates closing a recordset.

Modifying a Record

The commands for adding and editing recordsets are easy. Line 8 of Listing 7.2 demonstrates how to add a record. To save changes to an added or modified record, you use the `Update` command when you are finished modifying the data.

Assuming you have a recordset variable named `RS`, the code for adding a record is `RS.AddNew`; the code for editing a record is `RS.Edit`, and the code for updating changes, whether you're adding or modifying a record, is `RS.Update`. Listing 7.2, lines 8 and 17, demonstrate adding and updating one record, respectively.

Testing for the First and Last Record

The two methods you can use to test for the beginning and ending of a recordset are `BOF` and `EOF`. The method for testing for the start of a recordset is `BOF` (read *beginning of file*). The method that is used to test for the end of a recordset is `EOF` (read as *end of file*).

NEW TERM   *Method* refers to both functions and subroutines that are contained in objects. Methods define the capabilities of objects.

Assuming you have a recordset variable named `RS`, the code for a beginning-of-file test is `RS.BOF`, and the code for the end-of-file test is `RS.EOF`.

BOF and EOF are function methods that return a Boolean data type. BOF returns True if you are at the beginning of a recordset, and EOF returns True if you are at the end of a recordset.

Because Boolean values are good candidates for use in loops and conditional statements, you can use the BOF or EOF methods to iterate forward and backward through a recordset. Line 21 in Listing 6.5 (in Hour 6) provides an example of using EOF.

Changing Records

Several methods are available for changing records in an open recordset. Four valuable methods are MoveFirst, MoveLast, MoveNext, and MovePrevious.

One of the benefits of well-named methods is that they are (or should be) self-explanatory. MoveFirst positions the open recordset to the first record. MoveLast positions the recordset to the last record. MoveNext positions the recordset to the current record number plus one, and MovePrevious positions the recordset to current record number minus one.

Listing 6.5 in Hour 6 demonstrates how MoveFirst, MoveNext, and EOF can be used in concert to iterate through all records. It is important to note that these are all methods of Recordset objects. Therefore, their usage must always be prefixed with a declared Recordset variable and attached by a period, as demonstrated here:

Recordsetvariable.methodname

The preceding syntax is true, in general, of all objects. Left of the prefix is the variable name of the object, and to the right is the method or data you want to use.

Using Fields

A recordset points to one record at a time. A record may have one or many fields. The LIBRARY table has the TITLE, AUTHOR, ISBN, PAGECOUNT, PUBLISHER, and PUBLICATION columns. A single row and column intersection is referred to as a *field*.

When you write code, such as that in lines 10 through 15 of Listing 7.2, you are implicitly getting a field object. That is, RS("TITLE") (see line 5 of Listing 7.2) refers to the TITLE field at the current row position.

You can look at the Help file for fields by searching on the Field Object for ADO. The most important attribute of a Field object is the Value attribute.

NEW TERM   *Attribute* is an object-oriented term that refers to any data contained in an object.

7

The Value attribute has the same syntax as all other attributes of objects: *objectname.attributename*. The Value attribute is a Variant data type. This means that you can assign data of any type to the Value attribute, and the compiler will resolve the data type information. Lines 10 through 15 of Listing 7.2 demonstrate assigning strings, numbers, and dates to the Value fields of the LIBRARY recordset.

There are too many attributes and methods of field objects to cover in one hour. Rest assured that I will demonstrate many of them in later hours, and the Help files are an excellent resource of examples and explanations for all the objects defined by Microsoft developers.

Using the ADOX Object

The ADO Data Definition and Security Library contains objects that let you manage tables, views, and indexes and also administrate users and groups.

To use the ADO Data Definition and Security Library, open the Microsoft Visual Basic editor (the editor for Access programming). Select Tools, References. In the References dialog, check the Microsoft ADO Ext. 2.5 for DDL and Security reference. This will enable you to create ADOX objects.

Catalog

The Catalog object is the container for tables, stored procedures, views, users, and groups. In Listing 6.2, you used the Catalog, Table, and Key objects to dynamically create and add a table to the CONTACTS database (from Hour 6).

There is a one-to-one relationship between a Catalog and a Connection object. If you want to create a table and add it to your database with code, define new or additional indexes, or manage user and group permissions, you declare a Catalog object.

Excerpting from Hour 6, the code to define a Catalog object appears in Listing 7.5, which demonstrates how to list all the tables in a database.

LISTING 7.5   Using the ADOX.Catalog Object to List All the Tables in a Database

```
1:  Sub ListTables()
2:      Dim Catalog As New ADOX.Catalog
3:      Set Catalog.ActiveConnection = CurrentProject.Connection
4:      Dim I As Integer
5:      For I = 0 To Catalog.Tables.Count - 1
6:          Debug.Print Catalog.Tables(I).Name
7:      Next I
8:      Set Catalog = Nothing
9:  End Sub
```

ANALYSIS Lines 2 and 3 declare an `ADOX.Catalog` object and assign its `ActiveConnection` attribute to `CurrentProject.Connection`. Line 4 declares `Integer` `I` for indexing. Lines 5 through 7 define a `For Next` loop that iterates through all the tables in database. Line 8 releases the `Catalog` object's memory.

Expanding line 6 from Listing 7.5 illustrates all the work that is being performed in the statement `Catalog.Tables(I).Name`:

```
Dim Name As String
Dim Table As Table
Table = Catalog.Tables(I)
Name = Table.Name
Debug.Print Name
```

The phrase `Catalog.Tables(I)` returns the `Table` object in the `Tables` collection referenced by the index `I`. The `.Name` attribute gets the name of the table at the `I`th index. `Debug.Print Name` writes the name of the table to the Immediate window.

NEW TERM `Collection` is a kind of object that is defined for the express purpose of storing objects. A collection of items is usually the pluralized name of the data collected.

Listing 7.5 can be run against any database. I ran it against the database I used for Listings 7.1 and 7.2 and received the output in the Immediate window shown in Figure 7.1.

FIGURE 7.1

The table names for the `Catalog` object containing the LIBRARY table from Listings 7.1 and 7.2. The listing includes Access system tables and might vary based on your actual configuration.

7

The `ActiveConnection` Attribute

The `ActiveConnection` attribute of a `Catalog` object is an attribute that refers to the connection that the `Catalog` object refers to. You may assign the `ActiveConnection` attribute to `CurrentProject.Connection` if you want to have the `Catalog` object refer to the database you are working in. You also can create a new connection (to another database) and assign the `ActiveConnection` property to that connection.

Tables Collection

By convention, a collection of objects is usually the plural form of the object collected. Therefore, a collection of `Connection` objects would be named `Connections` by convention.

Hour 13, "Storing Information in a Collection," teaches you about using collections in general. After you learn how to use a collection, every use of collections is identical. This is also true for all objects. After you learn how to use a specific kind of object, every instance of that object works the same as every other instance of that object.

The `Tables` collection contains a `Table` object at every indexed position. Hence, `Catalog.Tables(I)` (where `I` is any valid index position from 0 to count –1) refers to one `Table` object.

`Table` objects contain collections of `Columns`, `Indexes`, `Keys`, and `Properties`. The `Columns` collection contains all the columns in a table. `Indexes` contains all the indexes for one table. The same is true of `Keys` and `Properties`. To learn about each one of these entities, read the rest of this book and use the Access Help file to look up the root of each collection name. For example, to get a comprehensive list of attributes and capabilities for an ADO column, look up "column (ADO)" in the editor Help file.

Groups, Users, and Views

`Groups`, `Users`, and `Views` are all collections in `Catalog` objects. You can define a user group by appending a `Group` object to the `Catalog.Groups` collection with the `Append` method. The same is true for `Users` and `Views`.

User permissions define read/write permissions for users of your databases. When you define a user permission, you are defining what a user, based on her user ID and password, can read and modify. (Refer to the "Users Collection (ADOX)" example in the Help file.) To find a complete code example for user permissions, follow these steps:

1. Click Start, Programs, Microsoft Access to run an instance of Access.
2. From the Task pane, open an existing database or create a new database.
3. Click Modules in the Objects view.
4. Click the New button to run the Microsoft Visual Basic editor.

5. Press the F1 key to display the Microsoft Visual Basic Help.

6. In the Microsoft Visual Basic Help file, click the Index tab.

7. In item 1, "Type Keywords," enter Users Collection.

8. Click Search.

9. In the Choose a Topic list (there should be several topics found), choose the Users Collection (ADOX) topic (see Figure 7.2).

FIGURE 7.2

Use the Help files aggressively to acquire experience and examples when you need them.

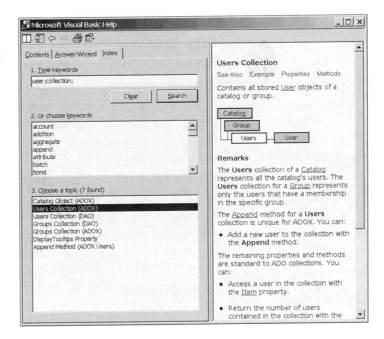

10. In the User Collection Help, click the Example tag (in blue).

The MSDN Help files contain about 2GB (2,000,000,000 bytes) of information, including articles and examples for all kinds of programming chores. That would never fit in this book, or a hundred such books. Learning to rely on vast resource files such as the Help file is an excellent way to acquire new techniques.

Summary

In this hour, I covered the ADODB and ADOX objects and others that you were exposed to in Hour 6. Because modern programs contain so much code written by others, before you write your first line of code, you must be able to use code written by others, even when you have no prior knowledge about how it was implemented.

7

Thousands of objects are in existence. You know how to use `Catalog`, `Table`, `Index`, `Key`, `Connection`, and `Recordset` objects now. You will see more examples demonstrating other aspects of ADO and Access programming in Hours 8 through 24. For more information on ADODB specifically, including examples, read Hour 15.

Q&A

Q **When should I use ADO and when should I use another protocol, such as DAO?**

A In general, stick with ADO. Microsoft will likely gear future development efforts towards ADO, and in most instances, ADO will require less effort on your part.

Q **How can I learn about all the objects you mentioned?**

A Learn about them when you need to solve a specific problem in the near future. Additionally, accumulate extemporaneous knowledge of Access programming tactics by reading more books like this one, talking to other developers, and contributing to the general programming dialog.

Q **When do I create `Catalog`, `Connection`, and `Recordset` objects?**

A It depends. To demonstrate code, it is often useful to perform all these tasks in one subroutine. However, in a real application, you will often want to perform some tasks more or less frequently than others. Experience will help guide you. In later hours, you will be able to practice with alternative examples.

Workshop

The Workshop includes quiz questions designed to help you test your understanding of the material covered and exercises to help put what you've learned to practice. You will find the answers to the quiz and exercises in Appendix A, "Answers."

Quiz

1. To how many records does a recordset refer at one time?
2. Which contains the `Tables` collection, a `Catalog` or a `Connection` object?
3. What objects does a `Catalog` object contain?
4. What two kinds of services does a `Catalog` object offer?
5. What methods are available for iterating over each record in a table?

Exercises

1. Create a query in your database. Open the query with code using the `Recordset` object.

2. Write code that iterates over every key in a `Catalog` object.

3. Write code that begins at the end of a `Recordset` object and iterates over every record backward.

7

PART III

Using Access Resources to Get the Job Done

Hour

HOUR 8

Solving Problems a Piece at a Time

A good way to solve complicated problems is to break them up into very small problems and solve each individual problem. A program is a collection of code that solves one or many related problems, depending on the scope of the problem. In earlier hours, you saw many examples referring to lines of code as statements. A statement can be one or more lines of code, much as a sentence can be simple (such as "Hello, Bob!") or more complicated (such as the sentence you are reading now). In programming, examples of statements include A = 5 and Dim A As Integer. Statements are the building blocks of functions and subroutines.

This hour teaches you how to find recurring and useful lines of code that can be placed at one location in your program and referred to by name. A named block of code, composed of one or more statements, is referred to as a *function* or *subroutine*. A function is distinguished from a subroutine by the specific way the code block is written.

Functions and subroutines have a precise syntax. It is the use of the keywords Function or Sub that specifically denotes whether a code block is a function or subroutine.

In Access, you will use functions and subroutines to define blocks of code that solve problems you cannot solve any other way.

Sometimes, you must write a program that consists of at least one function or subroutine when you need to automate multiple tasks. You might find there is no Access menu item or macro available for the task or the task might be too tedious to be performed manually. A perfect example is a task that must be run during the middle of the night when no one is at the office.

When you need to automate tasks or minimize mistakes and inefficiencies due to repetition or complexity, what you need is an Access program. An Access program is one or more functions or subroutines that run in Access and are written in VBA.

In this hour you will learn

- The mechanics of writing functions and subroutines
- Rules of thumb for functions, subroutines, and commenting
- By experimenting with practical examples
- From writing functions to import data from text files

The Mechanics of Writing Subroutines

You can write two kinds of code blocks: One is referred to as the *subroutine*, and the other is the *function*. I will begin with the subroutine. Subroutines are a little easier to write, and they're as good a starting place as any.

Subroutines evolved from an innate need, apparently caused by our short-term memory limitations, to consolidate complex ideas into simple named references. For example, social security numbers are composed of nine digits, but logically they are grouped into three distinct groups of digits. If you listen, you can frequently hear information collection in speech. Phone numbers are an example. I am the type of person who groups a phone number by area code, three-digit prefix, and four-digit suffix. Therefore, I am really remembering 3 numbers instead of 10. Subroutines evolved from our need to group many little things into named concepts to help combat our limited short-term memory.

A subroutine is a block of statements that can be referred to by name. The general principle is aggregation. Because it is natural for people to think of complex things by name, it is natural that programming languages evolved in a similar manner. For example, when I refer to Hogan, my dog, I am referring to an animal that we purchased from the pound. He is a yellow Labrador, mixed-breed, friendly, tail-wagging, male canine that is about five years old. Hogan captures all that information nicely for us.

NEW TERM To *aggregate* (as a verb) means to gather together parts of a program to create a named part. The noun form refers to the sum of the parts, and *aggregate* can be used as an adjective, too. Here is a sentence using aggregate in all three forms: I will *aggregate* the people and e-mail information from your black book and make an *aggregate* type, called Contacts, an *aggregate* of this information.

Subroutines enable you to gather, that is *aggregate*, statements for the common purpose of solving a problem. It is much easier to refer to many lines of code by one name than it is to repeat the individual lines of code many times.

Subroutines are comprised of a few basic parts: the first line, the statements that make up the subroutine, and the last line. The first line of a subroutine is comprised of the keyword Sub, the subroutine name, and the data that you want to pass to the subroutine. The data passed to the subroutine is called an *argument*. The subsections that follow describe each of the parts and how to use them.

Writing the First and Last Lines of Subroutines

The first and last lines of a subroutine are so important that they actually make up a valid subroutine by themselves. The subroutine they comprise doesn't do anything, but it is a valid subroutine, nonetheless.

The first and last lines of a subroutine basically have the same makeup. The general form of a subroutine is called the *syntax*. The syntax of the first and last lines of a subroutine is shown in the following lines:

```
Sub Name( [[Qualifier] DataName As DataType, ...] )
End Sub
```

The syntax example shows that you need the word Sub, the parentheses, and the words End and Sub. Arguments are optional, and the ellipsis means there can be as many arguments as you would like.

Programming languages, like spoken languages, have a grammar or syntax. The syntax is comprised of the rules that govern the use of the language. Formal Language Theory is the mathematical study of programming languages. For our purposes, it is enough to simply memorize the general form of a subroutine rather than the canonical form.

Naming Subroutines

Using good naming conventions makes your code understandable to the human reader and is also a good documenting technique. Often a good name and small subroutines can mitigate the need for other textual documentation. A good rule of thumb is to use a noun to name the thing a subroutine relates to and a verb to describe the action. Combing the noun and verb into a function name results in a good name. Here's an example:

```
Sub PostCommissions( RepresentativeRepID As String,_
  CommissionAmount As Double )
End Sub
```

The subroutine is `PostCommissions`. The subroutine name clearly depicts what is occurring. The arguments `RepresentativeRepID` and `CommissionAmount` are clearly descriptive. If this subroutine only posts the commissions for a representative, it is likely that very little additional commenting will be required. (Refer to the section "Programming Rules of Thumb," later in this hour, for more guidelines on writing subroutines and functions.)

Naming Subroutine Arguments

The data passed between the parentheses of a subroutine is referred to as its *arguments* or *parameters*. Blame the mathematicians for the word *arguments*. Mathematicians, being the first programmers, named everything. Mathematical terms can be challenging to learn for non-mathematicians, but precise terminology affords a more precise interchange of ideas. Our earlier discussion on naming applies to arguments as well as to subroutines. Name them well.

Avoid using nonstandard abbreviations, pseudowords, or nonsensical alphanumeric characters. The computer doesn't care what you name your argument, but the human reader will. Someone will eventually have to maintain what you write, and, in a few months, even you will forget what `mskCustTel` or `txpct` means. You probably won't forget `CustomerTelephone` and `TaxPercent`, however, because the these variables are self-descriptive.

 Using whole words, separating the words by a capital letter, and publicly posting any abbreviations that are standard in your industry will make your code much easier to maintain.

Defining Argument Types

The last piece of the subroutine puzzle is deciding what data you want to pass to the subroutine. The data passed to a subroutine is declared between the parentheses of the subroutine. This data is referred to as *arguments* or *parameters*. I will use the term *arguments*, but both are accurate.

You define an argument by placing a variable name, followed by the As keyword and the data type between the parentheses. You can have as many arguments as you like. If you have more than one argument, separate the arguments by placing a comma after the data type and before the next argument name. (You will always have one less comma than you do arguments.)

The brief code example that follows demonstrates a subroutine that calculates a total sale by multiplying the sale by the sales tax and adding it to the sale. The resulting total is stored in a global variable. Here is the example:

```
Global TotalSale As Double
Sub CalculateSalesTax( SaleAmount As Double, SalesTax As Double )
    TotalSale = SaleAmount * ( 1 + SalesTax )
End Sub
```

This simple subroutine is syntactically correct and demonstrates the passing of two arguments. The function is also logically correct. Syntactical and logical correctness are two standards that you must achieve. Syntactic correctness ensures that your code runs. Logical correctness ensures that your code produces the right answer. CalculateSaleTax passes both of these standards.

There are, however, two other standards. Is the code semantically correct and robust? The standard of semantics refers to whether the code conveys your intended use. Robustness has to do with whether the code is fault-tolerant and maintainable.

> *Robustness* will be discussed more in Hour 18, "Adding Code to Handle Errors." It is preferable to avoid using global data whenever possible.

Because the parameters SaleAmount and SalesTax are defined, as shown in the preceding code snippet, any changes made to these values inside of the subroutine are reflected when the subroutine is run. It is unlikely that you will want the SaleAmount parameter to be modified, so the intent or semantic meaning of the code is not communicated as well as it might be.

Access VBA enables you to precede arguments with qualifiers that convey information about their intended purpose, hence promoting semantic correctness. Although it is not absolutely necessary to use these qualifiers, your code will have fewer defects (and you will spend less time debugging in the future) if you learn to employ them. Read the following subsections for discussions on argument qualifiers. They will show you revisions that will improve the previous code sample.

Using ByVal Arguments

The ByVal qualifier precedes any arguments to a subroutine whose value you do not want to be changed outside of the subroutine. A ByVal argument will maintain the same assigned value after the last line of the subroutine executes as it had when you passed it into the subroutine.

You can modify the ByVal argument in the subroutine, but changes to ByVal arguments are only temporary. A ByVal argument actually gets a copy of the data passed to it. It is the copy you are changing. The following example uses the ByVal qualifier to ensure that the Sale and SalesTax values are not inadvertently changed:

```
Global TotalSale As Double
Sub CalculateSalesTax( ByVal Sale As Double, ByVal SalesTax As Double )

  ' changes made to Sale and SalesTax are not reflected
  ' outside of this subroutine
End Sub
```

Use the ByVal prefix for subroutine arguments when you want to ensure that the individual argument cannot be changed permanently. You may change ByVal arguments within the subroutine, but those changes will be lost after the last line of the subroutine is executed. To test your understanding of ByVal arguments, guess what values the code in Listing 8.1 reflects.

LISTING 8.1   Demonstrating the ByVal Qualifier for Subroutines

```
1:  Sub TestByVal( ByVal A As Integer )
2:     A = 5
3:     MsgBox A
4:  End Sub
5:
6:  Sub Test
7:     Dim A As Integer
8:     A = 10
9:     Call TestByVal(A)
10:    MsgBox A
11: End Sub
```

ANALYSIS If you guessed that line 3 will show 5 and line 10 will show 10, you have ByVal down pat. ByVal ensures that changes made to variables are only temporary. Another qualifier is the ByRef qualifier.

Using `ByRef` Arguments

The `ByRef` argument conveys to the reader and the compiler that the `ByRef` argument is supposed to be changed. Further modifying the sample fragment you have been using, you can eliminate the use of a `Global` variable. The following example calculates the total sale but passes in the value being calculated in `TotalSale` ByRef.

```
Sub CalculateSalesTax( ByVal Sale As Double, ByVal SalesTax As Double, _
  ByRef TotalSale As Double)
    TotalSale = Sale * (1 + SalesTax)
End Sub
```

The `ByRef` (by reference) qualifier signifies that the subroutine is getting a reference to the actual passed variable. Hence, any changes in the subroutine are equivalent to changes outside the subroutine. Use `ByRef` when you want to change the value of arguments permanently.

Using `Optional` Arguments

The `Optional` qualifier offers some flexibility in your subroutines. An `Optional` argument is one for which the user of the subroutine does not have to supply an argument. The `Optional` qualifier is best for data that might have the same value most of the time, but once in a while will have a different argument value.

In the sales tax example in the beginning of the section, suppose most of your sales are in Michigan. If you define the `SalesTax` argument as `Optional` and provide the default value of `.06`, users of the code will not need to pass that argument unless the sales tax is something other than `.06`, such as a sale in Washington, where the sales tax is 8 percent. The subroutine that calculates sales tax in Listing 8.2 demonstrates this technique.

If you use `Optional` qualifiers, they should be the last arguments in the subroutine argument list. If they are not, the VBA editor will display an error message, and your program won't run.

LISTING 8.2   Demonstration of the `Optional` Qualifier

```
1:  Sub CalculateTotalSale( ByRef TotalSale As Double, _
      ByVal SaleAmount As Double, Optional TaxPercent As Double = .06)

2:    TotalSale = (SaleAmount * (1 + TaxPercent))
3:  End Sub
4:
5:  Sub Test()
6:    Dim SaleAmount As Double
```

LISTING 8.2   continued

```
7:    Dim TotalSale As Double
8:    SaleAmount = 100
9:    Call CalculateTotalSale( TotalSale, SaleAmount )
10:   Dim WashingtonSalesTax As Double
11:   WashingtonSalesTax = .08
12:   Call CalculateTotalSale( TotalSale, SaleAmount, WashingtonSalesTax )
13: End Sub
```

ANALYSIS   Using Optional in line 1 enables you to accommodate sales (in Michigan and outside) and to anticipate the continual plague of increasing taxes. Note that you call CalculateTotalSale without and with a third argument. The Optional qualifier allows you that privilege. Line 9 demonstrates the subroutine call without the third Optional argument, and line 12 demonstrates the subroutine call with the third argument. Both are acceptable. (Insert a Debug.Print statement to evaluate the results of the calculations.)

> The proper use of the Optional qualifier requires that all Optional arguments be at the end of the argument list.

The Mechanics of Writing Functions

Functions are almost identical to subroutines. Functions and subroutines differ in one aspect only. Functions enable you to declare a return value. (If you have not read the previous section, I suggest you do so at this time.)

Functions and subroutines are identical except for the return argument. This section will show you how to assign a value to be returned by a function. The general syntax follows that of the subroutine in every aspect except for the use of the keyword Sub and the addition of a return data type. Look at the syntactical example that follows:

```
Function Name( [[Qualifier] ArgumentName As DataType, ...] ) As DataType
End Function
```

Recall that italicized portions should be replaced with an appropriate value, and nonitalicized words are literal values that you should copy precisely.

If you compare the preceding syntactical example with the syntactical example for subroutines, you will notice that subroutines and functions differ only in the use of different keywords, Function and Sub, and the presence of the return data type for functions. Use Function when your code block is written to return a value. A slightly better implementation of the code in Listing 8.2 is to revise the subroutine CalculateTotalSale as a function. Look at Listing 8.3.

LISTING 8.3 `CalculateTotalSale` Redefined from Listing 8.2 As a Function

```
1:  Function CalculateTotalSale(ByVal SaleAmount As Double,
    ➥Optional TaxPercent As Double = .06 ) As Double
2:    CalculateTotalSale = (SaleAmount * (1 + TaxPercent))
3:  End Sub
4:
5:  Sub Test()
6:    Dim SaleAmount As Double
7:    Dim TotalSale As Double
8:    SaleAmount = 100
9:    TotalSale = CalculateTotalSale( SaleAmount )
10:    Dim WashingtonSalesTax As Double
11:   WashingtonSalesTax = .08
12:   TotalSale = CalculateTotalSale(SaleAmount, WashingtonSalesTax )
13: End Sub
```

ANALYSIS The changes from Listing 8.2 to Listing 8.3 exemplify the differences between subroutines and functions. Note that the code example uses the keyword `Function` and doesn't require the `TotalSale` argument. `CalculateTotalSale` has a return data type at the end of the first line of code (see line 1) and assigns the return value to the name of the function (see line 2).

 Now that you understand the differences between subroutines and functions, I will use the word *function* generically to mean either a function or subroutine. If the difference is critical to the topic, I will intentionally specify `Sub` or `Function`, whichever is appropriate.

Functions are similar to subroutines. The difference is the use of the keyword `Function`, the appendage of the return data type, and the assignment of the return value to the function name in the body of the code. Deciding whether to use a function or subroutine is simple. Use a subroutine unless you need the code to return some value, and reserve the right to change your mind.

Programming Rules of Thumb

There are six rules of thumb that you can apply to writing your functions and subroutines. The rules described in this section were developed during the last five decades. If you learn and utilize these rules, they will help you get out of the office at five o'clock. Each of the relevant rules of thumb is described in the subsections that follow.

Rule 1: Make Recurring Code into a Function

The best way to get more mileage out of your code is to write less code. The best way to make your code work better and more consistently is also to write less code. If you see the same few lines recurring frequently in your program, make them into a function. Code occurring once is the easiest to maintain and test. It is also easiest to modify your code in one function.

Often code that recurs will be difficult to maintain. The result is that, as you modify the recurring code, you are more likely to make an error. In other words, if you have the same 5 lines of code in 20 places, any modification has to be done 20 times. If you miss any, your program will behave erratically. This won't happen if you use a function.

Rule 2: Keep Functions Short

A short function is one that is less than 5 lines long (10 with error-handling code). In most circumstances, if there are more than 5 or 10 lines, the function is doing too much. Writing short functions takes more practice to perfect than any other technique. Remember, getting the code to work right is the most important goal. Allowing for the code's maturation and keeping the cost of ownership low is the second most important goal. Keeping functions short increases the chance that the code can be reused and promotes a low cost of ownership.

Rule 3: Strictly Limit the Number of Arguments

The best functions only require a few arguments because they only performing one task. Keep it simple. A basic acronym in programming is K.I.S.S—that is, "Keep it simple, stupid." Although this is a little blunt, it means simple is best.

When you are making the first pass at writing a new solution, concentrate on getting your code to work. On a second, third, and fourth pass, work on making the code small and robust and ensuring you pass only the arguments your code actually needs.

Rule 4: Use Argument Qualifiers to Inhibit Variable Misuse

Use the `ByVal`, `ByRef`, and `Optional` qualifiers (refer to the section "Defining Argument Types," earlier in this hour, for examples) to clearly indicate to the compiler your intended purpose. Although the reader or editor of your code might not understand the intended meaning of the qualifier, the compiler will enforce your intentions. You can worry about using the qualifiers that signify the intended use for your arguments after you are sure your code works.

Rule 5: Use Contract Programming

Contract programming is the term used for writing functions that presume your variables have reliable values and certain preconditions are met. The author of the code is the *contractor*, who stipulates assumptions about preconditions. The user of the code has to meet those preconditions. The user of the code is the *contractee*. Preconditions can be stipulated with comments and enforced with error-checking code that stops the program's execution if the preconditions are not met.

> The contractor and contractee can be one programmer. Whether you are acting as a contractor or contractee depends on whether you are writing the code or using the code.

Listing 8.4 contains an example of contract programming. The contract stipulates, with a comment, that the contractee (the user) is responsible for ensuring that the file referred to by FileName exists.

LISTING 8.4   An Example of Contract Programming

```
1: Function OpenFile( ByVal FileName As String ) As Double
2:     ' Contract: File must exist
3:     Debug.Assert Len(Dir(FileName)) > 0
4:     OpenFile = FreeFile
5:     Open FileName for Input As #OpenFile
6: End Function
```

ANALYSIS   As mentioned, you should stipulate the contract in plain English with a comment, as demonstrated in line 2. However, a contract without enforcement is not very useful. Line 3, Debug.Assert Len(Dir(FileName)) > 0, acts as the contract enforcer. If the Dir function passed with the FileName argument returns an empty string, meaning that the file was not found, the code halts at line 3. The test code enforces the contract.

Contract programming is a technique you can use to keep your functions simple and to delegate responsibility. In Listing 8.4, the user of OpenFile is responsible for making sure the file exists. Use contract programming as a means of encouraging reliable preconditions.

Rule 6: Don't Be Afraid to Comment

There are millions of lines of code that don't contain comments. One of the favorite reasons I've heard for not commenting is, "It was hard to write, so it should be hard to understand." I hope that the programmer was kidding. However, some code is so well written that it doesn't require comments. Self-documenting code is an ideal worth striving for. Most code, however, will benefit greatly from some simple text that describes what the code does and how it does it as well as any assumptions made while the programmer was writing the code.

Take a moment when you write a function to add a couple of plain sentences that describe what the code does in nontechnical jargon and supply a few words explaining your reasoning at the time you wrote it. This provides the best documentation of your code. It takes a lot more time to decipher the intent of the code at a later date. For example, lines 1–3 in Listing 8.3 don't really need any comments. If your code is that plain, don't be afraid to skip a few lines of comments.

Tying It All Together

When several lines recur in your program, or you can name the task the code performs, you can create a function. Writing good functions that are highly reusable and robust takes some practice. Get your problem solved and spend time refining your solution when you can. This section contains some practical examples that show you how you can write functions for some of the problems you might encounter in your day-to-day business.

The specific problems were chosen at random and are fairly generic, but they will show you the mechanics of assembling reusable solutions and provide you with some good, practical examples on which to model your code.

Creating a Table with Code

A database table is the second largest level of abstraction after the database. A database is comprised of one or more tables. There can be times when it is convenient to create a table dynamically and drop the table during a single run of your program.

Access 2002 uses the Structured Query Language (SQL), which is discussed in detail in Hour 16, "Using Advanced SQL Techniques," as well as VBA. For now, it's only important that you know that SQL can be used to literally create the table. Nonetheless, you might not want to use raw SQL every time you want to add a table. By wrapping the creation of the table in a named function, you can write a function one time that creates a table. You can then pass the table name as an argument to a function. Examine Listing 8.5 for a demonstration.

LISTING 8.5   Creating a Function to Create a Database Table

```
Sub CreateTable(ByVal TableName As String)
Dim SQL As String
' Uses SQL "CREATE TABLE" Command
```

LISTING 8.5   continued

```
        SQL = "CREATE TABLE " & TableName & "(TotalSales Double);"
        Call CurrentDb.Execute(SQL)
End Sub
```

ANALYSIS   You have to determine the suitability of code such as that in Listing 8.5. The code shows you how to create a function to dynamically create a named table with one column, TotalSales. Every place you substitute the function for literal copies of the code, you reduce the size and cost of maintaining your code.

> As a general rule, Listing 8.5 demonstrates how simple your functions should be. Think of statements as atoms and functions as molecules. In the physical world, everything imaginable is comprised of atoms and molecules. Your programs can be as powerful as the physical world, if you solve problems by building modestly upon small, solid building blocks.

Importing a Comma-Delimited Text File

DoCmd is a property of the Application object. The Application object refers to Access itself. So think of DoCmd as a capability of Access. DoCmd is a complex property. That is, it has capabilities and data associated with it, including the capability to import text files.

NEW TERM   A *property* is data that belongs to an object. Properties can be simple data or objects.

The capability to import text files is named TransferText. The syntax for TransferText is

```
Call DoCmd.TransferText( [transfertype][, specificationname], tablename,
➥filename[, hasfieldnames][, HTMLtablename][, codepage])
```

Because TransferText belongs to DoCmd, you prefix the function call with its owner, DoCmd. The argument transfer type is one of a set of predefined values. The value you want is acFixedDelim. The specification name is optional. More complex text files can be imported if you specify an alternate transfer type and define an import specification. The table name you want to import to and the filename you want to import from are mandatory. *Hasfieldnames, HTMLtablename*, and *codepage* are optional. They aren't necessary, but if you want to learn about them, Access Help is a good resource for examples and explanations.

Many predefined Access capabilities have a wide variety of uses based on the value of the arguments and the number of arguments that you actually send them. A useful technique is to wrap an Access function in a function that you define to simplify the interface.

You can redefine a function for importing comma-delimited files that require only the arguments you need and perform some validation, too. Consider a simple text file with the first and last names and the e-mail addresses of associates. The file might look like the example in Listing 8.6.

LISTING 8.6   A Sample Text File Containing Names and E-mail Addresses

```
First Name, Last Name, Email Address
Paul, Kimmel, pkimmel@softconcepts.com
Lori, Kimmel, Lori_Kimmel@yahoo.com
Robert, Golieb, RobertGolieb@hotmail.com
```

ANALYSIS   In a simple sense, the file in Listing 8.6 is essentially a database containing one table. You might want to export such a comma-delimited file into an existing database. The TransferText function can do this easily. Listing 8.7 shows a function that simplifies using import text for the purpose of importing a simple comma-delimited text file.

LISTING 8.7   Creating an Interface for the Generic TransferText Function Makes It Easier to Use and Maintain

```
 1: Sub ImportContactFile(ByVal FileName As String, ByVal TableName As String)
 2:   Const HASFIELDNAMES = True
 3:   If( FileExists(FileName)) Then
 4:     Call DoCmd.TransferText(acImportDelim, , TableName, FileName, _
 5:       HASFIELDNAMES)
 6:   Else
 7:     MsgBox "File not found " & FileName
 8:   End If
 9: End Sub10:
11: Function FileExists(ByVal FileName As String) As Boolean
12:   FileExists = Len(Dir(FileName)) > 0
13: End Sub
```

ANALYSIS By defining `ImportContactFile`, you can extend the basic capability of `TransferText` and conceal the aspects of `TransferText` you do not need your users to see. Concealing some information goes a long way toward minimizing defects and reducing complexity.

Finding a Record

As a professional programmer, I encounter code that contains raw SQL littered just about everywhere in a database program. Unfortunately, this kind of code is difficult to read and maintain. As in the preceding section, you can minimize SQL's deleterious impact on the bulk of your application by placing SQL inside a function.

Listing 8.8 defines a function that uses SQL to dynamically find a contact in the CONTACTS table imported in Listing 8.7. As you can see in Listing 8.8, it can take approximately 14 lines of code to perform a simple query operation on one table.

LISTING 8.8   Embedding SQL in a Function

```
1:   Function FindContact(ByVal LastName As String) As String
2:     Dim RecordSet As New ADODB.RecordSet
3:     Dim SQL As String
4:     SQL = "SELECT [First Name] + ' ' +  [Last Name] As " & +
5:     "[Contact Name]" FROM CONTACTS WHERE [Last Name] = '" & _
6:     LastName & "'"
7:     Call RecordSet.Open(SQL, CurrentProject.Connection, adOpenDynamic)
8:     If (RecordSet.BOF And RecordSet.EOF) = False Then
9:       FindContact = RecordSet("Contact Name")
10:    Else
11:      FindContact = "Not Found"
12:    End If
13:    RecordSet.Close
14:    Set RecordSet = Nothing
15: End Function
```

Functions are powerful because they are separately testable and modifiable chunks of code. The code in Listing 8.8 uses DAO. If I wanted to use ADO, optimized SQL, or no SQL at all, all that is required is that the function implementation be changed. No other code changes are required.

ANALYSIS Using the code in Listing 8.8 only requires one line of code. Simply call the FindContact function, passing a string representing the last name of the contact you want to find. Often, putting your code in a separate function makes it more comprehensible.

Using the Windows Registry

The Windows registry is comprised of a hierarchical relationship of keys and values kept in a big file. The Registry is used much like a database to persist information between application runs. With database tools you might elect to store information in either place.

> You can view the registry on your computer by typing regedit in the Run dialog. Click the Start button and select Run. Type regedit and press enter.
>
> Generally, it is unwise to modify the registry directly. If you make a mistake your system may not run correctly or event re-boot. If you are going to modify the registry, select Registry|Export Registry File in the Registry Editor to store a copy of the registry before making modifications.

Probably the most common kind of information stored in the registry for database applications is information that will help you connect to the database. Instead of storing connection information as we have been doing in the code listings, in a real application we would store this information in the registry. Thus if we moved the database we would not have to modify code; we would only need to modify the registry setting.

> Storing registry information like connection information is less critical in Access than it is with other tools. In Access as long as we are working with data in the current database we can use the CurrentProject object to get the Connection information; that is we are connected by default.

To save and retrieve registry information we can use the SaveSetting and GetSetting to write and read registry information directly. Generally, we would read this information upon application initialization or whenever we opened a connection. Listing 8.9 demonstrates reading the connection information dynamically from the registry. (See Figure 8.1 for a shot of the registry with the added Connection String key.) If the information returned from the registry is empty then the code performs a one time initialization with a default value.

Figure 8.1

Registry value containing a valid connection string added to the registry in Windows 2000 with SaveSetting.

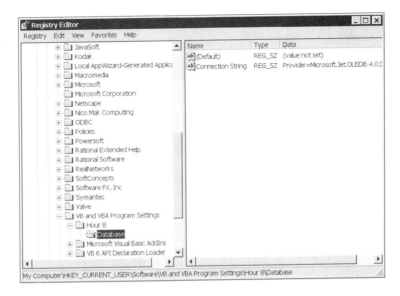

Listing 8.9 Reads a connection string value from the registry. If Connection String is empty then a default value is written to the registry.

```
1:  Function GetDefaultConnectionString() As String '
2:    GetDefaultConnectionString = _
3:     "Provider=Microsoft.Jet.OLDB.4.0;" & _
4:     "Data Source=C:\Books\Sams\Teach Yourself " & _
5:     "Access 2002 Programming in 24 Hours " & _
6:     "\Chapter 8\Hour8_1.mdb"
7:  End Function
8:
9:  Function GetConnectionString() As String
10:
11:   GetConnectionString = GetSetting("Hour 8", _
12:     "Database", "Connection String", "")
13:
14:   If (GetConnectionString = vbNullString) Then
15:     Call SaveSetting("Hour 8", "Database", _
16:       "Connection String", GetDefaultConnectionString())
17:
18:     GetConnectionString = GetSetting("Hour 8", _
19:       "Database", "Connection String", "")
20:   End If
21:
21: End Function
22:
23: Sub ConnectWithRegistryInfo()
24:   Dim Connection As New ADODB.Connection
25:   Connection.Open (GetConnectionString())
26:   MsgBox Connection.State = adStateOpen
27: End Sub
```

ANALYSIS   Line 23 defines a subroutine ConnectWithRegistry info. GetConnectionString()
on line 25 attempts to read the connection information from the registry with
GetSetting. If the registry doesn't contain the connection string then a default value is
written on line 15. Line 26 verifies the connection works properly, that is, the connection
string is correct.

Remember that the CurrentProject global object refers to the active database. If you need
to connect to an external data source then you may want to store that database's configuration information.

Use the registry if you need to store information about your application that you may
want available next time the user runs your database application.

Summary

Functions and subroutines are designed for collecting code that solves singular problems.
The landscape of your program is made up of these functions and subroutines and the
orchestration of their use.

This hour demonstrates how to write functions and subroutines. It also teaches you how
to pass arguments to them and how to use qualifiers that clarify the intended use of your
functions and subroutines to the human reader and the compiler. These are important for
both reliability and maintainability.

These rules of thumb can be applied to all the code that you write. They help you write
fewer lines of code that are higher in quality. The six rules of thumb help you get more
bang for you programming buck.

The hour wraps up with some practical examples of coupling SQL and database access
with functions, and it provides you with some ideas for the resources available to locate
other functions and subroutines. The following "Q&A" section provides you with some
additional tips.

Q&A

Q I want to test my function in Access. How do I do it?

A Open the module with your function and place the cursor in the function. Press the
F8 key.

Q How do I get my code to stop before it executes a certain line?

A In the Code view, click in the far-left column. A red bar will be drawn over that
line. This is referred to as a *breakpoint*.

Q **I want to view the value of my data while running my code. How do I do that?**

A While using the F8 key to step through your code, place the mouse over the variable in the code editor. A hint will display any relevant values.

8

Workshop

The Workshop includes quiz questions designed to help you test your understanding of the material covered and exercises to help put what you've learned to practice. You will find the answers to the quiz and exercises in Appendix A, "Answers."

Quiz

1. What is a good average length for a function?

2. If you want to define a function with an `Optional` argument, in what position should the argument be placed between the parentheses?

3. What would be one possible good name for a function that reads an e-mail address from a database?

4. What is the name of the object that refers to the current, open database?

5. What's the name of the application property containing many useful capabilities?

Exercises

1. In the section "Defining Argument Types," you created a subroutine that calculates sales. Implement this subroutine as a function.

2. In the section "Creating a Table with Code," you created a table in a demo database. Write a function that deletes or drops a table.

3. In the section "Importing a Comma-Delimited Text File," you imported a text file. Use the Access Help to rewrite the function to import an Excel spreadsheet.

HOUR 9

Using Macros As Learning Aids

A macro language is a programming language. A macro language has an interpreter that reads text written using special keywords and grammar. It then performs operations based on the macro text.

Access macros serve two purposes. An Access macro can solve problems. You can incorporate these solutions as part of your overall database solution. In Access, you also can use macros to learn how to write code.

Every programming language nowadays has some built-in capabilities. These capabilities consist of data types and functions. The Access macro language provides you with some of the same facilities that VBA does. Because macros can be written without data modules and test functions, you can use a macro as a quick-and-dirty means of testing and experimenting with different implementations of a solution. This hour shows you how to do that.

In this hour, you will learn

- How to write macros (a refresher course in creating macros)
- How to test a solution with a macro before implementing it

- How to use many different macros to solve common problems
- How to incorporate the capabilities found in macros into your code

Creating a Macro 101

Macros are stored as part of your database. To create macros, you need a test database. The test database that I will be using in this hour represents a simple concordance. A *concordance* counts and enters the number of words in a document.

The two tables used and referred to in this hour are a table named CONCORDANCE, which keeps and counts the words, and a table named DOCUMENT, which stores the filename and an index that is used to logically join the DOCUMENT table to the CONCORDANCE table.

Creating a Table with SQL

The CONCORDANCE database has two tables. The first table is the DOCUMENT table, which contains two columns, and the second is a table named CONCORDANCE (the same as the name given to the whole database). You can define the DOCUMENT table by running the following SQL statement:

```
CREATE TABLE DOCUMENT (DOCUMENTID AUTOINCREMENT CONSTRAINT
➡C1 PRIMARY KEY, FILENAME TEXT )
```

The CONCORDANCE table can be created with this SQL statement:

```
CREATE TABLE CONCORDANCE (ID  AUTOINCREMENT CONSTRAINT C1 PRIMARY KEY,
➡DOCUMENTID LONG, WORD TEXT, COUNT INTEGER)
```

To create a table using the CREATE TABLE SQL command, follow these steps:

1. Create a new database.
2. Click the Queries button in the Objects list.
3. Click New.
4. In the New Query dialog, select Design View.
5. Close the Show Table dialog.
6. Click the View, SQL View menu.
7. Type in the CREATE TABLE SQL, repeating the steps for both of the preceding SQL statements.

The relationship between the DOCUMENT and CONCORDANCE tables is "one to many." A one-to-many relationship means that for every one row in the DOCUMENT table, there are zero or more rows in the CONCORDANCE table.

The CREATE TABLE statement can be deciphered by referencing the Access Help file, searching on CREATE TABLE, and looking at the syntax and sample code. Here is the general syntax used for CREATE TABLE:

```
CREATE TABLE tablename (fieldname datatype [(fieldsize_in_parentheses)])
```

Type the literal SQL command CREATE TABLE. Immediately after CREATE TABLE, provide a table name and then place the field name, data type, and (optionally) the field size in parentheses. You can define as many fields as you need in the parentheses by separating the field descriptors with a comma.

The following is a revised version of the SQL that creates the DOCUMENT table, demonstrating how to specify a size for the FILENAME column:

```
CREATE TABLE DOCUMENT (DOCUMENTID AUTOINCREMENT CONSTRAINT
➥C1 PRIMARY KEY, FILENAME TEXT(255) )
```

You can follow along with the examples by using the CONCORDANCE database or by referring to the definition of the two tables in this section.

Creating a Macro

Macros are defined as objects in every database. You create an empty macro by clicking the Macros button in the database Objects view. Clicking the New button, with the Macros button selected, opens the Macro design view with the default name for the macro. The default naming convention for macros is Macro*n* where *n* is incremented to ensure a unique name for each macro. (see Figure 9.1 for an example of the Macro design view; the design view shows the naming convention at work, having created a unique named Macro2).

When you have added code to a macro, give the macro a good name, as you would for any other database object.

The macro definition interface is very similar to the table definition interface. The left column of the Macro design view contains a list of actions you can select. The column on the right is for adding comments. You can use the Comment column to add documentation for your macro.

After you select a Macro Action label, input text fields appear on the bottom-left half of the Macro design view. These are referred to as *action arguments*. Action arguments are just like function and subroutine arguments. Action arguments supply information the macro needs in order to run correctly.

FIGURE 9.1

The Macro design view.

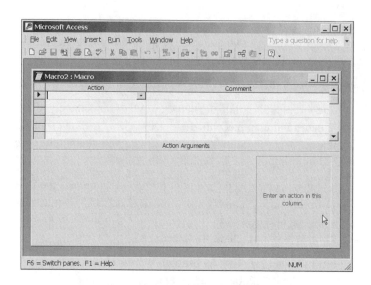

In the very first line of the Action column, select or type **RunMacro** in the cell on the top left. This will display three action argument input fields. These are Macro Name, Repeat Count, and Repeat Expression. By adding data for the action arguments, you can run the macro specified in the Macro name input field. (See Figure 9.2 to see the change in the Macro design view.)

FIGURE 9.2

The Macro design view with the RunMacro action arguments input fields displayed.

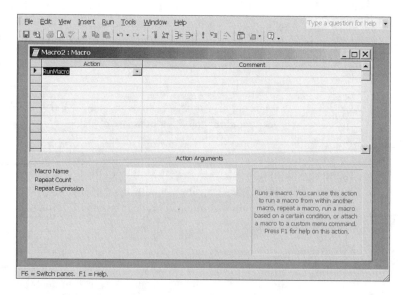

After you have defined a macro, you can run the macro by clicking the Run button (the button with the exclamation point on it) or by selecting the Run, Run menu item.

Defining Macro Names and Conditional Code

There are two additional columns you can define in each of your macros: the Macro Name column and the Condition column. The Macro Name and Conditional columns can be displayed when a macro is open in design mode. To view the Macro Name and Condition columns, select View, Macro Names and View, Conditions. To have the macro Names and Conditions columns displayed in the Macro design view by default, select Tools|Options|View and check Names Column and Conditions column in the Show in Macro Design group (see Figure 9.3)

FIGURE 9.3

The View tab of the Options dialog enables you to turn on the Macro Names and Condition columns in the Macro dialog.

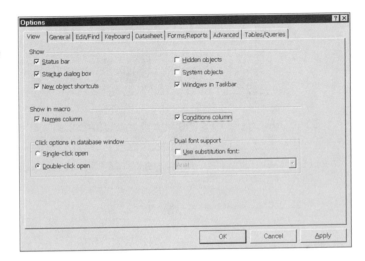

The Condition column is very useful. You can write statements in the Condition column that evaluate to a Boolean result. If the Condition result returns `True`, the macro statement will run. If the result returns `False`, the macro line won't run.

You can temporarily disable individual lines of macro code by placing a literal `False` in the Condition column on the Macro dialog.

A wide variety of code can be put in the Condition column. Figure 9.4 shows the Condition column defined to return the negation of the result returned by `TableExists`. The macro is an example of using a macro to test a function. The conditional statement is

```
Not TableExists("DOCUMENT")
```

Take a look at Figure 9.4, which shows the conditional test for the macro. The code for
`TableExists` is shown in Listing 9.1.

FIGURE 9.4

*The Condition column
lets you write condi-
tional code to deter-
mine whether a macro
statement will run.*

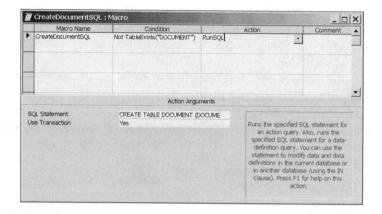

LISTING 9.1   `TableExists` Uses the `OpenTable` Command and Error Handling to
Facilitate Creating a Table with Macro Code

```
 1: Function TableExists(ByVal TableName As String) As Boolean
 2:     On Error GoTo Except
 3:     TableExists = True
 4:     Call DoCmd.SelectObject(acTable, TableName)
 5:     Exit Function
 6:
 7: Except:
 8:     TableExists = False
 9:     Err.Clear
10: End Function
```

Trying to open the table to determine if it exists or not, as demonstrated in
Listing 9.1, works fine unless you have the Visual Basic Editor "Break On All
Errors Checked" selected. (This feature can be set in the General tab of the
Tools, Options dialog in the Error Trapping group.

"Break On All Errors Checked" is a good design-time feature. I would not
ship a database to users with this option selected unless you want to visit
your users every time your database has an error. The only time you want
the application to stop is when you cannot handle an error condition, and it
doesn't make sense to continue processing.

When you right-click in the Condition column, a pop-up menu appears. The Build menu item will display the Condition Builder dialog. This dialog helps you build conditions and provides access to tables, queries, forms, reports, functions, constants, operators, and common expressions.

The Condition Build dialog has been around for a while. It is well documented in the Help files. You can handcraft conditional code or use the Condition Build dialog to help.

ANALYSIS Line 1 defines the function TableExists that is used in the macro `CreateTable`. Line 2 sets error trapping for this function. You will learn more about error handling in Hour 18, "Adding Code to Handle Errors." Line 2 instructs the compiler to go to the label Except in the event of any error condition. Line 3 establishes a default return value of `True`. (I am being optimistic.) In line 4, `DoCmd.SelectObject` calls the macro command `SelectObject`, trying to select the table referred to by `TableName`. (Unfortunately, SelectObject doesn't return a Boolean; otherwise, it could be used in the Condition column.) Line 6 exits the function. The code from line 8, including lines 9 and 10, is run only if an error occurs on line 4. If the error code runs, you know that the table wasn't found, and `False` is returned from the function (on line 9). Line 10 clears the `Err` object.

The `Err` object contains information about an error condition. `Err` information is set any time an error condition occurs. You can write your code to check the `Err` object any time you want. (You'll find more about `Err` in Hour 18.)

Testing and Debugging a Macro

After you have created your macro, test it. Macros do not offer as rich a testing and programming environment as VBA code in the Microsoft Visual Basic editor, but you can effectively test macros.

I will use the macro from the previous section to demonstrate. If you want to follow along, create the macro by performing these steps:

1. Click the Macros button in the database Objects view.
2. Click New.
3. Add **NOT TableExists("DOCUMENT")** in the Condition column.
4. Select RunSQL in the Action column.
5. In the SQL Statement input field, enter the code to create the DOCUMENT table.
6. Save the module and switch back to the macro view.

7. Click the Run button.

8. You will be prompted to save the macro. Click Yes.

You can run the code by clicking Run, Run. If the DOCUMENT table was already created because of an earlier exercise, it will fail because the table already exists.

To step through the macro, click the Step button. The Step button is adjacent and to the right of the Run button. Alternatively, you can select the Run, Single Step menu item. The Single Step menu button will toggle on and off. In single-step mode, clicking the Run button will run only one line of the macro for each click.

If you have a macro with multiple lines, stepping is a good way to run one line of the macro and then verify that the task is performed correctly. If you want to test the VBA code, you can place a breakpoint on the first line of the TableExists function (see Figure 9.5).

FIGURE 9.5

You can debug code used in your macro by placing a breakpoint in any functions that the macro calls.

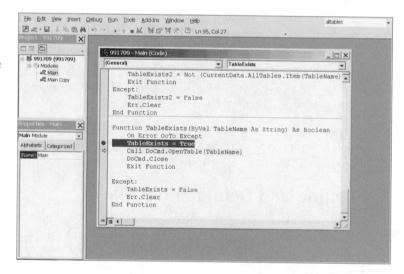

To place a breakpoint in code, open the module containing the code you want to step through. Click the line of code that you want to break on and then press the F9 key. You will know that the breakpoint is set because the line of code will be highlighted in red with a red circle in the left margin. Use the F9 key to toggle the breakpoint on and off.

Although you can use the Watch window, quick watches, and the Immediate window in the editor, you cannot use them in the macro window. After a complete step (one macro line of code) is executed, the Macro Single Step dialog, shown in Figure 9.6, will be displayed.

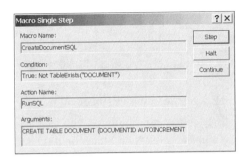

FIGURE 9.6

After each complete line of macro code is executed, the Macro Single Step dialog is displayed, showing the status of the macro code run.

Now that you know the basic mechanics of creating macros, you can test code ideas with macros before implementing complete solutions or create macros to support your database development. The rest of the hour contains some practical examples of macros.

Using CopyObject

The CopyObject macro action uses the term Object as a generic term, where Object refers to items such as tables, queries, macros, or modules. The CopyObject action can be used to copy a table, query, form, report, macro, module, or Data Access Page within the current database with a new name or to a new database.

Here, I use the CopyObject action to create a backup macro for the CONCORDANCE table. While following along with Figure 9.7, complete the numbered steps to create a backup macro:

FIGURE 9.7

A macro to back up the CONCORDANCE table.

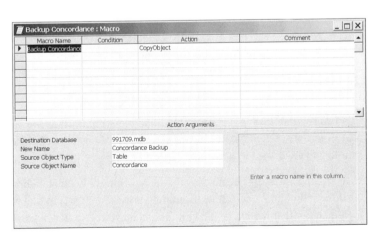

1. Click Macros in the Objects view.

2. Click New.

3. In the first row in the Action column, select `CopyObject`. This displays the action arguments for `CopyObject`.

4. Type the name of the database in the Destination Database input field. My database name is `concordance.mdb`.

5. Type **Concordance Backup** in the New Name input field.

6. Select Table in the Source Object Type field.

7. Type **Concordance** in the Source Object Name field.

Remember to save and test the macro. After you run the macro, you will see a table named CONCORDANCE BACKUP in the Tables view.

Using `DeleteObject`

You can combine `DeleteObject` with `CopyObject` and `TableExists` to implement a complete table-backup scheme. To complete a backup scheme for the CONCORDANCE table, you implement `DeleteObject` for the Concordance Backup table and reuse the `CopyObject` macro, which creates the backup file.

Using `DeleteObject` is easier than using `CopyObject`. To delete the Concordance Backup table, follow these steps:

1. Click Macros in the Objects view.

2. Click New.

3. In the Actions column, select the `DeleteObject` macro action.

4. In the Action Arguments input fields, enter **Table** for Object Type and **Concordance Backup** for Object Name.

Test the new macro.

If you run the `Delete Concordance` macro a second time, you will get an error, as shown in Figure 9.8, when `DeleteObject` attempts to delete Concordance Backup a second time. Now we need to add some error handling.

To create a backup scheme, you might be tempted to create a brand new macro and copy all the individual macro lines from the various macros into a new single macro. Remember that the reuse ideal applies to macros, too. If you copy the code, you will have to re-test. However, if you reuse the existing macros then you will only have one copy of the macro code and will not have to re-test.

FIGURE 9.8

A general error message is displayed when DeleteObject *is called a second time on the same table.*

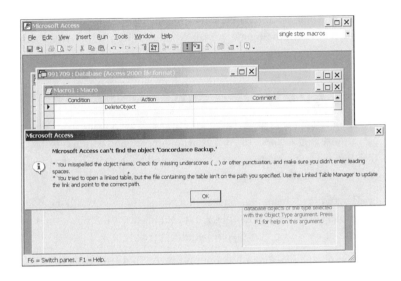

A backup macro must check whether the object exists—in this instance, the Concordance Backup table—before it attempts to delete the object. If the object exists, the DeleteObject macro should run, followed by the CopyObject macro.

A new macro and the RunMacro command can be used to facilitate creating the backup macro. Implementing the new solution in this fashion maintains the two previous macros as unchanged. A good technique for reducing debugging and testing time is to use something that works without changing it at all.

To implement the new macro, called Backup, complete these steps:

1. Click the Macros button in the Objects view.

2. Click the New button.

3. In the first row of the Condition column, reuse the TableExists function, passing Concordance Backup as the argument.

4. In the first row in the Action column, select RunMacro.

5. In the Macro Name field for the first row of the macro, select Delete Concordance.

6. Add a second row in the macro. Again, choose RunMacro.

7. In the Macro Name field of the second macro row, select Concordance Backup.

A general rule of thumb is that after you have tested a macro (this applies to functions and subroutines, too), you only need to test it again if you change the macro. By reusing macros you know that TableExists, Delete Concordance, and Concordance Backup all work correctly. Creating a new macro from existing macros means that you still can use the original macros by themselves. You don't have to retest those macros, and you can quickly reassemble new macros from existing macros. Macro and code aggregation will keep your code simple.

The Keys to the City

Using RunCommand is like getting the keys to the city. You can use RunCommand to manage almost every aspect of Access. The RunCommand action has one action argument command. The Command action is a required argument. To select a command, you can pick one of dozens from the Command input field.

There are so many RunCommand capabilities that a whole book could be written on the subject. (This is a good place to remind you of the power and benefit of the Help files and of consulting with your peers.)

The RunCommand action is both powerful and easy to use. To use RunCommand, create a new macro and then select the RunCommand action and a Command action argument. Figure 9.9 shows the database properties summary displayed when you run the RunCommand macro with the DatabaseProperties Command.

One of the new features of Access 2002 is the capability to remove author information (that is, database properties).

The General tab of the Tools, Options dialog allows you to remove all personal information from the database.

FIGURE 9.9

Using the RunCommand macro option to show the Database Properties dialog.

db1.mdb Properties	
General	Summary	Statistics	Contents	Custom
Title:	991709
Subject:	Teach Yourself Access 2000
Author:	Paul Kimmel
Manager:	
Company:	Software Conceptions, Inc
Category:	Learning to Program
Keywords:	
Comments:	
Hyperlink base:	http://www.softconcepts.com
Template:	
	OK	Cancel

Importing Data

Importing information from external sources is a common task. You might have spreadsheet data that you want in your Access database, text information exported from a mainframe computer, or data simply transferred from an existing Access database to a new one.

Transferring a Database

To transfer a database with a macro, you first create a new macro. The Action value for transferring a database is TransferDatabase. The action arguments for TransferDatabase are Transfer Type, Database Type, Database Name, Object Type, Source, Destination, and Structure Only.

Transfer Type can be Import, Export, or Link. Select Import if you want to bring data into the current database. Choose Export if you want to copy data from the current database to an external one. Choose Link if you want to create a logical attachment to an external data source. Linking data can be a good way to use existing data without making a copy that might get out of sync.

Specifying the Database Type

The database type can be any valid type for which your computer has a driver. The combo box list will contain all the types from which you can choose. The last type in the combo box list for Database Type is ODBC Database. If you choose ODBC Database, you must enter an ODBC alias in the Database Name field.

NEW TERM *ODBC (Open Database Connectivity)* is a protocol that specifies an interface design that all database manufacturers can use to facilitate reliable communication between computer programs and different databases.

Specifying the Database Name

The Database Name action argument is the physical file location of the database file from which the transfer will be made, or it is an ODBC alias.

Choosing an Object Type to Transfer

The Object Type action argument describes the object you want to transfer. You can select Table, Query, Form Report, Macro, or Module. However, the object type must be applicable to both the object from which you are transferring and the object to which you are transferring.

Specifying a Transfer Source and Destination

The Source action argument specifies where the data is coming from, and the Destination action argument indicates where the data is headed.

Replicating Structure Only

The last action argument is Structure Only. If this argument is False, you will get the object and data. If it is True, you will get only the object.

 The Structure Only action argument applies to Table objects only.

You can modify the backup macro from the earlier section to back up a single table or an entire database to an external database. To back up a single table, use TransferDatabase and Export instead of CopyObject.

Transferring Text Data

The TransferText macro action enables you to get data from any external text file in which the text is in a consistent format. (If the text is in mixed formats, you can write code to separate the file into separate files, one for each format.)

To use TransferText, you must do two important things. The first is to define a new macro, indicate TransferText, and specify action arguments. The second is to create a specification (more about that in a minute).

The action arguments for transferring text are Transfer Type, Specification Name, Table Name, File Name, Has Field Names, HTML Table Name, and Code Page.

Specifying a Text Transfer Type

Transfer Type can be one of three variations of importing, linking, and exporting. To transfer text from a comma-delimited file, choose Import Delimited. For a fixed-format file, choose Import Fixed.

Creating a Transfer Specification

Specification Name is actually the name of a record in one of the Access hidden tables. You will have to import or link to an external file that contains the specification that you want to use in order to create a specification.

To learn how to create a transfer specification, start by creating a text file named phone-book.txt with the following data:

```
Name, Address, City, State, Zip
```

The comma-delimited names will provide you with enough information to create the specification.

The specification is created as part of the process of importing, exporting, or linking. I will demonstrate this by walking you through importing the table represented by the text file phonebook.txt.

To create a transfer specification that can be reused automatically by macros, perform these steps:

1. Create a new blank database by selecting View, Toolbars, Task Pane and clicking Blank Database in the task pane. You will need to specify a name and location for your new database before you proceed.

2. Click Tables in the Object view.

3. Click New.

4. In the New Table dialog, click Import and click OK.

5. In the Import dialog's Files of Type input field, select the Text Files type.

6. Select the phonebook.txt file and click Import.

7. The Import Text Wizard will be set to use the Delimited type, but click the Advanced button so that you can see how to create a specification.

8. The Phonebook Import Specification dialog will be displayed (see Figure 9.10). In the five fields (temporarily named field1, field2, and so on), type the name of the fields (Name, Address, City, State, and Zip).

FIGURE 9.10

The Import Text Wizard's Phonebook Import Specification dialog.

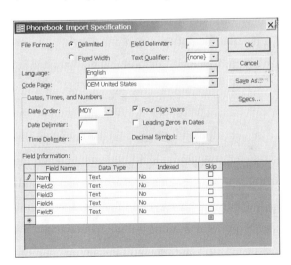

9. To save this specification, click the Save As button; use the default specification name of Phonebook Import Specification. Click OK to close the Phonebook Import Specification dialog.

10. Click Next to proceed to the next step of the wizard. Check First Row Contains Field Names.

11. Click Next.

12. Click Next. The third dialog of the Import Text Wizard enables you to indicate whether you want to use a new table or an existing table. Leave the default, In a New Table, checked.

13. Click Next.

14. The fourth step enables you to specify data type, field name, and index information about the table. Click the State column and change the indexed field to Yes (Duplicates OK).

15. Click Next.

16. Use the default to let Access create a primary key for you.

17. Click Next.

18. Use the default table name of Phonebook. Click Finish to create the table.

Steps 8 and 9 create and save the import specification. If you open the Phonebook table and the data and columns look correct, the import specification is correct.

The import specification you created will be an item in the input field after it is created and saved. To complete the macro, add the name of the specification you defined in steps 7, 8, and 9.

Specifying a Table Name

You must enter a unique table name in the `TransferText` macro's Table Name action argument field. You can use a macro similar to the `DeleteObject` macro from the earlier section "Using `DeleteObject`" to ensure that no table name collisions occur.

Specifying a Filename

You must specify the filename for the `TransferText` macro. There are many points of interest here. For instance, how will you ensure that the file from which to transfer exists? The answer is that you will write some conditional code and perhaps some VBA code.

One way to request a dynamic filename is to use the `InputBox` function for the File Name action argument. If you write

```
=Input("Enter filename to transfer:","File Name","phonebook.txt")
```

for the File Name argument (note the equal symbol) when you run the macro, the `InputBox` function will be called, and the user will be prompted to enter a filename to transfer.

Does the Text Source Contain Field Names?

If you want the TransferText macro to treat the first line of text in the transfer source file as the field names for your new table, change the Has Field Names action argument field to Yes.

If the first row contains the field names, as it does in this example, you don't want that data imported as data but rather as column names. This has the same effect as step 10 in the numbered instructions in "Creating a Transfer Specification."

Using HTML Table Data

You can import table data from an HTML page, too. If you choose Import HTML, Link HTML, or Export HTML in the Transfer Type action argument for the TransferText macro, your table will be transferred from (or *to*, if you choose Export HTML) an HTML table.

Indicating a Code Page

The Code Page action argument enables you to specify a Unicode language type for the transfer. The default is the code page configured for Access.

Using Macro Resources in Code

Every one of the macro action items can be used in code. The slight difference between running a macro from the macro Run menu and running the macro in code is that you have to use the predefined DoCmd object to run the macro in code. DoCmd contains all the macro action items as functions. The action arguments are arguments to the DoCmd function.

Therefore, if you want to transfer text in VBA code, write a statement using the TransferText function, as follows:

```
DoCmd.TransferText [transfertype][, specificationname], tablename,
➡filename[, hasfieldnames][, HTMLtablename][, codepage]
```

The DoCmd.TransferText function is written literally. The only two arguments you must supply are the *tablename* and *filename* arguments. The default transfer type is to import from a delimited text file. You do not need a *specification name* argument for delimited imports. The hasfieldnames argument is False by default. *HTMLtablename* is ignored by default, and *codepage* is the default language for your computer.

If you wanted to write a subroutine to import the phonebook, you could use the import specification defined in "Creating a Transfer Specification" and write a function such as the one in Listing 9.2.

LISTING 9.2   Writing Code to Import a Text File Using an Import Specification

```
1:  Sub ImportPhoneBook()
2:    Const DefaultFileName = "c:\temp\book\phonebook.txt"
3:    Const ImportSpecification = "Phonebook Import Specification"
4:    Dim FileName As String
5:    FileName = InputBox("Import file:", "Import", DefaultFileName)
6:    DoCmd.TransferText acImportDelim, ImportSpecification, _
7:      "Phonebook", FileName
8:  End Sub
```

ANALYSIS   Line 1 declares a `FileName` variable to store a dynamically entered text file to import. Line 3 uses the `InputBox` function to request the import file, and line 4 uses `DoCmd.TransferText` to import the file. The first argument to `TransferText` is a constant defined in Access to indicate a delimited file import. The second argument uses "Phonebook Import Specification", the import specification defined earlier. The table name is PhoneBook, and the dynamic variable `FileName` contains the reference to the file from which to import.

To Macro or Not to Macro

From a programmer's perspective, if you have a choice between using a macro and using code, use code. Macros are useful if you do not know how to program. Macros also are useful if you want to experiment with different parameters to use commands such as `TransferText`. Ultimately, you will need error-handling and dynamic aspects of code to create functional and robust solutions.

A great benefit of macros is that you can save them in such a way as to convert them to VBA code in a module. In this fashion, you get the ease of writing macros and the benefit of modifying them as code, making the code more robust if you need to. To save a macro as VBA code follow the numbered steps.

1. Select Macros in the Objects view.
2. Right-click on the macro you want to convert and select Save As.
3. In the Save As dialog provide a good name for the module and select Module from the As combobox. Click OK.
4. In the Convert macro dialog leave the defaults checked; you do want error handling and included macro comments.

When you click the Convert button the module will be created and the Visual Basic editor will be opened. Listing 9.3 demonstrates a macro named Backup Concordance macro converted to VBA code.

LISTING 9.3 The Backup Concordance macro saved as VBA code from a macro.

```
1:  Option Compare Database
2:  Option Explicit
3:  '------------------------------------------------------------
4:  ' Backup_Concordance_Backup_Concordance
5:  '
6:  '------------------------------------------------------------
7:  Function Backup_Concordance_Backup_Concordance()
8:  On Error GoTo Backup_Concordance_Backup_Concordance_Err
9:
10:    DoCmd.CopyObject "991709.mdb", "Concordance Backup", acTable,
"Concordance"
11:
12:
13: Backup_Concordance_Backup_Concordance_Exit:
14:    Exit Function
15:
16: Backup_Concordance_Backup_Concordance_Err:
17:    MsgBox Error$
18:    Resume Backup_Concordance_Backup_Concordance_Exit
19:
20: End Function
```

ANALYSIS The converted code doesn't do anything special. The most significant code is contained on line 10, the CopyObject command. Everything else is a vanilla error handler that displays the content of an Error if one occurs. You could use the macro generated VBA code as a learning aid, but generated code tends to be a little verbose. Macros are fine. Code gives you more control. Start with a macro. If you find it doesn't solve the problem, or provide enough protection against errors, generate the macro code as VBA code and make necessary modifications.

Summary

In this hour, you learned how to use the Macro design view. You learned how to use predefined macro actions and specify action arguments. There are many powerful uses for macros. Macros can be used to test implementation ideas, to learn to use new programming capabilities, and to perform housekeeping tasks.

Generally, before you ship your solution to your customer, you will profit by converting your macros to code. You can use the DoCmd object in code to get at the same resources that macros offer. You can exercise more control over your code than you can over your macros, and you can create dynamic and fault-tolerant solutions.

VBA code will be easier to implement, test, and debug. Macros are a useful resource, and you will be glad to have macros in your arsenal, but now that you know how to write code, that's the way to go.

Q&A

Q When should I use macros instead of code?

A If you are not creating an Access program, but just need a small task performed, a macro is a good choice.

Q Can I perform any tasks with macros that I can't perform with code?

A No. Macros are useful, but code is more so. Macros have been around longer, perhaps because a macro language was easier to implement than a database programming language. Because macros are older technology, at some point, they might disappear from the Microsoft Office landscape.

Q Are there other objects such as DoCmd that I can use?

A Absolutely. Because of object-oriented programming, there are many interesting objects. You may enjoy investigating the Application and CurrentDB objects.

Q How can I learn about all the things that Access already offers me as a programmer?

A Unfortunately, that is a hard question. The tools available are too vast to master easily. Reading books such as this one, writing code, interacting with your peers, and time will be the best teachers. You will find that those things you need 80 percent of the time will become familiar to you, and you will rely heavily on the Help files for everything else.

Workshop

The Workshop includes quiz questions designed to help you test your understanding of the material covered and exercises to help put what you've learned to practice. You will find the answers to the quiz and exercises in Appendix A, "Answers."

Quiz

1. What command can I use to transfer data from an Excel spreadsheet?
2. How is an import specification created?
3. What command uses import specifications?
4. What is the name of the object you can use to program macro commands in code?
5. Can commands such as DoCmd be used in other Office applications too?

Exercises

1. Write a macro to back up all tables to a database.

2. Write code to get the input filename from a user for transferring text.

3. Write the code equivalent of a backup macro that uses `DeleteObject` and `CopyObject`.

9

HOUR **10**

Employing Access Predefined Solutions

When you program in Access, you are programming in the Visual Basic for Applications language (VBA), which now exists in all of Microsoft's Office XP desktop tools. Until Microsoft Visual Basic.NET was invented (not yet released), Visual Basic and Visual Basic for Applications were converging on becoming a single language. Visual Basic.NET is a brand new language; only the basic constructs of Microsoft Access VBA and Visual Basic.NET are interchangeable. You no longer will be able to exchange VBA files between Access (or other Office XP applications) and Microsoft's Visual Basic.NET programming language. Currently, you cannot take advantage of the .NET framework with VBA, but VBA is a powerful desktop solutions programming language in it's own right.

VBA has its roots in PDP-11 B.A.S.I.C., which Bill Gates and Paul Allen ported to the MIPS Altair computer in the 1970s. There was ROM BASIC, GW-BASIC, BASIC for DOS, the first Visual Basic for DOS, Visual Basic for Windows, VBA, and most recently Visual Basic.NET. Visual Basic.NET is a brand new, "first-class," object-oriented programming language. The similarities between VBA and Visual Basic began to diverge radically after Visual Basic 6.

Because of its rich and diverse history, VBA is a powerful and easy-to-use language, especially when compared to languages such as Assembler and C++. VBA contains a tremendous amount of predefined code that you can tap into to solve your problems. Fortunately, you will not have to solve very many common kinds of programming problems because the code already exists.

In this hour, you will learn how to take advantage of existing capabilities in VBA

- By using string-handling functions
- By formatting data
- By managing basic, non-database file input and output

Using String-Handling Functions

All data, in a sense, is stored as strings of characters. It is often useful to convert even numeric data into string data. Working with contiguous lists of characters, or *strings*, is one of the most common tasks you will perform.

When you get dynamic input from users, it will probably come to you as string data. A rich library of string-handling functions and subroutines are available for your everyday use. Even so, there are so many operations you can perform on strings, you will no doubt want to create additional capabilities.

In this section, I will show you how to use existing string functions and derive others from these. Let's get started.

Converting Between String and Numeric Values

Str and Val are two useful functions that enable you to convert numbers to strings and strings to numbers. The syntax for Str is

Str(*number*)

The Str function and parentheses are literal values. The *number* argument is any valid numeric argument, whether a literal or a variable. You pass in the numeric value and receive a string value with the same information in return.

The Val function performs the inverse operation. Pass in a string containing contiguous numeric characters, and you get a numeric value in return. The syntax for Val is

```
Val(string)
```

Val and the parentheses are literal values, and the *string* argument is a contiguous string of numeric characters. Here are some valid values for the *string* argument:

```
"1234"
"-54321"
"-0.78"
"10e34"
```

Here, e is used to indicate an exponential number. If you pass in other nonnumeric alphabetic characters, they are ignored. Therefore, 1313 Mockingbird Ln. will be the number 1313 if passed as an argument to Val. Listing 10.1 contains some examples of Str and Val.

LISTING 10.1 Examples of Str and Val

```
 1: Sub StrAndVal()
 2:     Dim L As Long
 3:     Dim D As Double
 4:     D = Val("10e34")
 5:     Debug.Print D
 6:     L = Val("3i")
 7:     Debug.Print L
 8:     Dim S As String
 9:     Dim T As String
10:     S = Str(D)
11:     Debug.Print S
12:     T = Str(L)
13:     Debug.Print T
14:     Debug.Print TypeName(T)
15:     Debug.Print T
16: End Sub
```

ANALYSIS The conversions are straightforward. An interesting use of the TypeName function writes the type of T, a string, to the Immediate window. Debug.Print writes information to the Immediate window. The output for StrAndVal is shown in Figure 10.1. The Debug.Print D statement on line 4 shows that the string "10e34" converts to the value 1e35. Line 7 prints the value 3, demonstrating that the literal i was truncated from the conversion.

FIGURE 10.1

The last four lines of output from StrAndVal data conversions in the Immediate window.

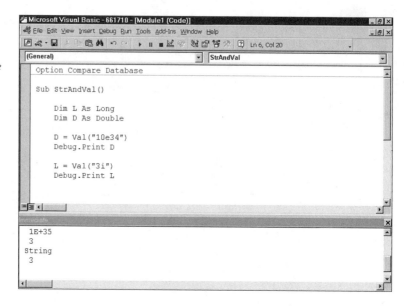

Dual Type String Functions

Table 10.1 contains a list of functions that have two versions. The functions in Table 10.1 can be used with or without the dollar sign ($) at the end of the function name. If you use the function without the dollar sign, the function returns a Variant data type. The same function with the dollar sign returns a String type.

TABLE 10.1   Dual-Mode Functions That Return a String When $ Is Used and a Variant When $ Is Not Used

Function	Description
Chr$(*charcode*)	Returns a string containing characters.
ChrB$(*charcode*)	A single-byte string containing a character.
Command$	Returns a string containing command-line arguments.
CurDir$[(*drive*)]	The current directory on the drive. The drive letter is optional.
Date$	The current date.
Dir$[(*searchmask* [, *fileattributes*])]	Returns the first file matching *searchmask*.
Error$[(*errornumber*)]	Returns the error message that coincides with *errornumber*. If the error number is omitted, this function returns the error message for the last error.

TABLE 10.1 continued

Function	Description
Format$(expression[, format[, firstdayofweek[, firstweekofyear]]])	Returns a formatted string based on the format instructions and the optional "day of the week" and "week of the year" arguments.
Hex$(number)	Returns a string representing the hexadecimal number represented by number.
Input$(number, [#]filenumber)	Returns a string of characters read from an opened file. number specifies the number of characters to return.
InputB$(number, [#]filenumber)	Returns a string containing the number of bytes from an opened file.
Lcase$(string)	Returns a string in lowercase.
Left$(string, length)	Returns the left substring of characters represented by length.
LeftB$(string, length)	Returns the left substring of bytes represented by length.
Ltrim$(string)	Returns a string with leading spaces trimmed.
Mid$(string, start[, length])	Returns a substring of characters starting at start to length.
MidB$(string, start[, length])	Returns a substring of bytes starting at start to length.
Oct$(number)	Returns a string representing the octal number.
Right$(string, length)	Returns a substring of characters from string, counting from the right, to length.
RightB$(string, length)	Returns a substring of bytes from string, counting from the right, to length.
Rtrim$(string)	Returns the right substring trimming removing trailing spaces.
Space$(number)	Returns a string of spaces of length number.
Str$(number)	Returns a string representing the number.
String$(length, characters)	Returns a string padded with characters repeated the number of times specified in length.
Time$	Returns a string with the current system time.
Trim$(string)	Returns a string with leading and trailing whitespace removed.
Ucase$(string)	Returns a string in uppercase.

For example, when you call the Chr(65) function, a Variant type is returned. If you call Chr$(65), a string type is returned, although both uses resolve to the character A.

The Variant type is more generic and flexible but requires more memory usage than the specific String type. Although the String type is specific, no implicit type conversion is performed on the data. Although variants are flexible and convenient, as a programming practice, it pays to write what you mean. If you know the type of the data you want, use that type. If the function you are using requires a variant value, use the variant form of the function.

General Data Type Conversion Functions

There are too many functions to cover in a single book. Help files remain unchallenged as the best source for facts. That said, there are several useful functions available for converting string or numeric expressions into specific data types. These functions all take the same form: Pass a string or numeric value as the only argument to the function and assign the result to a variable of the data type indicated as the return type for the function.

Because the functions all have the same form, I will only demonstrate a few of them. The conversion functions are detailed in the following list:

- CBool converts an expression to a Boolean type.
- CByte converts an expression to a Byte type.
- CCur converts an expression to a Currency type.
- CDate converts an expression into a Date type.
- CDbl converts an expression into a Double type.
- CDec converts an expression into a Decimal type.
- CInt converts an expression into an Integer type.
- CLng converts an expression into a Long type.
- CSng converts an expression into a single-precision floating-point number.
- CStr converts an expression into a String type.
- CVar converts an expression into a Variant type.

> You cannot declare a Decimal data type variable. You have to declare variables that you want to contain decimal numbers as Variant types.

To convert the string value "False" into a Boolean type, you use the CBool function:

```
Dim B As Boolean
B = CBool("False")
```

To convert a very big number stored as a string into a decimal type, you can declare a `Variant` variable and use the `CDec` function to convert the string into a `Variant` type with a `Decimal` subtype. The following code fragment demonstrates this:

```
Dim S As String
S = "1234567890123456789"
Dim D As Variant
D = CDec(S)
D = D * 10000
MsgBox D
```

The conversion functions are commonly used by programmers because you generally have to present data as a string to allow the user to modify that data and then you have to convert the data back to its original type to evaluate or perform calculations on it.

Searching Strings

The `InStr` function is used to perform substring searches. Extricating string data from text is a common and useful task. The `InStr` function has the following syntax:

```
InStr([start, ]searchin, searchfor[, compare] )
```

The `InStr` function accepts an optional starting index. The start index is useful when you're searching for repeated substrings. The `searchin` argument is the string to search. The `searchfor` argument is the substring you want to find in the search string. Valid values for the optional argument `compare` are `vbUseCompareOptions`, `vbBinaryCompare`, `vbTextCompare`, and `vbDatabaseCompare`.

`vbUseCompareOptions` tells the `InStr` function to use the setting expressed in the `Option Compare` statement. Use `vbBinaryCompare` to compare the underlying ASCII value, character by character. This is also considered a case-sensitive compare. Use `vbTextCompare` to perform a case-insensitive compare.

If `InStr` returns zero, the substring searched for is not in the search string. Any value greater than zero indicates the offset of the string being searched. By using the result value of the `InStr` function and adding one to the result, you can write code that finds all occurrences of the search string.

Listing 10.2 demonstrates the difference between the binary and text comparisons, and Listing 10.3 provides code that will perform a repeated search until it finds all occurrences of the search string.

LISTING 10.2 Case-Sensitive and Case-Insensitive String Comparisons

```
1:  Sub Search()
2:    MsgBox InStr(1, "Hello, World", "world", vbBinaryCompare)
3:    MsgBox InStr(1, "Hello, World", "world", vbTextCompare)
4:  End Sub
```

ANALYSIS Line 2 of Listing 10.2 performs a case-sensitive search, looking for "world" in "Hello, World". MsgBox, in line 2, displays a message with the value 0. The string "world" with a lowercase *w* does not have the same binary value as "World" with an uppercase *W*. Line 3 displays a message box with the value 8. The strings "world" and "World" are identical in a vbTextCompare (or case-insensitive) search.

LISTING 10.3   Finding Every Instance of a Substring with InStr

```
 1: Sub FindAll()
 2:    Const SEARCH_ME = "This is the way we wash our clothes."
 3:    Const SEARCH_FOR = "the"
 4:    Dim P As Integer
 5:    Do While (1=1)
 6:      P = InStr( P + 1, SEARCH_ME, SEARCH_FOR, vbTextCompare )
 7:      If( P = 0 ) Then Exit Do
 8:      MsgBox "'" & SEARCH_FOR & "' found at offset=" & P
 9:    Loop
10: End Sub
```

> To help you recognize and name idioms when you see them, it is worth pointing out that line 5 of Listing 10.3 represents an infinite loop, and line 7 is an exit point or loop short circuit. I prefer to use the term *short circuit*.

ANALYSIS To create a reusable function, you can add a static offset and pass in the string to search and the string to find to this subroutine. Using the arbitrary strings "This is the way we wash our clothes." and "the" in a case-insensitive search—using vbTextCompare—the Do While loop in line 5 displays three messages on line 8. The first one is at offset 9, the second at offset 25, and the third at offset 32, contained in the word "clothes".

Dynamically Allocating Strings

The string and space functions enable you to allocate string memory and clean up fixed-length string data after it is no longer needed. The string function takes a count and character value and fills a string with the character repeated "count" times. The space function returns a string filled with spaces "count" times.

If you want to fill a fixed-length string with a specific character, such as *, use the string function. To fill a string with the space character, use string(*n*, " ") or space(*n*). Both functions return a string with *n* spaces.

Formatting Data

Very basic formatting, as well as complex formatting of alphanumeric string data, can be accomplished easily with the Format function and the formatting characters @, &, <, >, and !. The syntax for the Format command is

```
Format( stringvariable, formatrule )
```

The Format command accepts a string literal or string variable as the first argument and a format rule as the second argument. The string variable can be any string containing alphanumeric characters. The rule can be special formatting characters combined with literal values. Table 10.2 contains the special formatting characters.

TABLE 10.2   Format Rule Characters

Character	Description
@	Character placeholder
&	Character placeholder
<	Forces lowercase
>	Forces uppercase
!	Forces left-to-right placeholder

The @ and & characters act as placeholders for text. Wherever you have @ or & in your format rule, your literal characters at the same ordinal position will replace the format characters. The < character applied to a string has the same effect as the LCase$ function, and the > character has the same effect as the UCase$ function. The exclamation (!) character bumps a literal from the string variable at the same ordinal position. Listing 10.4 contains some examples you can test in the editor's Immediate window. These examples demonstrate some combinations of the format characters.

LISTING 10.4   Formatting Character Demo

```
1:  Sub FormatDemo()
2:     MsgBox UCase$("bargain") = Format("bargain", ">")
3:     MsgBox LCase$("WALMART") = Format("WALMART", "<")
4:     MsgBox Format("5175551212", "(@@@) @@@-@@@@" )
5:  End Sub
```

ANALYSIS   Line 2 displays a message box with the word True displayed. The UCase$ and Format functions used with the > character produce the same result. Line 3 also displays a message box with True. LCase and < used with Format produce equivalent results. More useful combinations of literal and formatting characters can produce some nicely formatted text. Line 4 displays the formatted string `"(517) 555-1212"` in a message box. You are limited only by your imagination when defining formatting rules, but the best guideline for applying formatting rules to data is to model these rules after the way the data commonly appears.

Using Date and Time Functions

The `Date` and `Time` functions each have two versions. For example, `Date` returns today's date as a date variable, and `Date$` returns today's date as a string variable. `Time` and `Time$` exist for the current time, too. The `Date` and `Time` functions (sans $) return a double-precision value. The underlying value for `Date` and `Time` types is `Double`.

If you write the code `Print Date` in the Immediate window of the editor, you will get `6/28/01` on June 28, 2001. If you write `Print Time` at 3:55 P.M., you will get the exact time. (On my computer, it was `3:55:51 PM`.) If you write `Print Now`, you will get the complete date and time on your computer. (On my computer, the result was `6/28/01 3:56:55 PM`.)

The double-precision number that stores the date and time is a single value. The date is stored as the whole number part, and the time is stored as the decimal part. To see the underlying floating-point number, write `Print Now / 1`. This will cause the time to be implicitly converted to its underlying `Double` value. On my computer, the value for the date and time was `37019.0441435185`. The whole number is the number of days that have elapsed since December 30, 1899.

The following code will extract the whole-number date part of the `Double` date/time value and the time (or the decimal part) of the number:

```
Dim DatePart As Double
Dim TimePart As Double
DatePart = Fix(Now)
TimePart = Now - Fix(Now)
```

At 10:22 P.M. on March 7, 2001, `DatePart` was `36957` and `TimePart` was `0.933206`. The whole-number date part represents dates including and after December 30, 1899. Negative date-part numbers represent dates before 12/30/1899. The time part represents a fractional part of 24 hours. If the fractional time part is `0`, this represents 12:00 A.M.; `0.5` represents 12:00 P.M. The fractional value `0.75` represents three-quarters of a day, or 6:00 P.M. Date and time values are probably the second most useful values in database applications. You will use them a lot, and you might find it useful to use them in both numeric and date/time formats.

Managing File I/O

Many kinds of data are stored in binary and text formats. INI files are stored in text format and are still in limited use. Batch files, configuration files, HTML files, and data exported from other databases, word-processing documents, and spreadsheets can be stored in external files. Some basic facilities are available for managing file data that you will find useful on occasion.

VBA offers the `Open`, `Close`, `FreeFile`, `Line Input`, `Print`, `Write`, `Get`, and `Put` commands for managing basic file input and output. `Open` is used to open files for read, write, and read/write access. The `Close` function is used to close a file. Files still use what is referred to as a *file handle*. File handles represent finite resources in computer operating systems, so you must close file handles when you are done with any open files. The `FreeFile` function can ensure that you get a file handle that is not already in use by another process. `Line Input` is used to read a line of text from a text file. The `Print` and `Write` statements write text to a text file. `Write` wraps text in double quotes, but `Print` does not. The `Get` and `Put` functions can be used to read binary data and write binary data, respectively.

I will cover the commands in groups, starting with `Open` and `Close` with `FreeFile`, followed by `Line Input`, `Print`, and `Write`, and ending with `Get` and `Put`.

Using `Open` and `Close`

The `Open` function has a convoluted syntax. I will get to that in a minute. `Close`, however, is easy. To close a file, write

```
Close #filehandle
```

Here, *filehandle* is the double-precision variable returned from `FreeFile`, and `FreeFile` is a function that gets an available file handle from the operating system.

It is generally considered a best practice to use resources that are all within the same context. That is, if you open a file in a function, you should normally close it at the end of the same function. This procedure was adopted as a good programming practice because it decreases the likelihood that files will be corrupted from being left open accidentally.

If you need to keep a file open, it is a good idea to extend the context by wrapping the `Open` and `Close` functions in a class. That way, when the instance of the class is released, the class can be responsible for closing the file.

To learn more about classes for managing external data files, read about the `FileSystemObject` class defined in the Microsoft Scripting Runtime library in Hour 21, "Class Programming Basics."

Open is the more painful command to use. Open can be used to open text files for reading, writing, or both—in text or binary mode. The difference between text and binary mode is that, in text mode, the delimiter between discrete pieces of data is the carriage return–linefeed pair. In binary mode, delimiters are whatever sized chunk of data you want them to be. You can easily view a text file with any simple editor, but a binary file will look like mishmash in an editor. The Open command has the following syntax:

```
Open pathname For mode [Access access] [lock] As [#]filenumber [Len=reclength]
```

The *pathname* argument is a variable or string containing the location of the file. The mode argument indicates whether you will be reading, writing, or both and whether the data will be treated as text or binary characters. Valid values for mode are the keywords Append, Binary, Input, Output, and Random. Append means that the file is opened in write mode and positioned at the end of the file. Binary means the file will be opened as a binary file. Input means that the file is read-only text. Output means the file will be opened in write-only text mode, and Random means you can read and write text to the file without closing and reopening the file. If mode is unspecified, the mode will be Random. The Access part is filled out only when the mode is Binary. Binary access can use the Read, Write, and Read Write access specifiers. The file-access type indicates how you intend to use the file. The *lock* optional specification can be used to specify file sharing. You can specify that the file is Shared, Lock Read, Lock Write, or Lock Read Write.

The *filenumber* argument is an integer in the range of 1 through 511. It is best to use the FreeFile function to request an available file handle and use the handle immediately. In a multithreaded environment such as Windows, a file handle can be used by another process if you don't use it immediately. Use the *reclength* argument, which is an integer, to specify how much data represents a record for binary files. If you want to write one character at a time, specify Len=1. To specify an alternative size, use Len=Size(*type*) to get the correct size. Listing 10.5 provides a couple examples for opening and closing text and binary files.

LISTING 10.5   Opening and Closing Text and Binary Files

```
1:   Type Email
2:      Name As String
3:      Email As String
4:   End Type
5:
6:   Sub OpenAndClose()
7:      Dim Handle As Double
8:      Handle = FreeFile
```

LISTING 10.5 continued

```
 9:    Open "test.txt" For Output As #Handle
10:    Close #Handle
11:
12:    Handle = FreeFile
13:    Open "test.bin" For Binary Access Write As #Handle
14:    Dim Mail As Email
15:
16:    Do While (1 = 1)
17:      Mail.Name = InputBox("Enter name (Q=Quit): ", "Add Name", "")
18:      If( Mail.Name = "Q") Then Exit Do
19:      Mail.Email = InputBox("Enter email address: ", "Add Email", "")
20:      Put #1, , Mail
21:    Loop
22:    Close #Handle
23: End Sub
```

ANALYSIS Lines 1 through 4 define a type named Email. You will learn about user-defined types in Hour 11, "Making the Complex Simple: Creating Your Own Data Types." Line 7 declares a Double type that is used to store the file handle. Line 8 calls the FreeFile function to get an available file handle from the operating system. Line 9 opens a text file, named test.txt, for writing, using the handle returned in line 8. In line 10, the file is closed. Although not very useful, the code demonstrates the mechanics of opening and closing text files.

In line 12, I recycle the Handle variable and use FreeFile again. In line 13, I open a file named test.bin for binary writes. Line 14 declares an e-mail variable named Mail. Lines 16 through 21 define a Do While loop that uses the InputBox function to get a name and e-mail address. Line 20 demonstrates using the Put function for writing to the binary file. I will cover Put in the next section. The loop is terminated by entering Q in as a response to the request for a name. On line 22, remember to close the file.

If you try to view the binary file with a text editor, you get garbled data. But a quick peek with the very old debug.exe program enables the data to be read (see Figure 10.2).

Binary files are very useful for writing blocks of data, such as those with user-defined data types. Binary files are useful for storing specifically typed data, and text files are appropriate for data that is random text. For example, this chapter would be best stored in a text file, and a list of names and phone numbers would be best stored as user-defined types in a binary file.

FIGURE **10.2**

The data written to a binary file.

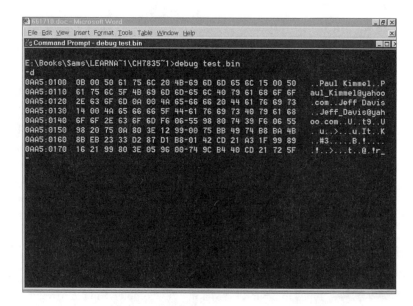

Reading and Writing Text Data

Text data is easy to read and write with the `Line Input`, `Input`, `Print`, and `Write` functions. If you know the format of your data, it is a matter of picking the correct function. Use `Line Input` if you want to read your data a line at a time. Use `Input` if you want to read delimited text. Use `Print` if you want to output fixed-length data. Use `Write` if you want to write comma-delimited data in quotation marks. The syntax for each of the four commands follows:

```
Line Input #handle, stringvariable
Input #handle var1 [,var2, var3, ...]
Print #handle, var1 [, var2, var3, ...]
Write #handle var1 [, var2, var3, ...]
```

`Line Input` needs a valid file handle and a literal or string variable and writes the output to the file represented by *handle*. `Input` requires a valid handle of an opened text file and writes field-level data to a text file represented by *handle*. In both `Input` and `Line Input`, the *handle* variable is a `Double` type and should be requested from the `FreeFile` function. `Input` enables you to read strings and non-`String` data types directly. The `Print` and `Write` commands both require a valid handle from a call to `FreeFile` and write one or more delimited literal or string values to a text file. The `Write` statement (from Listing 10.6 on line 7) creates output that is comma delimited and appears in the text file in this format:

```
"Robert Golieb","RobertGolieb@hotmail.com"
```

The same line of code written using the Print statement would produce the following output:

```
Robert Golieb  RobertGolieb@hotmail.com
```

Note the absence of any kind of delimiters. Text data in this format is referred to as *display-formatted data*.

By combining the Input command and the Write command, you can easily create a simple database using a text file as the data repository. Although creating a text database isn't a recommended practice, you might find occasions to manage data in this format. Such data can come from a number of sources: data downloaded from the Web, data from configuration files, or data exported from older technology databases. Listing 10.6 demonstrates how you can use a simple function to create a dynamic database of names and e-mail addresses.

LISTING 10.6 Using Input and Write to Store Data

```
1:  Sub UsingInputAndWrite()
2:
3:      Dim Handle As Double
4:      Handle = FreeFile
5:      Open "commadelimited.txt" For Output As #Handle
6:
7:      Write #Handle, "Robert Golieb", "RobertGolieb@hotmail.com"
8:
9:      Close #Handle
10:
11:     Handle = FreeFile
12:     Open "commadelimited.txt" For Input As #Handle
13:
14:     Dim Name, Email As String
15:
16:     Input #1, Name, Email
17:
18:     MsgBox "Contact: " & Name & ", " & Email
19:
20:     Close #Handle
21: End Sub
```

A key to writing fast, good code is to be consistent. A Double variable used as a file handle is, well, a Handle. Instead of trying to come up with unique names every time, be consistent; always use the same name when naming the same kind of thing. The more things you can accomplish without puzzling over them, the faster you go and the better the quality.

Files are resources. Because there are a limited number of file handles, you need to write code that ensures opened files are subsequently closed. If an error occurs between the line of code that opens a file and the line that closes a file, the file might never be closed. This could lead to a program that must be restarted and a corrupt data file. Hour 18, "Adding Code to Handle Errors," teaches you how to add all-important error-handling code.

ANALYSIS Line 3 of Listing 10.6 declares a `Double` variable named `Handle`. Line 4 requests an available file handle from the operating system using `FreeFile`. The very next thing you should do is use that handle so that some other thread (program or process) doesn't use the file handle. Line 5 opens a text file for writing, and line 7 writes one line to the file. Line 9 closes the file using the handle. Line 11 requests an available handle (don't rely on the original handle still being valid). Line 12 opens the file for reading. Line 14 declares two string variables to hold the data from the text file, and line 16 reads the data from the text file into the two variables. Line 18 displays the value of the inputted variables, and line 20 closes the file.

To make a simple data-management application out of this code, all you need to do is separate the code that writes the data from the code that reads the data and create a simple user interface. I will show you how to create a user interface in Hour 19, "Creating Custom Forms."

Reading and Writing Binary Data

Binary files are useful for storing data in a simplified record format. By specifying the size of a record, you can read and write data a record at a time with the `Put` and `Get` commands. Line 20 of Listing 10.5 demonstrates how to use the `Put` command. The `Get` command works the same way, but it is used for files opened in read or read/write modes. The syntax for `Put` and `Get` is as follows:

```
Put #handle, [recordnumber], variable
```

```
Get #handle, [recordnumber], variable
```

`Put` requires a file handle to a valid file opened for binary access writes, an optional record number, and a variable. The variable can be a simple type or a user-defined type, such as the `Email` type defined on lines 1 through 4 of Listing 10.5. Use the *record number* argument if you know the record index of the data you want to write. If you leave the record number blank in `Put`, the `Put` command will write the records sequentially. Using record numbers requires careful error handling, in case you try to "put" past the end of the file. The `Get` command reads binary data into simple variables or user-defined types. The same admonition applies when using the record number argument with Get as it does with Put. Read Hour 18 before delivering code with explicit record number requests. All the other variables in Get are the same as those in Put, except that Get requires that you open a file in binary access read or read/write mode.

With the information in this section, you could literally write your own data-management scheme. This is not a recommended practice, however. Use direct file access when you have little other choice. For most new data-management tasks, you will find that a database is much more powerful and easier to manage and requires much less work.

Dynamic User Input Functions

When you need to get a lot of user-added data, you will want to create a form. Hour 19 shows you how to design and build forms. However, when you want to communicate simple messages to your users or request simple data input, you will want to use the MsgBox function for displaying information and the InputBox for requesting information.

The MsgBox function is used in the following manner:

```
MsgBox(prompt[, buttons] [, title] [, helpfile, context])
```

A message box is a modal dialog. *Modal*, as opposed to *modeless*, means that all other screens are inactive until you close the modal dialog. The *prompt* argument is a variable, constant, or literal string value that makes up the text of the message box. The *buttons* argument, a numeric value, is one of several constants, such as vbOKOnly or vbOKCancel, that indicate which buttons will be displayed on the message box. You can get a complete listing of valid *buttons* values in the Help file for MsgBox. The *helpfile* and *context* arguments, when used together, contain the string path and filename of an HLP file and the Help context ID. A context ID is a number assigned to a Help topic when a Help file is created. If both *helpfile* and *context* are used together, Help documentation appears when the user presses F1 while the message box is displayed.

The InputBox function is used to get feedback from your users. An input box is easy to use—you have seen several instances of its use earlier in this book—and it has some additional features I haven't covered yet. Let's look at the syntax example first:

```
InputBox(prompt[, title] [, default] [, xpos] [, ypos] [, helpfile, context])
```

The InputBox function displays a modal dialog with OK and Cancel buttons. If you click OK, the function returns the user-entered data as a string. If you click Cancel, a null string is returned. The first argument, *prompt*, is the text that guides the user concerning what kind of data to enter. The optional *title* string enables you to provide a caption for the modal input box. The *default* argument enables you to specify a default value, which the user can accept (by clicking OK) or modify. The optional Cartesian coordinate arguments *xpos* and *ypos* enable you to indicate where the top-left corner of the dialog will appear. The default coordinates are screen center. The `helpfile` and `context` arguments enable the user to press F1, which will open the HLP file specified by `helpfile` to the Help context indicated by `context`.

The MsgBox function provides one-way communication to your users. Here's an example:

```
Call MsgBox("Warning division by zero will cause an error", vbExclamation)
```

MsgBox is commonly used to tell the user about a change state in your program or communicate ad hoc instructions. InputBox is used to elicit a response. Here's an example:

```
Dim UserName As String
UserName = InptBox( "Enter user name:", "User Name", "Guest" )
```

The preceding code displays an input box with a text field preceded by the prompt `"Enter user name:"`; it returns the value entered by the user if the user clicks OK, and it returns a null string if the user clicks Cancel.

Using Function, Method, Property, and Statement References

Literally dozens and dozens of functions, subroutines, properties, and statements have predefined uses and meanings in VBA. A good technique for finding and using them is to name the problem you have. Condense the problem to a noun and verb, and search in the Visual Basic editor's Help system for combinations of that noun and verb and their synonyms.

Thus far, you have learned about functions and statements. *Methods* and *properties* are object-oriented terms. A method is a function or subroutine defined as part of a class; a property is data assigned to a class. You will learn all about these object-oriented terms in Hour 21.

Summary

Thousands of predefined functions and subroutines exist for VBA programmers. All the code that has ever been written for BASIC and Visual Basic is also available to you now. This hour showed you how to use common functions for managing strings, performing data type comparison, and getting dynamic user input, file input, and output. The VBA Help file contains many more functions and subroutines. Third-party developers create commercially available products with still more predefined and tested solutions.

You now know how to manipulate common data types, get simple user input, and save that input to text and binary files. Until just a few years ago, this was the only problem-solving programming available. The essential skills you have acquired so far will enable you to solve many kinds of problems—from simple to complex.

In coming hours, you will learn how to employ what you have learned to build database solutions, create user interfaces, and define complex user-defined types. All programming from here forward is derived from and builds on the knowledge you have acquired in just 10 short hours. The following questions and answers will give you some additional insight into how to use the skills you have now.

Q&A

Q How can I perform search-and-replace tasks using strings, similar to the capabilities found in Microsoft Word?

A Well, you could write those functions. However, there is a lot of existing code, and it is likely that anything you need related to string manipulation already exists. With a little searching on the Web, you will probably find what you need.

Q Can I use the capabilities of Word or Excel to perform data-manipulation tasks?

A Yes. Word and Excel and the other applications in Microsoft Office XP have OLE Automation interfaces. What this means is that there is already a mechanism devised to enable you to use these applications and services for your Access programs. You will learn how to manage Outlook data via automation in Hour 24, "Managing Outlook Contact Information."

Q Should I use binary or text files to store my data?

A It really depends on the data. Either binary or text files will work adequately. However, if you want some other filereader to be able to read your data, like notepad, then you will want to store external data in a text file. If you want to conceal the contents from casual observers then use a binary file. Most of the time you will use a table to store informaiton; in that case neither is the appropriate answer.

Workshop

The Workshop includes quiz questions designed to help you test your understanding of the material covered and exercises to help put what you've learned to practice. You will find the answers to the quiz and exercises in Appendix A, "Answers."

Quiz

1. What is the function for finding a substring?

2. What is the difference between a modal and modeless dialog?

3. What is the statement for opening a text file for reading purposes?

4. What function can you use to get input dynamically from a user?

Exercises

1. Write a statement that formats a nine-digit postal code.

2. Write a subroutine to add a line of text to a named file. Pass the line of text and the filename to the subroutine.

3. Write a subroutine that searches a binary file for a specific name. Use the Email type and assume that more than one record exists.

PART IV

Defining Data Types and Using Arrays and Collections

Hour

HOUR 11

Making the Complex Simple: Creating Your Own Data Types

After 10 hours, you get a break. This hour is "shorter" in terms of text, but it is a significant hour in terms of content because Hour 11 is a precursor to advanced programming topics. This hour covers the user-defined type.

The type declaration—referred to as a *record* in some languages—was an early attempt at data aggregation. Early programmers discovered that sometimes it was more convenient to think of many pieces of individual data as one aggregate of data. Even though objects hit the mainstream in the early 1990s, the VBA Type construct is still relevant today.

User-defined data types are still in use today. Sometimes you might need to create a new type that contains many individual pieces of data in order to manage that data more easily. User types are much easier to use, although they're less powerful than objects. They make understanding and using objects much easier.

In this hour, I will be covering the important topic of data aggregation. You will learn

- How to create user types from native types
- How to declare instances of user types
- What kind of types can go into user types
- What enumerated data types are

Understanding Aggregation

Data aggregation evolved as a way for humans to cope with complexity. You and I, after thousands of years of adaptation, have learned to manage increasingly complex ideas by creating simple representations for complicated things.

Love, for example, is an extremely complex thing. Whether you think of love as butter-flies in the stomach, a biochemical reaction, a need to mate and procreate, or something expressed in a Byron poem, love is abstract. Abstract things in general are very complex. However, you and I can collect all these possible aspects of this human state in one word, *love*. The aggregate word *love* represents all those things and then some.

Technical concepts can be complicated. I can say "VBA" and communicate "a Windows programming language that has evolved over a couple decades from a mainframe lan-guage, somehow related to a guy named Bill Gates." That is a mouthful, but all that can be communicated in three letters, *V-B-A*. An additional benefit of aggregation is that, even if two people do not have the same understanding of the aggregate, the aggregate is a point of reference. Therefore, if a name is known to be a complex thing, understanding of it can be communicated in writing, by example, or through verbal analogies.

Data types are one of the earliest ways in which programmers inevitably began aggregat-ing many data elements into a singly named thing. By no means, however, have program-ming and human languages finished evolving. Human language and computer languages are evolving daily. The new Visual Basic.NET is a perfect example of evolving program-ming languages. Bill O'Reilly used *disrespected* as a verb on *The Factor* recently; *disre-spected*, as a verb, is an example of the evolution of a human language. In fact, the computer has introduced a whole new sublanguage, sometimes called *geek speak*.

User-defined types are not difficult to use. So, without further ado, let's get started.

Using the Type Declaration

The basic type definition requires at least three lines of code. The first line uses the key-word Type, followed by a unique name for the type. The last line contains the keywords

End and Type, and at least one member type must be added to the new type. The first and last line of a type definition takes the following form:

```
Type typename
End Type
```

 User-defined types must have at least one member.

Everything is typed into your code literally. You must supply a unique type name. The type name can be anything you want it to be, but it should convey the nature of the data that is contained in the type. A couple of other rules apply, too. User types must be written at the top of a code module, before any functions or subroutines, and must have at least one member. You cannot define user types inside functions or subroutines.

NEW TERM A *member* of a user type is a variable that is defined as part of the type; that is, it is declared between the first and last lines of the type declaration.

When you define a new type correctly, your type will show up in a pop-up object window (see Figure 11.1). Listing 11.1 demonstrates a simple type with one member, an integer.

FIGURE 11.1

The pop-up object list.

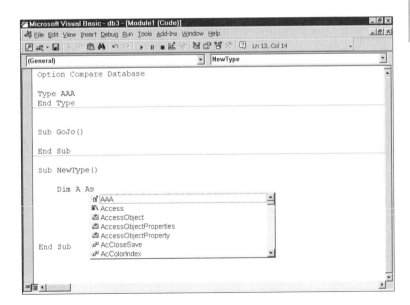

LISTING 11.1   A User Type Named AAA with One Member, an Integer

```
1:  Type AAA
2:     AnInt As Integer
3:  End Type
4:
5:  Sub NewType()
6:     Dim A As AAA
7:     A.AnInt = 5
8:  End Sub
```

ANALYSIS   The type AAA is defined on lines 1, 2, and 3. Line 2 defines the only member of
the type, AnInt. Lines 5 through 8 demonstrate how you can use the user type
AAA, with line 6 demonstrating the variable declaration and line 7 demonstrating the
assignment to the member AnInt.

The "member of" operator is the period. When you write *type.member*, the code is interpreted as "Give me the subtype of *type*, named *member*," where *member* is the variable
name of the subtype. When you write the line of code Dim A As AAA—refer to line 6 in
Listing 11.1—this is referred to as *declaring an instance* in the object-oriented world.
Just as *human* is a species, you are an instance of a human.

Every instance of a user type gets its own copy of the data in the type. The type itself is
like a blueprint from which instances of the type can be created. Therefore, each time
you write a declaration statement that defines a uniquely named variable of a user type,
you get a complete copy of the data members defined in that type. Therefore, modifying
line 6 in Listing 11.1 to Dim A As AAA, B As AAA creates two variable instances of the
AAA type. Assigning an integer value to A's copy of AnInt has no effect on B's copy of
AnInt, and vice versa.

What Kind of Data Can Go into My Type?

User-defined data types can contain many kinds of data. You can define strings, integers,
doubles, currency variables, data variables, and even other user-defined types. Objects
can be contained in user types, too. Just about any native data type and user-defined type
can be contained in a new type.

User types cannot, however, contain constant, static, or global types. Also, user types
cannot contain functions and subroutines. User types that can contain functions and subroutines in VBA are called *classes*, although other languages do permit functions in user
types.

Some languages, such as C, do allow you to define functions in user types. The equivalent of Type in C is struct. This is useful to know because Windows is implemented in C, and many Windows Application Programming Interface (API) functions can be used to extend the power of your VBA programs. Many of these Windows API functions require the use of equivalent user-defined data types.

Listing 11.2 demonstrates the various kinds of data that can be defined in a user type and how that data can be used. The exact number and data type of the elements in your types will be based on the needs of your program.

LISTING 11.2   A User Type with Many Elements, Including a Nested Type and an Object Reference

```
 1: Type LotsaData
 2:     AString As String
 3:     AnInt As Integer
 4:     ADouble As Double
 5:     SomeMoney As Currency
 6:     TheDate As Date
 7:     TheTime As Date
 8:     TripleA As AAA
 9:     RecordSet As ADODB.RecordSet
10: End Type
11:
12: Sub Initialize()
13:     Dim Data As LotsaData
14:     Data.AString = "Some string data"
15:     Data.AnInt = 13
16:     Data.ADouble = 34000000000000#
17:     Data.SomeMoney = 5000
18:     MsgBox Data.SomeMoney
19:     Data.TheDate = Date
20:     Data.TheTime = Time
21:     Data.TripleA.AnInt = 16
22:     Set Data.RecordSet = Nothing
23: End Sub
```

ANALYSIS   Lines 1 through 10 define a user type named LotsaData. Line 2 introduces a string member, line 3 an integer, line 4 a double, line 5 a currency, lines 6 and 7 a date, and line 8 a user type named AAA. Line 9 adds an ADO Recordset object reference.

Lines 12 through 23 demonstrate a fundamental use of each member of LotsaData: assignment. When you declare a variable of a type (line 13), you then use the variable name to access the members of the type. The dot operator (.) is used to indicate membership. To access a member of a nested user type, as line 21 does, you must daisy-chain the names together. In line 21, Data.TripleA.AnInt means "Give me the member AnInt, a member of TripleA, which is, in turn, a member of Data."

NEW TERM *Idiom* refers to the usual ways in which the words of a language are combined to express thoughts. A programming language idiom is something that expresses a whole idea; for example, a user-defined type is an idiom.

NEW TERM A *class* is a type that defines what instances of that type will be able to do and know. The "doing" is represented by functions and subroutines, and the "knowing" is represented by the variables. Think of classes as advanced types that can contain functions and subroutines.

NEW TERM An *object* is a variable whose data type is a class.

VBA was modified to support object-oriented programming in just the last few years. The member Recordset refers to a variable of the type ADODB.RecordSet, a class. The programmers who created VBA and developed it to include object-oriented idioms chose to make a distinction between simple type assignment and object type assignment. That's why line 22 uses the keyword Set. You will learn more about objects and the Set keyword in Hour 21, "Class Programming Basics."

Declaring Instances of User Types

User types are declared just as any other type is. You can declare data type variables inside and outside functions and subroutines. Remember, what is declared inside a function or sub is called a Local variable, and what is declared outside a function or sub is called a Global variable. You can explicitly declare a type variable outside a function or sub as a Global, and you can declare a type variable as Static inside a function or subroutine. Listing 11.3 demonstrates Local, Global, and Static type variable declarations.

LISTING 11.3 Local, Global, and Static Type Variable Declarations

```
1:  Type Type1
2:    NoData As Integer
3:  End Type
4:
5:  Dim T1 As Type1
```

LISTING **11.3**   continued

```
 6:  Global T2 As Type1
 7:
 8:  Sub OtherTypeVars()
 9:    Dim T3 As Type1
10:    Static T4 As Type1
11: End Sub
```

ANALYSIS   Line 1 declares a Type named Type1 with one member, an integer. Line 5 declares a variable, T1, that is implicitly global to the module it is defined in but local relative to any other modules that might exist in the program. You can use the variable T1 anywhere in the module in which T1 is defined, but you cannot use T1 in other modules. The relative accessibility of data, functions, and subroutines has to do with the notion of scope. You will learn about scope in Hour 21. Line 6 explicitly declares T2 as a Global variable of type Type1. There is no keyword to define local variables. Local variables are implicitly defined as such. When you define a variable as Global, it is accessible from anywhere in your program. Lines 8 through 11 define a subroutine that contains two Type1 variables, T3 and T4. T3 is local to—that is, it is accessible only from within—the subroutine OtherTypeVars. Line 10 declares a static Type1 variable named T4. Static variables maintain their value between successive calls to the function or subroutine in which they are defined.

Defining Enumerated Types

Enumerated types are roughly equivalent to constants. There are a few differences between the two, though. When you define a *constant*, it is a distinctly named, immutable value that represents some fixed data. An *enumeration* is a block of names that are assigned an implicit ordinal value relative to the order in which they are defined, or it's a mapped assignment integer value. I will elaborate in a moment, but for now, look at the following syntax of an enumeration to see how much like a Type it looks:

```
Enum enumname
    Elem1 [=integervalue]
    [Elem2 [=integervalue ]]
    [Elemn [=integervalue]]
End Enum
```

The Enum keyword and an enumeration name start the enumeration definition, and End Enum closes the enumeration. You can place as many elements in the enumerated type as you need. You can also assign an optional integer value to each or any element of the set.

11

Use an enumeration when you need an integral type that has only a range of valid values. By using an enumeration instead of an integer, users of your program—including other programmers—can only assign a variable that has the enumerated value of one of the elements in the enumeration. Consider Listing 11.4 for a demonstration.

LISTING 11.4 Two Versions of Equivalent Functions, One Using Enumerated Types and One Using Integers

```
 1:  Enum EmploymentStatus
 2:    esInterviewed = 1
 3:    esHired = 2
 4:    esTerminated = 3
 5:    esLeaveOfAbsence = 4
 6:  End Enum
 7:
 8:  Sub SetEmploymentStatus(ByVal CurrentStatus As EmploymentStatus)
 9:
10:    If(CurrentStatus = esHired) Then
11:      ' ProcessNewEmployee
12:    End If
13:
14: End Sub
15:
16: Sub SetEmploymentStatusWithInt(ByVal CurrentStatus As Integer)
17:
18:    If(CurrentStatus >= 1) And (CurrentStatus <= 4) Then
19:      If(CurrentStatus = 1) Then
20:        ' ProcessNewEmployee
21:      End If
22:    End If
23: End Sub
```

ANALYSIS In Listing 11.4, lines 1 through 6 define an enumerated type named EmploymentStatus. There are four possible statuses: esInterviewed, esHired, esTerminated, and esLeaveofAbsence. Lines 8 through 14 define a subroutine that uses the enumeration, and lines 16 through 23 define a subroutine that uses an integer to perform an equivalent task.

Notice how short the enumerated version is. Because only valid values can be assigned to variables of the enumerated type, no conditional code for checking valid values is necessary. However, in the nonenumerated subroutine, you must prudently check the variable for a valid range before you can be sure it is reliable. In fact, integer types that have a limited range of valid values should always be checked for validity if you do not use an enumeration. This adds a lot of overhead to your code.

> Use constants instead of literal values and use enumerations when you need a range of constant integral values.

Additionally, compare the specificity of the code in the first version to the ambiguity in the second version: If(CurrentStatus = esHired) Then versus If (CurrentStatus = 1) Then. The enumerated type is an idiom that is easily employed to avoid ambiguity and make your code more readable. In plain and simple terms, you will have to write more code that is less indicative of intent if you do not use enumerations whenever you have a limited range of valid values for integral data.

Putting It All Together

The user-defined type is a good idiom to use when you have to express a data type that can't be captured with a simple native data type or an existing aggregate type. For example, if you want to express the idea that a name and phone number pair represent contact information, you want to define a user type, called contact, that contains the simple data name and phone number.

You don't need a user-defined type if a type exists that includes all the subtypes or if the data exists in a table, for instance. However, it is always easier to pass a single piece of data to a function or subroutine than it is to pass a dozen arguments. Therefore, if you have a lot of related data that has to be passed to other functions and subroutines in your program, a good way to simplify the interface of those functions and subroutines is to put the data in a user-defined type.

Summary

This hour teaches you all about the VBA Type and Enum definitions. Types are useful for aggregating data, and enumerations are useful for defining ranges of valid data for integral types. As precursors to object-oriented programming, they are beneficial learning aids.

Learning to cope with the complexities of object-oriented programming is unavoidable. You will have to use objects to some degree every time you program, and it will be useful to master objects sooner rather than later.

In this hour, you learned how to define new types and enumerations. You learned how to declare variable instances of local, global, and static user types, and you learned the limitations of user types. Complete the "Q&A" and "Workshop" exercises to hone your understanding.

Q&A

Q Is creating my own types object-oriented programming?

A Creating user-defined types represents data aggregation. Data aggregation is a very small part of object-oriented programming, but defining new types is not object-oriented programming. Data types were introduced as part of structured programming. Object-oriented programming introduced a new user type, called the *class*. You will read about classes in Hour 21.

Q Can I nest types?

A You can include existing types in new types. The only criteria is subjective; the only requirement is that nesting the user-type should make sense.

Q Can I add functions and subroutines to my types?

A No. You will need to create a class to aggregate functions and subroutines.

Q Should I use enumerations instead of constants?

A Define an enumeration only if you need to specify a type that has a valid range of integer values. If the constant values are unrelated, use the Const keyword for each constant value.

Workshop

The Workshop includes quiz questions designed to help you test your understanding of the material covered and exercises to help put what you've learned to practice. You will find the answers to the quiz and exercises in Appendix A, "Answers."

Quiz

1. Can a user type contain an enumerated variable?
2. What is the difference between the uses for Type and Enum?
3. Can types contain functions and procedures?
4. Can types contain constant members?
5. Can types contain references to variables?

Exercises

1. Define a type that contains a name, address, and phone number.
2. Define a user type that aggregates the user type in exercise 1. Why might you want to create a new type and not just modify the old type to include the new data?
3. Define an enumeration that describes flavors of ice creams.

Hour 12

Managing Varying Amounts of Data

Getting data into memory and using it there is one of the fundamental tasks that a computer program performs. The array, the primary topic of this hour, is one of the most basic and widely used data structures.

An *array* is defined as a collection of one data type, containing zero or more variables of that type. This simplicity is both a strength and a weakness. Although arrays have some limitations, they are useful, easy to use, and powerful, if managed appropriately. In this hour, you will learn how to:

- Define arrays
- Write code that dynamically sizes arrays
- Use functions to limit errors introduced by array usage
- Learn to use arrays to perform common tasks, such as sorting data

Understanding Arrays

The array was one of the earliest kinds of data types that could store data. There are many uses for arrays. You can use arrays when you want to store data in memory that is not in a database table. Arrays are useful as in-memory storage places for data. Arrays can be used in lieu of `Select Case` statements (a technique demonstrated in Hour 21, "Class Programming Basics"), resulting in faster code.

If data is already in a collection or table, you probably won't need to use an array. However, if you have temporary data-storage needs, you can use an array as a place to store and manage more than one piece of data.

An array is a contiguous block of assigned memory addresses that are treated as a single variable. It just so happens that an array variable contains a certain number of elements of some other type. The array mechanism enables you to treat the memory as a subdivided block of memory where every ith position can contain a variable. Variables stored in arrays are generally of the same type. However, with the advent of the dynamic `Variant` type, arrays can contain *heterogeneous data* (different kinds of data).

Arrays can be multidimensional. In fact, a computer's capability to manage arrays of data exceeds the human mind's ability to grasp the complexity. In our world, there is a perceptible three-dimensional physical world; time is the fourth dimension, and space is the fifth dimension. Five-dimensional structures probably define the limit of the mind's potential to grasp complexity. A computer array can have as many dimensions as you want, limited only by the amount of memory your computer has. Fortunately, in most instances, one- or two-dimensional arrays will suffice.

Currently, an integer is 16 bits, or 2 bytes. Defining an array of 10 integers sets aside roughly 20 bytes of memory. You can think of the array as being laid out in your computer's memory as depicted in Figure 12.1. Each element of the array is accessed by using an index that falls within the range of the lowest indexable position to the highest indexable position, inclusive of the low and high boundaries.

FIGURE 12.1
Physically contiguous memory is used for arrays.

34	56	66	31	78					

☐ = 16-bits, or 2 bytes

Array arithmetic is based on the idea that an array has a base memory address. By multiplying the base address and adding the index multiplied by the size of the elements, the address of the indexed position can be found:

```
Baseaddres + (index * sizeof_datatype)
```

Fortunately, the array construct performs all the arithmetic for you. Only in languages such as Assembler and C will you find array index arithmetic still prevalent.

Declaring Arrays

The hardest thing about using an array in VBA is determining the size and data type. The syntax for an array is slightly different from that of single variables, as shown here:

```
Dim arrayname([initial_size]) As datatype
```

If you try to "redimension" a fixed-size array—that is, an array declared with Dim and a size—you will get "Array already dimensioned" error. You can resolve this problem by declaring the array with ReDim and leaving the parentheses empty (that is, don't specify the array size at the point of declaration).

You can use the ReDim and Static keywords for arrays, too. I will get to these keywords in a few minutes. The basic syntax of an array is to use Dim followed by an *arrayname* argument, expressing the size in parentheses. If you leave the parentheses (which you must include) empty, the array initially has no storage space. The end of the array is expressed with the keyword As and the data type. The type can be any valid native type or user-defined type.

Declaring Fixed Arrays

A *fixed array* is an array for which you indicate the number of elements at the time you declare the array. Such an array will always have the same number of elements. The general syntax from the preceding section applies, except that a fixed array requires that you specify a size. Listing 12.1 demonstrates a fixed array.

LISTING 12.1   Declaring and Initializing a Fixed Array

```
1:  Sub FixedArrays()
2:      Dim Ints(100) As Integer
3:      ' Initialize the array
4:      Dim I As Integer
```

12

LISTING 12.1   continued

```
5:     For I = 1 to 100
6:        Ints(I) = I
7:     Next I
8:
9:     For I = 100 to 1 Step -1
10:       Debug.Print Ints(I)
11:    Next I
12: End Sub
```

ANALYSIS   Line 2 demonstrates the application of the array syntax. The fixed array named
Ints contains room for storing 100 integers. Lines 5, 6, and 7 demonstrate how
to iterate through all 100 (if Option Base is 1) or 101 (if Option Base is 0) elements of
the array. Code such as that in lines 5 through 7 can be useful in initializing an array to
some value other than zero before using it. By default, array elements are initialized to
zero or its equivalent, depending on the data type. For example, an array of strings is initialized to null strings by default. Lines 9 through 11 demonstrate how to iterate through
each element of the fixed array backward.

Accessing array elements using different indexing schemes can be useful. As you will
see in the section "Sorting Array Data," forward and backward directions can be used to
create ascending and descending sort orders.

Declaring Dynamic Arrays

A *dynamic array* is an array whose size can be changed at runtime, unlike a fixed array,
whose size is fixed at programming time (or design time). A dynamic array is declared
with no size stipulated for the array, if you declare the initial array with the Dim keyword.
If you use the ReDim keyword, a size must be used. Here is the syntax:

ReDim *arrayname*(*size*) As *datatype*

Using the word ReDim indicates that the array size can be changed. Everything else is the
same as a static array. Simply name the array variable, specify an initial size in the
parentheses, and tack on a data type at the end.

After you add data to a dynamic array, you might want to preserve the contents of the
array before resizing it. Array contents can be preserved by creating a temporary array,
copying the elements from the original array to the temporary array, resizing the original
array, and copying the old elements back to the original array. However, the complicated
procedure just described is not the way you should preserve an array. Instead, use the keyword Preserve between ReDim and the array name during the redeclaration. The Preserve
keyword will carry the current values into the resized array unharmed. Listing 12.2
demonstrates resizing an array using Preserve.

LISTING 12.2   Declaring and Resizing a Dynamic Array Using *Preserve*

```
1:  Sub DynamicArray()
2:    ReDim Strings(5) As String
3:    ReDim Strings(10) As String
4:
5:    Strings(1) = "Greetings"
6:    Strings(2) = "Wilkommen"
7:    Strings(3) = "Bienvenido"
8:    Strings(4) = "Howdy"
9:    Strings(5) = "Hello, World! "
10:
11:   ReDim Preserve Strings(30) As String
12:
13:   Dim Elem As Variant
14:   For Each Elem In Strings
15:       Debug.Print Elem
16:   Next Elem
17: End Sub
```

ANALYSIS   Lines 2 and 3 declare and redeclare an array of strings named Strings. There is no need to use Preserve on line 3 because Strings contains no data; line 3 simply demonstrates the technique for redeclaration. Lines 5 through 9 demonstrate how to put data into an array: You indicate the index between the parentheses using the array name. Line 11 resizes the array Strings to contain 30 elements, using the Preserve keyword to ensure that existing data is maintained in good order. Lines 13 through 16 demonstrate that the original five pieces of data are still intact. The only time you will lose data when resizing a dynamic array is if you forget to use the keyword Preserve or if you shrink the array. Even Preserve can't maintain elements that no longer exist.

Declaring Static Arrays

All static variables are declared inside functions or subroutines. This holds true for a *static array*—that is, an array declared using the keyword Static. A static array, like any other static variables, will maintain its value between successive calls to the function or sub. This can be a useful idiom.

The declarative difference between a static array—whether the array is dynamic or fixed—and an array that isn't static is the use of the preceding keyword Static. An example of a static array follows:

```
Static Dim Array1(10) As String
```

Changing Dim to ReDim makes the array static and dynamic: The array values are maintained between successive calls to the function containing the array, and you can also resize the array. The array name is Array1, and the data type can be any valid data type,

12

including objects. There are some interesting applications for static arrays, which I will cover in the second half of this hour.

Setting Array Base Indexes

Some languages, such as C, have zero-based arrays. Hence, if you define an array containing 10 elements in C, valid indexes are 0 through 9. VBA enables you to specify the base element.

You specify the base with the `Option Base` command:

```
Option Base 0|1
```

The `Option Base` command is placed at the top of the module containing your code. The default is `0`. `Option Base` only affects the lower bound of the array. Therefore, if you do not specify `Option Base 1`, remember that arrays will contain an element at index position `0`, and in an *n*-size array, *n* will be the upper bound for the array. Specify the `Option Base` type you are comfortable with and stick with it. If you are comfortable in counting starting from zero, use the default; if not, set `Option Base` to `1`.

Using Arrays to Store Data

It is possible that another developer might work on your code eventually. That person might not be comfortable working with arrays that start with zero or one. Therefore, it is best to write code that is indifferent to the first and last indexes.

There are two ways you can write code that ignores whether the first number is zero or one. You can use the `For…Each` loop, or you can use the `Lbound` and `Ubound` functions. I recommend using `Lbound` and `Ubound` every time you index an array in a loop, if you actually index the array. The syntax for `Lbound` and `Ubound` follows:

```
Lbound(arrayname, [dimension])
```

```
Ubound(arrayname, [dimension])
```

`Ubound` and `Lbound` both accept, at a minimum, one argument. The first argument is the name of the array. The optional second argument is the dimension of the array for which you want to return the bounding limit. By default, both `Ubound` and `Lbound` return the limit of the first dimension.

The `Option Base` argument does not affect the *dimension* argument of the `Ubound` and `Lbound` functions. When you're referring to array dimensions, the dimensions always start with one in VBA.

Consider the following two- and three-dimensional arrays and `Option Base 1`:

```
Dim Array1(5, 20) As String
Dim Array2(5, 5, 10) As Integer
```

The first array, `Array1` is a two-dimensional array, called a *matrix*. `Array2` is a three-dimensional array, also called a *matrix*. (Any *n*-dimensional array can be referred to as a *matrix*.) `Array1` has 100 indexable positions for strings. If you call the `Ubound` function with `Array1` as the only argument, you get the value 5 as your result. Calling `Ubound` with `Array1` and 2 as the dimension argument results in `Ubound` returning 20.

You can use the `Lbound` and `Ubound` functions to make sure that an index is within the valid range of indexes for an array. You can also use these two functions as loop-control functions, as demonstrated in Listing 12.3.

LISTING 12.3   Declaring Multidimensional Arrays and Using the *Lbound* and *Ubound* Functions for Loop Control

```
 1:  Sub DisplayBounds()
 2:
 3:      Dim I As Integer
 4:      Dim array1(5, 10) As Integer
 5:      Dim array2(100) As Integer
 6:
 7:      Debug.Print UBound(array1, 2)
 8:      Debug.Print UBound(array2)
 9:
10:      For I = LBound(array2) To UBound(array2)
11:          array2(I) = I: Debug.Print array2(I)
12:      Next I
13:
14:  End Sub
```

ANALYSIS   Line 4 declares a two-dimensional array containing five indexable positions in the first dimension and 10 indexable positions in the second dimension. `Array1` can store 50 integers (with `Option Base 1`)and 66 (with `Option Base 0`). Line 5 defines an array of a single dimension of 100 integers. Line 7 demonstrates how the second argument of `UBound` can be used to return the upper bound of the second dimension. Line 8 displays the upper bound of the default first dimension. Lines 10 through 12 demonstrate using the lower and upper bounds to manage the `For Next` loop. The second statement—`Debug.Print array2(I)`—following the colon on line 11 prints the value of the array to the debug window.

Using the two bounds functions for array management is a good idea because the code can be changed more easily, and the bounds functions automatically accommodate

12

dynamically resized arrays and a change in `Option Base`. The reason the code is also generally more portable is that, even if you modify a fixed array's size at design time (when you are writing the code), you do not have to change `For Loop`.

Listing 12.4 demonstrates how to index elements of a multidimensional array. In general, you will use a loop of some kind for every dimension of the array. This can get very expensive in terms of processing speed because the loops have to be nested; an n-dimensional loop has an exponentially deteriorating performance penalty. As n, the number of elements, gets larger, the amount of memory grows and the speed at which the array can be processed deteriorates quickly.

Assume that it takes one second to process one item at an index. If there are two 100-element dimensions, it will take approximately 10,000 seconds to process all elements. Add a third 100-item dimension, and it will take 1,000,000 seconds to process all elements, not including the amount of memory it would take to hold that much data. Keep this in mind when declaring multidimensional arrays.

> Keep in mind that the processing speed in the preceding paragraph is based on an arbitrary, fictitious unit of time, and there are algorithms that process data more efficiently than nested for loops.

LISTING 12.4   Touching Each Element of a 10-by-10 Matrix

```
1:  Option Base 1
2:  Sub TwoDimensions()
3:    Dim two_d_array(10, 10) As String
4:    Dim I As Integer, J As Integer
5:    For I = LBound(two_d_array, 1) To UBound(two_d_array, 1)
6:      For J = LBound(two_d_array, 2) To UBound(two_d_array, 2)
7:        two_d_array(I, J) = I & "x" & J
8:        Debug.Print two_d_array(I, J)
9:      Next J
10:   Next I
11: End Sub
```

ANALYSIS   The 10-by-10 array is declared on line 3. Line 4 declares two index variables: I and J. I, J, and K are commonly used for indexing in mathematics, so there is some carry over into computer programming. (It pays to be consistent. If you use I for your first index, always use I. Save your creative energy for problem solving.) Line 5 sets up the outer For Next loop, and line 6 sets up the inner For Next loop, both using Lbound and Ubound for loop control. Note the use of the dimension argument with Lbound and Ubound. Line 7 demonstrates how to index a two-dimensional array. Use commas to delimit every index.

Most arrays beyond one or two dimensions do not have many applications in business software. Generally, only complex equations and mathematical applications require multidimensional arrays.

Functions for Managing Arrays

Several other useful array functions are available, including the Array, Erase, IsArray, and ParamArray functions. The Array function returns an array created from an argument list. The syntax is

```
Array( [arg1, [arg2, arg3, ...]] )
```

The Array() function returns an array containing the elements passed to the function. If you elect not to pass any arguments, Array() will return an empty array.

The Erase function sets each element of an array to its equivalent null value. In String arrays, this is an empty string. Erase sets each integer element in an Integer array to zero. In an array of objects, Erase sets each element equal to Nothing (that is, the keyword Nothing). An array of Variant data is set to Empty. All the other arrays have indexable positions containing a null equivalent, except the Variant array, which cannot be indexed after an Erase function. Listing 12.5 demonstrates technically accurate uses of the Array and Erase commands.

The tests for arrays of different types are different. Erasing Variant arrays sets the entire array to Empty. Erasing an array of objects sets each element to Nothing. An erased array of strings contains "" (null strings) at each index, and an erased array of integers contains 0 at each index. The data type–dependent behavior of Erase is an inconsistency in VBA that should be resolved by Microsoft, but for now you just have to be aware that erasing arrays of different types yields slightly different results.

12

LISTING 12.5   Examples of Using the *Erase* and *Array()* Functions

```
1:  Sub ArrayFunction()
2:    Dim A()
3:    A = Array(1, 2, 3, 4, 5)
4:    Dim I As Integer
5:    For I = LBound(A) To UBound(A)
6:      Debug.Print A(I)
7:    Next I
8:    Erase A
9:  End Sub
```

ANALYSIS In Listing 12.5, line 2 declares a `Variant` array named A. In line 3, the array A is assigned to the array created by the call to the `Array` function. The returned array contains five elements: 1, 2, 3, 4, and 5. Lines 4 through 7 are familiar to you now; they display each element of the array in the Immediate window. Line 8 erases the array. The `Variant` array A is empty after line 8 executes.

> If you use the UBound or LBound function on an erased Variant array, you will get a runtime error (see Figure 12.2). You can use the bounds functions on erased arrays of all other types, including arrays containing user-defined types.

FIGURE 12.2

The Subscript Out of Range error displayed when an array index exceeds the upper or lower bound of the array.

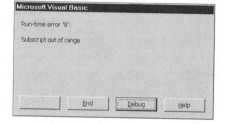

Testing Variables with `IsArray`

The IsArray function takes a variable argument of any type and returns a Boolean indicating whether the variable represents an array. You may pass a variable or literal to the IsArray function. Functions such as IsArray are useful when you have Variant data types where the actual type of the variable is not obvious. Listing 12.6 provides examples of statements that employ the IsArray function.

LISTING 12.6 Examples of Statements That Display a Boolean Value Indicating Whether the Argument Represents an Array

```
 1: Dim A
 2: MsgBox IsArray(A)     'Displays False
 3:
 4: Dim B()
 5: MsgBox IsArray(B)     'Displays True
 6:
 7: Dim C As Variant
 8: C = Array("A", "B", "C")
 9: MsgBox IsArray(C)     'Displays True
10:
11: Dim D As Integer
12: MsgBox IsArray(D)     'Displays False
```

LISTING **12.6** continued

```
13:
14: Dim E As ADODB.Recordset
15: MsgBox IsArray(E)     'Displays False
16:
17: Dim F(10) As String
18: MsgBox IsArray(F)     'Displays True
19:
20: MsgBox IsArray(Array(1, 2, 3))     'Displays True
```

As a general rule, avoid writing or using code that is so ambiguous you need these interrogative types of functions, such as IsArray. However, you may find yourself in the unavoidable situation of needing the function. Again, if code is ambiguous, consider revising the code to mitigate the ambiguity.

Passing Arrays of Parameters to Procedures

You may define the last argument of a procedure as a ParamArray parameter (an array of Variant types). This allows you to pass a variable number of arguments to a procedure, and the procedure will pack them into an array. Listing 12.7 demonstrates this.

LISTING **12.7**   Defining a *ParamArray* Parameter

```
1:   Sub CallTest()
2:     Call TestParamArray("Paul Kimmel", "(517) 555-1234", _
3:       "pkimmel@softconcepts.com")
4:   End Sub
5:
6:   Sub TestParamArray(ContactName As String, ParamArray ContactInfo() _
7:     As Variant)
8:     Dim S As String
9:     S = ContactName
10:    Dim I As Integer
11:    For I = LBound(ContactInfo) To UBound(ContactInfo)
12:      S = S & vbCrLf & ContactInfo(I)
13:    Next I
14:
15:    MsgBox "Contact Info for: " & S
16: End Sub
```

ANALYSIS   Begin testing the procedure by running the CallTest procedure. CallTest calls TestParamArray with three arguments. As you can see, TestParamArray only has two arguments. The first is ContactName, and the second is ParamArray. The test data "Paul Kimmel" is placed in the ContactName argument, and everything else is

12

placed in the `ParamArray` argument. To determine what is placed in `ParamArray`, simply subtract all the other literal arguments, and everything else goes in `ParamArray`. The result of this code is to display a message box with all the contact information, regardless of the amount.

 Assembly language programmers are probably more comfortable with parameter arrays because this mirrors the way in which data is placed into the stack frame prior to a function call and retrieved from the stack at the beginning of a function call. Although all this is hidden by the compiler, it was just a few years ago that programmers had to manually manage the stack frame.

There are two reasons `ParamArray` was developed and works. The C programming language supported a variable number of arguments in functions, so Visual Basic probably inherited the capability from old C programmers. The technique works because data is passed to functions by argument information being placed in the stack frame. Essentially the stack frame is an array of data. Although the stack frame is managed by the computer and the compiler adds stack frame code automatically, the array of arguments is already there. It probably requires more work for compiler writers to convert data from the stack into specific variables than it does to provide access to the stack frame as an array.

Returning Arrays from a Function

You cannot return an array type from a function in VBA. However, you can return an array. You accomplish this is in the same way the `Array()` function returns an array: You return a variant.

 Returning an array as a variant demonstrates an example of when you might want to use the `IsArray` function.

The `Variant` type is really a compilation of many types. The compiler adds special code to help determine what type is contained in variants, based on the way you use them in code. One of the types the variant code can decipher is an array type.

If your problem requires that a function return an array, remember that it can be done with a variant. Listing 12.8 demonstrates how to return an array from a function using a variant.

LISTING 12.8   Returning an Array from a Function As a *Variant* Data Type

```
 1:  Function GetMyArray() As Variant
 2:    Static Data(100) As Integer
 3:    GetMyArray = Data
 4:  End Function
 5:
 6:  Sub TestReturnArray()
 7:    Dim MyArray As Variant
 8:    MyArray = GetMyArray()
 9:    If( IsArray(MyArray)) Then
10:      MsgBox UBound(MyArray)
11:    End IF
12:  End Sub
```

ANALYSIS Lines 1 through 4 define a function that declares an array and returns the array from the function GetMyArray. It is best to declare local variables that are used outside the function in which they reside as static, as I did on line 2. Using a static array ensures that the memory for the array is valid after the function containing the array exits. Lines 6 through 12 of TestReturnArray demonstrates that the array returned by GetMyArray can be treated just like any other array.

You may use the strategy of binding the allocation and initialization of an array to a function, providing you with a tidy little package for your arrays. Essentially the combination of allocation and initialization is the definition of an array constructor. *Constructor* is an object-oriented term, loosely applied here. In object-oriented programming, a *constructor* is a special kind of class method that performs allocation and initialization of classes. Read Hour 21 for more on object-oriented programming.

12

Things You Should Do When Using Arrays

Arrays are easy to use, but they are also fragile. An array has a limited amount of memory, based on the amount you allocate when you declare the array. To use arrays effectively, without introducing bugs into your code, you should do certain things everywhere you use your arrays.

Before you request an indexed item from your array, you should check the index to make sure it is not out of bounds. If you are using a For…Next loop with the Lbound and Ubound functions, you can count this as range validation. However, if you arbitrarily pass an index to a function that indexes an array, you should write code to validate the index. Again, you can use Ubound and Lbound to validate the index.

For global arrays, consider writing one function to grow dynamic arrays and a second function to validate indexes. Although the code for either of these operations will be very short, it will be more readable and maintainable. One function is easier to change than a few lines of code repeated many times.

Sorting Array Data

Array data is convenient and easy to use for collecting and organizing similar kinds of data. One common operation applied to arrays of data is the sort. There are many kinds of sorts. Among these are the infamous Bubble sort, the Selection sort, the Quick sort, the Radix sort, and many others.

Classic algorithm books, including *Numerical Recipes in C: The Art of Scientific Computing* by William H. Press, et al. (Cambridge University Press, 1993) are available to you. *Numerical Recipes in C* is an exhaustive algorithms book, but you must translate C algorithms to VBA. There is also a Visual Basic book, *Ready-To-Run Visual Basic Algorithms*, by Rod Stephens and Kenneth R. Stephens (John Wiley & Sons, 1998) from which you can take algorithms directly (probably with little or no translation).

I have included three algorithms that are easy to write and very fast, even for large data sets. With modern processing exceeding gigahertz speeds, even the old Bubble sort works well on data sets of 10,000 elements or so. However, for very large data sets, the difference in performance between a Bubble or Selection sort and a Quick sort can be staggering.

Bubble-Sorting an Array of Strings

The Bubble sort performs well on random or mostly sorted data of up to about 10,000 elements. The Bubble sort works by comparing every element to every other element and swapping every time the comparison test passes. To sort in ascending order, every element at index I is checked to see whether the value is greater than every element at I + 1, to the last element. Descending sort orders compare to see whether the Ith element is less than the I+1 element. The algorithm for the ascending Bubble sort is shown in Listing 12.9.

LISTING 12.9   A Bubble Sort Algorithm for an Array of Integers

```
1:  Sub Swap(ByRef Data() As Long, ByVal I As Long, ByVal J As Long)
2:      Dim Temp As Long
3:      Temp = Data(I)
4:      Data(I) = Data(J)
5:      Data(J) = Temp
6:      Debug.Print "Swap:" & Data(I) & " with " & Data(J)
7:  End Sub
```

LISTING 12.9 continued

```
8:
9:  Sub BubbleSort(ByRef Data() As Long)
10:    Dim I As Long, J As Long
11:    For I = LBound(Data) To UBound(Data) - 1
12:        For J = I + 1 To UBound(Data)
13:            If (Data(I) > Data(J)) Then
14:                Call Swap(Data, I, J)
15:            End If
16:        Next J
17:    Next I
18: End Sub
19:
20:
21: Sub FillArrayAndSort()
22:
23:    Const Size = 10
24:    Dim Data(Size) As Long
25:    Dim I As Long
26:    Randomize Time
27:    For I = LBound(Data) To UBound(Data)
28:        Data(I) = Rnd * Size
29:    Next I
30:
31:    Debug.Print "Start: " & Time
32:    Call BubbleSort(Data)
33:    Debug.Print "Stop: " & Time
34:
35: End Sub
```

12

ANALYSIS You will need two indexes for a Bubble sort. The letters I and J are acceptable index variables. Line 11 sets up the outer loop, and line 12 the inner loop. To compare the I index to every I + 1 index, you need two loops. Line 12 demonstrates how to start the inner loop using the I + 1 index. Line 13 performs the comparison of Data(I) and Data(J), where J = I + 1, to the upper bound index. The test on line 13 (using greater than) will create an ascending order sort. Change > to < (less than) to sort in descending order. Line 14 refers to a function that swaps the I and J elements. The Swap subroutine was repeated here for clarity. Run the FillArrayAndSort subroutine to test the bubbleSort.

The Bubble sort gets a bad rap. It is used so often because it is easy to remember and easy to implement. When it comes to sorting data, it is worth spending the time to learn the characteristics of your data and find the right sort to suit your data and performance requirements.

If you want to sort some other data type, you must modify the type of the data passed as the argument to the sort routine. Everything else stays the same in the sort function. Note also the use of Ubound - 1 in the outer loop on line 3. The outer loop needs to go only to the upper bound minus one, because the inner loop checks the last element.

The subroutine in Listing 12.9 took 51 seconds to sort 10,000 longs on my Pentium 800 PC with 256MB of RAM. This is by no means fast, but it might be fast enough for your application. A Bubble sort's performance is described by the algorithm $O(n^2)$. This means that the performance is measured by the time it takes to process one element multiplied by the number of elements squared. Thus ten thousand elements squared results in one hundred million comparisons and swaps. More than 10,000 elements cause performance to begin to deteriorate even on very fast machines.

Selection-Sorting Arrays

The Selection sort has the same performance characteristics as the Bubble sort, $O(n^2)$, except that the Selection sort swaps only when it finds exactly the right location in which to place the elements. This differs from the Bubble sort, which swaps each time the test passes.

Listing 12.10 demonstrates the Selection sort. You will get good performance up to 10,000 or so elements, but the Selection sort will deteriorate quickly for very large arrays of data.

LISTING 12.10   Using a Selection Sort, a Modified Variant of the Bubble Sort

```
1:  Sub SelectionSort(ByRef Data() As Long)
2:    Dim I As Long, J As Long, SwapIndex As Long
3:    For I = LBound(Data) To UBound(Data) - 1
4:      SwapIndex = I
5:      For J = I + 1 To UBound(Data) - 1
6:        If( Data(SwapIndex) > Data(J)) Then
7:          SwapIndex = J
8:        End If
9:      Next J
10:     Call Swap(Data, I, SwapIndex)
11:    Next I
12:End Sub
```

ANALYSIS   On my PC, the Selection sort took 19 seconds to sort 10,000 elements, about a 40-percent reduction in time compared to the Bubble sort. The difference in performance will vary depending on the number of swaps actually required, which in turn is dependent on the relative sorted order of the array. The differences between sorts are few.

Notice that on line 2, I added a third integer, `SwapIndex`. On line 4, I set `SwapIndex` to the `I` value. On line 7, instead of swapping every time the comparison passed, I recorded the index as the new `SwapIndex` value. Future comparison will compare the now-indexed higher value with the element at `J`. The swap is moved outside the inner loop; therefore, it is called only once every pass through the outer loop (that is, only *n* times instead of potentially *n*-squared times). This slight difference results in the difference in performance between the Bubble sort and the Selection sort.

Quick-Sorting Arrays

The Quick sort has average performance characteristics of $O(n\ln n)$. This refers to the number of elements multiplied by the natural logarithm of the number of elements. Natural logarithmic numbers grow very slowly.

The Quick sort is a "divide and conquer" sort. The Quick sort works by logically partitioning the array into ever smaller partitions and then sorting the very small partitions. On randomly sorted data, the partitions will roughly be equal to half of the original partition. If the data is highly sorted already, the partition is very small to begin with, instead of half, and the Quick sort performance will deteriorate rapidly. Listing 12.11 contains a Quick sort algorithm in VBA using recursive calls to the Quick sort subroutine.

NEW TERM *Recursion* refers to a technique whereby part of the solution of a function or subroutine is for the function or sub to call itself. Such a function or sub is called a *recursive function* or a *recursive subroutine*.

LISTING 12.11   Blazing Speed for Large Data Sets

12

```
1:  Sub QuickSort(ByRef Data() As Long, ByVal Left As Long, ByVal Right As Long)
2:
3:     Dim I As Long, J As Long
4:     Dim Elem As Long
5:
6:     If (Right > Left) Then
7:
8:       Elem = Data(Right)
9:       I = Left - 1
10:      J = Right
11:
12:      Do While (True)
13:        Do
14:          I = I + 1
15:        Loop While (Data(I) < Elem)
16:
17:        Do
18:          J = J - 1
```

LISTING 12.11　continued

```
19:         If (J < LBound(Data)) Then GoTo Break
20:       Loop While (J >= LBound(Data)) And (Data(J) > Elem)
21: Break:
22:       If (I >= J) Then Exit Do
23:       Call Swap(Data, I, J)
24:     Loop
25:
26:     Call Swap(Data, I, Right)
27:     Call QuickSort(Data, Left, I - 1)
28:     Call QuickSort(Data, I + 1, Right)
29:   End If
30: End Sub
31:
32: Sub FillArrayAndSort()
33:
34:   Const Size = 10
35:   Dim Data(Size) As Long
36:   Dim I As Long
37:   Randomize Time
38:   For I = LBound(Data) To UBound(Data)
39:       Data(I) = Rnd * Size
40:   Next I
41:
42:   Call Dump(Data)
43:
44:   Debug.Print "Start: " & Time
45:   Call QuickSort(Data, LBound(Data), UBound(Data))
46:   Debug.Print "Stop: " & Time
47:   Call Dump(Data)
48:
49: End Sub
50:
51:
52: Sub Dump(ByRef Data() As Long)
53:   Dim Elem As Variant
54:     For Each Elem In Data
55:       Debug.Print Elem
56:   Next Elem
57: End Sub
58:
59: Sub Swap(ByRef Data() As Long, ByVal I As Long, ByVal J As Long)
60:   Dim Temp As Long
61:   Temp = Data(I)
62:   Data(I) = Data(J)
63:   Data(J) = Temp
64:   Debug.Print "Swap:" & Data(I) & " with " & Data(J)
65: End Sub
```

ANALYSIS The Quick sort on lines 1 through 30 performs at blazing speeds for even large data sets—up to 100,000 integers in random order sorted in less than one second. One million elements are sorted in 10 seconds, and 10 million elements sorted in 124 seconds.

In Listing 12.11, the dump function can be reused to view the data in the Immediate window, although I wouldn't recommend dumping data sets that number more than a couple hundred.

Lines 59 through 65 define a generic Swap function that is referred to in Listings 12.9, 12.10, and 12.11. The idea is to copy one variable into a temporary variable to facilitate swapping between two indexed items.

The FillArrayAndSort subroutine fills an array with random integers and calls the sort algorithm that I want to test. Replace line 49 with a call to a Selection sort or Bubble sort to test those algorithms.

Lines 1 through 30 demonstrate the kind of code that can make it necessary to exceed more than a couple lines of code per subroutine. (This subroutine can be made shorter, however, by creating a separate subroutine for lines 12 through 24.) Line 1 defines the subroutine signature. The Quick sort takes three arguments: the array, the lower bound, and the upper bound. Because this implementation partitions the array into smaller logical arrays and calls itself recursively, the logical boundaries are indicated by the Left and Right arguments. Line 3 declares two indexes: longs I and J. Line 18 declares a variable of the data type of the array's elements; this value is used in several places to partition the array into logically smaller arrays.

A check to make sure that the Right bound is greater than the Left bound is made first on line 6. Line 8 copies the sentinel value used to partition the array. The I index is set to Left - 1, and J is assigned the value Right. An infinite loop on lines 12 through 24 is used to find the next partition point of each half of the logical array. This is done for both the right and left halves of the logical array (lines 13 through 15 and lines 17 through 20). If the I index is greater than the J index, the infinite loop is exited; otherwise, the data at I and J is swapped. This is repeated until I is greater than or equal to J. Line 26 performs a swap, and lines 27 and 28 call a Quick sort on the Left and Right logical partitions.

Advanced sorts can get complex. There are many sorts that make sense for different sizes and kinds of data. An exhaustive survey is beyond the scope of this book, but there are several good books on algorithms, including *Algorithms in C++*, by Robert Sedgewick, and the other books mentioned earlier. Any book but those written for VBA will require

12

you to translate the algorithm to the VBA language. Fortunately, programs for sorting algorithms comprise a small part of business programs, and, with some searching on the World Wide Web, you can find many already in existence.

Summary

Arrays are powerful and useful. An array can hold millions of pieces of information and can be used to sort and manage that information in memory. You can create arrays of native data types, user types, or objects.

An array's simplicity is what makes it easy to use. However, its simplicity is also a drawback. You learned that when you use arrays, you have to perform bounds checking, declare variables to index elements of the array, and manage the size and elements with code external to the array. If you can bind all this code to the array, the array requires less code to manage.

Binding code to concepts to make them whole is what object-oriented programming is about. In the next hour, you will learn about the modern-day array—the collection. Arrays are easy to use, making themselves accessible to programmers at all skill levels. Use them when they seem appropriate, but don't limit yourself only to arrays. Complete the following "Q&A" and "Workshop" sections to polish your array skills.

Q&A

Q Can I declare an array with more than one data type, a heterogeneous array?

A Yes. Declare the array as a variant, and you will be able to store many kinds of data in the same array.

Q Should I erase every array after I am done with it?

A It isn't necessary. If you do, be consistent and perform an Erase operation on every array.

Q How much memory can I allocate in one function for an array?

A The size of arrays used to be limited by smaller stack memory a few years ago, but 32-bit operating systems such as Windows 2000 allow for very large arrays declared in subroutines and functions.

Q Are there other sorting algorithms that have better performance characteristics than the Bubble sort, Selection sort, and Quick sort?

A Yes. In part, the performance depends on the data set. If sorting speed is critical to your program, you will need to write code that samples the data and then apply the sort based on the data set.

Workshop

The Workshop includes quiz questions designed to help you test your understanding of the material covered and exercises to help put what you've learned to practice. You will find the answers to the quiz and exercises in Appendix A, "Answers."

Quiz

1. What is the name of the function that returns an array?

2. What function initializes the memory of an array to the data type's equivalent to null?

3. Does Erase perform exactly the same operation on all arrays?

4. How do you resize an array dynamically (that is, when your program is running)?

5. Which sort type is faster: Bubble, Selection, or Quick?

Exercises

1. Write the statement for a sort that tests string data.

2. Modify the dump subroutine to write to an output file. Why is it better to use a function instead of writing code, such as the Dump code, directly where you need that behavior?

3. Modify the Bubble sort to sort in descending order. (Hint: Listing 12.7 sorts in ascending order.)

12

HOUR 13

Storing Information in a Collection

For many years, computer science curricula at universities taught data structure classes that included instructions on how to manage dynamic arrays. A *dynamic array* is a very simple data structure (see Hour 12, "Managing Varying Amounts of Data"). Object-oriented programming hit the PC mainstream around 1990. Since then, many PC programming languages, including VBA, have adopted object-oriented idioms. What this means to you and me is that code, once written, can be used more easily by many developers.

A *collection* is just the sort of advantage object-oriented programming provides. In the most basic sense, a collection is a dynamic array, written as a class and incorporated as part of the VBA language. Where programmers might have chosen to use arrays in the past, they now find a collection is a better alternative. You will still encounter arrays in existing code, but for new code, the collection is the preferable alternative.

In this hour, you will learn to program with collections by

- Becoming familiar with object terminology
- Learning how to declare collection objects
- Learning to use the capabilities built in to a collection
- Recognizing collections in existing database and visual component objects

Understanding Collections

A *collection* is an indexable data structure that enables you to add, remove, and iterate over items within it. The items in a collection can be as diverse as those in an array. You can put simple types, user types, and objects in a collection. The data in a collection can be either homogeneous or heterogeneous—that is, of one type or many types. The added benefit is that the collection already knows how to grow according to your data-storage needs, and collections have built-in error handling.

The collection is the most powerful, general-purpose storage medium available to you as a VBA programmer.

Uses for Collections

Collections are used everywhere in existing code. Visual components such as list boxes and combo boxes use collections. ADODB uses collections to represent fields; ADOX contains collections to represent tables and keys, among other things. You will need to know how to manage collections to use the visual controls and ADO objects that are collections.

When you need to store or manipulate data in memory, a collection will be a useful object to know how to use. A common example of when you will encounter collections is when you list data in list boxes or combo boxes or manipulate field data in a recordset. You have already done so in earlier hours, as you might recall.

The Terminology of Object-Oriented Programming

There is code built in to VBA that defines what a collection is. This code is called, collectively, the Collection class. Think of a class as the blueprint that describes what the class will be capable of knowing and doing.

A simple integer type is capable of knowing the value assigned to integer variables. A class is somewhat like a type in that it can contain many subtypes. Each of the subtypes in a class can know information relevant to that type. A class also includes procedures that describe what instances of the class can do. Instances of classes are referred to as *objects*. The "doing" part of an object is defined by the subroutines and functions defined in the class.

Code written in a class module (.cls file) defines the class. When a programmer writes code that declares a variable of the class, the variable instance is referred to as an *object* or an *instance* (these terms are synonymous).

In general, the data in a class is referred to as the class's *attributes*, or those things that define what a class can know. Data attributes are referred to as *properties* in VBA. Properties are the same as variables, except that the term property means that the variable belongs to a class. Classes also have *methods*, which are the functions and subroutines that define what a class can do. The difference between methods and plain-old functions and subroutines is that the term *methods* infers that the named methods belong to a class.

When properties and methods are defined as part of a class, we say that the class *encapsulates* the properties and methods. Before object-oriented programming became mainstream, the programming paradigm was referred to as *structured programming*. Table 13.1 provides you with a visual map of object terms and their structured programming counterparts.

NEW TERM *Paradigm* in this context refers to a technique or style of programming. Object-oriented programming, for example, is an approach—a paradigm—for which the decomposition of a problem centers around the object rather than the process.

TABLE 13.1 A Visual Map of Structured Versus Object-Oriented Terms

Structured Term	Object-Oriented Term	Meaning
Variable	Property	Stores data
Function or subroutine	Method	Code that performs a task

New terminology is not created to be confusing, although sometimes it seems that way. The new terms encompass both the old meanings and the new dimension added by object-oriented programming. For example, *variable* refers to data by itself, whereas *property* refers to data as part of a whole class. When the definition evolves, naturally, so must the descriptive terms.

You do not have to master object-oriented terms before using objects, but mastering the terminology is a good initial step. Other programmers can more effectively and precisely communicate with you about objects if you are able to use object-oriented terms correctly.

The Collection class defines four attributes. The Count property defines the number of items in a Collection object. The Add method enables you to add items to a Collection object. The Remove method lets you remove items from a Collection object, and the Items method allows you to reference data in a Collection by index.

In this hour, I will emphasize mastery of these four collection attributes.

13

Declaring Collection Variables

Class data types are user-defined types. The user who defined them might be you or some other programmer. A collection is a type defined and incorporated by Microsoft into the VBA language. A collection contains the four attributes described in the preceding section.

Object-oriented idioms were introduced into VBA in the last couple years. The variable declarations are similar, but before an object is assigned memory (that is, before it is initialized), you must use a slightly different technique than you would use to initialize simple data types or simple user-defined types. (For now, I will stick with collection declarations, but the syntactical examples presented next apply to all objects.) The syntax for declaring a collection is

```
Dim MyCollection As Collection
```

As you might have noted already, the declaration of objects is identical to the declaration of non-objects. Replace *MyCollection* with the name you want to use, and you are all set. However, it is important to note that *MyCollection* refers to Nothing after the previous line. Nothing is the object equivalent of Null or Empty. This means that you cannot use the object after it is declared, as in the preceding example.

NEW TERM To *allocate* means to assign memory to. For example, you might say "An instance is a class variable that has memory assigned to it."

To use a collection after you declare a variable, you must assign it to an existing collection or allocate memory to the collection variable with the New command. You can allocate memory on the same line as the collection declaration or on a later line, but you must assign *MyCollection* to a valid Collection object. To allocate memory to a collection on the same line as the declaration, insert the New command between As and Collection, as shown here:

```
Dim MyCollection As New Collection
```

This tells the compiler to allocate memory to the object. You can also declare the collection variable and allocate memory to it later, like this:

```
Dim MyCollection As Collection
Set MyCollection = New Collection
```

Notice the use of the keyword Set. Whenever you assign an object reference to an object instance, you will need to do so with the word Set. This makes objects a little trickier to use than simple types. If you forget to use the Set keyword, the compiler will remind you. Learn to recognize the error in Figure 13.1 to mean that you forgot the Set keyword.

FIGURE **13.1**

Use the Set keyword when assigning an object to an object reference; otherwise, you will get the error shown.

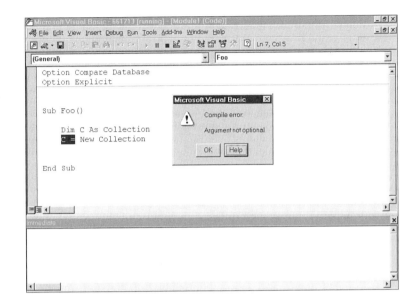

When you are finished with a Collection object, you will want to return the memory to the computer memory pool by setting the Collection object to Nothing. The following line of code demonstrates this:

```
Set MyCollection = Nothing
```

The New keyword was introduced in languages such as C++ to allocate memory on the Heap. Think of heap memory as your computer's available RAM allocated by Windows to a program. Objects require much more memory than simple types do. By allowing allocation of memory to be performed separately from declaration, a strategy referred to as *lazy instancing* can be employed. Lazy instancing refers to assigning memory to something only when and if it is really needed.

Imagine for a moment that every program has to request all the memory it might use over the course of the program's run duration. Some programs use millions and millions of bytes of RAM from beginning to end. If all the memory had to be requested up front, many programs would fail because of lack of memory.

For now, it is enough to remember that you can declare a collection and assign it an object reference at the point of declaration or at some later time.

13

Managing a Data Collection

A collection is basically a smart, dynamic array that knows how to contain items and grow automatically when necessary. The Count property answers the question of how many items are in a collection. The Add and Remove items enable you to deposit or withdraw items from the collection, and you can also access individual elements with the Items method or by using the For Each loop.

By convention, collections use pluralized names of the type of data they will contain. For example, the variable for a collection of strings might be named Strings.

Adding Data to a Collection

The Add method is used to add items to a collection. The syntax for Add follows:

```
Call collectionobject.Add( item, [key, [before, | ,after]] )
```

Here, collectionobject refers to the name of a collection object. The method is Add. Because Add is a member of the Collection class, you use the "member-of" operator to attach collectionobject with the Add method. (The use of Call is optional for subroutines. If you use Call, you need the parentheses. If you do not use Call, do not use the parentheses.) The basic use of Add is to pass the item argument only. The value of item can be a literal, variable, expression, or object reference. For example, A = 5 would place a Boolean into the collection: True if A is equal to 5, and False if not. If you use only the item argument, Add appends the item to the end of the collection.

The Key argument enables you to establish an associated name with the item. If you add a Key argument, you can access the item by an integral index or the key name. (Refer to the section "Using the Item Method and Count Property" for more details.) You can specify the optional Before or After argument, but not both. If you specify the After argument, remember to use the extra comma for the blank Before argument. If you specify a Before argument, item will be placed in the collection before the item represented by the Before index or key name. The After argument, which can also be an index or key, will place item after the item in the collection represented by the After index or key name. Listing 13.1 demonstrates several examples of Add.

LISTING 13.1   Using the Add Method for Collections

```
1:  Sub CollectionDemoAdd()
2:      Dim Strings As New Collection
3:      ' with parentheses
4:      Call Strings.Add("1")
5:      ' without parentheses
6:      Strings.Add "2"
7:      Call Strings.Add("3", "Three", , 2)
```

LISTING 13.1   continued

```
 8:    Call Strings.Add("4", "Four", "Three")
 9:    MsgBox Strings.Item("Three")
10:    MsgBox Strings.Item(1)
11:    Dim I As Integer
12:    For I = 1 To Strings.Count
13:        Debug.Print Strings.Item(I)
14:    Next I
15:    Set Strings = Nothing
16: End Sub
```

> You will have to use the parentheses when calling a function and assigning the return value to a variable. This means that you will have parentheses used for functions. To be consistent, I use them for both functions and subroutines, although it is not required to use parentheses when calling subroutines.

ANALYSIS   Line 2 declares and allocates a new collection named `Strings`. Line 4 demonstrates the basic append behavior of `Add` when you only pass the data to add to the collection. Line 6 demonstrates the same type of usage without `Call` and the parentheses. Line 7 adds the string `"3"` with the key `"Three"` after the second item added. Notice the extra comma to represent the unused `Before` argument. Line 8 adds the string `"4"` with the key `"Four"`. As with element `"3"`, this means that items with key names `"Three"` and `"Four"` can be accessed by an index or their key names.

Lines 9 and 10 of Listing 13.1 demonstrate accessing items by index and key name, respectively. Lines 11 through 14 iterate through each element of the collection, creating the output in the Immediate window shown in Figure 13.2.

> Visual Basic for Applications and the Java programming language do not require you to explicitly deallocate memory. The compiler builds in code to perform this task automatically. This process is referred to as *garbage collection*. However, releasing allocated memory is a good indicator of when you are done with your objects, and it makes your code more precise. I do it.

13

Line 15 releases the memory allocated to the collection, although VBA will do this for you automatically. The end of the subroutine is on line 16.

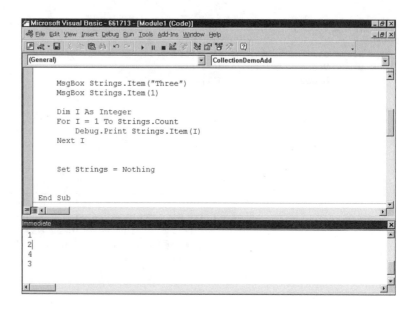

FIGURE 13.2

Output from Listing 13.1, which writes the elements of a collection to the Immediate window.

Removing Data from a Collection

The Remove method takes one argument: *Index*. The *Index* argument can be an integer from one to Count or a string expression resolving to one of the key names. The syntax is

```
Call collectionobject.Remove(Index)
```

Use Call and parentheses as you see fit. (I use Call and parentheses in subroutines in all the code examples in the rest of the book.) In the preceding syntax, *collectionobject* is an instance of a collection. The member-of operator attaches the Remove method to *collectionobject*, and *Index* is a variable, literal, constant, integer, or key string. If you use a string, the string must resolve to a key associated with an element of the collection. (See Listing 13.2, later in this hour, for examples of using Remove.)

Using the Item Method and Count Property

The Count property returns the actual number of elements in a collection. This might not be the actual number of elements allocated to the collection, but that information isn't necessary.

Remember in the dynamic array of the last hour that you had to write code to track the size and growth of an array. Some form of sizing and growing also exists in a collection, but it isn't necessary for you to be aware of it. This not knowing is referred to as *information hiding* or *complexity hiding*—a powerful benefit of object-oriented programming. Because of the inherent limitations of the short-term memory, you are unable to grapple with many details all at once. Information hiding enables you to focus on isolated problems, regardless of all the details.

The Item method gives you access to one element of a collection at a time. The Item member takes one argument: an integer or a key name. Listing 13.2 demonstrates how to use Item.

Iterating Through a Collection with For Each Loops

You learned how to use the For Each loop in Hour 5, "Learning to Write Conditional Code." Collections are ideal candidates for For Each loops. Listing 13.2 demonstrates all the methods and the Count method used in concert to manage a collection.

LISTING 13.2   A Collection of Strings

```
 1: Sub CollectionDemo()
 2:    Dim Strings As New Collection
 3:    Call Strings.Add("The")
 4:    Call Strings.Add("time")
 5:    Call Strings.Add("has")
 6:    Call Strings.Add("come, ")
 7:    Call Strings.Add("the")
 8:    Call Strings.Add("Walrus")
 9:    Call Strings.Add("said.")
10:    Dim Str As Variant
11:    Dim Text As String
12:    For Each Str In Strings
13:      Text = Text & " " & Str
14:    Next Str
15:    Debug.Print Text
16:    Dim I As Integer
17:    For I = Strings.Count To 1 Step -1
18:      Debug.Print "Removing " & Strings.Item(I)
19:      Call Strings.Remove(I)
20:    Next I
21:    Set Strings = Nothing
22: End Sub
```

13

ANALYSIS   Line 2 declares and allocates a collection named Strings. It is important to remember that almost any type of data can go into a collection. Lines 3 through 9 add a line from Lewis Carroll's "Walrus and Carpenter" from *Alice in Wonderland*. Line 10 declares a variant named Str, and line 11 declares a String variable named Text. Remember, For Each requires a Variant data type. The Str variable is used as the recipient of each element (line 12) of the collection, and Text is used on line 13 to create one string to write to the Immediate window on line 15.

Lines 16 through 20 demonstrate how to remove each item using the Count property. The Item property writes each element to the Immediate window and then removes each element on line 19. Line 20 performs cleanup on the collection itself.

If you want to remove all items using Count, do so in reverse order. When you remove an item, Count changes. If Count is your outer loop control value, you will get a Subscript Out of Range error when your index exceeds the number of elements actually left. Unfortunately, you cannot use For Each to iteratively remove all elements of a collection.

Places You'll Find Collections

The best technique to quickly identify collections in other objects is to search for a pluralized property. Often a plural property is indicative of a collection. This is one of the reasons conventions are useful; they provide us with a reference point for further learning.

If you encounter a property or object that seems to be a collection, you can place your cursor on the word in the editor and press the F1 key. The Help file will let you know for sure.

Collections are used in many places. Visual controls such as list boxes and combo boxes use collections to store the data in their lists. Collections are used in numerous places. For example, there are table, field, key, column, and index collections used in the ADO library. Collections are easy to use and powerful. After you learn to use an object of any given type, such as a collection, you know how to use all occurrences of it.

Summary

A *collection* is essentially a dynamic array (see Hour 12, which covers arrays). A collection is a generic data structure that can be used to store simple data or user-defined data. You can place data of the same type or of different types into a collection.

Objects, in general, are much more powerful than unrelated code. A well-crafted object can be designed to hide information, thereby reducing the complexity of using the object. Where you might consider using an array in new code, I would suggest you consistently employ a collection instead. Collections require much less management and can grow dynamically without any additional code from you.

Collections show you that recurring code can be made more powerful and easy to use when wrapped up tight in a class. Before you and I finish our journey together, you will know how to write classes too. I encourage you to complete the "Q&A" and "Workshop" sections to solidify your understanding and hone your skills.

Q&A

Q **When writing new code, should I use an array or a collection?**

A Use a collection for new code, although you are likely to encounter arrays often in the old VBA code still out there.

Q **Can I extend the capabilities of classes, such as `Collection`?**

A Yes. This is referred to as *subclassing*. You will learn how to subclass in Hour 21, "Class Programming Basics," and the chapters that follow it.

Q **Should I always set objects, such as `Collection` objects, to `Nothing` when finished?**

A I do, but you are just as likely to find programmers who don't, because VBA performs garbage collection. The most important thing is to develop consistent habits.

Q **Do all collections work alike?**

A Yes. If you encounter a variable that is a VBA collection, it will contain, at a minimum, `Count`, `Item`, `Add`, and `Remove`, although subclasses of collections may have more capabilities.

Workshop

The Workshop includes quiz questions designed to help you test your understanding of the material covered and exercises to help put what you've learned to practice. You will find the answers to the quiz and exercises in Appendix A, "Answers."

Quiz

1. What is the difference between a method and a function or subroutine?
2. What is the name of the method that appends items to a collection?
3. What effect does `Nothing` have on objects?
4. Do you have to remove items from a collection before assigning the collection variable to `Nothing`?
5. What is one of two ways to iterate over the items in a collection?

Exercises

1. Create an instance of a collection and add 10 integers to it.
2. Write a subroutine that writes all the collection items in exercise 1 to the Immediate window.
3. Modify the Bubble sort algorithm from Hour 12 to sort elements in a collection.

13

PART V

Database Programming in Access

Hour

HOUR 14

Managing Your Code

The term *spaghetti code* was coined to define code that looks like a snarled mess. It is no wonder that some code is messy because the software industry has set no standards for code writing, nor do many college curriculums teach how to write code.

In part, this might be because programmers can't even agree on what constitutes good code or bad code. I wrote my first code in 1978, but I began programming professionally in 1987. In 12 years, I have seen everything in production from poorly written code—written by both professional programmers and college students—to some of the best code in the world. I have adopted strategies based on what I have learned from both kinds of code and techniques deemed to be best practices by recognized industry leaders. I use the coding strategies presented in this hour in real code for successful business solutions and commercial retail software.

Writing good code is as important for the lone developer trying to pump out a one-time-only program as it is for the team programmer. There are many reasons why this is true, but an important one is this: When you write code, you are the author, but when you return to the code to modify or maintain it, you become a user of the code. From experience, I can tell you that code you wrote just a few weeks earlier can seem foreign to you. Therefore, even if you program alone and your code is never read by another soul, you will help yourself by adopting the strategies demonstrated in this hour. At some point in the lifetime of your code, however, another person will probably become the code user. This person might be your supervisor, a colleague who will use your program, a fellow Access power user evaluating the quality of your program for a variety of reasons, or someone who is helping you find a pernicious error.

In this hour, you will learn some strategies that will help you get more mileage out of your code and make your job a lot easier. For me, doing a good job means I get to move onto some other interesting project sooner. That very likely also means more money in my pocket.

In this hour, you will master good code writing strategies by learning

- How to use good naming conventions
- How to use whitespace and comments to make code readable
- How to manage complexity and maximize code reuse
- The guidelines for testing and tracking modifications
- How to make data easier to manage

Naming Conventions

The readability of your code is determined in part by how well you name your code. Considering the typing required, the effort to create a comment is roughly equivalent to the effort required to write a statement. In most circumstances, if your code is well named, you will not need comments. If your code is ambiguous, you need comments too—effectively doubling your labor. Uncommented, ambiguous code exists, but it is not something you want to emulate. This kind of code can be a nightmare to manage and will ultimately cost you more in terms of time, effort, and quality than any other kind of code.

There are two schools of thought on what constitutes a good name. One school uses naming conventions based on a prefix notation. The notation is most commonly called the *Hungarian notation*. The Hungarian notation was developed by Charles Simonyi in the 1980s. The Hungarian notation suggests that an abbreviated prefix be devised for each data type and that you prefix every variable, function, procedure, and user-defined type with the appropriate prefix. For example, *i* might be the prefix for `Integer` types, so every integer variable would be prefixed with an *i*. Applying the convention, you would name `Age`, an integer variable, `iAge`. There is much more history involved, but you get the general idea.

New Term A *weakly typed* language is a language that does not strictly enforce parameter data types. You might, for example, have declared a parameter as an integer, but the language allows you to pass data of many types for that argument. The C programming language is a weakly typed programming language.

New Term A *strongly typed* language is a language that strictly enforces parameter data types. This means that parameter data must exactly match the indicated type. The C++ programming language is a strongly typed language. VBA, the Access 2002 programming language, is a strongly typed language, although not as strongly typed as most implementations of C++.

In this book, I do not use any derivative of the Hungarian notation, nor do I use any notation. My arguments against using a prefix notation are simple:

- Many of the original reasons for using a prefix notation do not exist today. For example, the Hungarian notation was developed to support the weakly typed C programming language, which is not an object-oriented language. Most languages now are strongly typed (see the definitions of weakly typed and strongly typed languages).

- Most languages (implemented after the Hungarian notation was developed) are object oriented, and object-oriented languages allow an infinite variety of new types. New types require new prefixes. This adds significant overhead to maintaining a list of prefixes.

- No single master list exists containing the prefixes for existing types, which means there are many variations of prefixes for the same type.

> If you are compelled to adopt a prefix notation, keep a master list of the prefixes you will be using and use them consistently.

Instead of using a prefix notation, I use whole words and context. Whole words and context convey meaning very precisely and do not require any additional learning. Using simple, general rules is easier than remembering specific chunks of data. Here are the basic rules I use to create well-named code:

- Use whole words to clearly convey meaning.
- Use verb and noun pairs for subroutines and functions.
- Use only standard abbreviations; that is, abbreviations that can be found in any dictionary.
- Publish any industry-standard abbreviations (a simple list) that you intend to use.

14

Creating a list of industry-standard abbreviations—abbreviations that are standard in the industry you work in—exemplifies one of the many good reasons for establishing an intranet. You can build an intranet on your PC and make it available to everyone on your network. Publishing project information on an intranet cuts down on paper, makes information instantly accessible, and ensures a central repository for accurate information.

The previous list of rules is easier to remember than a list of dozens of specific prefixes. If you need to know the data type, you can prefix the whole-word data type to the variable. Whole word prefixes require only a little more effort than typing an abbreviated prefix and no effort to memorize. For example, if you have a `Form` variable representing the main form, you can name the variable `FormMain`. Easy. If you use a whole-word prefix once, use it consistently. Applied to the `Form` example, if you use `Form` for one form, use it for all forms.

Meaning Is Conveyed with Whole Words

When you pass a variable to a function, a whole word conveys meaning clearly. Additionally, if that function is very short, there is little room for misunderstanding. Consider the function in Listing 14.1.

LISTING 14.1   Context and Whole Words Convey Meaning Clearly

```
Function GetTotalSale(ByVal Sale As Double, _
    Optional SalesTax As Double = 0.0825) As Double
  GetTotalSale = Sale * (1 + SalesTax)
End Function
```

I recommend you use functions instead of inline code, even for functions as simple as `GetTotalSale`. Reading the line of code `GetTotalSale` conveys much more meaning than does reading an inline equation.

ANALYSIS   `GetTotalSale` conveys exactly what the preceding function will do—it gets the total sale. (It would also be perfectly acceptable to name the function `CalculateTotalSale` or `AddSalesTax`.) The parameters `Sale` and `SalesTax` are also quite clear. Because the function is clear, no prefixes or comments are required.

There are several variations you might encounter that demonstrate how other programmers write code, such as that in Listing 14.1. The `Get` verb might be written as `Calc`; `Tax` might be written as Tx. However, there is no real savings obtained using these partial words, and they result in code that is less clear. (Tx could imply *Texas*.)

Pairing Verbs and Nouns Make Subroutines and Functions Clear

Precede subroutine and function names with a verb to describe the action taken, and use a noun to describe the thing acted upon. A noun and verb pair are sufficient enough information to make a whole sentence; therefore, used in code, they are capable of conveying a complete meaning. If you limit the code in the function or subroutine to what the procedure name states, your code is eminently clear.

In Listing 14.1, Get is the verb. By convention, Get is used to indicate a function that returns data. Total is an adjective that, combined with Sale (as in GetTotalSale), conveys exactly what the function does.

NEW TERM A *procedure* is the generic word for a function or subroutine. Unless it is necessary for clarity in the discussion, I will use *procedure* to mean either a function or a subroutine.

Abbreviated procedure and variable names were used historically because compilers and interpreters had built-in physical limits for name lengths. Out of habit perhaps, many programmers still use short, arbitrarily abbreviated names. No such limit exists in VBA; therefore, you can have names that are as long as you need them to be.

As a general rule, if your procedure name is really long, you are probably doing too much in that procedure. Consider breaking the code into several smaller procedures.

When you define a new procedure, find a verb that describes what action the code takes and a noun that describes what data is acted upon.

Avoid Nonstandard Abbreviations

Many industries have abbreviations that are commonly understood in the context of that industry. As a general rule, you should avoid nonstandard abbreviations and acronyms. If the abbreviation cannot be found in an abbreviation list in a dictionary, it should be avoided; use the whole-word version instead.

If everyone in your line of work knows what an abbreviation means, by all means, use it. I would suggest, however, that you create a list of the abbreviations and their meanings.

14

In my case, I write software to assist other developers in many industries. There is no way someone like me will remember the hundreds of different industry-specific abbreviations. I need a list. You might also be working with industry outsiders or initiates who do not know what certain abbreviations or acronyms mean. The list will assist them, too.

Using Whitespace Consistently

Whitespace is any space that does not contain a visible character. Spaces and tabs are examples of whitespace. By being consistent in your use of whitespace, you make your code neater and easier to read. Compare Listings 14.2 and 14.3: Listing 14.2 uses whitespace inconsistently, and Listing 14.3 uses it consistently.

LISTING 14.2   Poor Use of Whitespace

```
 1: Function GetIQText(ByVal IQ As Integer) As String
 2: If IQ < 79 Then
 3: GetIQText = "A score less than 79 indicates severe retardation"
 4:     ElseIf IQ >= 79 And IQ < 90 Then
 5:            GetIQText = "Indicates moderate to low intelligence"
 6:         ElseIf IQ >= 90 And IQ < 105 Then
 7:              GetIQText = "Normal Intelligence"
 8: Else: GetIQText = "Above Normal"
 9:        End If
10: End Function
```

[ic:analysis]I have seen tens of thousands of lines of code like the code in Listing 14.2. To be fair, I don't think anyone sets out to write code like this. Code usually ends up like this after several modifications. It is up to you to keep your code neat. Many times, I have heard a programmer say something like, "I am not worried about it right now; I will clean it up later." It is amazing how often later never comes.

The code in Listing 14.2 takes an intelligence quotient (IQ) score and returns text that indicates the relative meaning of the score. However, the code is extremely difficult to read because whitespace is used inconsistently. (It is so bad that I had trouble writing it.) Compare Listing 14.2 to Listing 14.3.

LISTING 14.3   Good, Consistent Use of Whitespace

```
 1: Function GetIQText(ByVal IQ As Integer) As String
 2:
 3:     If IQ < 79 Then
 4:         GetIQText = "A score less than 79 indicates severe retardation"
 5:         ElseIf (IQ > 79 And IQ < 90) Then
```

LISTING 14.3 continued

```
 6:            GetIQText = "Indicates moderate to low intelligence"
 7:        ElseIf (IQ >= 90 And IQ < 105) Then
 8:            GetIQText = "Normal Intelligence"
 9:        Else
10:            GetIQText = "Above Normal"
11:        End If
12:
13: End Function
```

ANALYSIS The code in Listing 14.3 illustrates a better implementation of the same function shown in Listing 14.2. The code uses whitespace consistently. Note the blank line before and after the code block; notice also that the code in the function is indented at one level, and the code subordinate to that code is indented one more level. Using whitespace in this manner indicates ownership as well as neatness. Listing 14.3 makes it clear that the If conditional code belongs to the function, and the resultant text strings (each subordinated to its individual test) belong to the conditional tests. Listing 14.4 represents a best implementation of the function.

LISTING 14.4 Using a Select Case Statement to Block Code

```
 1:  Function GetIQText(ByVal IQ As Integer) As String
 2:
 3:    Const RETARDED = "A score less than 79 indicates severe retardation"
 4:    Const LOW = "Indicates moderate to low intelligence"
 5:    Const NORMAL = "Normal intelligence"
 6:    Const ABOVE_NORMAL = "Above normal intelligence"
 7:
 8:    Select Case IQ
 9:      Case Is < 79
10:        GetIQText = RETARDED
11:      Case Is < 90
12:        GetIQText = LOW
13:      Case Is < 105
14:        GetIQText = NORMAL
15:      Case Else
16:        GetIQText = ABOVE_NORMAL
17:    End Select
18:
19: End Function
```

14

ANALYSIS Listing 14.4 is the best example of the code. The text is separated from the conditional tests, making it easier to discern the test from the test result. The code uses whitespace consistently and is very easy to read. Read the next section, "Managing Complexity," for a continued discussion on what makes code more manageable.

Managing Complexity

You can employ some specific strategies to make your code more manageable. The strategies described in this section are not difficult to use. With a little practice, they will become second nature to you and will help you gain control of your code. Here's a list of the general strategies discussed in this section:

- Avoid nesting conditional statements.
- Use procedures to implement conditional code.
- Keep procedures short and to the point.

Practice writing code, applying the strategies listed. Using these three strategies will result in code that is easier to reuse and easier to extend and customize.

Avoid Nesting Conditional Statements

Nested conditional statements are `Select Case` and `If…Then` statements that contain other conditional statements. The code might look like the following:

```
If test Then
    If test   Then
    End If
Else
    If test Then
    ElseIf test Then
        If test then
        End If
    Else
    End IF
End If
```

Real code with this many levels of complexity will not be this sanitized. Add some real test code and some code for each test condition, and you will end up with a tangled mess—spaghetti code. Again, in fairness, it is unlikely that programmers set out to write code like the preceding. Code evolves—sometimes poorly and sometimes nicely. How code evolves depends on the application of the guidelines mentioned.

NEW TERM   *Refactoring* is similar to the mathematical term *factoring*. In programming, refactoring means to move recurring code into procedures or classes so that they only appear one time in your program. As an example of refactoring, if the same 10 lines of code appear several times, move that code into a procedure. Everywhere the code exists, replace it with a call to the new procedure.

The fragment refactored, applying the rules given earlier, will look something like the following:

```
If test Then
    call_procedure
Else
    call_else_procedure
End If
```

The *call_procedure* code implements the first code path, and the *call_else_procedure* code implements the Else path. The fact that the two code paths contain conditional code is concealed in the procedure calls, thus mitigating the potential for complexity in this algorithm.

Use Procedures to Implement Conditional Code

Wrapping code in procedures helps you keep code easy to read and easy to extend. Consider a Select Case statement. If you write the code for each case in the same procedure as the one containing Select Case, you will be limited to using the code in the context of the case statement only. Consider the following fragment:

```
Select Case test
Case value1:
Case value2:
Case Else
End Select
```

If you write the code for each case in the Select Case code, you can't reuse it. However, if you define a procedure for each case, you have procedures that you can reuse in other instances.

Remember this rule is a *caveat*, a cautionary guideline that will help you manage your code. If the code is as simple as that in Listing 14.4, write the code in the Select Case statement. If code in any case statement grows modestly in complexity or appears to acquire greater utility, separate the code into its own procedure.

Keep Procedures Short and to the Point

Earlier, I suggested that, when defining procedures, you adopt a style that uses a verb to describe the action and a noun to describe what is acted upon. The application of this rule means that you only write code that implements the behavior described by the procedure name.

Often, you want to add conditional error code to make your program more robust. Consider a function that opens a file and returns a file handle. If your implementation requires that the file exist, you can write two functions: an outer and an inner function. Listing 14.5 demonstrates the technique.

14

LISTING 14.5   You Can Use Procedures in Pairs to Manage Complexity

```
1:  Function DoOpenFile( ByVal FileName As String ) AS Double
2:    DoOpenFile = FreeFile
3:    Open FileName For Random As #DoOpenFile
4:  End Function
5:
6:  Function FileExists( ByVal FileName As String ) As Boolean
7:    FileExists = Len(Dir(FileName)) > 0
8:  End Function
9:
10: Function OpenFile( ByVal FileName As String ) As Double
11:   If( FileExists(FileName)) Then
12:     OpenFile = DoOpenFile(FileName)
13:   Else
14:     ' Error code
15:   End If
16: End Function
```

ANALYSIS   The first function, on lines 1–4, implements open file behavior. That is, DoOpenFile actually opens the file and returns the file handle (a number that represents the file). The second function, FileExist, implemented on lines 6 through 8, encapsulates the test in a well-named function. The OpenFile outer function is the one you would actually call directly. OpenFile performs the test for existence and calls DoOpenFile if the test succeeds. The end result is three very readable functions that combine to support one behavior, or that can be reorchestrated to form new behaviors.

In a nutshell, the technique is to define an inner and outer function. The one you call implements the error handling behavior, and the inner one is prefixed with Do (the inner function performs the action).

Commenting Guidelines

When you are writing code for the first time, you have some assumptions about the code's utility. Take a moment to document those assumptions. It is much easier to put them down when writing the code than it is to re-create them later. Here a few suggestions that will help you document your code when necessary:

- Write comments in complete sentences when you first write the code.
- Comment lengthy code.
- Comment ambiguous code or code copied from an external source.

Write Comments in Complete Sentences

This rule is self-explanatory. Write whole sentences. Whole sentences are easier to read and can help you produce external documentation at a later date, if you need to.

> JavaDoc.exe is a program that automatically produces documentation from Java code. It is possible that you can find an equivalent program for your VBA code, if needed. Whole-sentence documentation can help automate the creation of programmer-user documentation.
>
> The .NET environment is capable of producing external documentation from code comments, and it is highly likely that VBA will too, eventually.

Comment Lengthy Code

If a single procedure is more than two or three lines, consider writing a couple of sentences in plain English that document the code. This might include a sentence that describes the intended use and preconditions for use of the procedure.

Comment Ambiguous Code or Code Copied from an External Source

If you copy code from an external source or the code implements a specific kind of behavior, such as a sorting algorithm, write a comment or two. If the code is copied, cite the complete reference where the code was obtained, including file or document name, edition, author, publication date, publisher, and page or listing number. It is likely that the source will have additional, extended details that might help you in the event you encounter a defect.

Understanding the Benefits of Code Reuse

Code reuse is a multibillion-dollar industry. The name for this industry is *object-oriented programming*. One of the most touted problems that object-oriented programming was developed to address was code reuse. (You will learn more about object-oriented programming in Hour 21, "Class Programming Basics.") However, moderate-to-high reusability can be achieved with and without objects. This section demonstrates how.

Code that has already been written is code that is waiting to be used again. Reused code has already been tested; unless you change it, you do not have to retest it. Because existing code has been used by you and perhaps your colleagues, it is likely that it more completely solves a specific kind of problem. Finally, by extending existing code with a procedure wrapper, you only have to test the wrapper function. Listing 14.5 demonstrates a function wrapper. If you implement a function equivalent to DoOpenFile, you could extend it by adding error handling in the wrapper, OpenFile. Consequently, only the new function OpenFile would have to be tested.

> It is important to stabilize procedure names as soon as possible. The reasoning is simple: If you change a procedure name, you must change all the code that refers to that name. All the changed code will need to be tested. However, assume you have a procedure. If you prefix the existing procedure with Do and add a new procedure—a wrapper—with the name of the old procedure, all your code still works, and you will only need to test the wrapper.

Code is more likely to be reused when it is short. Code is also more likely to be used again if it is commented, well named, and neat. Essentially, code is more likely to be reusable and reused when you apply techniques such as those described in this hour.

Testing and Debugging

Hour 17, "Removing Bugs," and Hour 18, "Adding Code to Handle Errors," covers testing and debugging techniques in detail; therefore, I won't provide that information here. I do want to offer a few cautionary words. If you change code, test it. Even if the change seems simple, untested code will come back to haunt you.

In the absence of a tool for managing defects, you can use historical commenting to track modifications. Listing all the changes you make to a procedure, in an effort to eradicate a defect, can reduce redundant effort. You will learn all about bug hunting and writing fault-tolerant code in Hours 17 and 18.

Managing Data

You can also apply some specific strategies to variables to make your code more manageable. To summarize, the following tips will help:

- Use constants instead of literal values.
- Pass arguments with the ByRef, ByVal, Optional. Or ParamArray qualifiers to convey intended use.
- Eliminate global data.

If you find yourself writing literal string or numeric data in procedures, define a constant with a good name. Replace the literal with the constant name. Listing 14.2 demonstrates this.

When you want to ensure that a procedure doesn't change the value of an argument, make the argument a pass-by-value argument. If you intend that your argument be changed by a procedure, make the argument a pass-by-reference argument. If you have an argument that satisfies most conditions, use the Optional argument type. Listing 14.1 demonstrates how to use the keyword Optional.

Summary

How you write your code is a subjective matter. There is no perfect way to write code, but having a method to your madness will make writing code much easier. Adopting a set of strategies for writing code will leave you with more brainpower for thinking about what you will write.

In this hour, you learned that code reuse can be obtained by keeping procedures short. A good naming convention for a procedure is to use a verb and noun combination that describes what the procedure does. Subdividing conditional code and the code that each condition executes is another good technique for writing code that can be used in many contexts. Another good technique is to extend existing code with a code wrapper, reducing the number of modifications to other code and the amount of additional testing needed.

The techniques in this hour will take some practice, but if they become second nature to you, you will get a lot more mileage out of the code you write. Complete the "Q&A" and "Workshop" sections to gain a better understanding of writing manageable code.

Q&A

Q Is there any one best way to write code?

A No. That's one of the things that makes programming challenging. However, there are best practices you can employ to make the job easier. The first thing to do is get the code to work right.

Q Should I worry about these techniques on the first pass at a solution?

A No. If applied diligently, like any habit, they can become second nature. But I encourage you to refactor your code as it evolves—several times if possible. In this way, your technique and your code will become as good as they can be.

14

Q Are there other techniques I should learn?

A The best techniques are those acquired through experience and those that help you work more efficiently. Some techniques might not seem natural to you. If a particular technique seems too difficult, try a variation of the technique or develop your own.

Workshop

The Workshop includes quiz questions designed to help you test your understanding of the material covered and exercises to help put what you've learned to practice. You will find the answers to the quiz and exercises in Appendix A, "Answers."

Quiz

1. What is a good way to derive procedure names?

2. What is one benefit of code reuse?

3. Hungarian notation refers to a prefix notation based on the abbreviation of variable types. True or false?

4. *Procedure* is a generic term for both functions and subroutines. True or false?

5. What is a good generalization to describe the amount of code contained in a procedure?

Exercises

1. Define a name for a function that sums a principal and interest amount.

2. Define names for function pairs that close a file, verifying that the handle is greater than zero.

3. Define a name for data that stores a file handle, calculates the interest amount (given the principal and interest rate), and stores a constant for a bad file handle.

Hour 15

Data Programming Made Easy with ADODB

Database technology has changed rapidly. Its history makes interesting coffee-table talk, but the important point is that database technology has evolved to the stage that database programming is much less complicated than it was just a few years ago.

As part of this development, Microsoft established *Open Database Connectivity* (ODBC), a standard for database connectivity. ODBC defines a similar standard for connecting to all databases that use it. Microsoft has made database programming even easier with ADODB. Among the many ways of talking to databases, ADO (ActiveX Data Objects) is Microsoft's latest and greatest. I will be focusing solely on ADODB in this hour.

ADODB is prereferenced in the Visual Basic editor (Tools, Reference), automatically making it easy for you to create instances of ADODB objects and use the capabilities stored within. ADODB provides objects that represent tables, queries, rows, columns, and many other object-oriented types and associated capabilities. This makes it much easier for you to focus on solving your programming problems, rather than on writing code to manage the data. ADODB manages the data for you.

In this hour, you will learn:

- How to connect to a database and use recordsets
- How to perform insert, update, and delete operations
- How to add database data to collections, such as those contained in list box controls
- How to use the attributes and methods of ADODB objects that enable you to precisely manage data
- Where to find resources that contain tons of examples
- About the new AddItem and RemoveItem methods for collection management

Connecting to a Database

Much of programming databases with Access is simplified by the fact that the code resides in the database. The first thing to learn when programming a database is how to connect to one.

The Tools, References dialog in the Visual Basic Editor shows all the ActiveX libraries that your VBA code is using. ActiveX libraries are compiled programs that contain code your program can call. ADODB is available to your project by referencing msado26.tlb. The title of the current version of ADO is Microsoft ActiveX Data Objects 2.7 Library. ADO is the name of the protocol, and ADODB is the name of the actual object in the library.

ADODB contains a Connection object. By default, the Visual Basic editor contains a reference to ADO, so you can use the ADODB object. To connect to your database with code, you need to perform these steps:

1. Define a subroutine.
2. Declare a new ADODB.Connection variable.
3. Open the connection specifying the OLE DB provider information (that is, the database).

NEW TERM   A *provider* is the OLE DB (a new protocol with which Microsoft wants to replace ODBC) version of the data source. Because OLE DB allows for many

15

more things besides traditional database servers storing data, the term *data source* will be supplanted with the term *provider*. In loose terms, a provider refers to the data source.

4. Open the connection.

5. Release the allocated memory for the Connection object.

These five operations are demonstrated in Listing 15.1.

LISTING 15.1   Using an ADODB Connection Object

```
1:  Sub DemoADO()
2:    Const Provider = "Provider=Microsoft.Jet.OLEDB.4.0;"
3:    Const DataSource = "Data Source=C:\Data\Hour15.mdb"
4:    Dim Connection As New ADODB.Connection
5:    On Error Goto Finally
6:      Call Connection.Open( Provider & DataSource )
7:      Connection.Close
8:  Finally:
9:    If( Err.Number <> 0 ) Then
10:     MsgBox Err.Description
11:    End If
12:    Set Connection = Nothing
13: End Sub
```

Declare long strings of text as constants. This will make the code more readable.

  ANALYSIS   Lines 2 and 3 define constants containing the provider and data source information; together they form the connection string argument. The OLE DB provider string is

```
Provider=Microsoft.Jet.OLEDB.4.0
```

The data source is the path to your database. In the sample code, the data source is

```
Data Source=C:\Data\Hour15.mdb
```

The Open method of an ADODB.Connection object is probably the most challenging part of creating a connection to a database because the provider information looks like mumbo jumbo. Don't be afraid to copy existing code or experiment with different connection strings to get it just right.

Note that you will need to supply the actual path to your database. Also, notice that the connection string is a single, contiguous string with the provider and data source information separated by a semicolon.

NEW TERM The properties and methods of an object are referred to as its *interface*. You will learn more about interfaces and other object-oriented elements in Hour 21, "Class Programming Basics."

Line 4 of Listing 15.1 demonstrates how to declare a new Connection object. Remember that Connection is a member of ADODB, so you have to use the ADODB object. Because Connection is a class of ADODB, you must use the New keyword to create an instance of Connection. Line 5 sets up an error-handling mechanism (which you will learn about in Hour 18, "Adding Code to Handle Errors") that ensures the code from lines 8 to 13 is run, even if an error occurs.

Line 6 uses the new Connection object's Open method to open the database. After line 6, you insert the code to perform whatever operation you are interested in. After your code runs, close the connection, as demonstrated on line 7.

Lines 9 through 11 display an error, if one occurs, by polling the Err object. (To learn about the Err object, read Hour 18.) Line 12 releases the memory allocated to the Connection object.

Open Method's Connection Arguments

The Open method requires a connection string argument. The connection string recognizes four arguments in the form of *name = value*. These arguments are separated by semicolons. The four statements are *Provider*, *File Name*, *Remote Provider*, and *Remote Server* (see Table 15.1 for a description of each). All other commands are passed to the provider without processing from ADO. Therefore, if you specify a user ID or password, for example, this information must be in the form that the provider supports.

TABLE 15.1   Connection String Arguments Supported by ADO

Name	Description
Provider	Specifies a provider to use for the connection (see Listing 15.1)
File Name	Specifies a provider file (that is, a file containing data)
Remote Provider	Specifies the name of a provider used by a client application
Remote Server	Specifies the name of a server application used by a client application

You can specify password and user ID information in the connection string. The information in Table 15.1 is used by ADO, and everything else is passed through to the provider. Listing 15.2 demonstrates the same code as in Listing 15.1, using an ODBC alias instead of provider information.

LISTING 15.2   Opening a database with an ODBC alias.

```
 1: Sub ProviderWithODBCAlias()
 2:
 3:     Const ConnectionString = "DSN=Hour15;UID=;PWD="
 4:     Dim Recordset As New ADODB.Recordset
 5:     Dim Connection As New ADODB.Connection
 6:
 7:     On Error GoTo Finally
 8:
 9:     Call Connection.Open(ConnectionString)
10:
11:     Connection.Close
12:
13: Finally:
14:     If (Err.Number <> 0) Then
15:         MsgBox Err.Description
16:     End If
17:
18:     Set Recordset = Nothing
19:     Set Connection = Nothing
20: End Sub
```

ANALYSIS   The only difference between Listing 15.1 and 15.2 is that Listing 15.2 uses an ODBC alias on line 3 to access the data. ODBC has been the database connectivity standard for a few years. Using ODBC requires that you add an ODBC alias, as described in the following section.

With the popularization of Web software development, data can come from additional sources now. These new repositories require new code to facilitate alternative data sourcing. Because database connectivity requires extended capabilities to support Web programming, Microsoft has extended database connectivity. The new standard is called *OLE DB*. You can learn more about OLE DB at http://www.microsoft.com/data/oledb/default.htm.

Creating an ODBC Alias

An ODBC *alias* is a name stored in the Registry with associated information that enables applications to connect a particular database in an application. ODBC is a standard defined by Microsoft. Using ODBC means that you will be using a dynamic link library that provides the services defined in the ODBC standard.

To create an ODBC alias, follow these steps:

1. In Windows, click Start.

2. Click Settings, Control Panel.

3. In the Control Panel, click the Administrative Tools applet. Click the ODBC Data Sources applet icon to run the ODBC Administrator (see Figure 15.1).

FIGURE 15.1

Click the ODBC Data Sources applet in the Explorer view of Administrative Tools to configure ODBC aliases.

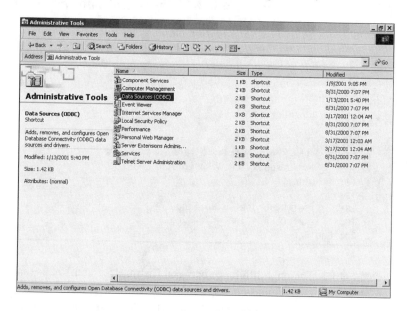

4. On the User DSN tab, click the Add button (see Figure 15.2).

FIGURE 15.2

The ODBC Data Source Administrator program.

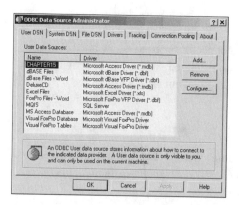

5. In the Create New Data Source dialog, click the Microsoft Access Driver (*.mdb) from the scrolling list box.

6. Click Finish. (You are not finished configuring the ODBC alias yet, though.)

7. In ODBC Microsoft Access Setup, enter a name for your alias. (For Listing 15.2, I entered Hour15.)

8. In the Database Group box, click the Select button.

9. Use the file browser to find your database file. (I entered the path from line 3 of Listing 15.1, c:\Data\Hour15.mdb.)

10. Click OK to close the setup dialog.

11. Click Apply to save your changes and then click OK to close the ODBC Administrator program. (Step 11 completes the process, adding the alias to the ODBC Administrator, as shown in Figure 15.3.)

FIGURE 15.3

Configuring a Microsoft Access 2002 data source.

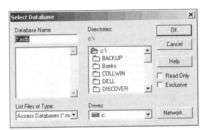

It is worth noting that the process defined earlier will change, depending on the data source you provide. Some data sources require more information; others require less. Read your database manufacturer's documentation for more assistance.

What Is a Provider?

In the blink of an eye, the term *data source* is being packed up and relegated to the scrap heap. Well, not quite yet. If Microsoft has its way, you and I will be using *provider* exclusively soon enough.

When a term takes on an extended meaning, it is often customary to create a new word that means the old thing and something more. *Data source* is an ODBC term usually meaning a database. *Provider* is the OLE DB term meaning *a data source and something more*. The "more" part is that a provider can be other kinds of data besides database servers, such as MS SQL Server, MS Access, Oracle, or text files.

OLE DB was developed to facilitate managing the many kinds of data that programmers have to work with, including old legacy systems written in COBOL with fixed-length records, modern relational database servers such as Oracle, and now Web data.

Specifying a Username and Password

If your database is password protected, you can specify a username and password in the connection string. Remember that connection strings can contain providers as well as other information.

Use the *name* = *value* syntax for username and password. Line 2 of Listing 15.2 demonstrates specifying a username and password; in this listing, the user ID and password are empty. You can specify the user ID and password as part of the connection string or as the second and third argument to ADODB.Connection.Open.

> Using the second and third arguments for user and password information overrides any user and password information passed as part of the connection string.

Selecting a Connection Mode

An ADODB.Connection object's Open method can have as many as four arguments. The second and third arguments can be a user ID and password, if these are not passed with the connection string argument. The fourth argument is an optional mode, enumerated value.

The two choices are adConnectUnspecified and adAsyncConnect (the former is the default). The adConnectUnspecified argument opens the database connection in synchronous mode. When something is *synchronous*, this implies that when it has code running, the ADO process won't return to the calling program until the ADO process is finished.

New Term A *thread* is a subprogram that runs in an application. A single-threaded application has only one internal process running at a time. A multithreaded application may have many subprocesses running at the same time.

> In single-threaded applications, subprocesses are called and returned before other processes run. In multithreaded applications, processes are spawned and returned to the spawning process even though they are not necessarily complete. A thread may be as simple as a function or as complicated as a subprogram.

The adAsynchConnect argument is the opposite of the adConnectUnspecified mode. Opening a connection in adAsynchConnect mode means that ADO requests can run in a different thread, returning to the calling program before the ADO process is complete.

15

When code runs synchronously, a subprocess returns only after it has finished. An asynchronous process starts and runs independently of the starting process. This means that when the subprocess returns, the asynchronous process is not necessarily finished. Running asynchronous ADO processes requires more care because you have to respond to the completed subprocess in another location in your code.

Managing a Recordset

The `Connection` object lets you send requests to a provider. However, it is at the recordset level where the real work gets done. If `Connection` is an object that represents a digital link to all the data, `Recordset` is an object that represents a link to some specific subset of the data. Generally, unless you are managing an entire database (for instance, performing backups or housekeeping), you are modifying only a small part of the data at a time.

A recordset facilitates modifying data a row or field at a time. The term *record* was used to indicate one row of data from one table, but it is an antiquated term. Recordsets in relational databases, such as Access 2002, can contain data from more than one table. Hence, the new term *row* was used to indicate something different from a record. The newer, correct terminology is *row*. The object used to manage the data in one row is the `Recordset` object.

Before you can manage data, you have to know how to declare recordsets and open and close them. Let's look at how to do that next.

Opening and Closing Recordsets

The `Recordset` object is defined as part of ADODB. Because I am referring to the ADODB `Recordset`, as opposed to the DAO `Recordset`, I will use the ADODB object when declaring an ADO `Recordset`. You will have to, also.

In ADODB, `Recordset` is an object; therefore, you will have to use the `New` keyword when declaring a `Recordset` object and the `Set` keyword when assigning an object reference to it. The syntax for declaring an ADODB `Recordset` object is as follows:

```
Dim varname As New ADODB.RecordSet
```

Everything is typed literally except for *varname*. Use any variable name you would like. Some programmers like to use `RS` as an abbreviation for `Recordset`. You might see other code that uses an `ado` prefix to indicate that the recordset is an ADO `Recordset` object and not a DAO `Recordset` object. I generally use plain `Recordset` or some variation. You are welcome to use whatever you want, but be consistent in the naming style; a consistent style of naming your code will make it more readable and professional.

After a recordset is declared, you will need to open the `Recordset` object before you can manage data. The `Recordset` object's `Open` method has the following syntax:

```
Call recordset.Open( [source], [ActiveConnection], [CursorType],
➡[LockType], [Options])
```

The reference to *Recordset* means that you should use the name of a declared recordset in that location, attaching the `Open` method with the dot operator. All the arguments for `Open` are optional. In this instance, the arguments being optional does not mean you don't need them, but it does mean that you can set the values using the `Recordset` object and the appropriate properties before calling `Open`. Refer to the Editor's Help documentation on the ADO `RecordSet.Open` method for exhaustive detail.

The final method of the `Recordset` object is the `Close` method. `Close` remains completely unadorned—that is, there are no arguments—and it closes the `Recordset` object. You should close recordsets when you are through with them. Listing 15.3 expands Listing 15.1 to include a `Recordset` object.

LISTING 15.3 Opening and Closing a Recordset Is Necessary If You Want to Update Data

```
 1:  Sub ProviderWithODBCAlias()
 2:     Const Provider = "Provider=Microsoft.Jet.OLEDB.4.0; "
 3:     Const DataSource="Data Source=C:\Data\Hour15.mdb"
 4:     Dim Recordset As New ADODB.Recordset
 5:     Dim Connection As New ADODB.Connection
 6:     On Error Goto Finally
 7:       Call Connection.Open(Provider & DataSource)
 8:       Call RecordSet.Open("MUSIC", Connection, adOpenDynamic, _
 9:         adLockOptimistic)
10:       Recordset.Close
11:       Connection.Close
12: Finally:
13:     If( Err.Number <> 0 ) Then
14:       MsgBox Err.Description
15:     End If
16:     Set RecordSet = Nothing
17:     Set Connection = Nothing
18:  End Sub
```

ANALYSIS All the code in Listing 15.3 is the same as Listing 15.1, except for the `Recordset` code on lines 4, 8, 10, and 16. Line 4 declares a new ADODB `Recordset`. Line 8 demonstrates opening the recordset MUSIC in the demo database. (In this example, the `Recordset` object can be an Access table, so the schema of MUSIC is not important.) In Listing 15.3, you place the code to modify the MUSIC table between lines 9 and 10.

15

Line 10 closes the `Recordset` object, and line 16 sets the `Recordset` object to `Nothing`. This has the effect of releasing the memory allocated to the object.

The `Open` method call on line 8 and 9 is the most interesting line of code. The first argument is the record source, a table named MUSIC. The second argument is a reference to the `Connection` object. The third argument on line 8 defines the cursor type. This recordset uses `adOpenDynamic`; the adOpenDynnamic cursor is used to allow the addition and deletion of records, and the changes other users make will be visible to all other users in this process. The fourth argument is `adLockOptimistic`. *Optimistic locking* means that the record is locked when you call the `Update` method. An optimistic lock is equivalent to assuming that the data hasn't changed between the time you got a copy of the data and the time you want to save your changes.

The Ingredients in a Recordset

The source argument in the `Recordset.Open` method represents the data. `Recordset` can be a `Command` object (see the Editor's Help for ADO commands), literal SQL code, a table, a query, a stored procedure, or the name of a persisted recordset.

Command Objects

A `Command` object is an ADO object that can contain code to return records or modify the database. A `Command` object is one of the choices you can pass as the source argument of the `Recordset` object's `Open` method.

Stored Procedures

The source argument of the `Recordset` object's `Open` method can be a (stored) procedure object. A procedure object contains stored procedure text; a stored procedure is SQL wrapped in a function—a hybrid of SQL. You will learn more about using procedure objects in Hour 16, "Using Advanced SQL Techniques."

Literal SQL Code

Literal SQL code means that you can pass SQL text as the source argument for `Open`. This gives you a tremendous amount of flexibility in describing the action your `Recordset` object's `Open` method actually performs. You will learn more about advanced SQL techniques in Hour 16.

You can also learn a lot more about writing SQL in *Sams Teach Yourself Microsoft Access 2002 in 21 Days* and the companion book to this book from Sams, *Sams Teach Yourself Microsoft Access 2002 in 24 Hours*. Visit the Sams online bookstore at `http://www.samspublishing.com` and search on "SQL" for advanced books that emphasize SQL programming.

From Listing 15.3, here is the equivalent code using literal SQL:

```
Call RecordSet.Open("SELECT * FROM MUSIC", Connection,
➥adOpenDynamic, adLockOptimistic)
```

Notice that the MUSIC table is now represented by a query. I wrote this fragment to pinpoint the modification to the source argument. Preferably, the preceding code should include a string constant containing the SQL, and the source argument is passed to the string constant instead of the literal text.

Tables and Queries

The most common kind of source is a table or a query. Access 2002 enables you to define table and query objects. A *table* is the representation of a single recordset, and a *query* can be a conglomerate recordset composed of many tables, depending on the SQL used to define the query or the SQL that performs an action, such as APPEND or DELETE.

Listings 15.1, 15.2, and 15.3 demonstrate how to use a table for the source argument of the `Recordset.Open` method. The fragment from the last section demonstrates a literal query, but you can also predefine queries and use those, too. Follow these steps to learn how to use an Access query as the source:

1. In Access, click the Queries button in the Objects view.
2. Click New.
3. In the New Query dialog, select Design View and click OK.
4. Select a table. To use the MUSIC table, create a database and add these fields:
   - ID—Autonumber
   - FIRST_NAME—Text(30)
   - [LAST_NAME]—-Text(30)
   - TITLE—Text(50)
   - FORMAT—Text(50)
   - PUBLISHER—Text(50).

     Save the table as MUSIC.
5. In the Show Table dialog, double-click the MUSIC table (see Figure 15.4). Click Close.
6. In the MUSIC table view, double-click the asterisk to add the asterisk (the select all fields indicator) to the fields list (see Figure 15.5).
7. Click the View, SQL View menu to verify that you have the SQL SELECT MUSIC.* FROM MUSIC;.

FIGURE 15.4

In the Show Table dialog, double-click the table name to add it to the query definition.

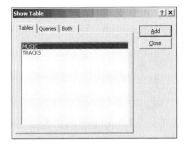

FIGURE 15.5

Selecting the asterisk field from the table means that you want all records in the query result set.

8. Close the query, saving it as ALL_MUSIC.

9. Replace "MUSIC" in the source argument in line 8 of Listing 15.3 with "ALL_MUSIC".

Run the code to test the new query. You will see that the query ALL_MUSIC has the same effect as the original code. The mechanics are the same, whether you are writing simple or complex SQL. Sometimes it is beneficial to predefine your queries in this manner because you can change the query without modifying code, and your code will be easier to read. Other times you want maximum flexibility in the values that go into the SQL statement. In the latter case, it can be more beneficial to write the SQL in the code instead. Either method is okay; it really depends on your needs.

Adding and Updating Data

Common tasks you will need to perform include adding rows to existing recordsets and editing existing data. Adding a row and editing a row are very similar operations. First, you will need an opened Connection object. Then you will have to open a recordset in write mode. This means that you will need to specify adOpenKeySet or adOpenDynamic for the CursorType argument of RecordSet.Open.

After the record is open, if you want to add a new record, call

```
RecordSet.AddNew
```

where `RecordSet` is the name of a valid `Recordset` object. Assign appropriate values for each field and call

`RecordSet.Update`

to save your new record.

Editing existing data is very similar. Instead of calling `AddNew`, you write code that finds the record you want to modify. You can find a record by iterating over each record using a `Do While` loop and the `EOF` method or by writing SQL to return the correct record in recordset. Either technique is valid; however, writing the SQL will result in faster performance.

Listing 15.4 demonstrates adding a new record to the MUSIC table. (Refer to step 4 in the previous section, "Tables and Queries," to create the MUSIC table.)

LISTING 15.4 Adding a New Record

```
1:  Sub DemoADODB()
2:      Const Provider = "Provider=Microsoft.Jet.OLEDB.4.0;"
3:      Const DataSource = "Data Source=C:\Data\Hour15.mdb"
4:      Const ConnectString = Provider & DataSource
5:
6:      Dim Recordset As New ADODB.Recordset
7:      Dim Connection As New ADODB.Connection
8:
9:      On Error GoTo FINALLY
10:
11:     Call Connection.Open(ConnectString)
12:     Call Recordset.Open("MUSIC", Connection, adOpenKeyset, adLockOptimistic)
13:
14:     Recordset.AddNew
15:
16:     Recordset("FIRST_NAME").Value = "Natalie"
17:     Recordset("LAST_NAME").Value = "Merchant"
18:     Recordset("TITLE").Value = "TIGERLILLY"
19:     Recordset("FORMAT").Value = "CD"
20:     Recordset("PUBLISHER").Value = "Elektra"
21:
22:     Recordset.Update
23:     Recordset.Close
24:     Connection.Close
25:
26: Finally:
27:     If (Err.Number <> 0) Then
28:        MsgBox Err.Description
29:        Err.Clear
30:     End If
31:     Set Recordset = Nothing
32:     Set Connection = Nothing
33: End Sub
```

ANALYSIS The change from Listing 15.3 to Listing 15.4 is the insertion of lines 14 through 22. Line 14 adds a new record. Lines 16 through 20 use the default `Fields` property of the `Recordset` object to modify the value of each field. On line 22, the changes are committed to the database with the `Update` method.

> If you don't specify a property, but your code implies a property, the object uses a default property if one is available and is suitable for the data.
>
> Lines 16 through 20 in Listing 15.4 demonstrate using the default `Fields` property. The statement `Recordset(columnname)` is the same as `Recordset.Fields(columnname).Value` because `Fields` is the default property of a recordset.

To edit existing data, you can modify the code on line 14, removing `AddNew` and replacing it with code to find the record you want to modify. Lines 16 through 33 remain the same.

You can also specify all the columns and values as parameters to the `AddNew` method. `AddNew` takes two arguments. These arguments can be a single field name and value or an array of fields (the first argument) and an array of values. The following code fragment demonstrates this:

```
Dim Fields As Variant
Dim Values As Variant
Fields = Array("FIRST_NAME", "LAST_NAME", _
  "TITLE", "FORMAT", "PUBLISHER")
Values = Array("Faith", "Hill", "Breathe", "CD", "Warner Bros.")
Call Recordset.AddNew(Fields, Values)
```

The code declares and initializes the field and value arrays and passes these two arrays to the `AddNew` method. When you are testing your code, it may be easier to discover bad field names if you assign values to fields one at a time.

Modifying Field Data

A recordset contains a `Fields` collection property. Recall from an earlier hour that I defined a *property* as data contained in a class. Properties can be simple data or objects themselves. The `Fields` property happens to be a collection.

The `Fields` collection is the default property. That's why `Recordset(fieldname)` is equivalent to `Recordset.Fields(fieldname)`. You need to know that a separate class called `Field` exists. Now that you know a `Fields` collection containing `Field` objects, you can use the Help file whenever you want to look up the properties and methods of `Fields`.

The three important properties of Fields are OriginalValue, Value, and Name. The Value property is a variant; use this property to modify the value of a field. Use the OriginalValue property, also a variant, to get or restore the original value. The Name property can be used to assist you in referring to fields by name.

It is important to remember that when you write code such as that in line 17 in Listing 15.4—Recordset("ARTIST")—you are returning a reference to a property of a Field object. The Field object has capabilities and data all its own. The .Value part of lines 16 through 20 in Listing 15.4 is the Value property of a Field object. Rewritten, lines 16 through 20 equate exactly to the following:

```
16:  Recordset.Fields("FIRST_NAME").Value = "Natalie"
17:  Recordset.Fields("LAST_NAME").Value = "Merchant"
18:  Recordset.Fields("TITLE").Value = "TIGERLILLY"
19:  Recordset.Fields("FORMAT").Value = "CD"
20:  Recordset.Fields("PUBLISHER").Value = "Elektra"
```

It is a common object-oriented technique to promote the interface of contained objects to the interface of containing objects. The end result is that the code is much simpler to write. As an example, compare the original lines 16 through 20 to the verbose version.

Deleting Data

There are two ways to delete rows with code. One way is to write a DELETE SQL statement and run the SQL. The other way is the brute-force method—you write code to visit each record you want to delete and call the Delete method of a Recordset object.

The Delete method has the following syntax:

```
Call recordset.Delete([AffectRecords] )
```

The default behavior is to delete the current record. This means that you will have to write SQL or code that finds the records you want deleted. The AffectRecords command can be one of the values defined in Table 15.2.

TABLE 15.2   The AffectRecords Argument of the Recordset.Delete Method

Enumeration Name	Effect
adAffectCurrent	The default. Deletes the current record.
AdAffectGroup	Deletes a limited subset of records based on the Filter property.
AdAffectAll	Deletes all records (equivalent to SQL DELETE FROM tablename).
AdAffectAllChapters	Deletes all chapter records.

15

The `Delete` method for ADO is almost as powerful as the SQL `DELETE` command. The equivalent form of

```
Call RecordSet.Delete( adAffectAll )
```

is

```
DELETE FROM tablename
```

You can, of course, specify a `WHERE` clause to limit the rows deleted, and the SQL `DELETE` will also enable you to specify a nested `SELECT` statement to further refine deleted rows. Read Hour 16 for more details.

Finding Records

Operations are usually performed on a subset or group of records. When you create reports, update data, or remove old records, generally you want to perform these operations on a data subset. This means that you have to write code to limit your result set.

Finding rows of data can be easily accomplished via two means: You can create a query or write literal SQL to refine your result set, or you can open an existing table and use brute-force data comparisons to determine which records meet your criteria.

Writing SQL relegates finding the records to the database server, which often results in faster performance. However, writing code often provides the greatest flexibility and power. Usually, a combination of the two methods yields the best overall result.

When you create a query, your code is easier to read and write. When you use a pure-code find algorithm, the code is messier. Although the quality and appearance of the code is a secondary consideration, subordinate to getting the job done right, code quality should be a consideration. There is significant added cost in poor-quality code.

In this section, I will demonstrate both methods of finding records. After you have established how to refine or limit a result set, what you do with it is relatively easy.

Using a Table

You can use the name of a table as the source when you want to write code to find specific records. An all-code solution results in the greatest flexibility. Listing 15.5 demonstrates code that finds records that meet specific criteria.

LISTING 15.5   Brute-Force Searching of a Recordset

```
1:  Sub Test()
2:    Call FindRecords("LAST_NAME", "Merchant")
3:  End Sub
```

LISTING 15.5   continued

```
 4:
 5:  Function OpenConnection() As ADODB.Connection
 6:    Const Provider = "Provider=Microsoft.Jet.OLEDB.4.0;"
 7:    Const DataSource = _
 8:      "Data Source=C:\Data\Hour15.mdb"
 9:
10:
11:    Set OpenConnection = New ADODB.Connection
12:    Call OpenConnection.Open(Provider & DataSource, "", "")
13:
14:  End Function
15:
16:  Sub FindRecords(ByVal SearchFieldName As String, ByVal FindValue As String)
17:
18:    Dim Connection As ADODB.Connection
19:    On Error GoTo Finally
20:    Set Connection = OpenConnection
21:
22:    Dim Recordset As New ADODB.Recordset
23:
24:    Call Recordset.Open("MUSIC", Connection, adOpenDynamic, adLockOptimistic)
25:
26:    Recordset.MoveFirst
27:    Do While Not Recordset.EOF
28:      If (Recordset(SearchFieldName) = FindValue) Then
29:        Debug.Print Recordset(SearchFieldName)
30:      End If
31:
32:      Recordset.MoveNext
33:    Loop
34:
35:    Recordset.Close
36:    Connection.Close
37:
38:  Finally:
39:    If (Err.Number <> 0) Then
40:      Call MsgBox(Err.Description)
41:      Err.Clear
42:    End If
43:    Set Recordset = Nothing
44:    Set Connection = Nothing
45:  End Sub
```

NEW TERM   A *scaffold* is test code that you write to incrementally test your code. The best time to write scaffolding code is when you write the original algorithm that you want to test.

Line 41 of Listing 15.5 calls the Clear method of the Err object. You do not have to explicitly clear the error under all circumstances. An Err object is also cleared when the code reaches the end of the procedure in an error-handling block or when an Exit Function, Exit Sub, Exit Property, any Resume, or another On Error statement is executed.

I explicitly use the Err.Clear method when I am finished with the Err object rather than remembering the implicit rules for clearing the error.

ANALYSIS Lines 1 through 3 define a test function that calls the target algorithm, FindRecords. Lines 5 through 14 define a function that conceals the connection steps in a separate function. Note the return type in line 5: ADODB.Connection. Simple test functions, such as the one on line 1, are referred to as *scaffolds*. Scaffolding is a technique of writing simple test subroutines and functions that enable you to test code incrementally. When the testing is done, the scaffolding can be removed. You can remove scaffolding code with compiler directives. (Read Hour 17, "Removing Bugs," for more on scaffolding and compiler directives.)

Lines 16 through 45 demonstrate the searching code. Line 18 declares a Connection variable; notice the absence of the word New. Because memory is allocated in the OpenConnection method, you don't need New on line 18. Line 19 establishes an error-handling condition. The code after the label FINALLY is always run. Line 20 establishes the new connection. Notice the use of the word Set. Set is used in object assignment.

Line 24 opens the table MUSIC. Line 26 moves the cursor to the first record. Lines 27 through 33 establish a Do While loop that iterates over every record. The conditional test on line 28 is the actual searching algorithm. Note the use of MoveFirst on line 26 and MoveNext on line 32. Without these two lines of code, the Do While loop might never run or might never stop running. Matching records are written to the Immediate window with the Debug.Print statement on line 29.

In Listing 15.5, lines 35 through 45 contain the cleanup code you have seen before in this hour.

Using a Query

The benefit of using a query over a table is that a table draws data from one recordset, whereas a query can represent data from multiple recordsets. Queries also make it much easier to limit the number of fields in the result set. Additional queries enable you to filter the result set by writing a WHERE clause. When you use the code in Listing 15.5, only a few changes are necessary to convert the code to use a query. The query is represented by literal SQL code.

The partial listing in Listing 15.6 contains all the changes necessary to demonstrate the technique.

LISTING 15.6   Using a Query Instead of a Table As the Data Source

```
22:  Dim SQL As String
23:  SQL = "SELECT * FROM MUSIC WHERE " & SearchFieldName &
     ➥"='" & FindValue & "'"
24:
25:  Dim Recordset As New ADODB.RecordSet
26:  Call Recordset.Open(SQL, Connection, adOpenDynamic,
     ➥adLockOptimistic)
27:
28:  Recordset.MoveFirst
29:  Do While Not Recordset.EOF
30:      Debug.Print Recordset(SearchFieldName)
31:      Recordset.MoveNext
32:  Loop33:
```

ANALYSIS   Notice the new string variable SQL. The query is assembled (line 23) with a constant string and the SearchFieldName and FindValue arguments embedded into the SQL text. Line 26 uses the string SQL instead of the literal "MUSIC", and the If conditional test in the Do While loop is no longer necessary.

As a refresher, remember that the WHERE clause in SQL takes as text arguments in the form FieldName = 'Value' (use single quotes for strings and no quotes for other data types). You can use as many predicates in the WHERE clause as you like, forming the clause with Boolean operators AND and OR and others. Here's the syntax:

... WHERE *fieldname*= *value* [[OR|AND] [*fieldname* = *value*], ...]

One form of the WHERE clause (with ... representing valid SQL) is at least one predicate in the form *fieldname* = *value*, where *fieldname* is a field name in the recordset and *value* represents data to find in that field.

SQL WHERE clauses can also have nested queries; that is, the result of the right side of a WHERE predicate can be derived from SQL. The next hour covers SQL programming in greater detail.

Using the Filter Property

The Recordset object has a property named Filter, which is a variant that essentially performs the same function as the WHERE clause in SQL. A common use of the Filter property is to assign it a string in the form *fieldname* = *value*.

You can daisy-chain logical predicates together to create simple or complex filters. Do this by inserting the following line of code after line 20 in Listing 15.5:

```
Recordset.Filter = SearchFieldName & "='" & FindValue & "'"
```

The filter mitigates the need for the `If` conditional test on line 28 of Listing 15.5. As you can see, you have several choices available when it comes to finding data. Choosing the right one for your needs is up to you. All things being equal, choose the technique that yields the tidiest code.

Copying Data to a Collection Object

Collections are useful in many situations. A recordset contains a `Fields` collection. Visual components such as list boxes and combo boxes contain collections. A common task involves getting data from a storage collection to a visual collection, such as a list box, to present the data as a list of choices to the user.

No existing method copies collection items; however, the code to copy data from one collection to another is straightforward. I will describe it and then give you an example. The following steps describe copying elements in a collection in general terms:

1. Identify the source collection.
2. Identify the target collection or declare a collection instance.
3. Use a loop to iterate over each item in the source collection, adding the items from the source collection to the target collection with the target collection's `Add` method.

That's all there is to it. Listing 15.7 demonstrates an example.

LISTING 15.7   Copying the Artist Names from a `Fields` Collection to an Alternative Collection

```
25:  Dim Target As New Collection
26:  Recordset.MoveFirst
27:  Do While Not Recordset.Eof
28:    Call Target.Add( Recordset("FIRST_NAME").Value & " " & _
29:      Recordset("LAST_NAME").Value)
30:    Recordset.MoveNext
31:  Loop
32:
33:  Dim Artist As Variant
34:  For Each Artist In Target
35:    Debug.Print Artist
36:  Next Artist
37:  Set Target = Nothing
38:  Recordset.Close
```

ANALYSIS Note that you can insert the code in Listing 15.7 into Listing 15.5 after line 24
(that is, after the Recordset object is open.) Target, line 25, is an arbitrary collection. Because a recordset represents the source collection, you use the EOF test demonstrated on line 27. A collection can hold variant objects, so you specifically indicate that
you want the field value stored in the Target collection by using the Value property. The
code on line 28 without the Value property actually stores the field, not the field value,
in the collection. That's okay, if that is what you want to have happen, but you must
know the difference.

Lines 33 through 35 use the For Each Next loop control to verify that the field values
are, in fact, in the collection. The rest of the code is the remaining code in Listing 15.5
after the recordset is closed.

The code changes little for other kinds of collections. The biggest difference between the
code fragment and an actual program is that you are unlikely to open a collection,
Recordset, and allocate a target collection all in the same function. For instance, the target collection might be a list box on a form.

Using AddItem and RemoveItem

Microsoft Access 2002 has added two methods to the combo and list box controls to
facilitate managing items displayed in these controls. These methods are AddItem and
RemoveItem.

AddItem takes two arguments and adds an element to the collection represented by the
combo or list box. RemoveItem takes a single index and removes the item represented by
the index from the collection. The form of each method follows:

```
Object.AddItem(string, index)
```

```
Object.RemoveItem(index)
```

If you have a combo box named ComboNamesList, you could initialize the combo box
as a value list using an array (or some other source for the data) with code similar to that
shown in Listing 15.8. If you are going to add data manually to the combo box, versus
using a data source, you will need to change the Row Source Type property to Value List
in the Properties dialog. You can also change the RowSourceType property programmatically, as demonstrated in the listing.

LISTING 15.8 Using the New AddItem Method to Populate a Combo Box with Code

```
1:  Private Sub Form_Load()
2:    Dim Data As Variant
3:    Data = Array("Paul Kimmel", "Jack Blanton", "Jackie Gooding", _
```

LISTING 15.8   continued

```
 4:     "William Jones", "Toni Johnson")
 5:     ComboNamesList.RowSourceType = "Value List"
 6:     Dim I As Integer
 7:     For I = LBound(Data) To UBound(Data)
 8:       Call ComboNamesList.AddItem(Data(I), I)
 9:     Next I
10: End Sub
```

ANALYSIS   This code listing uses an array of names to simulate a source of data. To populate a combo box manually, you will need to set RowSourceType to "Value List", as demonstrated in line 5. The loop (lines 7 through 9) simply copies the data from the array to the combo box. The first argument to AddItem is the data to add to the combobox. The second argument is position of the item in the list. To delete elements from the combo or list box, use the RemoveItem method. Keep in mind that the number of elements will change when you are deleting elements, so you cannot use a low-to-high loop when deleting items. The following code will work sufficiently when you need to delete all items:

```
Do While (ComboNamesList.ListCount > 0)
  Call ComboNamesList.RemoveItem(0)
Loop
```

This sample fragment deletes the zero-index item until there are no more items.

You also have the choice of populating the combo box with data from a data source. If RowSourceType is "Table/Query", you will need to define the row source. When you add a combo or list box to a form, the Combo or List Box Wizard will walk you through the process. Refer to Hour 19, "Creating Custom Forms," for more on using visual controls.

Finding ActiveX Data Objects Resources Online

An infinite combination of code can be written, and a tremendous amount of information supports these combinations; no single book can comprehensively cover all the information. Publishers create several books on the same topic because it requires that much information and that many perspectives to begin to dent the wealth of possibilities. This brief section points you to additional resources on the Web that will help you use ADO more efficiently.

What this means is that one *Sams Teach Yourself in 24 Hours* book can start you on your journey, but the road is long. People who love programming might not mind reading thousands of pages of technical material, but thousands of pages can be overwhelming to beginners.

The best advice I can give you is to learn what you need to solve immediate problems on one front. Then you can tackle the tremendous job of learning the theoretically best practices and techniques on an alternate front. You will be able to program Access applications when you finish this book; however, how good a programmer you become depends on what you do after you read this book.

NEW TERM An *object model* is a hierarchical diagram of the classes that make up a program. The term *program* is used loosely to mean an executable, dynamic link library, or component.

There is a wealth of information on the World Wide Web. Useful information on ADO can be found at `http://www.microsoft.com/data/ado`. The ADO homepage is the first word on ADO.

Summary

Database programming is one of the best reasons to program with VBA in Access 2002. In this hour, you learned how to use ActiveX Data Objects, represented by the ADODB objects, to perform many common programming tasks.

Perhaps 80 percent of database programming is moving data out of the database and into memory (in a form that can be modified by code or a user) and then moving it back into the database. Managing connections and recordsets are the two most common tasks you will perform, with the greatest amount of code being written to manage recordsets.

There are a tremendous number of objects in ADODB, and each has its own attributes—both properties and methods. Each property and method requires certain kinds of data, values, and arguments.

After hundreds of hours of programming, it is unlikely that you will know everything about ADO. By that time, more will have been added, or Microsoft will change the protocol from ADO to something else, such as ADO.NET. For this reason, I encourage you to rely on the work of other developers, to read as much as you can on the subject (including reading and writing code), and to rely heavily on the Help system.

The "Q&A" and "Workshop" sections that follow provide you with an opportunity to experiment with the techniques discussed in this hour.

Q&A

Q **What is a good way to learn SQL programming?**

A Sams offers many good books on SQL programming, and your database vendor may have additional resources. Not all SQL implementations are identical.

Q **What benefit is derived from an object model?**

A An object model is a visual representation of the classes that compose a software system.

Q **How can I sort data in a recordset?**

A You can write a query using the ORDER BY clause, the Order property of a record-set, or the SortOrder property of an ADOX Column object.

Workshop

The Workshop includes quiz questions designed to help you test your understanding of the material covered and exercises to help put what you've learned to practice. You will find the answers to the quiz and exercises in Appendix A, "Answers."

Quiz

1. To what does the term *provider* equate?

2. What clause filters data in a SQL query?

3. What property limits the data available in a recordset?

4. What is the name of the property that contains the data in a field? To what object does it belong?

5. What is the name of the collection in a recordset that holds the data?

Exercises

1. Modify the query in Listing 15.6 to order the query in ascending order by *SearchFieldName*. (Hint: Use the ORDER BY clause).

2. Explain how you might make the code in Listing 15.7 more generic—that is, more generally useful.

3. Demonstrate how you could associate the elements in an arbitrary collection to the rows in the recordset. (Hint: Use the Key property inherent in collections.)

Hour **16**

Using Advanced SQL Techniques

Access programming is Visual Basic for Applications programming. That is, when you program with Access, you are writing Visual Basic (VBA) code. Structured Query Language (SQL, pronounced *sequel*) is not the same thing as VBA. VBA and SQL are two separate languages. VBA is an all-purpose programming language, and SQL is a language designed specifically for programming databases.

No book on Access programming would be complete without a tour of SQL programming because SQL is especially useful for programming databases. In the last hour, you had an opportunity to write code using the ADODB object. What might not be readily apparent is that the ADODB object converts a lot of the VBA code that you write into SQL code before it passes the code to the database. That's right: ADODB and other tools like it often pass requests for data transactions to the database as SQL. Exactly when this occurs and to what extent depends specifically on the implementation of the tool; the important piece of the puzzle is why it does so.

The answer to why programming languages revert to SQL when communicating with databases is that SQL is a powerful tool for programming databases. Although VBA code can offer the ultimate in flexibility, sometimes the convenience and power of SQL is useful, too. Specifically, you can program in Access and use another database server besides Access to warehouse your data (for example, SQL Server). Microsoft SQL Server and other powerful database servers often reside on computers other than the desktop computers where the programs run. Database servers are often more powerful and faster than desktop computers. For this reason, code run on the server is often capable of running many times faster than code on a desktop PC.

When you program in SQL, it is possible to run the SQL code on the server side; that is, the code can be run on the faster computer that stores the actual database. Access databases can be stored on network servers, which are often more powerful than desktop PCs. In Access 2002, you can also run SQL on the server.

Convenience is another important factor. SQL was designed for database programming. Therefore, it is often easier to write SQL statements that require much less coding than VBA to perform an equivalent task.

All SQL languages are not the same, however. Although most implementations of SQL are based on ANSI (the American National Standards Institute), many databases deviate slightly. In this hour, you will learn to write SQL that works with Access 2002. However, the same SQL might need minor modifications to work correctly with other databases. It might be necessary to check with the database vendor's technical documentation if you find that the SQL used in this hour does not work with other databases.

In this hour, you will learn to write SQL for Access 2002 databases. Specifically, you will learn

- All about using the SELECT statement, including how to write JOIN and UNION statements and nested subqueries
- How to maintain data with INSERT, UPDATE, APPEND, and DELETE
- How to use the ADODB Procedure object to facilitate writing stored procedures for Access databases

Using the SELECT Statement

The SELECT statement is the most common and versatile SQL statement. The SELECT statement returns a result set of data based on the criteria in the statement. SELECT queries can be written with a few essential elements or contain very complex logic that enables you to return a precise set of data.

SELECT statements enable you to specify filtering criteria, define calculated fields, sort and group data, and perform calculations. In this section, you will learn how to write both simple and complex SELECT statements. I will start with the basic SELECT statement that you saw demonstrated in the last hour.

Writing a Simple SELECT Statement

A simple SELECT statement uses the keyword SELECT followed by the names of the fields that you want in the result set and a FROM clause that indicates the table in which the data resides. The syntax is as follows:

```
SELECT fieldlist FROM tablename
```

By convention, many SQL programmers write all SQL keywords in uppercase letters, as demonstrated in the syntax example. You can choose to follow this convention or not, but be consistent.

An interesting side note is that in virtual social gatherings, uppercase words are considering *shouting*. However, SQL existed before e-mail and chat groups.

SELECT and FROM are keywords in SQL. SELECT is the command, and the FROM clause indicates the table name. The *fieldlist* argument can be an asterisk (*), indicating that all fields should be in the result set, or a comma-delimited list of the actual fields you want returned. You can return one field or as many as you like.

I will be using the database from the last hour. You can create the database by creating a table named MUSIC with the following fields:

- ID—AutoNumber
- ARTIST—Text 50
- TITLE—Text 50
- FORMAT—Text 50
- PUBLISHER—Text 50

A second table, named TRACKS, will be used to store the music tracks. The TRACKS table has the following fields:

- ID—AutoNumber
- MUSIC_ID—Number
- TRACK_TITLE—Text 50
- TRACK_LENGTH—Date/Time

For example, if you want to return all the rows in the MUSIC table, the SQL would be

```
SELECT * FROM MUSIC
```

You can test the preceding SQL code by creating the MUSIC table (see the sidebar) and adding a couple of titles of your favorite music to the database. To run the SQL code follow these steps:

1. Open the database containing the MUSIC table.
2. In the Objects view, click Queries.
3. Click New.
4. In the New Query dialog, click Design View and click OK.
5. The Show Table dialog will be displayed. Click Close. This will leave the Query Designer open.
6. On the Access menu, click View, SQL View.
7. Enter the SQL **SELECT * FROM MUSIC**.
8. Click Query, Run to run the query.

Unless specifically instructed to do otherwise, you can use this process to test all your SQL. Exercises in this hour will demonstrate the use of tools that assist you in developing SQL so that you don't have to write code.

> It is always a good idea to save your work frequently.

You can save any query you create by selecting File, Save at any time while you are editing your queries.

Filtering the Recordset with the WHERE Clause

The WHERE clause can be used to select records containing specific information that you want a query to return. The WHERE clause is useful with SELECT statements, but it's not limited to SELECT statements only. The information in this section applies to SELECT, UPDATE, and DELETE.

You append a WHERE clause to the end of your SELECT statement after the FROM clause. The syntax for WHERE follows:

```
SELECT * FROM  tablename WHERE fieldname =|<>|LIKE value
➥[OR|AND fieldname = value, [...]]
```

The preceding syntax example shows the placement of the WHERE clause after the FROM clause. WHERE requires predicates in the form of *fieldname* = *value*. You can have as many predicates in a WHERE clause as you like. The *fieldname* argument is a field in the table (or tables) specified in the SELECT clause, and *value* is a value of the type of the field represented by *fieldname*.

You can use the NOT keyword before a predicate to negate the result of a WHERE predicate. You may use the equal-to operator (=), not-equal-to operator (<>), or LIKE operator between the left and right operands in the WHERE clause predicates. You can also daisy-chain additional predicates with AND or OR. These combinations enable you to write a wide variety of filtering WHERE clauses. Listing 16.1 demonstrates several queries that you can test in the Access 2002 Query Editor. Each query runs against the MUSIC table.

LISTING 16.1   Several Examples of Queries Using the WHERE Clause

```
1:  SELECT * FROM MUSIC
2:  SELECT * FROM MUSIC WHERE ARTIST = "Elvis Presley"
3:  SELECT * FROM MUSIC WHERE PUBLISHER = "Elektra" and ARTIST <>
4:  ➡ "Natalie Merchant"
5:  SELECT * FROM MUSIC WHERE ARTIST LIKE "Natalie*"
6:  SELECT * FROM MUSIC WHERE ARTIST = "Elvis Presley" OR ARTIST LIKE "Elvis*"
7:  SELECT * FROM MUSIC WHERE NOT( ARTIST LIKE "Natalie*")
```

ANALYSIS   Each of the lines of code is a separate query. Line 1 returns all rows in the MUSIC table. Line 2 returns only rows containing titles by Elvis. Line 3 returns all Elektra artists, except for Natalie Merchant. Line 5 demonstrates how to use the LIKE operator, which performs masked searches. The asterisk (*) is the "any characters" mask. Line 5 returns any row containing Natalie, such as Natalie Cole and Natalie Merchant. Line 6 returns Elvis Presley or Elvis. If you change the predicate after OR in line 6 to ARTIST LIKE "Elvis*", you would get Elvis Costello (if he were in your collection). Line 7 demonstrates NOT combined with LIKE. You may use parentheses to group predicates, as demonstrated on line 7.

Operators for the WHERE Clause

SQL is a rich database language. Access 2002 is still ANSI-89 SQL compliant by default. You can change the version of ANSI-SQL to ANSI-92 by selecting Tools, Options, Tables/Queries and checking the This Database option. To make the default ANSI compatibility ANSI-92, change the Default File Format setting to Access 2002 on the Advanced tab of the Tools, Options dialog. You will want to change to ANSI-92 compatibility if you plan on upscaling your database to the SQL Server engine. Expect the possibility that some of your existing queries may not run if you switch the SQL compatibility mode of a database. If you are interested in the benefits of switching between ANSI-89 and ANIS-92 standards, you can find out all about SQL standards at the American National Standards Institute site at http://www.ansi.org.

Operators that you might find useful are the logic operators and the BETWEEN and IN operators, used with WHERE clauses. The BETWEEN operator enables you to specify an upper and lower range of acceptable values for a field, and the IN operator performs set arithmetic.

Specifying a Range with BETWEEN

The BETWEEN operator is used in a WHERE clause, in conjunction with AND, to specify a starting and ending value. The BETWEEN operator is an inclusive operator. The start and end values will be included in the result set. Listing 16.2 demonstrates this.

LISTING 16.2   An Example of Using the BETWEEN Operator

```
SELECT * FROM MUSIC WHERE LAST_NAME BETWEEN "Cash" AND "Martin"
```

This single line of SQL will return all artists whose last name ranges from Cash to Martin. Both Johnny Cash and Dean Martin will be in the result set.

Performing Set Operations with IN

The IN operator compares the values in a field to a set of literal values. The syntax for the IN operator is

```
SELECT fieldlist FROM tablename  WHERE fieldname  in ( value1, value2, ...)
```

Applied to the MUSIC database, an example demonstrating the IN operator might be

```
SELECT * FROM MUSIC WHERE PUBLISHER IN ("Polygram","Elektra", "Capitol")
```

This SQL statement returns all recording titles published by Polygram, Elektra, and Capitol Records.

Using Logic Operators

The logic operators AND, OR, and NOT work the same way in SQL as they do in VBA. The AND and OR operators are binary operators requiring two operands—one on each side of the operator. The NOT operator is a unary operator. The SQL NOT operator negates the test result of a predicate. NOT is used in the prefix position, as demonstrated in line 7 of Listing 16.1.

If you have many predicates in your WHERE clause, use parentheses to group expressions. SQL operators have a precedent order, but it might be more difficult to remember an implied precedence than to remember a stipulated order. Relying on implied precendence order may yield unexpected results as illustrated by the two, almost identical SQL statements that follow.

```
SELECT *FROM MUSIC
➥WHERE  PUBLISHER = "Capitol" AND
➥LAST_NAME = "Cocker" OR LAST_NAME ="Merchant"
SELECT *FROM MUSIC
➥WHERE  PUBLISHER = "Capitol" AND
➥(LAST_NAME = "Cocker" OR LAST_NAME ="Merchant")
```

 The AND operator is equivalent to multiplication, and OR is equivalent to addition in Boolean logic. Therefore, the order of precedence is AND, OR, and NOT. That is, AND predicates are evaluated first, then OR predicates, followed by NOT predicates (that is, unless you use parentheses to change the order).

The two SQL statements contain almost identical text but return different results. Because AND has precedence, the first SQL statement evaluates PUBLISHER = "Capitol" AND LAST_NAME = "Cocker" and then evaluates OR LAST_NAME = "Merchant". The result of the first query returns Joe Cocker and Natalie Merchant.. The second statement using parentheses to indicate ordering evaluates PUBLISHER equal to Capitol and artist's LAST_NAME equal to Cocker or Merchant. The second statement indicates that we only want Capitol recording artists in the result set. Comapred to the first statement which indicates that we want Capitol recording artist Joe Cocker or Natalie Merchant.

 If you have more than two predicates in your WHERE clause, use parentheses to explicitly express your intended order of operator evaluation.

In the second SQL statement, the parentheses change the meaning. The SQL ARTIST LIKE *MERCHANT* OR ARTIST LIKE *NATALIE* returns True for all instances of Natalie and Merchant, but combined with AND, ARTIST = "Dean Martin" results in False because the text "Dean Martin" does not contain "NATALIE" or "MERCHANT". Whereas the first query returns all instances of Natalie and Merchant, the second query, although it has the same text, returns no rows because it has the parentheses added.

Using Nested SELECT Statements in WHERE Clauses

The *value* proposition of a WHERE clause can be a simple value, as demonstrated in the last section, or it can be another SQL SELECT statement. Like other programming languages (such as VBA), SQL languages have parsers that are capable of interpreting the code you write.

When you write a nested SELECT statement, the innermost SELECT statement is processed first. Although you can nest SQL statements several layers deep, anything beyond one level of nesting is likely to have deleterious effects on your database server. A nested SELECT statement can be as basic or as complex as any other SELECT statement.

A nested SELECT statement is placed as the right-side argument of a WHERE predicate. The following demonstrates a nested SELECT statement:

```
SELECT * FROM MUSIC WHERE TITLE IN (SELECT TRACK_TITLE FROM TRACKS)
```

The single line of SQL text can be understood by reading the query inside out. The nested query says to select TRACK_TITLES from the TRACKS table. The outer query says to select all columns from the MUSIC table where TITLE is in the set returned by the nested query. In essence, this query returns all music titles containing title tracks; *title tracks* are songs that have the same name as the album or CD. A word of caution applies. What might not be immediately evident is that the nested query does not distinguish whether the title track is actually a track on the recording in the MUSIC table. Therefore, although the SQL is syntactically correct, it is logically incorrect.

The correct result can actually be obtained with a simpler query that equates the primary key ID in the MUSIC table with the foreign key in the TRACKS table, MUSIC_ID. The SQL to accomplish this is

```
SELECT* FROM MUSIC, TRACKS WHERE MUSIC.ID = TRACKS.MUSIC_ID
➥AND (MUSIC.TITLE LIKE TRACKS.TRACK_TITLE)
```

NEW TERM   A *primary key* is a column (or columns) in a table that constitutes a unique value for a single row in the table. A primary key is the main indexed value for a table. This terminology is associated with relational databases.

NEW TERM   A *foreign key* is an indexable value that comprises one or more columns associated with a primary key in another table. This terminology is associated with relational databases.

> You can look up information about nested queries by searching on the word *subquery* in the Help documentation.

When two or more tables are linked by equivalent fields in a WHERE clause, this linkage is referred to as an *implicit join*. Read the section "Joining Tables," later in this hour, to learn about table joins.

I am not suggesting that a nested query is never needed. There might come a time when it is exactly what you need. I am, however, suggesting that nested queries require care and are not used very often.

Sorting Queries

The SELECT statement enables you to order data by column in ascending or descending order. You can specify a comma-delimited sort order using a *columnname order* pair, where *columnname* is a column in one of the tables in the FROM clause and *order* is one of two possible values—ASC or DESC. Ascending (ASC) order means that the column will be sorted from the lowest to highest value. Descending sort order (DESC) means that you want the column to be sorted from highest value to lowest value. The following SQL SELECT statement sorts the result set by ARTIST in descending order and by TITLE in ascending order:

```
SELECT * FROM MUSIC ORDER BY ARTIST DESC, TITLE ASC
```

The default sort order is ascending order. If you specify a column in the ORDER BY clause without an order qualifier, that column will be sorted in ascending order.

Grouping Columns

The GROUP BY clause is used to group data by columns. This is necessary when you're performing aggregate operations, such as using the SUM function.

The GROUP BY clause, like the ORDER BY clause, takes a comma-delimited list of fields that is returned in the group.

When you group any columns in a result set, you must group all columns in the result set or include those fields that aren't specifically grouped in an aggregate function.

Use a GROUP BY clause when you want only one row of identical data. For example, the TRACKS table has the foreign key MUSIC_ID. If you were to write

```
SELECT MUSIC_ID FROM TRACKS
```

you would get as many rows as there are tracks. However, each row may only be associated with one MUSIC table ID. To get an accurate picture of the number of distinct titles from the TRACKS table, you could use the GROUP BY clause:

```
SELECT MUSIC_ID FROM TRACKS GROUP BY MUSIC_ID
```

The preceding SQL would only return one row per unique MUSIC_ID. If you want to figure out the number of Tracks per MUSIC title, the GROUP BY clause is just what you want. The following SQL returns one row with the number of tracks per MUSIC title:

```
SELECT MUSIC_ID, COUNT(MUSIC_ID) FROM TRACKS GROUP BY MUSIC_ID
```

One row for each distinct track would be found, including the count of the number of tracks. The COUNT function counts the number of rows, and GROUP BY MUSIC_ID ensures that only one row is actually returned.

Using the HAVING Clause to Filter Result Sets

SQL does not allow you to use aggregate functions in WHERE clauses. However, sometimes you might want to validate that a result set has certain conditions met. The HAVING clause is similar to the WHERE clause in that it helps limit the data returned in the set.

You may have as many predicates in the HAVING clause as you like. HAVING clauses use Boolean operators to combine multiple predicates.

Listing 16.3 demonstrates a HAVING relationship and a valid use of a nested subquery.

LISTING 16.3   The HAVING Relationship and a Nested Subquery

```
1: SELECT *  FROM MUSIC WHERE ID =
2:   (SELECT MUSIC_ID FROM TRACKS
3:    GROUP BY MUSIC_ID
4:    HAVING CDate(Sum(TRACK_LENGTH)) > CDate("0:6:0"))
```

ANALYSIS   The outer query starts on line 1. The nested subquery begins on line 2 and ends on line 4. The nested subquery groups rows in the TRACKS table by MUSIC_ID. The HAVING clause in line 4 performs a test to determine whether the sum of all tracks is longer than exactly six minutes.

A complete row from the MUSIC table is returned based on the ID in the MUSIC table matching any foreign key MUSIC_IDs from the TRACKS table. Line 4 provides one example of using the CDate function, which converts a number or string to a Date and Time type. In this example, CDate is converting the sum of all the times (Double) to Date and Time and comparing the converted type to the string "0: 6:0" (converted to a Date and Time type). The CDate function, along with other functions, is described in the section "Calling Functions in SQL Code," later in this Hour.

Joining Tables

A relational database is designed to combat waste. Historically, when database programmers wanted to store data, they had to determine how many items, such as phone numbers, of a certain type might go in each record. Problems arose because a developer might choose two as the maximum number of phone numbers, but, on occasion, storage for three numbers was needed.

In a *flat* database—a database where all data is kept in one monolithic record—a database programmer must modify the database to allow for three phone numbers. What happens to all that extra storage space in records that contain just two phone numbers? If you guessed that it is wasted, you are right.

Database designers who overestimated storage requirements ended up with large databases that contained lots of wasted space. Database designers who allocated a minimal amount of storage space per data type often ended up not having sufficient space for exceptions.

Relational databases were the solution. A relational database spreads the data out over many tables instead of placing it in one monolithic table. Each table is responsible for storing certain kinds of information.

For example, a customer database might have a name, account number, and a separate table for credit cards. This would result in each customer having exactly as many rows of credit card information as needed—nothing more or less.

Relational databases require a mechanism for combining data in many tables into one coherent picture. In a flat database, all that is necessary is to move to a client record, and all the data is right there. This makes flat database files easier to manage but wasteful of storage space.

In a relational database, the data in one table is associated with data in two, three, four, or more tables. The means of reassembling the data is to store extra indexed columns in the tables. The value of the indexes, called *keys*, makes it possible to assemble the data. This makes relational databases more difficult to program well, but it often makes faster and much less resource intensive.

The process of reassembling data from two or more tables is referred to as *joining* the tables. As you read in the section "Using Nested SELECT Statements in WHERE Clauses," earlier this hour, one kind of join is an *implicit* join. In it, columns with matching data in disparate tables are compared in a WHERE clause. Such a join returns rows where data in all equivalencies are returned. Of course, this is useful. However, in the case of two tables mentioned earlier (one containing customers and the other credit cards), what if a customer doesn't have a credit card?

As demonstrated using pseudo-SQL, the SQL would approximate the following:

```
SELECT * FROM CUSTOMER, CREDIT_CARDS WHERE CUSTOMER.ID =
➥CREDIT_CARDS.CUSTOMER_ID
```

If a customer does not have a credit card, the WHERE clause would fail, and the customer rows that contain customers without credit cards would not be returned. Consider the consequences of this behavior if you are processing invoices. All your customers not paying by credit card are really happy, and you get fired just before your company goes bankrupt.

This is where the join statement comes in. A join requires two tables. The first table is referred to as the *left table*, and the second table is referred to as the *right table*. There are three kinds of join statements—INNER JOIN, LEFT JOIN, and RIGHT JOIN. Each of these joins has a specific purpose, which I will cover next.

Using the INNER JOIN

An INNER JOIN is identical to an equivalency test in a WHERE clause. The INNER JOIN returns all the rows in both tables in the join, where each column has a matching value. An INNER JOIN can be written as follows:

```
SELECT * FROM MUSIC INNER JOIN TRACKS ON MUSIC.ID = TRACKS.MUSIC_ID;
```

The preceding SQL statement will return all rows in MUSIC and TRACKS, where MUSIC.ID = TRACKS.MUSIC_ID. The preceding INNER JOIN is identical to

```
SELECT * FROM MUSIC, TRACKS WHERE MUSIC.ID = TRACKS.MUSIC_ID;
```

The inner join has the same problem as joining tables in a WHERE clause; that is, if both tables don't have their half of the match, the row is not returned at all.

Using the LEFT JOIN

Use a LEFT JOIN when you want all the rows from the left table and only rows in the right table that match rows in the left table. Therefore, you might get null values for fields in the right table. Here's an example:

```
SELECT * FROM MUSIC LEFT JOIN TRACKS ON MUSIC.ID = TRACKS.MUSIC_ID;
```

The preceding query returns all MUSIC table rows, even if you have not added TRACKS data yet. Therefore, you might have empty fields for TRACKS data.

Using the RIGHT JOIN

A RIGHT JOIN is the opposite of a LEFT JOIN. In a RIGHT JOIN, you will get all the rows in the second (or right) table and only those rows with matching data in the first (or left) table. Here's an example:

```
SELECT * FROM MUSIC RIGHT JOIN TRACKS ON MUSIC.ID = TRACKS.MUSIC_ID;
```

In this example, you get all the TRACKS data and only the MUSIC rows that have matching tracks. In the `RIGHT JOIN`, you get tracks that don't have music data—perhaps singles in your music collection. (Remember the old 45 records? That's a `RIGHT JOIN`; single music tracks without an album title.)

Creating a Union of Tables

A `UNION` statement is used with two queries. Each query is separate from the other, but two queries in a `UNION` statement are run as one SQL statement. The results are combined into one result set. Duplicate values in a `UNION` statement are discarded by default. If you specify the `ALL` predicate, duplicates are returned, too.

You can write a `UNION` statement that acts like a single `SELECT` statement with an `OR` clause. This type is not very useful. A better use for `UNION` is to combine data that is similar in nature but resides in more than one table into one coherent table. The following is an example of a `UNION` statement that returns the ID columns of both the MUSIC and TRACKS tables:

```
SELECT ID FROM MUSIC UNION SELECT ID FROM TRACKS
```

The result of the query is that all ID values in use are returned. For the most part, this SQL demonstrates the technique and is not very useful. However, if you use an existing MUSIC table—suppose your wife has her own music collection and is willing to share her CDs with you—you can link to an Access database, and a `UNION` statement would provide you with one coherent view of the collective music.

Defining a Column Alias

At times, it may be useful to combine two or more columns into a single column. Consider the ARTIST column in the MUSIC table. If I want to sort the artists by last name, I would be hard pressed to do so without code to separate the columns. As a result, I might decide to separate the ARTIST column into FIRST_NAME and LAST_NAME columns. However, this would result in losing the nicely formatted artist's whole name. Consider Alice Cooper. Originally, that was a reference to the group rather than an individual; therefore, it would be semantically wrong to split Alice Cooper into last name and first name columns. What's more, how would you split Aerosmith, Sade, and Everclear into two fields.

For the sake of argument, suppose you are working with two columns where it makes sense to have two separate columns. You can use column aliasing to recombine the columns when you need to.

SQL enables you to combine two fields and rename the combination with the AS operator. Assume for the sake of argument that I now have FIRST_NAME and LAST_NAME
columns (instead of ARTIST). A SQL statement to return both parts of the name nicely
formatted might look like the following:

```
SELECT FIRST_NAME + ' ' + LAST_NAME As ARTIST FROM MUSIC ORDER BY LAST_NAME
```

The new MUSIC table no longer has an ARTIST column. The data was separated into
FIRST_NAME and LAST_NAME columns. The preceding SQL statement combines the
two columns separated by a literal space into a unified, aliased column: ARTIST.
Because the columns are separated, I can easily use ORDER BY LAST_NAME.

> A good use for the AS predicate is to alias columns in existing databases that
> have poorly defined or unsightly names when preparing to display those
> names on forms or reports.

Separating the ARTIST data into two columns represents a more powerful solution. The
change enables you to sort by first and last name and to format the name in any way you
like—first name first or last name first. Use the AS clause to name combined columns,
provide meaningful names for calculated columns, or simply modify a name to provide
neater output.

Inserting New Data

The INSERT INTO SQL statement enables you to append records to tables. The INSERT
command can be used to input fields into all columns in a table or a specific subset of
the columns. It can also be used as a means of copying data from one source to another. I
will discuss four basic kinds of INSERT commands in the next four subsections.

Inserting into Specified Fields Only

The most common use of the INSERT INTO command is to add new data to an existing
table. The following line of SQL demonstrates the syntax:

```
INSERT INTO tablename (field1[, field2, field3, ... ])
➥VALUES ( value1[, value2, value3, ...] )
```

All the capitalized words are SQL keywords. After the SQL command INSERT INTO, you
indicate a table name. The fields list follows. Specify those fields to which you want to
assign a value. The number of fields must match the number and type of the VALUES
list—one field, one value, and so on.

The following SQL statement demonstrates the technique by inserting Johnny Cash's *Folsom Prison* CD into my eclectic music collection:

```
INSERT INTO MUSIC ( FIRST_NAME, LAST_NAME, TITLE, FORMAT, PUBLISHER )
➥VALUES ("Johnny", "Cash", "JOHNNY CASH AT
➥FOLSOM PRISON AND SAN QUENTIN", "CD", "Columbia")
```

Running this SQL statement will append one row to the MUSIC table where FIRST_NAME equals "Johnny", LAST_NAME equals "Cash", TITLE equals "JOHNNY CASH AT FOLSOM PRISON AND SAN QUENTIN", FORMAT equals "CD", and PUBLISHER equals "Columbia". Notice I did not specify a value for the primary key ID. ID is an AutoNumber field and will be assigned a value by Access automatically.

Inserting into Implied Fields

A similar style of INSERT statement is one in which the fields are implied. The implicit INSERT statement works because you supply a value for every field, and the data items in the VALUES clause will be added to the table in the order in which they are listed. An implicit INSERT statement has a slightly shorter syntax than an explicit INSERT statement:

```
INSERT INTO tablename VALUES ( value1[, value2, value3, ...] )
```

The basic command is the same, except you do not need the fields list. Enter a value of the right type of data and in the right order for each column in the table. You also add a value for AutoNumber columns. Use the literal 0 for AutoNumber columns; Access will replace it automatically with the next number in the sequence before the row is written. Here's an example:

```
INSERT INTO MUSIC
➥VALUES(0, "Jewel", "Kilcher", "PIECES OF YOU", "CD", "Atlantic")
```

I generally write SQL by line-breaking the SQL text at each clause, indicated by a SQL keyword. For example, INSERT INTO is on the first line, the VALUES clause is on the second, and so on.

INSERT INTO MUSIC indicates that the data will be appended to the MUSIC table. Notice that there is no fields list immediately following the table name, and the last part of the statement is a fields list. There is one data value for each field. That's all there is to inserting values without the fields clause.

Inserting with Parameters

You indicate parameter values by placing names in brackets ([ ]) in a SQL statement in the VALUES list. The dynamic INSERT statement, where the operator has to enter values dynamically, can be written so that the fields are explicitly or implicitly declared.

If you use an explicitly declared fields list, you only need parameters for those fields to which you want to add data. If you want to write the INSERT statement so that the fields are implicit, you will need a literal or parameter for every column.

The syntax difference between specified and parametric INSERT statements is that, in the latter, the VALUES clause contains parameter names in brackets. The following two SQL statements demonstrate both explicit (Listing 16.4) and implicit INSERT (Listing 16.5) statements using parameters.

LISTING 16.4   A SQL INSERT INTO Statement That Uses Implicit Field Names and Dynamic Parameters

```
1: INSERT INTO MUSIC
2: VALUES( 0, [First Name], [Last Name], [Title], [Format], [Publisher] )
```

LISTING 16.5   A SQL INSERT INTO Statement That Uses Explicit Field Names and Dynamic Parameters

```
1: INSERT INTO MUSIC ( FIRST_NAME, LAST_NAME, TITLE, FORMAT, PUBLISHER )
2: VALUES ([First Name], [Last Name], [Title], [Format], [Publisher]);
```

ANALYSIS   Listing 16.4 contains five parameters. When you run the query in Listing 16.4, you will be prompted to input values for each of the five parameters (see Figure 16.1), depicting the input dialog for First Name in Listing 16.4. Notice that there is the same number of values as columns in the MUSIC table; there are four parameters and one literal, 0.

FIGURE 16.1

A generic dialog is displayed, prompting you to enter a value for replaceable parameters in INSERT INTO statements.

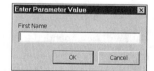

Listing 16.5 explicitly indicates those fields for which you want data values to be dynamically entered. Each dynamic value is represented by a parameter.

You can mix values and parameters in the same statement. For example, you may know what values you want in several columns and only want to specify parameters for one or two fields. That is perfectly acceptable.

Inserting from a Table with SELECT

16

A useful application of the INSERT INTO statement is to use it to import data from one table into another. This is accomplished using a SELECT statement in place of the VALUES clause. Consider the following syntax example:

```
INSERT INTO destination_table( field1, [field2, field3, ...] )
➥SELECT source_table.field1 [, source_table.field2, source_table.field3,
➥ ... ] ) source_table;
```

In this example, everything is the same except for the VALUES clause. An INSERT INTO statement with a SELECT clause starts with INSERT INTO, a table name, and fields list. However, instead of the usual VALUES clause, you use a SELECT statement. The fields in the SELECT clause must match the type and number of fields in the INSERT INTO fields list.

Remember the scenario where your wife is going to share her CDs with you? Suppose she has her own MUSIC collection and database, in addition to your own. The two of you are now a couple, and you want to combine your MUSIC collection database. You could use the following INSERT INTO statement with a SELECT clause to get the job done (see Listing 16.6).

LISTING 16.6   A SQL INSERT INTO with a Nested Subquery Used to Import Data from an Identical Table

```
INSERT INTO MUSIC (ID, ARTIST, TITLE, FORMAT, PUBLISHER)
SELECT 0, ARTIST, TITLE, FORMAT, PUBLISHER FROM MUSIC2
```

ANALYSIS   The INSERT INTO statement is identical up to the point where it includes the fields list. Because we are using an autonumbered primary key, the first value in the SELECT statement will be a literal, 0. After the literal value 0, each field in the source table (in the nested subquery) is in the fields list of the SELECT statement.

There is quite a bit of flexibility in the INSERT statement. As you know, the SELECT statement is diverse in its capabilities. Combining INSERT INTO and SELECT statements offers tremendous computing power.

Updating Data

The UPDATE statement is used to modify one or more rows with one statement. The basic syntax enables you to update an indicated subset of columns to contain new field values. An extended version of UPDATE, using a WHERE clause, enables you to conditionally modify data that meets criteria in the WHERE clause.

As with WHERE clauses in general, you can specify a nested subquery (a SELECT statement) in the WHERE clause of UPDATE statements. An UPDATE statement has the following general syntax:

```
UPDATE tablename
SET field1 = value1[, field2 = value2, field3 = value3, ...]
[WHERE where_clause]
```

SQL keywords, by convention, are uppercase. UPDATE, SET, and WHERE are all keywords. You must use the UPDATE and SET keywords; the WHERE clause is optional. The SET clause must have at least one predicate, as indicated by the syntax example. You can have as many predicates in the SET clause as you would like. The WHERE clause is optional and works exactly the same with UPDATE SQL statements as it does with other kinds of SQL statements. Listing 16.7 demonstrates several arbitrary UPDATE statements that modify data in the MUSIC database.

LISTING 16.7   UPDATE Statements That Modify Data

```
1:   UPDATE MUSIC SET TITLE = UCase(TITLE);
2:   UPDATE MUSIC SET FIRST_NAME = ICap([FIRST_NAME]);
3:   UPDATE MUSIC SET PUBLISHER = "Columbia Records" WHERE PUBLISHER = "Columbia"
```

ANALYSIS   Each of the three lines in Listing 16.7 is a separate query. Line 1 calls the VBA function UCase to modify all titles to uppercase letters. Line 2 calls a function I wrote to capitalize the first letter of the field FIRST_NAME (the ICap function is shown in Listing 16.8). Line 3 demonstrates using a WHERE clause to update only those PUBLISHER fields that contain Columbia to Columbia Records.

LISTING 16.8   You Can Call User-Defined Functions from Your SQL Statements

```
1:   Function ICap(ByVal FieldValue As String) As String
2:       ICap = UCase(Left$(FieldValue, 1)) & LCase(Mid$(FieldValue, 2))
3:   End Function
```

ANALYSIS The ICap function is quite simple. The first letter is copied with the Left$ function and uppercased. The rest of FieldValue is extricated with the Mid$ command and lowercased. This kind of UPDATE statement ensures that data, such as the kind that might end up in a report, is nicely formatted. Functions and subroutines do not have to be long to be worth writing; neither do they have to be complicated. Short and simple functions are the best kind.

> In commercial software, you can add what is euphemistically called *sanity checking* to the function in Listing 16.8. Sanity checking is a fun-to-computer-geeks way of saying that error checking is needed.
>
> In Listing 16.8, if the field contains a null value, the function will explode. An error handler can handily keep your program from crashing. Read Hour 17, "Removing Bugs," coming up next.

Deleting Data

What goes into a database may eventually have to come out. The DELETE statement is responsible for removing rows of data from a database. The DELETE command is easy to use. (As with most things, it always seems easier to destroy than to create.) The syntax for the DELETE SQL statement is

```
DELETE FROM tablename [WHERE where_clause]
```

> Be careful when using DELETE. Consider using a prompt to allow the user to abort the operation before actually deleting the data. The MsgBox function can be used for this purpose.

> SQL programming and databases should not be taken lightly. There are many considerations that go into good programs. For example, if you have several tracks for a music selection, and you delete the MUSIC row associated with those tracks, what happens to the TRACKS data? The rows are orphaned.
>
> *Orphaned rows* are rows that logically belong to rows (in another table) that have been deleted. When you delete a row in one table, you often have to delete rows in other tables. The same is true for updates.

16

> Many databases support cascading deletes and updates. A cascaded process means that the database takes care of logically associated data. However, you often have to do some extra work to turn cascading features on. If you do not turn them on, you will have to use SQL or VBA code that ensures that related data is kept up-to-date relative to its associated data.
>
> Good tools make programming seem deceptively easy. Don't be afraid to seek experienced help to assist you through any hard spots. Many well-known experts in various fields are available through e-mail and chat groups, and they are often willing to help newcomers.

If you write DELETE FROM MUSIC without a WHERE clause, you are instructing Access to delete all rows. If you write a WHERE clause, only those rows that have data matching the criteria in the WHERE clause will be deleted.

Calling Functions in SQL Code

As I demonstrated in Listing 16.7, you can call built-in Access functions, such as UCase, and user-defined functions, such as ICap, in SQL code. If you find your SQL getting too complex, consider using an existing function or writing a new function to do some of the work. SQL is great at managing data, but you might encounter some limitations when trying to perform everyday tasks such as capitalizing the first letter of a field.

Functions such as counting rows (COUNT) and summating fields (SUM) are defined as part of the SQL language. Several listings in this hour demonstrate how to use functions. For example, Listing 16.3 demonstrates using the SUM and CDate (date conversion) functions.

The rules for using functions in SQL are the same as those in VBA. You must indicate the name of the function and pass any required arguments of the correct type to the function. Time, experience, and a rational reliance on all the documentation available will aid you in mastering using functions in your SQL code.

Writing Stored Procedures

Introduced with ActiveX Data Objects in the ADOX library is support for stored procedures. A *stored procedure* is SQL's equivalent of a function. Stored procedures have existed in large-scale database servers, such as Oracle, for a long time. (The Oracle procedural language is called PL/SQL.)

Stored procedures are beneficial for at least two important reasons: First, they run on faster database servers, and, second, they enable you to define an interface. Typically, a stored procedure runs on the server faster than it will run on a desktop computer. A stored procedure might run faster in Access 2002, even if the database is on your desktop, because it is running inside the database kernel. Because the stored procedure allows you to specify a named interface, stored procedures are almost as easy to use as any other kind of function. You pass the arguments required, the operation defined is run, and the data specified is returned.

Procedures are stored in your database in a collection, `Procedures`, in the database's `Catalog` object. Each item in a `Procedures` collection is a `Procedure` object. A `Procedure` object contains the `DateCreated`, `DateModified`, `Name`, and `Command` attributes. The `Command` attribute actually contains the stored procedure code.

A stored procedure is stored in the `Procedures` collection of a `Catalog` object. (Physically, it resides in your database's system tables, but you won't ever need to use it at that level.) You must add the procedure to a `Catalog` object before you can use it. The basic syntax of a stored procedure is similar to that of a query:

PARAMETERS [*param*] *type* [[*param2*], *type2*, ...]; *SQL text*

The procedure is a string. Use the keyword PARAMETER to add parameters that you can pass to the procedure. The [] tokens are literal values. You can have as many comma-delimited parameters and type-pairs as you need. End the parameter list with a semicolon, followed by the SQL text that makes up the procedure code. Listing 16.9 contains two stored procedure statements. The first returns MUSIC rows by the parameter passed in for PUBLISHER, and the second returns MUSIC rows by PUBLISHER and FORMAT.

LISTING 16.9 Two Stored Procedure Statements

```
1:  PARAMETERS [APUBLISHER] Text;
2:  ➡SELECT FIRST_NAME & ' ' & LAST_NAME As ARTIST, TITLE, FORMAT, PUBLISHER
3:  ➡FROM MUSIC WHERE PUBLISHER = [APUBLISHER]
4:
5:  PARAMETERS [APUBLISHER] Text, [AFORMAT] Text;
6:  ➡SELECT FIRST_NAME & ' ' & LAST_NAME As ARTIST, TITLE, FORMAT, PUBLISHER
7:  ➡FROM MUSIC
8:  ➡WHERE PUBLISHER = [APUBLISHER] AND FORMAT = [AFORMAT]
```

ANALYSIS Lines 1–3 constitute one stored procedure. You would assign this as a single string to the CommandText property of an ADODB Command object. The same is true of the second procedure, on lines 5–8.

The first stored procedure accepts a text argument, APUBLISHER, and selects all rows where the publisher is equal to the value of the parameter. The second stored procedure requires two parameters: APUBLISHER and AFORMAT. The procedure returns a recordset containing all rows where the publisher and format match the parameter values.

Adding a Stored Procedure to a Catalog

A stored procedure is added to a database's Catalog object, which is an ADOX attribute (that is, Catalog is an object that is part of the ADOX library). You already know how to write most of the code necessary to add a stored procedure. Listing 16.10 contains sample code that demonstrates how to create and store a procedure.

LISTING 16.10   Adding a Stored Procedure to the Database Catalog

```
 1:  Sub CreateProcedure()
 2:    Dim Connection As ADODB.Connection
 3:    Set Connection = CurrentProject.Connection
 4:    Dim Command As New ADODB.Command
 5:    Dim Catalog As New ADOX.Catalog
 6:    Set Command.ActiveConnection = Connection
 7:    Command.CommandText = "PARAMETERS [APublisher] Text;" & _
 8:      "SELECT ARTIST, TITLE, FORMAT," & _
 9:      "PUBLISHER From MUSIC Where PUBLISHER = [APublisher]"
10:    Set Catalog.ActiveConnection = Connection
11:    Call Catalog.Procedures.Append("Artist By Publisher", Command)
12:    Set Command = Nothing
13:    Set Catalog = Nothing
14:    Set Connection = Nothing
15:  End Sub
```

Notice that the SELECT part of the stored procedure object uses the MUSIC table containing the ARTIST column instead of the two separate FIRST_NAME and LAST_NAME columns.

ANALYSIS You will need to add a reference to Microsoft ADO Ext, 2.6 for DDL and Security from the Tools, References dialog in the Visual Basic Editor. You also

need an instance of an open connection. At this point, you already know how to open a new connection, so we will switch our focus to `CurrentProject.Connection`, which represents the current database connection. The procedural text is stored in a `Command` object, created on line 4. The `Command` object containing the procedural text is stored in the catalog, so you will need a `Catalog` object. `Command.CommandText` is assigned to the store procedure text on lines 7, 8, and 9. Line 11 appends the `Command` object with the name `"Artist By Publisher"`, and the rest is cleanup.

Lines 1–15 store a procedure in your database. It is worth pointing out that all the code written here is for demonstration purposes; it is not necessary to open and close connections and catalogs in every subroutine. Generally, you can use the `CurrentProject`'s `Connection` object and open a catalog only when you need one. Read more about this in Hour 19, "Creating Custom Forms."

Executing a Stored Procedure

Now that you have the stored procedure, you can use it any time you want. Stored procedures are run with a `Command` object's `Execute` method. If the stored procedure, such as the one in Listing 16.11, returns a result set as `SELECT` statements do, you will need to assign the value of the `Command.Execute` statement to an `ADODB.Recordset` variable. However, if the stored procedure contains an `INSERT`, `DELETE`, or `UPDATE` statement, you do not need a `Recordset` object.

Listing 16.11 demonstrates how to execute a stored procedure in your database.

LISTING 16.11 Executing a Stored Procedure

```
 1:  Sub ExecuteProcedure()
 2:    Dim Connection As ADODB.Connection
 3:    Set Connection = CurrentProject.Connection
 4:
 5:    Dim Catalog As New ADOX.Catalog
 6:    Set Catalog.ActiveConnection = Connection
 7:
 8:    Dim Command As ADODB.Command
 9:    Set Command = Catalog.Procedures("Artist By Publisher").Command
10:
11:    Dim Publishers As ADODB.Recordset
12:    Dim RecordsAffected As Long
13:    Command.Parameters("[APublisher]").Value = "Elektra"
14:    Set Publishers = Command.Execute()
15:
```

LISTING 16.11   continued

```
16:    Publishers.MoveFirst
17:    Do While Publishers.EOF = False
18:      Debug.Print Publishers("ARTIST")
19:      Publishers.MoveNext
20:    Loop
21:
22:    Publishers.Close
23:    Set Publishers = Nothing
24:    Set Command = Nothing
25:    Set Catalog = Nothing
26:    Set Connection = Nothing
27: End Sub
```

ANALYSIS   You have seen most of this code several times by now; therefore, I won't go over it again. Instead, let's go over the highlights. You will need an open connection and the catalog. Note that I did not create a new instance of a Recordset object on line 11. This isn't necessary because the Command.Execute statement on line 14 returns a Recordset instance. All you need is a named variable without memory on line 11. On line 13, I set the value to be passed to the command parameter and call the Execute method on line 14, which returns the recordset representing the results of the query in the stored procedure.

From line 16 to line 26 everything else is identical to the code you have seen before. After you have the valid Recordset object from line 9, you can use it as you would any other Recordset instance.

Querying a SQL Server Database

You can use SQL in your Access projects in three ways: You can establish a connection to a SQL database, upsize the Access database to SQL, and link to a SQL table using the File, Get External Data, Link command. The choice you makes depends on the objectives you are trying to achieve. If you need a more robust server, you may want to upsize to SQL Server. If you only need some data in a SQL Server database, you can link a table or use a Connection object.

If you plan on linking or connecting to a SQL Server database, it will be helpful to create an ODBC alias to the SQL Server database. Alternatively, you can use OLE DB and

ADO to provide the `Provider` information directly. You learned how to perform these operations in this and earlier hours.

Once you have made SQL data accessible, working with the SQL database is a lot like working with Access data. You will need to get a `Recordset` object, define the query based on the operation you want to perform, and open that recordset. The operations from there are roughly identical to those in Access; you can write SQL or VBA code (or a combination of both) to manage the data.

One final thing to keep in mind is that SQL Server is a different database server. The specific query text may be slightly different, depending on the specific version of SQL Server you are accessing. A good book on your version of SQL Server, experimentation, and patience will be helpful.

Summary

This hour contained a lot of information. This book is not a SQL book. If you need more information on SQL than what's covered in this hour, I urge you to get a book devoted only to SQL, such as *Sams Teach Yourself SQL in 24 Hours* (ISBN 0-672-31245-X) by Ryan Stephens. The SQL language is a powerful programming language. There are almost as many flavors of SQL as there are databases. If you are using a database other than Access, I suggest you get a SQL book that's written for your database.

In this hour, you learned how to write SELECT statements with JOIN and UNION statements and nested subqueries. You will use SELECT statements for a large percentage of your database programming. You also learned how to insert, update, and delete records. The WHERE clause enables you to filter the records affected by SELECT, UPDATE, and DELETE operations.

Stored procedural programming, thus far, has been the purview of very expensive database programs. With ADO, Access programmers now can write stored procedures. A stored procedure is comprised of the kind of SQL you wrote in the first half of the hour and is stored in a catalog via the Command object. If you learn to write SQL well, you will be able to write good stored procedures. Complete the "Q&A" and "Workshop" sections to wrap up this hour.

Q&A

Q Does SQL have its own grammar and keywords like VBA does?

A Yes. All languages, including programming languages, have a grammar and vocabulary. The vocabulary consists of the words that make up the language, and the grammar consists of the rules that define its usage. So, you now have been introduced to two programming languages: VBA and SQL. How well you learn them depends on your need and interest.

Q Is there a limit to the size of a single query?

A No. You can write very complicated queries. However, SQL is a monolithic language. There is always one long block of text in a query, even though the statement is comprised of many parts. SQL code looks messy, and it is difficult to maintain if it is too long.

Q What can I do to manage my SQL?

A Good programming rules for VBA apply to SQL, too. Limit the SQL to solving a single problem per query and consider combining code and SQL to get intermediate results. This will enable you to break up complicated queries into smaller, simpler queries.

Q Where can I go to find out about a specific version of SQL?

A You can go to the ANSI Web site at `http://www.ansi.org`, or you can request suggested SQL book titles from your database vendor.

Workshop

The Workshop includes quiz questions designed to help you test your understanding of the material covered and exercises to help put what you've learned to practice. You will find the answers to the quiz and exercises in Appendix A, "Answers."

Quiz

1. What is a subquery?
2. What does the `ALL` keyword do in a `UNION` statement?
3. Can you use a nested subquery in a `DELETE` query? If so, why might you?
4. Are stored procedures limited to `SELECT` statements?

Exercises

1. Write a WHERE clause containing an IN predicate that returns all Elektra and Empire music publishers.

2. Modify the update query in Listing 16.6, line 2, to capitalize the first letter of the first and last name data in the MUSIC table.

3. Write the text of a stored procedure that would delete a specific artist from your music collection.

16

PART VI
Mastering Error Handling

Hour

HOUR 17

Removing Bugs

A *bug* is a programming error that causes a program to act erratically, produce incorrect results, or crash. The term *buggy* refers to programs that are fraught with such errors and are, therefore, unreliable and frustrating for users. This hour gives you some specific strategies that will help you reduce the number of bugs in your code, help you find bugs more quickly, and make it easier for you to extend your code without rewriting testing code from scratch a second time.

Generally, finding bugs is intractable only if comprehending the code is an intractable solution. This hour helps you write better code that is less likely to have bugs—and the bugs you do have will be easier to find. In this hour, you will learn about:

- Testing your code in small pieces, when it is easy to test
- Effective debugging techniques, adopted from expert solutions originally implemented for the C programming language
- Using conditional compiler directives that facilitate testing and debugging
- The differences between testing code that is shipped and testing code that is not shipped

Scaffolding

There is a famous problem in computer science called the *halting problem*. It has been rigorously demonstrated that no algorithm can possibly verify whether code is correct under all conditions. The *halting problem*, to date, has not been solved. This means that no matter how much code anyone writes, no one can absolutely stipulate that his or her code is bug-free.

NEW TERM An *algorithm* generally refers to a function or subroutine. Occasionally, the term *algorithm* may be used to refer to more than one function, including supporting functions.

There is no provably bug-free code. Therefore, it is assumed that all code will have some bugs. (How much code has really nasty bugs? Well, on January 1, 2000, we found out that things weren't as bad as predicted relative to Y2K anyway.) Because you cannot write *completely* bug-free code, code that is *relatively* bug-free is the best you can do. But, how much code must you write to achieve a *mostly* bug-free solution? This is the question I am going to answer in this hour.

I will present you with some guidelines that help you decide how much code to write so that you get the most bang for your buck. The first important strategy is called *scaffolding*. As an adjective, *scaffolding* means *testing code*; as a verb, it refers to the act of writing test code.

 Two positive innovations have been popularized in recent months. The first is a suite called *JUnit*. JUnit helps automate self-testing for Java. I expect that additional JUnit-like test suites will be written for other languages in coming months. The second innovation is the growing acceptance of *refactoring*, which is the process of finding commonality in code and converging that code into single occurrences of the code. Refactoring defines an almost algebraic approach to revising code on a going-forward basis. A good book on refactoring, if you are interested, is Martin Fowler's *Refactoring: Improving the Design of Existing Code*, published by Addison-Wesley.

Fowler's book on refactoring is an advanced programming book, but it's a good source of ideas on how to proactively manage code.

Almost all the programmers I have ever met claim that they test their code. Scaffolding is not merely about testing your code; scaffolding is about testing the right amount of code at the right time.

Test your code a little bit at a time. If you write a function that is an important part of your solution, write a scaffold to test it separately. For example, each of the sort algorithms in Hour 12, "Managing Varying Amounts of Data," is an ideal function for scaffolding. Each sort algorithm represents a complete and independent solution to a problem. Therefore, you should write a small program (or subroutine, at least) to test the sort algorithms.

> You can use the Immediate window in the Visual Basic Editor to test individual lines of code separately from you program or simply step through a single procedure to test that one procedure. Using the Immediate window to test code is a good first step, but it is not as enduring, nor as reusable, as writing additional test procedures in the module.

17

In general, functions, subroutines, classes, and modules all make good approximations as to the size of the code you should scaffold independently of your program. That is, if you write an algorithm that is nontrivial, it is a good candidate for scaffolding. Entire modules should be tested, but you may have to write code to test the functions and subroutines independently. Also, a class is an excellent candidate for scaffolding. Classes represent whole solutions and subsequently should be tested independently of any other non-related code.

Why Scaffolding Early Is Important

Programmers make assumptions about the state of their programs all the time. When a programmer writes a function or subroutine, there is generally an anticipated state that the programmer believes the program will be in.

For example, when a programmer modifies an ADODB.Recordset, he or she usually assumes that the data set is open and pointing to the right record. Programmers typically make this kind of assumption while they are writing algorithms.

In other words, you, as a programmer, probably know more about what state your program is in when you are writing an algorithm than at any other time. Consequently, you should write your testing code at the same time you write your solution code, not later. Later, you might forget some of the assumptions you made about the program's state.

Understanding What to Look For

It is important to understand what to look for when you scaffold code. When you are scaffolding code, you should write code that tests the assumptions you have made about your code, and you should write code that tests the positive and contrapositive assertions about your code. Typically, if programmers write test code, they write code that validates their assumptions. You should write that kind of code because your code should definitely work when it gets the data it expects. However, what about when your code ends up with data it didn't expect? By writing scaffolding code, you validate your assumptions and perhaps illuminate possibilities you haven't considered. This is because scaffolding forces you to think of the piece of code as a whole solution by itself.

Even if you only effectively test your assumptions, your scaffold code provides a legacy for other developers. Your scaffold will show others what you have and haven't tested. A second or third pair of eyes is likely to find holes in your assumptions.

When scaffolding, you should also look for dependencies. A *dependency* is when one piece of code depends on the existence of some external data or algorithm. Generally, external dependencies are signs of half-baked code. For example, in Hour 12, if the Quick sort didn't work as a separate function, I would reconsider its implementation.

> Scaffolding code separately helps you write better code because it gets you in the habit of writing code that is not dependent on other code.
>
> It is okay to write code that is dependent on other code by design. However, you should remove unplanned, accidental dependencies.

In general, code should have few external dependencies. The same is true for classes; a class should know everything it has to know about solving its piece of the problem. Checking for dependencies is the reason you should test code separately from your program.

How to Scaffold Access Code

To scaffold code in Access, it is best to have a testing database. An empty database is a good place to start because this forces you to think about instances when data doesn't exist. The following list explains how to scaffold Access code:

1. Start with an empty database with the same schema as your program's database.
2. Create a new module if you are testing an algorithm or add the class you want to test if you are testing a class.
3. Write a subroutine that calls your subroutine with the correct number and type of arguments.
4. Start the process by starting the test subroutine in the debugger.

If your code passes each item in the following checklist, it is in good shape:

- The code compiles and runs without error; for example, the code doesn't refer to something that doesn't exist or is unintentionally referenced.
- The code solves the problem intended, producing the right output.
- The code can handle any serious errors without shutting down in an unplanned way.

If your code survives up to this point, you must determine the next step. If the code is very important to your program, you should get another set of eyes to look at the code and determine whether there are potential arguments or program states you might not have anticipated. Alternatively, you can elect to document what you have done and move on. Choose the second condition if there is a testing group whose job it is to find what you might have missed.

If your code falls short of one of the three standards, you must take further action.

What to Do If Your Code Has Dependencies

Whether the code doesn't compile because of a global variable, another function, or some other dependency depends on how you write the code.

If your code refers to an external object reference or variable, consider adding that variable to the interface of the function or class. That is, pass it as an argument to the subroutine or function or make it a property of the class. (Read Hour 21, "Class Programming Basics," for more on properties.) A general caveat is, Don't ship code that has dependencies across function or class boundaries.

If the dependency is to a global variable, consider making that variable an argument, too. Choose carefully which variables you leave as global variables. Global variables are often a source of pernicious bugs.

If the dependency is to another function or subroutine, decide whether it actually must exist. If the dependency is part of the implementation of the algorithm or class, consider passing the argument rather than leaving the dependency.

What to Do If the Code Doesn't Solve the Problem

If the code doesn't provide the intended solution, determine why. If the code is wrong because the data was bad, consider using a contract style of programming. *Contract programming* is when you stipulate that the arguments must be within a certain range of data that is valid for your algorithm. Contracts are enforced with conditional code and assertions. Read the section "Asserting Assumptions," later in this hour, for more information on contract programming.

17

If the algorithm is wrong because, well, it's wrong, you should fix it. Take some solace in the fact that a function or class is always easier to fix in a scaffold than it is as part of a bigger program. A scaffold is smaller and simpler and allows you to focus your attention on resolving the problem and perfecting the solution.

What to Do in the Event of Unhandled Errors

If the code causes a critical error to occur, you have to first determine how you want to handle the error. The first step is to determine the cause of the error. If the error is caused by a dependency, see the section related to dependencies. Often, you can resolve a critical error with an error handler, or perhaps you just have to document the error.

If the error is supposed to occur when the situation that caused the error occurs, that's just the way things are. A good comment might be sufficient to resolve the problem. Consider a program that dials up a network. If you can't connect, the program can't run. That's an error. Report it to the user and exit the program gracefully.

You can write some specific kinds of code in your scaffolds to find out whether the code is satisfactory. I will cover those strategies next.

Trapping Code

I did not develop the strategies in this section or the next two sections. The credit belongs to Dave Thielen, who is the person responsible for shipping DOS 5. If you were computing in those days, you might remember that DOS 4 was a mess. It had a lot of bugs. One might imagine that the mandate came from the almighty Bill Gates, himself, that DOS 5 better be good or no more employee stock options.

DOS 5 was a success. It was well received by users and had relatively few bugs. David Thielen subsequently wrote the book *No Bugs!: Delivering Error-Free Code in C and C++* (Addison-Wesley, 1992). I loved the book for two reasons: One, it is only about 180 pages long (compared to many computer books, which are around 1,000 pages); two, it is full, from beginning to end, of tips that make good sense and work. Since 1992, I have adapted the strategies in Thielen's book to every language in which I have programmed (if these strategies were not native to the language). Language vendors since have adopted some of these strategies, including *assertions*, which is part of VBA now, too.

An assertion is extra code that conditionally checks data values and stops if the tests fail. *Tracing* is when extra code reports, in a log file or output window (such as the Watch window), what the program is doing. Visual C++ has tracing and asserting. Delphi (Object Pascal) has assertions. Visual Basic and VBA support writing assertions and the equivalent of tracing, implemented in the Debug object. This section and the two after it demonstrate how to use these powerful techniques.

What Is a Trap?

A *trap* is just what it sounds like. You step in it, and it's triggered. In code, a *trap* is a line of code that lets you know when it has been executed. The purpose of the trap is to let you know that the code "got there."

Using a trap is a good way to ensure that every code path is actually tested. Suppose, for example, you have an If…Then…Else statement, and you test the code but have no way of validating whether the Else condition is tested. How do you know that the Else condition doesn't cause your program to hiccup? The answer is, you can't know unless you write code that tells you if the code path has been exercised. Traps are designed for exactly this purpose. In addition, trapping code can help you find code that is unnecessary, allowing you to trim some fat.

Using Traps

You can implement a trap method quite easily in VBA. Listing 17.1 demonstrates a trap implementation and a demonstration.

LISTING 17.1 Implementing Code Trapping in VBA

```
1:  Sub Trap(ByVal FileName As String, ByVal TrapNumber As Long)
2:    Debug.Print "Trapped: " & FileName & "(" & TrapNumber & ")"
3:    Stop
4:  End Sub
5:
6:  Sub SomeCodeToTest()
7:    Dim Condition As Boolean
8:    If( Condition = True ) Then
9:     Call Trap("Module1", 1)
10:   Else
11:     Call Trap("Module1", 2)
12:   End If
13: End Sub
```

ANALYSIS Lines 1 through 4 implement a subroutine called Trap. Lines 6 through 13 represent some code you want to trap. Trap is easy to implement. You have to implement the Trap subroutine only once and then import it into the database (or other VBA code) in which you want to use it. Trap takes two arguments: FileName and TrapNumber. In this case, FileName is the module from which the trap was thrown, and TrapNumber is a unique number you assign each trap. The number is unique to the file, allowing you to find the trap easily by searching a particular file for the reference number.

17

When the trap is thrown, the filename and trap number are written to the Debug window. After you run your code, simply examine the Immediate window and comment out any traps that have been thrown. Don't remove the trap, because the presence of a commented trap indicates that, indeed, a particular code path has been exercised.

Lines 6 through 13 represent some arbitrary code you want to ensure has been tested. Use traps for important code and all code paths of algorithms. It isn't necessary to trap all code, but it isn't a bad idea, either. When you modify code, uncomment the trap and then run the code again to make sure that it is tested. If you find any traps that haven't been commented out, you must devise a test that will explicitly exercise that code. If you find that you cannot devise a test for untrapped code, you might have found code that safely can be removed. The best way to ensure that code doesn't introduce bugs is to remove it if it isn't necessary.

Tracing Code

The purpose of tracing code is to document the order and state of the code. You also can determine how many times certain lines of code are run. The number of times an algorithm is run can help you determine which code to optimize.

A tracing procedure takes arguments similar to the trapping subroutine. A tracing subroutine takes a filename, a trace number for reference purposes, and what you want to record about the trace (the message). The filename is the name of the module containing the trace. The trace number is a reference number that is unique to each trace statement in a particular module; it helps you locate the trace using the Edit, Find menu in the editor. The message can be the name of the function or subroutine, the value of a variable, or anything else you need it to be. The idea is that what you trace helps you keep track of what your program is doing.

Only within the last five years or so have programming tools come with integrated debuggers. An integrated debugger lets you perform watches, inspect the call stack, and set breakpoints. You can equate using watches and the call stack to tracing, and you can equate breakpoints to traps and assertions.

However, implementing the simple but useful strategies described in this hour is still beneficial because, at times, you might run your program outside its development environment, as your testers might likely do. You certainly can use the Immediate window to help you trace code in the IDE, but you cannot use the Debug window outside of the IDE. Also, breakpoints set in the Visual Basic editor will not be available after you close the database.

I would recommend that you use the techniques in this hour in conjunction with the integrated debugging tools. When it comes to finding bugs, it is wholesale warfare. Use everything that helps.

The best thing about tracing is that you can write the trace to a log file instead of the Immediate window, and you have an audit trail of what your program really does. Comparing what code paths your program is expected to take versus the code paths taken when an actual user is running the program can provide you with invaluable feedback. Listing 17.2 implements a subroutine called Trace.

LISTING 17.2 Implementing the Trace Subroutine

```
1:  Sub Trace(ByVal FileName As String, ByVal TraceMessage As String, _
2:    ByVal TraceNumber As Long)
3:    Dim Output as String
4:    Output = "Traced: " & FileName & "(" & TraceNumber & ") on " & _
5:      Now & vbCrLf & TraceMessage & vbCrLf
6:    Debug.Print Output
7:  End Sub
```

ANALYSIS Listing 17.2 implements the Trace subroutine. Add the Trace subroutine to the same module as the Trap subroutine, and you have the makings of a good tool set. (To use the module in other databases, remember to export the module with the File, Export File command. To reuse testing code, use File, Import to add the module containing Trace and Trap to new databases.)

Line 3 declares a variable that makes formatting easier. Lines 4 and 5 format the output as *filename(tracenumber) on date_and_time*. Here, vbCrLf is a constant defined in VBA that adds the carriage return/newline pair to the formatted output. Line 6 logs the text to the Immediate window.

An alternative version of Trace would be to write the output to a text file. I have used both in the past, so I typically have both forms implemented. To log the output to a text file, you might append .log to the filename, open *filename*.log for the append operation, write the output string, and close the file.

It is a good idea to have these tools on hand before you run into bugs. They will save you a lot of extra time and frustration when you have to find bugs.

Asserting Assumptions

Without assumptions, it would be impossible to program. When you make an assertion, you are stipulating that a condition must exist for the code to work correctly. Assertions are considered so important to programming that the Assert method has been implemented in most mainstream programming languages.

The Assert method is a member of the Debug object. Assert takes one argument, a Boolean, and stops program execution if the assertion fails. This is exactly what you want the Assert method to do. Assert is your program's sheriff. If certain assumptions must be true for your code to work correctly, an assertion is the means to ensure that those assumptions are sustained.

There are as many examples of using assertions as there are examples of code. The general rule is to use an assertion to verify that a certain condition exists. For example, suppose you write an algorithm that updates a text file. A condition for updating the text file might be that the file has to exist—not that the file should exist, but that it *has* to exist. Certainly, you could write code that checks for the existence of the file, like the following:

```
If (Len(Dir(FileName)) > 0 ) Then
```

For runtime purposes, this code will verify that the file exists, but it won't notify the programmer in a timely manner if the file does not exist. However, if you couple this fragment with an assertion, the code will work correctly, and if the test fails, program execution will be halted while you are testing:

```
Debug.Assert Len(Dir(FileName)) > 0
If (Len(Dir(FileName)) > 0 ) Then
```

If the assertion fails, the program pauses at that line of code. Perhaps another process has deleted the file. Perhaps the FileName argument has invalid path information. For whatever reason, the assertion will notify you that the assumption is invalid.

> Don't use code such as Len(Dir(FileName)) > 0. Rewrite code like that with a function that names exactly what the code does. It is preferable to wrap code such as Len(Dir(FileName)) > 0 in a function wrapper, such as FileExists(ByVal FileName As String). Such a revision makes code much more readable.
>
> The revision described is an example of a refactoring. The preceding example of refactoring is referred to as an *extract method*.

Instead of putting a breakpoint on the If…Then statement, you can place the assertion there and worry about it only if the assertion fails. You can test code much more quickly if the code stops only when something is wrong.

Clearly, you can put a conditional breakpoint on the line of code containing the test, but you need the editor to be running for a breakpoint to be useful. The assertion travels with the code; the breakpoint does not. Both the breakpoint and the assertion are useful, but only the assertion is a self-documenting stipulation.

Contract Programming

Contract programming is a style of programming that is especially effective when working in teams. A *contract* is a stipulation that certain prespecified conditions must occur and that the code works correctly if those conditions are met. For example, if you write a function that appends text to a file, you might stipulate that the user of the function must ensure that the file exists, because the function doesn't do it.

Such a stipulation is a contract. The `FileExists` contract allows you to focus only on the update, keeping the update smaller than it would be if you had to verify that the file exists, too. How do you stipulate a contract? Well, one way is to write a comment and hope that it is read. A better way is to write an assertion. If the assertion fails, the programmer who forgot to check for the file's existence will see your assertion and, in effect, read the contract.

Use assertions to enforce contract-style programming. This is an effective technique for single programmers because it reminds you of preconditions that you set for the code. Also, contract programming is a great technique for groups of programmers working together or remotely, because contracts delegate responsibility and eliminate redundant effort.

Reusing the Debugging Techniques

Test code, like all code, has to be debugged. It is not my intention that you write `Trace`, `Trap`, and `Assert` methods every time you start a new module or program. Instead, write them once, export the module as `Debug.bas`, and import `Debug.bas` into every program you write.

You can use the functions themselves to make sure you get the implementation of each correct. This way, removing bugs will be easier from now on.

Using Compiler Directives

It would be a mistake if we went this far and I allowed you to use the debugging tools incorrectly. It is important to remember that code has a shelf life beyond when you originally write it. This means that you will likely have to trap, trace, and debug your code again at a later date.

If you write good debug code but then strip it out before you make your program available to other users, you will have to write the debug code all over again when you modify your program. What a drag! Instead use conditionally compiled code and let the compiler remove the code or leave it in.

A *compiler directive* is an instruction to the compiler to include or not include code. A compiler directive is preceded by the pound symbol (#). You can define constant values as compiler constants and use these constants to conditionally compile your code. Therefore, you can define a #const compiler directive and wrap debug code in an #If #Then compiler directive, disabling or enabling the code based on the value of the compiler constant.

> The code If…Then is not the same as #If…Then. The former is runtime code, and the latter is compile-time code.

Instead of removing debug code, you can wrap it in a compiler directive and modify the value of the directive #const. The compiler will automatically include or not include the code, based on the value of the compiler constant and the conditional compilation test. Listing 17.3 demonstrates using a constant and a conditional test to include or not include debug code.

LISTING 17.3   Using Conditional Compilation

```
1:  Sub Test()
2:    #Const DebuggingOn = True
3:    #If DebuggingOn Then
4:      Debug.Assert BooleanValue
5:    #Endif
6:  End Sub
```

ANALYSIS Listing 17.3 demonstrates a technically correct use of compiler directives. Because DebuggingOn is True, line 4 will actually end up in the compiled program. If DebuggingOn were False, line 4 would not end up in the compiled program. Regardless of the value of DebuggingOn, the compiler code in lines 2, 3, and 5 is not compiled into the program.

Although Listing 17.3 is technically correct, it demonstrates poor usage of compiler directives. The reason is that you would have to write the #If test everywhere you had used the Assert statement. For this reason, it is best to write a separate subroutine for Assert, implement it with Debug.Assert, and place the conditional code inside the new Assert subroutine. Listing 17.4 demonstrates the best way to use the compiler directives.

LISTING 17.4   A Better Way to Use Assert

```
1:   #Const DebugginOn = True ' or False
2:   Sub Assert( ByVal Test As Boolean, ByVal FileName As String,
3:   ➡ByVal AssertNumber AS Long )
4:       #If DebuggingOn Then
5:             Debug.Assert Test
6:       #End If
7:   End Sub
```

ANALYSIS   The drawback with this method is that you will have to look in the call stack or examine the FileName and AssertNumber arguments to determine where Assert has failed. However, this is the only drawback, and this method is much easier than writing three lines of code for every line of debug code (instead of just one line of debug code).

> Assert works well in the C and C++ programming languages because these languages implement Assert as a macro. Therefore, the Assert code is automatically placed at the location of the call to Assert. VBA does not include macro capabilities. (Don't confuse preprocessor macros with Access macros; they are different things.) In this context, I am not referring to Access macros. Rather, I am referring to macros as an extension of compiler directives.

To view the call stack (remember that the program will stop when it hits the line Debug.Assert), select View, Call Stack. The second-from-the-top item in the call stack is the line of code that has failed the assertion. Assuming that I call the Assert subroutine from a subroutine named SomeCodeToTest, where Test equals False, the call stack would look like the one in Figure 17.1.

FIGURE 17.1

The call stack when an assertion fails from a subroutine named SomeCodeToTest.

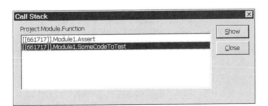

The nature of a call stack is that entries are placed in the stack in reverse order, so the last item called is the topmost item in the stack. Function and subroutine calls are the items placed in a stack. Therefore, every time a function or subroutine calls another function or subroutine, an entry goes into the stack. By clicking an item in the call stack (refer to Figure 17.1) and then clicking the Show button, you can go to the line of code where the code branched. Therefore, by clicking `Module1.SomeCodeToTest` in the call stack shown, the cursor would be placed on the line of code containing the `Assert` call.

Conditional code eliminates the need to strip debug code. Write debug code and leave it in; let the compiler remove the debug code from your program before you make it available to other users, such as your co-workers. The debug code can be turned on or off by changing the state of the compiler directive, and only one change is necessary.

If you write the conditionally compiled code inside a function or subroutine, you only have to write it once per subroutine or function. Another added benefit to leaving debug code in place is that debug code documents the code you have tested and how you have tested it. A completely revised `Debug.bas` module appears in Listing 17.5.

LISTING 17.5   `Debug.bas`—A Complete Debugging Module

```
 1:  Option Compare Database
 2:  Option Explicit
 3:  #Const DebuggingOn = True
 4:  Private Sub DoTrap(ByVal FileName As String, ByVal TrapNumber As Long)
 5:      Debug.Print "Trapped: " & FileName & "(" & TrapNumber & ")"
 6:      Stop
 7:  End Sub
 8:  Sub Trap(ByVal FileName As String, ByVal TrapNumber As Long)
 9:      #If DebuggingOn Then
10:          Call DoTrap(FileName, TrapNumber)
11:      #End If
12: End Sub
13: Private Sub DoTrace(ByVal FileName As String,
14: ➥ByVal TraceMessage As String, ByVal TraceNumber As Long)
15:      Dim Output As String
16:      Output = "Traced: " & FileName & "(" & TraceNumber & ") on " &
17:      ➥ Now & vbCrLf & _
18:          TraceMessage & vbCrLf
19:      Debug.Print Output
20: End Sub
21: Sub Trace(ByVal FileName As String, ByVal TraceMessage As String,
➥ByVal TraceNumber As Long)
22:      #If DebuggingOn Then
23:          Call DoTrace(FileName, TraceMessage, TraceNumber)
24:      #End If
25: End Sub
26: Private Sub DoAssert(ByVal Test As Boolean, ByVal FileName As String,
➥ByVal AssertNumber As Long)
27:      Debug.Assert Test
28: End Sub
29: Sub Assert(ByVal Test As Boolean, ByVal FileName As String,
➥ByVal AssertNumber As Long)
30:      #If DebuggingOn Then
```

LISTING 17.5 continued

```
31:         Call DoAssert(Test, FileName, AssertNumber)
32:     #End If
33: End Sub
```

As mentioned before, I prefer very short functions and subroutines. If you look at Listing 17.5, you will see that no function is more than two or three lines in length. I separated the conditional compilation code from the implementation code so that DoAssert implements Assert, and so on.

I have met a few programmers who are vehemently opposed to this level of decomposition. I use this style of coding based on the divide-and-conquer principle of warfare: Divide a problem into very simple parts, and every problem becomes easy to fix.

ANALYSIS In Listing 17.5, I separated the implementation of the debug code from the conditional compilation code. This would ultimately enable me to use the debug code if I wanted to, even if debugging is off. However, I declared the implementation versions as Private subroutines, prohibiting their accidental use outside the module in which they are declared. (Read Hour 21 for more on using keywords such as Private.)

Making Debug Code Read-Only

Debug code should be read-only code. In other words, debug code should not change the value of data. What this means in application terms is that you should not modify code in a conditional compiler directive that won't get modified when the compiler directive is toggled. Also, you should avoid executing code in a conditional compiler directive that won't get executed when the directive is toggled back on.

Either of the practices mentioned will cause your program to behave erratically because you will ultimately have a different program when the conditional code is enabled versus when it is disabled. The meaning of the code should be the same whether or not debugging code is compiled in.

Development Versus Deployment Error Handling

Development error-handling code is intended to let you, the programmer, know at the earliest possible opportunity when something is wrong. Deployment error-handling code is intended to make the program run correctly even when things go wrong and, in a worst-case scenario, exit gracefully.

Often, this means that you will duplicate your debug code alongside your runtime code. For example, if a file must exist before it can be opened, then write an assertion and the if conditional statement which both check to ensure the file exists. The assertion tells you, the programmer, if the calling procedure sent a valid file. The If Then test ensures that the program behaves correctly for the end user. Here's an example:

```
Call Assert( FileExists(FileName), "ModuleName", 1 )
If( FileExists(FileName)) Then
        ' Do something
Else
        ' let the user pick the file or something else
End If
```

The assertion will let you know that something is wrong while you're developing, and the If Then conditional test will allow your program to recover even after the debug code is stripped out by the compiler.

Summary

Programming can be hard enough. If you have programmed for even a short time, you've experienced putting in long hours while accomplishing relatively little. To reverse that and become a hyperproductive programmer requires solid problem-solving techniques, consistency, and practice.

In this hour, you learned about some methodical ways to eradicate bugs from your code. If you apply these techniques consistently, you will become a hyperproductive programmer. Rules of the road include keeping code simple, writing debug code at the same time you write your production code, leaving debug code in place, and using compiler directives to toggle debug code on and off.

The debugging strategies in this hour are tried and true. When used in conjunction with modern coding environments, such as the Visual Basic editor, you'll be writing bulletproof code in no time. Definitive signs of progress will include fewer syntax errors at compile time, followed by fewer bugs at testing time, and ultimately better, more reliable software.

There is a story about a tourist in the Big Apple who stops one of New York's finest and asks, "How do I get to Carnegie Hall?" The cop replies wryly, "Practice, practice, practice!" Practice applying these techniques, and programming will be a pleasurable, success-filled endeavor for you, too. The following "Q&A" and "Workshop" sections will help you get to Carnegie Hall.

Q&A

Q Does VBA include debug functions already?

A Yes. The `Debug` object includes `Print` and `Assert`. The `Print` method can be used to implement tracing, and `Assert` can be used to implement assertions. I recommend that you wrap these two methods in a subroutine. This will allow you to modify the interface and strip the code out with a compiler directive.

Q Why can't I pass the line number to the debug subroutines you described?

A Line numbers and preprocessor macros would be great. Unfortunately, neither is supported in VBA.

Q Are there any more functions I can implement to facilitate debugging?

A Yes. I have found using a modified `Trace` function that writes to a dialog box and one that writes to a file to be useful over the years. The file-logging version makes a useful auditing mechanism.

Q What about logging errors to a database?

A A good idea. Of course, this will slow your program down some, but logging to a database is an excellent auditing mechanism. In fact, it is exactly what Microsoft does in the Windows 2000 operating system. When you have an interface (subroutines and functions) for tracking defects, you can implement all kinds of useful tools. Consider a lookup table that converts generic system errors to user-friendly, plain English text as an example.

Workshop

The Workshop includes quiz questions designed to help you test your understanding of the material covered and exercises to help put what you've learned to practice. You will find the answers to the quiz and exercises in Appendix A, "Answers."

Quiz

1. What is the name of the object that contains basic debugging capabilities?
2. What two methods does the object from question 1 offer in support of debugging?
3. What is a good security use for tracing?
4. Should debug code be removed with the editor or the compiler before you ship your program?

Exercises

1. Implement a function that returns `True` or `False` based on whether a file exists.

2. Create a scaffold to test the implementation of the function you write in in exercise 1.

3. Write a version of `Trace` that writes output to a text file.

Hour **18**

Adding Code to Handle Errors

Hour 17, "Removing Bugs," taught you how to hunt down, find, and remove bugs in your program. This hour will teach you how to handle the errors in your program that aren't bugs. It's important to understand this distinction: Bugs are problems in the code, such as syntax errors, that interrupt execution of the code or produce incorrect results. On the other hand, if a user enters an invalid date into your program, that constitutes a user error. User errors are not the same as bugs. Users make mistakes, and you need to gently encourage them to do better, or, compensate so your users will not have to try so hard.

Other kinds of errors occur when a user tries to open a file that was deleted, when your program runs out of disk space, or when an Internet connection is dropped. These kinds of errors constitute runtime errors, not bugs. In this hour, you will learn how to write code that handles runtime errors.

If you have never taken a programming course, and this book is your first brush with programming, this hour is definitely for you. Similarly, if you took programming classes more than four or five years ago, this hour is for you, too. Error handling has evolved significantly in the last few years. I will show you how to write robust code, using modern runtime error-handling techniques. In this hour, you will learn:

- How to handle exceptions
- How to write error-handling blocks
- How to write resource-protection blocks
- How to work with the Err object and raise errors

Comparing Error-Handling Styles

When I was in college, I was taught that error handling meant writing If conditional statements that tested for error conditions. The idea was that you could write enough conditional tests up front, before any code ran, to ensure that data was valid and your code was in a valid state. This wasn't wrong; rather, it represented the state of technological innovation and understanding at the time. An alternate method of handling errors existed, but it hadn't been implemented in many mainstream languages. That alternate method is *exception handling*.

NEW TERM   An *exception* is an error condition. Therefore, an *exception handler* is code that handles an error condition.

The software development industry, as a collective body, has revised its thinking on robust code. *Robust code* is code that uses exception handling instead of If conditional checks. This doesn't mean every programmer uses exception handling, but exception handling is the preferred methodology. First, let's review conditional error checking.

Conditional Error Checking: The Old Way

Conditional error checking means you write all your code, testing for error conditions in advance. If you write If conditional tests for all the error conditions you can anticipate, it is exactly like walking a high wire without a net. When the human cannonball knocks you off the tight rope, you will wish you had the net. Exception handlers comprise the net.

An added concern is that programmers sometimes get lazy and forget to check for errors. What's more, the practice of performing all error checking upfront means that your program takes a performance hit—in the form of the time it takes to run the error-checking code—even when everything is right.

In the past, when an unhandled error condition did occur, programs crashed. Usually they stopped accepting user input, stopped running, or the computer rebooted. These conditions are sometimes jokingly referred to as *vapor lock*. But, all joking aside, if it's your data that is lost, vapor lock is not funny.

Because programmers can't know everything that might go wrong, because they sometimes get lazy, and because upfront error checking incurs a cost, a better way to handle errors was sought and found.

Exception Handling: A Better Way

Exception handling works differently from conditional error checking. The idea behind exception handling is that instead of playing 20 questions, you stretch a net under the tight rope. Exception handlers provide blanket coverage for all errors and only take action when an error occurs.

This means you don't spend time on conditional checking up front, and your code can catch every error. Because error handlers catch every error, a default behavior can be defined. The default behavior for most exception handling is to return the program to the state it was in before the error occurred. Although this won't eliminate the error, it may keep the computer from going into vapor lock.

In addition to providing default behavior, exception handlers enable you to define the safety net. The handling behavior involves some code that attempts to resolve the error condition. If you can resolve the condition with the handling code, you can also write code to pick up where you left off.

If you cannot solve the problem, you can still choose to notify the user and shut down the program gracefully. A graceful termination of the program can often preclude serious loss of data and preserve good will.

One of the jobs I do involves evaluating code for other companies. If code returns error codes and has a lot of upfront error checking, I give it a lower rating. If code uses exception handling, I give it a higher rating. Code that uses exception handling is more robust.

As I have said in earlier hours, much of what constitutes good programming is subjective. You can successfully write good code using conditional error checking, but it is unlikely that it will be as good as code that uses exception handling effectively. Any programmer worth his salt will use exception handling instead of error codes.

The capability to catch all errors, provide a default behavior, handle the error or shut down gracefully, and only run the error code in an error condition makes exception handling far superior to conditional error handling. The collective industry has voted, and exception handling won by a landslide.

The bad news is that VBA doesn't support full-blown exception handling, yet. The good news is that Visual Basic and, subsequently, VBA support a form of error trapping that is pretty good and can be used in a way that resembles exception handling.

> Visual Basic.NET supports structured exception handling.

Throughout the rest of the hour, I will demonstrate effective techniques for using the error trapping supported by VBA. What you will learn to write in the following sections will be effective in helping you produce robust code—and that's what counts.

Writing Error Handlers

For our purposes, an error-handling block is equivalent to an exception handler. Microsoft doesn't use the term *exception handling*, so I won't either. (I suspect that Microsoft doesn't use this term because error handling in VBA is not true exception handling.) Currently, in VBA, the correct terminology is *error handling*, so I will stick with this convention when referring to the code you write.

An error-handling block has a beginning, a middle, and an end. When writing an error handler, you place it before the first line of code in a function or subroutine that might cause an error. The actual handling code goes at the end of the function or subroutine—unlike conditional code, which is written at the beginning of a procedure. Conditional code is always run; error-handling code is run only when an error occurs.

Starting an Error Handler

An error handler is started with the On Error Goto statement. The syntax for On Error Goto is

```
On Error Goto Label
```

> I will use *procedure* to mean function, subroutine, or method for the rest of the hour, unless the distinction is relevant.

You literally write On Error Goto and a text label that indicates the line where your error-handling code is located. Error-handling code must be defined in the same procedure as the On Error Goto statement. By convention, error-handling labels and code are written at the end of a procedure. Listing 18.1 demonstrates an error block with a label.

LISTING 18.1 An Empty Error Handler

```
1: Sub Test()
2:     On Error Goto Except
3: Except:
4: End Sub
```

> I consistently use Except for error labels. This eliminates the need to contrive clever labels. However, you can use the same label only once per function. Therefore, if you have another error handler in the same function, you can use Except1, Except2, and so on. However, if you keep your procedures short then you will not need too many error handling labels.

ANALYSIS Line 2 contains the start of the error handler with the label Except. Line 3 is the actual label. Notice the use of the colon (:); you must use a colon to indicate a label. The Goto statement does not require the colon. After line 2 is run, any error that occurs causes the program execution to immediately jump to the line containing the label indicated in the On Error Goto statement.

Naming Labels

Be consistent with your label names. I used to use uppercase labels, but uppercase text can look awful. Therefore, I consistently use Except for the error-handling block; this word is distinct enough that it doesn't need to be adorned with special letter casing. You might use a specific name or name-casing combination for labels, but remember to be consistent. Consistent code is more professional, and consistency enables you to write code more quickly.

Writing Your Exit Statement

Listing 18.1 has a shortcoming. If you write the code for Test in Listing 18.1 between lines 2 and 3, as you should, the error-handling code will always be run. Remember, you want error-handling code to run only when an error occurs. Listing 18.2 demonstrates a revision of the code, which involves adding the Exit statement.

18

LISTING **18.2**   Demonstrates the basic error handling code.

```
1: Sub Test()
2:     On Error Goto EXCEPT
3:     Exit Sub
4: Except:
5: End Sub
```

ANALYSIS Listing 18.2 is correct. When you write an error handler, it is a good idea to write all three lines—the Goto line, the Exit line, and the label line, followed by the colon—at the same time. This way, you won't forget to write the Exit statement. If you forget the Exit statement, your error-handling code will always run, but it will probably induce errors instead of resolve them.

The Exit statement is specific to the procedure type. If the procedure is a subroutine, you write Exit Sub. Use Exit Function for functions and Exit Property for Property methods. (Read Hour 21, "Class Programming Basics," for more on Property methods.)

In Listing 18.2, you write the code that implements the subroutine between lines 2 and 3 and the code that implements the error handler between lines 4 and 5.

General Rules for Error Handlers

Only write an error-handling block if you actually have an idea about the kinds of errors you want to handle and how you want to handle them.

The default behavior implemented by VBA displays a dialog box with the error and plays a warning WAV file—usually a bell sound. If you do not have a better solution to the error than the default behavior, don't write an error handler. An exception to this rule occurs when you want to log the error.

If you are creating an audit trail for your application, you might want basic error handling to log the error, in addition to executing the error-handling code.

Default error-handling behavior only occurs when you don't write an error handler. If you write an error handler and also want to mimic the default behavior, use the Err object to access the error information. See the section "Using the Err Object" for more information.

Clearing the Error Handler

Error handlers have function-level scope. When you write an error handler, it is only valid within that function. If you want to clear error handling at the function level, use the following command:

```
On Error Goto 0
```

This command disables any previous error handlers and clears the properties of the `Err` object. (Refer to the section "Using the `Err` Object," later in this hour, for more information.)

Writing Silent Error Handlers

A *silent error handler* is an error handler that simply proceeds to the next line rather than jumping to an error-handling block. A silent error handler uses the `Resume Next` clause:

```
On Error Resume Next
```

The preceding code is interpreted to mean that if an error occurs on any line after the `On Error Resume Next` statement, simply go to the next line after the line where the error occurred. However, because `Resume Next` is still an error handler, you will not get the default error-handling behavior; instead, `Resume Next` will gloss over any errors and keep on trucking.

You should seldom use `Resume Next` to simply gloss over errors. If it is valid in your solution to just continue processing on an error, `On Error Goto Resume Next` is what you want.

An example of when to use `Resume Next` is when you are copying data from recordsets, and individual fields might be null. If it is okay to ignore null field data in your program, `Resume Next` works nicely.

Using Resume in an Error-Handling Block

The `Resume` command, by itself, is useful in error-handling blocks. For example, if you handle an error successfully and want to retry the same line of code again, you can use the `Resume` command in an error handler to do it. `Resume` alone runs the line of code that caused the error, so make sure you resolve the error before you use `Resume`.

Listing 18.3 provides an example of using the `Resume` command. As you will see, the front-loaded code is very simple. It is only when things go wrong that the code does anything special.

LISTING 18.3 Using the `Resume` Command

```
1:  Sub Test()
2:    Call DeleteFile("somefile")
3:  End Sub
4:
5  Sub RaiseError(ByRef Err As Object)
6:    Call Err.Raise(Err.Number, Err.Source, Err.Description, _
```

LISTING 18.3   continued

```
 7:    Err.HelpFile, Err.HelpContext)
 8: End Sub
 9:
10: Function FileExists(ByVal FileName As String) As Boolean
11:    FileExists = Len(Dir(FileName)) > 0
12: End Function
13:
14: Sub DeleteFile(ByVal FileName As String)
15:    On Error GoTo EXCEPT
16:    Kill FileName
17:    Exit Sub
18: Except:
19:    Const FILE_NOT_FOUND = 53
20:    If (Err.Number <> FILE_NOT_FOUND) Then Call RaiseError(Err)
21:    If (MsgBox(Err.Description & "(" & FileName & ") try again?", _
22:      vbRetryCancel) = vbRetry) Then
23:      FileName = InputBox("Enter file path:", "File Name", "")
24:      If (FileExists(FileName)) Then Resume
25:    End If
26: End Sub
```

ANALYSIS Lines 1 through 3 test the subroutine `DeleteFile`. Lines 5 through 8 are optional. I could have placed the code on line 6 or line 20, but I might want to re-use the `RaiseError` subroutine, and it makes the error handler shorter. Line 10 through 12 is my implementation of `FileExists`. Because this function was written in the last hour, I do not have to write it again. Lines 14 through 26 implement `DeleteFile`.

Line 16 is the heart of `DeleteFile`. I could call `Kill FileName` in my code right where I need it, but I would have to clutter my code with error handling. It is worth wrapping up `DeleteFile` in my implementation because I have reasonable error-handling code that I want to bundle with deleting a file. Now, everywhere I want to delete a file, I only need the call to the `DeleteFile` subroutine. `DeleteFile` presumes everything will go all right. It is only when something goes wrong that extra code is needed.

Lines 18 through 26 of Listing 18.3 handle any errors. If the error is not Error 53 (File Not Found), the error is raised again. If the error is Error 53, the user is prompted to enter a new filename. If the user enters a file that exists, the `Resume` statement on line 24 retries line 16.

I could have written the code as

```
If( FileExists(FileName)) Then Kill FileName
```

Many other versions of this code could be written. For example, I could add an `Else` condition that enables the user to input the file, checks for the file's existence, and then kills the file. Any such variation is not wrong—it's just less right. For instance, what happens if the file still doesn't exist? Would I add a loop to keep trying perhaps? How about if the file exists but is opened by another user, or what if the file is read-only?

There are times when conditional checking is adequate. If you want to verify one condition or a set of specific conditions, a conditional test is acceptable. For example, you might want to validate whether an expression is a valid date. If all you care about is the answer to that question, you should write code such as IsDate(*expression*), where *expression* is the date in question.

As a general rule, if you want answers to specific questions, use conditional statements; if you want general fault tolerance, use error handling. Most of the time you'll want general fault tolerance.

A number of things could preclude you from successfully deleting the file on the first try. That's why error handlers are useful. An error handler presumes everything will work but enables you to write code in case something goes wrong. The Resume statement allows you to rerun the code after a problem is cleared up.

Using Resume Next in an Error-Handling Block

The Resume Next command can be used on a Goto line as a silent error handler, or it can be used in the error-handling block. Resume Next continues the line of code after the line that caused the error.

Using the preceding example, suppose you wanted to delete an old file before you add new data. Perhaps the file is a daily log file. You could write this:

```
On Error Resume Next
Kill FileName
' Process File
```

The old file is deleted if it exists and the program continues processing normally. The Resume Next command ensures that cleaning up the old file doesn't cause the program to stop if the old file doesn't happen to exist; the old file is not central to the algorithm in this example, so we don't want general housekeeping to slow down processing.

Using the Err Object

The Err object is maintained internally. When an error occurs, the Err object's properties are set, providing you with a means to determine what went wrong. The Err object has two methods, Clear and Raise, and six properties. The methods of the Err object describe the things you can do with it, and the properties describe the last error condition. The six properties are `Description`, `HelpContext`, `HelpFile`, `Source`, `Number`, and `LastDLLError`.

Err Object Properties

The `Description` property is a text description of the error. The `HelpContext` property is the number of the Help context item in an associated Help file. The `HelpFile` property is the name of a Help file; you can pass an argument for `HelpFile` if you are sure a Help file exists. You can assign `HelpFile` and `HelpContext` when raising an error. If you do this, users can press F1 when an error message is raised. This way, help for that error will be displayed.

The `Source` property is a string containing the name of the object or the application that is the source of the error. The `Number` property is the error number. This may be an error number that is meaningful to VBA, such as Error 53 (File Not Found) in Listing 18.3. It can also be an error number you define.

A separate tool for DLLs is available. The `LastDLLError` function returns errors returned by DLLs written in Visual Basic.

Err Object Methods

The `Clear` method is called as `Err.Clear`. This clears the last error. `Clear` is automatically called when the program executes a `Resume`, `Exit`, or another `Goto` statement.

The `Raise` method has the following syntax:

```
Call Err.Raise(Number [,Source, Description, HelpFile,
➡ HelpContext])
```

At a minimum, you must pass an error number. If you pass a number, such as 54, this will raise the error associated with the error number. (Error 54 is Bad File Mode.) If you want to raise a user-defined error with the error number only, write

```
Call Err.Raise(vbObjectError + number)
```

where *number* is the number of your error. You only have to supply an error number with `Err.Raise`. The Source argument is usually an object or module name in which the error occurred. `Description` is used for a textual description that explains the error. `HelpFile` and `HelpContext` are used when you have a Help file and context ID that you want to associate with the error. Listing 18.3, line 4, demonstrates the mechanics of raising an error.

There are two circumstances in which you will use the `Err` object: The first is in responding to errors raised when an error occurs, and the second is when you want to raise an error to let a user or another programmer know that some preconditions haven't been met. In Listing 18.3, I re-raise the error if it is a File Not Found error. `Delete` was intentionally designed to only handle File Not Found errors. All other errors are re-raised.

Using Error Handlers to Validate User Input

Use an error handler when you want to write a block of code that recovers from an error. In this hour, you have already seen a couple of examples showing you how to do this. You can also use an error handler for simple validation. For example, the user may add some data as string data but the value is of another type. You can use a conversion function to validate the input data and an error handler to catch the error when the data is unconvertible. Consider Listing 18.4, which uses error handling to determine leap years.

LISTING 18.4 Using Error Handling to Determine Leap Years

```
 1:  Sub Test2()
 2:    MsgBox IsLeapYear(2000)
 3:  End Sub
 4:
 5:  Function IsLeapYear(ByVal Year As Integer) As Boolean
 6:
 7:    On Error GoTo Except
 8:
 9:    IsLeapYear = True
10:    Dim ADate As Date
11:    ADate = CDate("2/29/" & Year)
12:    Exit Function
13:
14: Except:
15:    IsLeapYear = False
16:
17: End Function
```

ANALYSIS Listing 18.4 effectively determines whether a year is a leap year with some sleight of hand. (Lines 1 through 3 are a test subroutine.) Line 7 sets the error handler. Line 8 initializes the default return value to `True`. The function is optimistic about the year being a leap year. Line 11 appends the year to the 29th of February. The `CDate` function attempts to convert `2/29/year` to a date. If the entire date is valid, the function exits and the year is a valid leap year; if not, the error-handling block properly returns `False`.

18

There is also an `IsDate` function that returns a Boolean: `True` if the expression is a valid date and `False` otherwise.

Clearly you could write code to parse the day, month, and year. An algorithm exists to calculate the leap year. I had to find my copy of *C Programmer's Toolkit* by Jack Purdum, published in 1989, and convert the C algorithm to VBA. Listing 18.5 contains an actual leap year algorithm, ported from C.

LISTING 18.5   A Leap Year Algorithm Ported from C

```
1:  Function LeapYear( ByVal Year As Integer ) As Boolean
2:      LeapYear = (Year Mod 4 = 0) And ((Year Mod 100 <> 0) Or Year Mod 400 =
0)
3:  End Function
```

Attempting to convert the data to the right type inside of an exception handler is a down-and-dirty way of validating data.

Leap years are evenly divisible by 4 or 400, except years that are divisible by 100 years. It is likely that the CDate function has the leap year algorithm on line 2 of listing 18.5 in it. In the event you don't have a copy of Jack's book, you can use the trick in Listing 18.4.

Creating the Resource-Protection Block Idiom

Another use for error handlers is to protect resources. In programming, a resource worth protecting is anything that is in limited supply. There are only so many file handles available, only so much memory, and a limited amount of disk space. If you don't make sure your program cleans up after itself, you are likely to run out of these precious resources.

A resource-protection block refers to an exception handler where the handler part is always executed. Code to release a resource is placed in such a block. Although VBA doesn't support this idiom directly, you can implement resource-protection blocks. In VBA, you are less likely to run out of memory because of unreleased objects (as you might in C++, for example), but there will be times that you will want to ensure a file or database is closed, and cleaning up memory is a good idea.

The resource-protection block is implemented just as any other error handler would be. However, because you want the code in the handler block to run every time, you eliminate the Exit statement before the label. That's it. Listing 18.6 demonstrates a resource-protection block that always ensures a file is closed, whether an error occurs or not.

LISTING 18.6 A Demonstration of a Resource-Protection Block

```
1:  Sub ProtectedResource()
2:    On Error GoTo Finally
3:    Dim Handle As Double
4:    Handle = FreeFile
5:    Open "C:\autoexec.bat" For Input As #Handle
6:    Dim Line AS String
7:    Do While (EOF(Handle) = False)
8:      Line Input #Handle, Line
9:      Debug.Print Line
10:   Loop
11: Finally:
12:   Close #Handle
13: End Sub
```

You may not find the resource-protection block used by many VB programmers. Programmers who have programmed in languages with structured exception handling are more likely to use this technique. Microsoft has acknowledged its practicality by supporting structured exception handling in Visual Basic.NET, and you might anticipate structured exception handling showing up in VBA eventually.

The fact that the method is simple and only needs one error handler is supported by strategies described in the subject of refactoring. Again, you may encounter many long, convoluted procedures, but that does not mean long procedures are good.

ANALYSIS Line 2 establishes the start of the protected resource. In Listing 18.6, I am making sure the file handle is returned to the system and the file is closed. Lines 3 and 4 obtain a valid file handle. Line 5 opens the file. Lines 6 through 10 represent some processing (here I am writing the contents to the Immediate window). Line 12 always gets executed whether the function is successful or not. The file represented by the handle is always closed. Notice that there is no Exit statement before the label on line 11. By convention, I use the word Finally to distinguish protected resources from error handlers.

Reviewing the Debug Object

You have seen the Debug object used throughout this book. The Debug object is a global resource. There is only one Debug object. Debug is useful at design time. It has two methods and no properties. You can call the Print method with string data that you want to write to the Immediate window, and you can call the Assert method, which pauses code execution if the Boolean argument passed to Assert is False.

 One global object is referred to as a *Singleton*. Just in case you get the question "What is a Singleton?" on *Who Wants to Be a Millionaire*.

In the last hour, I demonstrated an extended use of Assert. You will find the Debug object's Print and Assert methods useful every time you write code.

Summary

You can do several things to ensure you build a good, quality product. For example, spend some time designing what you are going to build before you begin writing code. Keep your code simple and reuse as much of it as possible. Test your code, test it some more, and after that, have someone else test it. Finally, for all other problems, employ the techniques you learned in this hour.

If you have a single, specific test, use a conditional statement. If you want blanket protection against anything that might go wrong, use an error-handling block. Write an error handler if you can provide any error handling beyond the default mechanism. Remember, by default, VBA displays an error message notifying the operator that an error has occurred. If you can't offer more than that, rely on the default error handling. Use the resource-protection block idiom to ensure that files and recordsets get closed and objects are set to Nothing.

Use the Err object to determine what is going wrong inside your application, and, instead of returning error codes, use the Raise method to notify users of your code about error conditions. Follow these guidelines, and you and your users will have fewer headaches and instances of vapor lock. The "Q&A" and "Workshop" sections that follow will help you further your understanding of the topics covered in this hour.

Q&A

Q What is the `Err` object?

A The `Err` object contains information about the last program or DLL runtime error.

Q Where can I find information about error numbers?

A Look in the Help reference under Trappable Errors.

Q What is the difference between protecting a resource and error handling?

A Not much. Error handling involves code that is written to handle errors. Resource protection involves code that is written to ensure that your cleanup code is always run, too. They are both implemented using the `On Error Goto` statement.

Q Should every function have an error handler?

A No. Only those functions that are critical to your application and are likely to have an error for which you can define a resolution should have an error handler.

Q What do I do about code that I do not have a resolution for?

A The default error-handling mechanism and Windows 2002 are much more robust than earlier designs. Error handling is ultimately designed to help your program run better, but it should also help to limit outright crashes. The default error-handling mechanism and Windows do a pretty good job of protecting against the latter. With practice, you will be writing good, robust code.

Workshop

The Workshop includes quiz questions designed to help you test your understanding of the material covered and exercises to help put what you've learned to practice. You will find the answers to the quiz and exercises in Appendix A, "Answers."

Quiz

1. What two arguments must you provide to associate Help information with an error?

2. What is the name of the object that sends output to the Immediate window while you're testing your code?

3. What is the difference between a resource-protection block and an error-handling block?

4. Can you raise errors? If so, when should you do it?

Exercises

1. Write a resource-protection block to set a `Recordset` variable, `RS`, to `Nothing`.

2. Write code for Listing 18.3 that prompts the user to delete a file set to read-only.

3. Write a line of code that handles a case where a file does not exist. The line of code should raise a user error with error number 100 from Module1.

PART VII

Creating Access User Interfaces

Hour

HOUR 19

Creating Custom Forms and Reports

In just 19 hours, you are ready to tie together into a user interface and a program everything you have learned. In some ways, the user interface is one of the most exciting aspects of programming because this is what everyone sees.

Access has built-in support for a graphical user interface. This distinction is worth noting because, just a few years ago, creating a graphical user interface was pretty difficult stuff; creating a Windows user interface was left up to technical gurus who understood C programming and the Windows API in depth.

However, good fortune and timing shine upon us. You will find creating a user interface a comparatively easy task in contrast to writing code that solves business problems. Access 2002 makes creating a user interface a task that you can accomplish using your mouse, and a lot of the initial work can be accomplished using wizards.

This style of programming is called *rapid application development* (RAD); VBA is a great programming language, and Access 2002 is a great RAD tool. In this hour, you will learn how to use Access to build user interfaces and deliver a completed business solution. In particular, you will learn:

- How to use form wizards to get started quickly
- How to customize wizard forms
- How to use properties and events that enable you to define the behaviors of your applications
- How to test and run your application

Using Form Wizards

RAD tools are great because they make it easy to perform common tasks and smooth the process of building applications. If you write good code behind user-friendly graphical user interfaces, you get great programs.

Access 2002 makes it easy to create user-friendly interfaces with little or no code. You can then proceed to write the code that solves the underlying problem for creating an application. When you are just beginning, a good place to start is with the form wizards. The form wizards contain a variety of predefined form styles that you can use to produce a professional-looking user interface in only a few minutes.

NEW TERM   A *form* is an instance of the Form class. The Form class has properties, methods, and events that define its behaviors and capabilities, just as any other object does. In addition, because the Form instance has a visual presence, graphical data is stored in the object. The graphical data defines what the form will look like on your screen. In Windows, all graphical user programming is "form centric"; that is, every visual component is presented on a form.

There are several predefined form wizards that will yield several different styles of forms. Let's go over the different wizards briefly and then jump right in and build a user interface.

An Overview of Each Form Design Type

You have nine choices available to you when creating a new form. You can choose the Design View, the Form Wizard, a Columnar AutoForm, a Tabular AutoForm, a Datasheet AutoForm, the Chart Wizard, the PivotTable AutoForm, or PivotChart AutoForm. The choices are available when you select the Forms button in the Objects View and click the New button. The New Form dialog is shown in Figure 19.1.

FIGURE 19.1

Select a form design type. The wizard types shown will do a lot of the initial work for you.

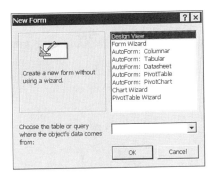

Design View

The Design View opens a blank form. A *form* is the window in Windows; everything visual in Windows programming is presented on or in association with forms. The Design View is for free-style development. You will have to do a lot more legwork if you start with the Design View.

Form Wizard

The Form Wizard presents you with several dialogs in succession. The information you enter in each dialog is used to determine what the final form will look like. The Form Wizard adds all the components to the form and assigns the necessary properties to make the form ready to use.

You will start with the Form Wizard in a moment. Using wizards is a good way to get a jumpstart on the visual part of programming.

Columnar AutoForm

The AutoForm: Columnar Wizard selection creates a form with the data presented in a column.

This is a simple layout. Select AutoForm: Columnar and the table name from the combo box (refer to Figure 19.1) and click OK. In just two steps, you will have a complete graphical interface for the table. The columnar style form is shown in Figure 19.2.

FIGURE 19.2

A columnar style form created by the New Form Columnar AutoForm Wizard.

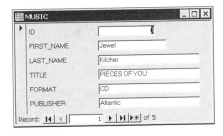

19

Tabular AutoForm

The Tabular AutoForm Wizard works just like the Columnar AutoForm Wizard. Follow these steps to create a Tabular AutoForm:

1. In the database Objects View, click Forms.
2. Click the New button.
3. In the New Form dialog, select the AutoForm: Tabular option (refer to Figure 19.1).
4. Find the prompt Choose the Table or Query Where the Object's Data Comes From. From the combo box to the right of this prompt, choose the table or query that represents the data you want to manage on the form you're creating.
5. Click OK.

That's all there is to it. The first couple steps are identical for all the wizards in the New Form dialog, except the Design View. After completing steps 1 through 5, you have a tabular-style form. To see how easy the process is, try it on one of the sample databases or tables I have defined in previous hours. Take a moment to become familiar with the appearance of the tabular-style form.

Datasheet AutoForm

The AutoForm: Datasheet option creates a form that looks identical to the view you get when you open a table or query using Access. This is the simplest kind of form style. Repeat steps 1 through 5 from the previous section, except select the AutoForm: Datasheet option in step 3, to create a datasheet form.

PivotTable AutoForm

The PivotTable AutoForm Wizard allows you to dynamically configure filter, row, and column fields in a pivot table and rearrange the presentation and organization of the data. The PivotTable View is a powerful means of presenting data. Pivot table data can be added to reports, forms, and Web pages. (Refer to Hour 20, "Creating Data-Aware Web Pages," for examples of using a PivotTable in a data-aware Web page.)

Suppose, for example, you want to create a customizable PivotTable View of the Music Collection database. You could create a PivotTable View showing all recording labels and organize the view by recording artist, including a total of all media by artist. Using the Music Collection database from Hour 15, "Data Programming Made Easy with ADODB," performing the following steps would yield a satisfactory result, as shown in Figure 19.3, with the media count of Johnny Cash selected:

1. Open or create the Music Collection database from Hour 15.
2. In the Objects list, select Forms and click the New button.

FIGURE 19.3

A Music Collection PivotTable with the added total of recordings by artist.

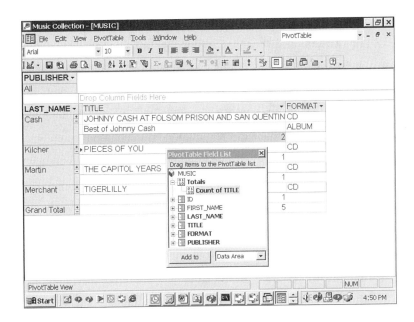

3. In the New Form dialog, select AutoForm: PivotTable and then select the MUSIC table from the combo box. Click OK.

4. Thus far, you have created a blank PivotTable in Design View. The PivotTable Field List should display the list of fields from the MUSIC table. (The PivotTable Field List is shown in Figure 19.3.)

5. Notice the region titled Drop Filter Fields Here. We want to filter on recording labels (PUBLISHERS). From the PivotTable Field List, click and drag the PUBLISHER field to the Drop Filter Fields Here region of the PivotTable form. This will allow you to select which publishers to show in the results. (By default, all publishers are selected.)

6. To group rows by artist, drop the LAST_NAME field into the Drop Row Fields Here region of the PivotTable Design View.

7. To view recording titles and media format, drag and drop the TITLE and FORMAT fields to the Drop Totals or Detail Fields Here region of the PivotTable form. (After step 7, your PivotTable view should appear very similar to Figure 19.3. You will not see the media totals, and your collection will be different from the demo collection, so the field values will be different.)

19

8. Select one of the TITLE fields and click the Sum Σ button (refer to Figure 19.3). Then select the Count option. This will create a count of titles by artist.

9. Close and save the PivotTable to preserve your changes.

Notice the bottom of the view shows the grand total; that is, the total number of titles. The PivotTable allows users to rearrange the view of data to answer questions about the data. The PivotTable allows you to add calculated subtotals, as well as base PivotTable Views on more complex recordsets, such as queries.

PivotChart AutoForm

The PivotChart AutoForm works like the PivotTable AutoForm. PivotCharts allow you to arrange series and axes of data to get a graphical presentation of your data. To switch the example from the last section to a graphical view, select View, PivotChart View to imme-diately see a (very plain) chart indicating the number of recordings byartist. The added benefit is that you can customize the presentation of data in a PivotTable and PivotChart visually and enhance the quality of the view by modifying properties such as color, style, and data format. PivotTables and PivotCharts can be included in forms, Web pages, and reports. To learn more about PivotCharts and PivotTables, refer to Hour 20.

Chart Wizard

The Chart Wizard creates a data-bound form containing a graphical chart. The chart is an object. After the wizard takes care of the basics, you can modify the chart to make the data presentation as basic or as elaborate as you need.

PivotTable Wizard

The PivotTable Wizard uses Excel to create a PivotTable, and then it stores the `PivotTable` object created from your data in a form. A pivot table enables you to dynam-ically modify the way that data is presented. When you change the layout of a pivot table, the results are immediately recalculated.

Creating a Form with the Form Wizard

To demonstrate creating a Form, I will use the MUSIC database created from Hour 15. I chose this database because it will be easy for you to create (if you don't already have it from Hour 15), thus enabling you to follow along. The steps for using the Form Wizard to create the MUSIC table form are identical for all table-based forms. Therefore, if you have some data you have been waiting to use, the steps in this section will help you cre-ate forms for that data, too. Use your own table where I refer to one of the MUSIC data-base tables.

RAD tools are comprised of solutions to well-understood problems, like creating form-based Windows applications. RAD tools make getting projects started easy, because the tools are so good. However, solving problems beyond painting forms is still challenging. You will be more successful if you spend a substantial part of your time defining and understanding the problem and designing a solution, before you begin programming.

Defining the database and painting forms is only a small part of a solution. The code that supports the interaction between user, form, and data is important, but more important is the actual code that solves the original problem.

I will demonstrate the Form Wizard by walking you through each step and providing you with·a screenshot for the major steps required by the wizard. The first step is to choose a database and open the New Form dialog (mentioned at the start of this hour). Let's continue from there. Here are the steps to follow:

1. In the New Form dialog of the MUSIC database, select the Form Wizard.

2. In the Choose Table or Query combo box, select the MUSIC table, as shown in Figure 19.4.

FIGURE 19.4

Selecting the Form Wizard to create a form for the MUSIC database from Hour 15.

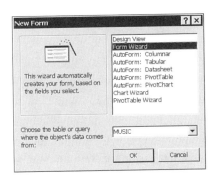

3. Click the OK button to proceed to step 1 of the Form Wizard.

4. The first step of the Form Wizard is to select those fields that will be displayed on your form. Remember, the MUSIC.ID field is an AutoNumber field; therefore, your users will not need to modify it. Using the arrow buttons shown in Figure 19.5, select every column of the MUSIC table except for the ID column.

5. Click Next.

6. In step 2 of the Form Wizard, select a form layout type. Choose the Columnar style, as shown in Figure 19.6, and click Next.

FIGURE 19.5

Selecting the fields to display on the form in step 1 of the Form Wizard.

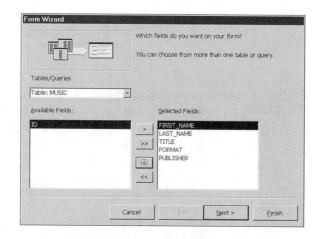

FIGURE 19.6

Selecting the Columnar style form in the Form Wizard.

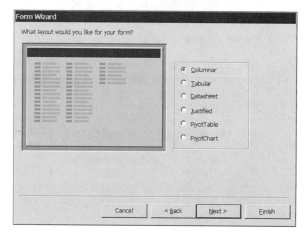

7. The final step enables you to select a style that presents several visual effects. After all the information necessary to create the form has been selected, click Finish to generate the form.

NEW TERM A *control* is the generic term for a visual object. Examples of controls are TextBox, Label, and Form.

Congratulations! The resultant form is shown in Figure 19.7. This form, made up of the form code and the MUSIC table, is an application, albeit a small application. If you set the MUSIC form, shown in Figure 19.7, as the startup form for this database, every time you open the database you run this form. The wizard puts enough controls on the form to enable you to manage data in the associated table.

FIGURE 19.7

The completed Form Wizard form.

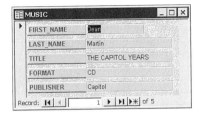

Figure 19.8 points out the features of the completed form. The field names on the left are Label controls, used to indicate the names of the values associated with the controls. The controls on the right half of the form are TextBox controls. The TextBox controls are bound to fields in the MUSIC table. In a graphical user interface, the TextBox control is one of the controls with which users can modify data. Along the bottom is the Navigation control. From left to right, the control enables you to navigate to the first record, navigate to the previous record, display the current record count, navigate to the next record, navigate to the last record, and append a new record.

FIGURE 19.8

The layout of a wizard-created form.

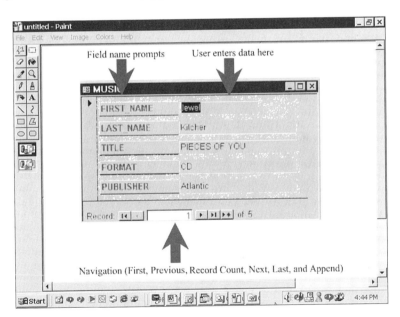

From the View menu in Access 2002, you can toggle between Design, Form, and Datasheet Views. By selecting View, Design View, you can customize the form. The Form View is the mode you want to be in to use the form to manage data. The Datasheet View is identical to the view you see when you open the table, except that only the fields you select in the wizard are available in the Datasheet View.

Using Data-Management Menu Items

In Form View mode, the Access menu has additional menu items that help you manage the data. You can delete, select, find, replace, and go to a record from the Edit menu. You can insert a new record with the Navigation control (refer to Figure 19.8) or use the Insert, New Record command. The Records menu, available in Form View and Datasheet mode, enables you to apply and remove filters and sorts, save the changes to the current record, refresh the recordset, and place the form in data-entry mode. (Select Records, Remove Filter/Sort to exit data-entry mode.)

All the menu items mentioned here are immediate menus, except for the Records, Filter submenus. That means the operation stated in the menu is performed without further input from you when you click the menu.

Filtering Form Records

The Filter submenus offer four possible means of filtering records. (Remember, a filter is equivalent to a WHERE clause on your recordset; it refines the records returned in the set.) You may choose Filter by Form, Filter by Selection, Filter Excluding Selection, and Advanced Filter/Sort.

Using Filter by Form

The Filter by Form option displays a form that looks just like the original wizard form. The data you enter in this form is used in the same manner as a predicate in a query's WHERE clause. For example, in the MUSIC table is a last name field. To use the Filter by Form option on the LAST_NAME field, follow these steps:

1. With the MUSIC form open, select Records, Filter, Filter by Form. The MUSIC: Filter by Form dialog is displayed, as shown in Figure 19.9.

FIGURE 19.9

The MUSIC: Filter by Form dialog.

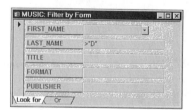

2. You can pick a last name from the combo box next to the LAST_NAME prompt or enter > "D", as shown in Figure 19.9. The filter shown will filter the result set, excluding anyone's name greater than CZZZZZZ....

3. To apply the filter, click Filter, Apply Filter Sort.

When the Filter by Form dialog closes, the recordset will only return those artists whose last name begins with *D* or a letter greater than *D*. To clear the filter, click Records, Remove Filter, Sort.

It is worth pointing out at this point that the Access 2002 menus are context driven. Depending on what operations you are performing, the menus will vary. Menu items germane to available tasks will be displayed, and others will be hidden if they are not available in the current context. For example, in the Form View, there is no Filter menu; however, in the Filter by Form View, a Filter menu is displayed.

Using Filter by Selection

The Records, Filter by Selection menu item is available in the Form View or Datasheet View. Select the data in any text box and click Records, Filter by Selection. Only those records containing the same data in the same field will be in the filtered result set.

Using Filter Excluding Selection

The Records, Filter Excluding Selection menu item is available in the Form View or Datasheet View. Select the data in any text box and click Records, Filter Excluding Selection. Those records that do not contain the value expressed in the Filter field will be returned in the result set.

Building Advanced Filters

In the Datasheet or Form View, you can also build filters that compare simple data values to fields or call functions. An advanced filter dialog is shown in Figure 19.10. This dialog is similar to the Query Builder View and works much the same way.

FIGURE 19.10

In this advanced filter dialog, the filter is
FIRST_NAME =
"Jewel" *and the sort order is* Ascending.

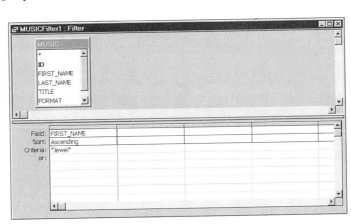

To apply the filter, click Filter, Apply Filter Sort. To build advanced filters or use subqueries, tables, or functions in a filter, use the Expression Builder. To open the Expression Builder, follow these steps:

1. In Form View, choose Records, Filter, Advanced Filter Sort.
2. In the Filter dialog, right-click the Criteria field (refer to Figure 19.10) to select the data field for which you want to create a filter.
3. The context menu pops up. Click the Build menu item, as shown in Figure 19.11.

FIGURE 19.11

Accessing the Expression Builder from the conext menu.

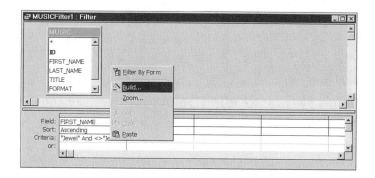

The Expression Builder dialog enables you to enter simple expressions, such as the one shown in Figure 19.12, which filters the artist's first name for "Jewel". You can enter simple text expressions, such as "Jewel", right in the Criteria field, shown previously in Figure 19.10. For complex expressions containing many predicates or expressions that use fields, functions, or nested queries, the Expression Builder is easier to use.

FIGURE 19.12

The Expression Builder dialog.

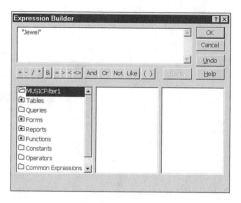

You can enter text free form in the Expression Builder or use a combination of operators (by clicking the operator buttons) and picking from the column of choices. The possible places from which you can get data for a filter include tables, queries, forms, reports, functions, constants, operators, and common expressions. In other words, filter data can be derived from almost anywhere.

Customizing Wizard Forms

Some wizard forms might suit your purposes right out of the box. However, at some point, you will need to add additional code and customizations to these forms. This section tells you about all the different kinds of modifications you can make to forms.

In Hour 21, "Class Programming Basics," you will learn about writing classes. Recall that a variable instance of a class is an object. In this section, you will learn more about using objects.

When you look at a form created by a wizard, you are looking at several objects. In the MUSIC form shown previously in Figure 19.7, there are three commonly used objects: the TextBox, the Label, and the Form object itself. The biggest difference between these objects and a Collection object, for example, is that these objects have visual attributes. That is, some of the data in these objects is used to determine what they look like.

Visual objects have three facets that I will introduce to help you understand how to program forms.

Understanding the Three Facets of Visual Objects

Let's review what I have covered thus far. A class is a user-defined type, where a user is any programmer. An object is a variable instance of a class. For example, the statement

```
Dim MyCollection As New Collection
```

defines an object, MyCollection, as an instance of the class Collection. Every instance of a class is capable of storing the same kinds of data and doing the same kinds of things as every other instance of that class.

In an object, the variables that are defined as part of the object are referred to as that object's *properties*. The word *property* is an object-oriented term that means *data that is part of a class*. Objects are capable of knowing and doing. The "knowing" is captured by properties, and the "doing" is captured by methods. *Method* is an object-oriented term for functions and subroutines—that is, *procedures*—that are defined as part of a class.

You have already read about methods and properties in earlier hours. The third facet of Visual Objects is the *event*. All three facets together are properties, methods, and events. An *event* is something that happens involving an object. When you type in a text box or click on a form, these actions are events.

19

NEW TERM A *message* is the data that Windows sends to a program in response to an external or internal occurrence. For example, a mouse click is an external occurrence that is sent to a program as a message.

NEW TERM *Event* is the term used to refer to a message being created by Windows and sent to a program. For example, the mouse-click message, when sent to a program, is called a *mouse event*.

NEW TERM An *event handler* is a procedure written to respond to events.

When you hit a key on your keyboard or click a mouse button, the computer's hardware responds first. The Windows operating system converts that physical occurrence into data. That data is called a *message*. When Windows has a message, it determines what program currently running should get the message and then sends the message to that program. The code that receives the data (the message) is referred to as an *event handler*. An event handler is a procedure that is registered with Windows to respond to Windows messages.

To synopsize, properties are pieces of data that programmers add to classes. Methods are procedures that programmers add to classes. Events are occurrences that your program must respond to. Event handlers are the procedures you write to respond to events. The last part is a bit tricky. Events are, in part, properties and procedures. To a computer, a procedure is an address (that is, data). In an object, an event property is a property that contains the address of an event handler.

Don't worry. Visual objects are easier to use than they were for programmers to invent. I will cover each of the three facets by example in this hour.

Assigning Data to Properties

Access 2002 is a visual programming environment. This means that some of the programming related to forms is accomplished with the aid of Access 2002.

Every visual object has properties. When you are viewing a form in Design View, you can look at the properties of the form. To look at the properties of the MUSIC form, open that form and click View Properties. The properties for my MUSIC form are shown in Figure 19.13.

The properties shown in the Form dialog are data. You modify a property at design time by finding the name of the property on the left and modifying the data associated with it on the right. To change the caption of the MUSIC form to "Music," follow these steps:

1. Open the MUSIC form.
2. Click View, Properties.

3. Click the Format tab in Form dialog.

4. Find the `Caption` property and modify the value on the right. Change `MUSIC` to `Music`.

FIGURE **19.13**

Properties in the Form dialog.

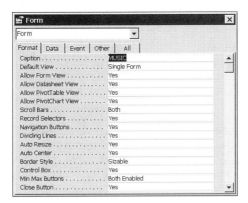

This is actually easy to do—after you get the hang of it. Instead of writing the code, a visual environment lets you modify the properties by just writing the data. You can modify properties with code, too; I will get to that in a moment.

The properties that are listed in the dialog are the properties of the control that has the focus. Click the FIRST_NAME text box on the `MUSIC` form, and the FIRST_NAME text box's properties will be displayed.

Calling Methods

Methods are called using the object name, followed by the member-of operator (`.`) and the method name. In Hour 13, "Storing Information in a Collection," you learned how to use objects and methods. Recall that the `Add` method of a `Collection` object is called by using the *name*`.Add` method and passing the arguments to the method. (Listing 13.2, line 4 demonstrates adding a string to a collection named `Strings`.)

When you write the code, you can indicate that you want to call a method by typing the object name, immediately followed by a period (the member-of operator) and the method. This applies to visual controls, like forms, and non-visual controls, like and ADODB.Recordset.For example, the `Form` object has a `Repaint` method that redraws the form and its controls. The name of the MUSIC form is `Form_Music` (you can get the form name from the `Name` property). To call the `Repaint` method with code, you would write this:

```
Form_Music.Repaint
```

19

`Repaint` takes no arguments, so the code is written exactly as shown. Most objects have some methods. The methods of any object can be identified and their use determined by reading the Help documentation for that object.

Programming Event Handlers

Event handlers are written in a module, along with any other code that solves your business problem. Before you learn to write event handlers, you must tell the MUSIC form that it will have code. (Recall that the form is capable of performing basic editing operations without code.)

> To learn about any property, open the properties dialog for an object, click a property, and press F1. You will get context Help related to that property, which may include references to related topics, code examples, and a complete description of that property.

You indicate that a form has code by changing the `Has Module` property to `Yes`. To modify the `Has Module` property, follow these steps:

1. Select the `Form` object by clicking the outline of a square box in the upper-left corner of the form (see Figure 19.14).

FIGURE 19.14

Select the Form *object by clicking the box in the upper-left corner, indicated by the dark square.*

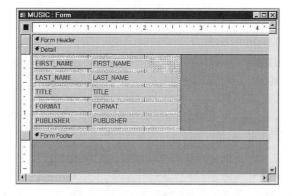

2. Click the View, Properties menu. The Form dialog appears, showing the form's properties.

3. Click the Other tab of the Form dialog.

4. As the second-from-the-last property, you will find the `Has Module` property. Change the value to `Yes` by selecting Yes from the combo box on the right, adjacent to the property name (see Figure 19.15).

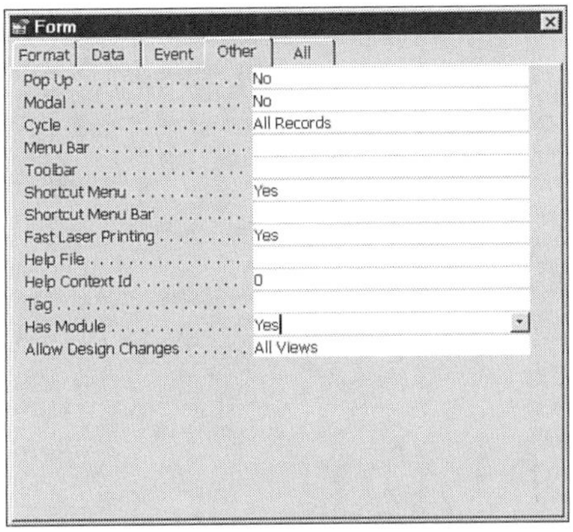

FIGURE **19.15**

To write code for a specific form, set the Has Module *property to Yes for that form.*

Now you will be able to write event handlers and associate them with a form.

The value of an event property is the procedure you write to respond to that event. To write an event handler for a specific event, find the event name on the Event tab of the Form dialog. Click that event and then click the ellipsis (…) button. Let's try an example. To change the caption at runtime (that is, dynamically), complete the following steps:

1. Click the form.

2. Open the properties dialog for the form using View, Properties.

3. Click the Event tab.

4. Click the On Load event property.

5. Click the Build button (the button with the ellipsis) to the right of the event. The code module for this form will be displayed. (If you do not have Tools|Options Forms/Reports "Always use event procedures" checked then you will have to indicate whether you want to build an Expression, Macro, or Code.)

6. Type **Form_Music.Caption = "Paul's Music Collection"** for the Load event handler. The complete listing is shown in Listing 19.1.

LISTING 19.1 Code Added to the On Load Event to Modify the Caption Property of the Form Dynamically

```
1:  Private Sub Form_Load()
2:    Form_MUSIC.Caption = "Paul's Music Collection"
3:  End Sub
```

No matter how simple or complex the code is, the process for associating events with code is the same every time.

Adding Controls to Your Form

The controls on a form are added from the Toolbox. The Toolbox can be displayed by selecting View, Toolbox. The Toolbox is shown in Figure 19.16.

FIGURE 19.16

The Toolbox contains the controls—such as ListBox, TextBox, and Label—you can put on your form.

Putting a control on a form is referred to as *painting the control on the form*. To paint a control on a form, click the control and then click and drag the shape and size that you want the control to be painted in. After the control is on the form, modify the properties and events for that control to make it appear the way you want it to look. Follow these steps to place a bitmapped image onto the MUSIC form:

1. Open the form in design mode.
2. Open the Toolbox by selecting View, Toolbox.
3. Click the Image control. (Each control has pop-up Help that displays the name of the control.)
4. Move the mouse over the form where you want the control placed and click the left mouse button.
5. The Image control will automatically open the Insert Picture dialog, filtering for compatible image files.
6. Find the image that you want displayed in the control and click OK.

The steps for painting controls on your form are the same for each control. However, different controls will require that you modify different kinds of properties. There are thousands of controls you can use in VBA, even though the default Toolbox only shows 18 of them. Programmers around the world are writing new controls all the time.

Selecting Additional Controls from the Toolbox

You can select additional controls from the Toolbox by clicking the More Controls button in the lower-right corner of the Toolbox (represented by the crossed hammer and wrench).

There are so many tools available that it would take a 10,000-page reference guide to cover all the properties, events, and methods of a small subset of those available. Instead, choose tools from vendors other than Microsoft that offer context-sensitive Help. Rely on the Help documentation to teach you about the attributes available for each control. All tools will have a number of events, properties, and methods.

Making Non-Component Objects Available to Your Programs

Controls are useful pieces of reusable code, represented by an icon and displayable in the Toolbox. Controls can be both visual and nonvisual and may have properties, methods, and events. Additional objects are available to your application that do not have a control representation displayable in the Toolbox. The Microsoft ActiveX Data Objects 2.5 Library is a perfect example. ADO is contained in an application with the filename `msado25.dll`. There is no cute icon representing a single component that is displayed in the Toolbox, but you still can use ADO in your application.

To make additional capabilities, such as ADO 2.5, available to your program, add a reference to the library you want to include. Add a reference to external tools by selecting Tools, References in the Visual Basic Editor. In the References dialog, select the library containing the classes you want to use and click OK. If you open the Tools, References list, you will note that Visual Basic for Applications, Microsoft Access 10.0 Object Library, OLE Automation, and Microsoft ActiveX Data Objects 2.5 Library are added by default.

The names of references are DLLs, OCXs, and OLE Automation servers that are registered in the Windows Registry. These libraries reside on your computer's hard disk as files with `.TLB`, `.DLL`, `.OCX`, or `.EXE` extensions. As with controls, each of these libraries contains classes, and each of those classes has methods and properties. Some will have event attributes that you can learn to use when you need them.

Writing Code

Once you have set the form's `Has Module` property to `Yes`, Access 2002 creates a module that is associated with your form. The form module appears in the Project Explorer under the Microsoft Access Class Objects folder. After you open the form, you can modify the code by selecting Code, View, or you can open the Visual Basic Editor and select the object from the project Explorer view.

Form code can be used to write code that adds capabilities to the form. There are two kinds of code you will write in a form module: event handlers and regular procedures. The form code is written in the same way as any other code. Generally, though, code written in a form is code that extends or supports the capabilities of only that form.

You can call any code from an event handler or procedure in a form. As a general rule, you should implement the code that handles the event in a separate procedure rather than

19

in the event procedure itself. For instance, in Listing 19.1, I modified the caption in the Form_Load handler. Generally, I prefer writing a separate procedure. This makes the code self-documenting and makes it easier to reuse the code in other places beside the event handler. Listing 19.2 contains a modified version of Listing 19.1 that demonstrates the technique.

LISTING 19.2   Modified Version of Listing 19.1 That Makes the Code More Reusable and Self-Documenting

```
1:  Public Function GetCurrentUser() As String
2:    GetCurrentUser = "Paul"
3:  End Function
4:  Private Sub SetCaptionToCurrentUser()
5:    Caption = GetCurrentUser() & "'s Music Collection"
6:  End Sub
7:  Private Sub Form_Load()
8:    SetCaptionToCurrentUser
9:  End Sub
```

ANALYSIS   The style of coding in Listing 19.2 looks more complicated than the code in Listing 19.1. However, each of the three functions is simple and well named. Lines 7 through 9 contain the event-handling code. The actual capability provided is delegated to the function SetCaptionToCurrentUser. Lines 4 through 6 are responsible for formatting the caption, and lines 1 through 3 return the current user.

It is worth noting that each line of code is self-documenting; therefore, no comments are necessary. Both GetCurrentUser and SetCaptionToCurrentUser are procedures that can be used by other code. In Listing 19.2, the code is intentionally trivial to illustrate the technique. However, code seldom stays this simple. It is precisely when code becomes complex that this kind of code (that is, the code in Listing 19.2) helps you better manage the complexity of your programs. It is also likely that in a real application, you would derive the actual username from the database or from the data entered by the user when he enters a username and password. Code that is not specifically related to supporting the form is best written in a separate module. Avoid writing large event handlers and putting too much code in a single form. When choosing whether to put code in a form module or a non-form module, ask yourself whether the code is useful only to this form. If the answer is yes, put the code in the form module. If the answer is no, put the code in a separate module. You can call the code in a module (that's not a form), of course. You can always move code around, but it is harder to do if your code becomes too complex.

Enhanced Editing Capabilities

Access 2002 has added some additional editing shortcut keys to help you manage your development experience. These capabilities include the following:

- The F7 key and the Shift+F7 key combination toggle between the code and object view of a form, respectively.

- The F4 key is a shortcut for displaying the Properties window.

- The Ctrl+< and Ctrl+> keyboard combinations cycle you backward and forward between the available for views. For example, if you are viewing a form in Design View and you want to quickly switch to Form View, press Ctrl+> one time.

  What's more, the Ctrl+< and Ctrl+> keys cycle whatever views are contextually available. If you are viewing Table objects, these keys cycle between Design, DataSheet, PivotTable, and PivotChart View.

Small revisions like these in Access 2002 will help you work more smoothly with the design environment. With a little practice, you will be able to quickly find your way around.

Extended Capabilities for Forms and Reports

Keep a look out for some enhanced properties, events, and methods for forms and reports in Access 2002. As with the enhanced editing revisions, the number of changes is small but useful.

New Properties for Forms and Reports

In Access 2002, the Tools, Startup menu contains an Application Icon property. You can add a custom icon that will be used for your forms and reports with this new feature.

Report objects have acquired some additional properties. Reports can be displayed as modal dialogs. (A modal dialog is a form that maintains focus until it is closed. The user must close a modal report before continuing with other activities.) Besides displaying reports as modal dialogs, you may modify a Report object's BorderStyle, AutoResize, AutoCenter, MinMaxButtons, CloseButton, and ControlBox properties.

To modify a Report object's properties, select the report from the list of objects. Open the report you want to modify by selecting from available reports. When the report is open in Design View, press F4 to display the Properties window. The new features are simple Yes/No values that indicate whether you want the features. For example, to display a report without the control box, open the properties for the report. Select the Data tab of the Properties View and set the Control Box property to No. In case you are not familiar with the control box, Figure 19.17 shows the Mouse pointer pointing at the Size menu item in the control box of a report containing data from the MUSIC table.

19

Figure 19.17

The control box is shown with the Size menu selected.

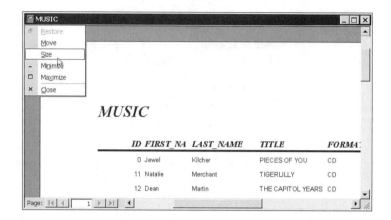

Refer to the section "Defining a Report" for an example of displaying a report as a modal dialog.

New Form Events

Access 2002 has added the OnUndo and OnRecordExit form-level events and the OnDirty and OnUndo control-level events. The OnUndo event for a form is called when the user selects Edit, Undo or presses the Esc key in Access. The control OnUndo event is called when the user hits the Esc key when editing the value contained in a control. OnDirty occurs when the contents of a form or combo box change or the user navigates to a new page in a Tab control. OnRecordExit occurs anytime a new record is navigated to.

Each of these events contains a single Cancel integer argument. If Cancel is True, the operation—be it Undo, Dirty, or RecordExit—is not performed. For example, if the Form_OnDirty event handler always sets Cancel = True, you would never be able to change data in the form.

New Methods for Forms and Reports

Form and Report objects have a new Move method. Pass the new values for Left, Top, Width, and Height locations of a form or report to position the form or report in a single statement. The following statement demonstrates the Move method:

```
Call Me.Move( 0, 0, 2000, 1500 )
```

The new Left and Top values of Me will be 0; Width will be 2000, and Height will be 1500. These units are in twips, which is equivalent to about 1/1,440th of an inch.

Live Subreport Form

When you define or add a subform or subreport, you may now view the subform or subreport in its own Design View. In Design View in Access 2002, select the subform or subreport. Then right-click and select View, Subform in Own Window.

Testing Your Form

If forms contain code, that code must be tested. If you use the form "as is" after generating it from the wizard, you can view the form in Form View and quickly make sure that you can add, edit, and delete data as well as navigate through the recordset.

If you add code to events or write additional procedures for your forms, you will need to employ the testing strategies discussed in Hours 17, "Removing Bugs," and 18, "Adding Code to Handle Errors," to ensure that all the code works correctly and is robust.

Defining a Report

Reports, just like forms, can be defined initially with wizards. Once you have a basic report, you need to keep in mind that a instance of a report is an object replete with its own methods, properties, and events. In Access, all object properties are managed at design time through the Properties View and at runtime by code. To use an object, such as a `Report` object, learn what events, properties, and methods are available and write code to manipulate the report based on the desired appearance or behavior as well as the available events, properties, and methods.

Open Access and select the Reports item from the Objects View. Double-click Create Report by Using Wizard. It becomes immediately apparent that the Report Wizard works just like the Form Wizard. For the MUSIC database, select the MUSIC table. Select all available fields and click Finish. What you get is a vanilla report, just like the one shown in Figure 19.18.

Figure 19.18 is displaying the Print Preview mode of the `Report` object. To modify the report, select View, Design View. The Design View of a report looks similar to that of a form. You can customize the appearance and behavior of the report by modifying the properties of controls on the report or by writing code behind the report.

Using the New `Printer` Object

A new `Printer` object has been added to facilitate the management of printer properties. The `Printer` object allows you to manage the printer port, the page margins, the number of copies to print, the orientation, and more.

FIGURE **19.18**

A plain vanilla report
that takes less than a
minute to create with
the Report Wizard.

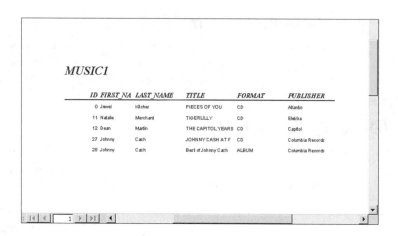

To print the MUSIC table report from the previous section use code similar to that in
Listing 19.3.

LISTING **19.3**   Opening and Printing a Report in Landscape Mode Using the
`Printer` and `DoCmd` Objects

```
1:  Sub PrintReport()
2:    Dim Report As New Report_ALL_MUSIC
3:    Printer.Orientation = acPRORLandscape
4:    Printer.Copies = 1
5:    Call DoCmd.OpenReport("ALL_MUSIC", acViewPreview)
6:    DoCmd.PrintOut
7:  End Sub
```

Add the preceding code to a module in the MUSIC database and test it by stepping
through the code with the F8 key. This example demonstrates the kind of code you will
need in order to open and print a report programmatically. The new `Printer` object is
used to manage printer properties, and the `DoCmd` object is a general-purpose object we
have used many times in past hours. To incorporate the report in your form, allowing the
user to print a report of the MUSIC table, add a button to the form. Set the button's caption to "Print" and use code identical to that in Listing 19.3 to open and print the form
when the user clicks the Print button.

Adding a Menu Item to Access to Print the Report

Access facilitates adding custom menus to your database solutions. Suppose, for example, you want to add a menu item to the Tools menu. You can define the report-printing

behavior as a macro and add that macro to the Tools menu. Perform the following steps to add a Print Report menu item that displays the MUSIC collection report:

1. Modify the `Test` function in Listing 19.3 to be a function with an undefined return type. (The return type will be `Variant` by implication.) The rest of the code remains the same.

2. From the Database Objects View, select Macros. Click the New button to create a new macro.

3. Select the `RunCode` action. For the `Function Name` action argument, click the ellipsis button to invoke the Expression Builder.

4. In the Expression Builder dialog select the `PrintReport` function as the code to run (use Figure 19.19 as a guide). Close the macro and save it as `PrintReport`.

5. In Access, select the Tools, Customize menu item. From the Customize dialog, select the Commands tab. Scroll down to All Macros in the Categories list box.

6. Select the All Macros category. The `PrintReport` macro should show up in the Commands list. Click and drag the `PrintReport` macro from the Commands list over to the Access Tool menu. Continue to hold down the left mouse button and drag the `PrintReport` macro over to the Tools menu. When you do, the Tools menu will open.

7. After the Tools menu opens, drag the `PrintReport` macro to the last position on the Tools menu. The Customize dialog and the Tools menu are shown in Figure 19.20 and Figure 19.21.

8. Change the name of the menu from PrintReport to Print Report in the Name menu item or by modifying the Caption field in the Tools Control Properties dialog.

FIGURE 19.19

Selecting a user-defined function from the Expression Builder.

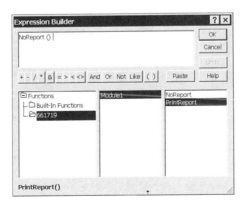

19

FIGURE 19.20

Adding a custom menu item macro to the Tools menu—a drag and drop procedure.

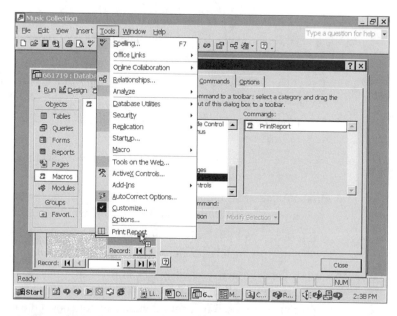

FIGURE 19.21

Modify the custom menu item while the Customize dialog is displayed using the Modify Selection button or the context pop-up menu.

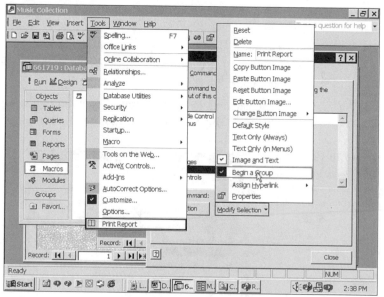

With steps 1 through 8 complete, your Music Collection report is fully integrated into the MUSIC database and is as convenient and easy to use as any other feature in Access.

You will need the Customize dialog open to add, modify, and remove custom menus. From Figure 19.21, it is apparent that you may use the Modify Selection pop-up menu item to modify the button text and icons and to add hyperlinks to menus. The Customize dialog enables you to add new menu and toolbar items as well as customize existing ones.

Setting the Startup Point for Your Program

You now know the essential steps for creating an Access 2002 program, complete with forms and reports. The difference between a one-form program and a large, complex program is one of degree, practice, and managing code complexity. By default, your database will open in Database View mode. If your database is to run as a program in User mode, you will need to set the startup properties. The Startup dialog is shown in Figure 19.22.

FIGURE 19.22

Use the Tools, Startup dialog to specify the form or code that will run when your database is opened.

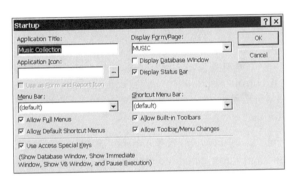

To make the MUSIC database run like an application when you open it, make the following modifications to the Startup dialog (following along with Figure 19.17):

1. Modify the application name to Music Collection.
2. In the Display Form/Page combo box, select the MUSIC form. This will be the startup (or main) form.
3. Uncheck Display Database Window. All check boxes should have a check in them.
4. When you open the database next, it will display the form, ready to edit.

If you buy the Developers Tools for Office XP, you can distribute your application with the Access runtime library. With the Developers Tools for Office, users can run your database application without having a copy of Access installed.

19

Summary

Almost all Windows programs are comprised of code and a user interface. Access 2002 lets you create databases and write code, and it has a rich visual interface development environment. In other words, Access 2002 contains everything you need to create Windows programs.

In this hour, you learned that controls are visual objects that enable you to paint the appearance of a form or report and define how those controls will look at design time and runtime. You learned that there are three facets to visual programming: properties, which describe how controls look, methods, which enable you to write code to use the controls, and events, which respond to messages sent by Windows. Windows is a message-based system; events are properties that keep track of event handlers. Event handlers are procedures that respond to events.

Controls are shown in the Toolbox. You can add controls to a blank form or modify Wizard-generated forms. When you put a control on a form, the verb used to describe that action is *paint*. To use any control, you select the control from the Toolbox and paint the control on the form. After the control is on the form, you can open the properties dialog to modify the properties that are necessary to make the control look and respond the way you want. Controls respond to events. You only have to write code to respond to those events in which you are interested. If you do not define a handler for an event, no code will run for that event.

Defining user interfaces and reports is a matter of painting the controls on forms and reports. Responding to user input and other kinds of events requires that you associate event handlers with controls. The rest of the code you write is geared toward supporting the user interfaces or solving the business problem that brought you to your keyboard and Access in the first place. Read the "Q&A" section and complete the "Workshop" section to practice what you have learned in this hour.

Q&A

Q How do I manually associate a data source with a form?

A This is accomplished by setting the Record Source property of that form to the object that contains your data. This can be a table, query, or other valid provider.

Q How do I associate an alternative data source to a control other than a form?

A Controls, such as text boxes, have the Control Source property. The *control source* is the name of the field in the record source from which the control will read and write its data.

Q How do I add multiple tables to a form?

A You can add more than one table in step 1 of the Form Wizard. For the wizard to know how to present the data, though, you must describe the relationships between the tables in Access 2002 with the Tools, Relationships menu item.

Q Can I distribute my application without Access 2002?

A Yes, Developer Tools for Office XP (which can be purchased separately from Office XP) has a distributable runtime library that can be shipped with your application.

Workshop

The Workshop includes quiz questions designed to help you test your understanding of the material covered and exercises to help put what you've learned to practice. You will find the answers to the quiz and exercises in Appendix A, "Answers."

Quiz

1. What is the object-oriented term used to describe data belonging to a class?
2. Methods require an object prefix. True or false?
3. What are events?
4. What are event handlers?
5. How are controls added to a form?

Exercises

1. Create a relationship between the MUSIC and TRACKS tables from Hour 15 in Access 2002.
2. Use the new relationship to define a master detail form from the wizard.
3. Save the new master detail form. Modify the startup properties so that the new master detail form is the startup form.

19

Hour 20

Adding Data to Web Pages

Software tools evolve as frequently as other types of software. Current emphasis in software tool evolution is on providing capabilities that allow you to build solutions for the World Wide Web. If you follow any of the e-commerce initial public offerings in the stock market, you have probably noted the meteoric rises in their stock prices followed by their equally meteoric fall. Perhaps this demonstrates the adage that what goes up must come down, but more importantly it illustrates the pervasive interest in Web technologies and the fact that you can't time the market. The hottest program topic for the foreseeable future is Web programming, and Cinderella stories are cropping up every day.

Until about 1995, Windows programming was the coolest thing around. A Windows program is a program that runs under Windows, has a graphical user interface (GUI) based on the window paradigm, and can be a single-user or multiuser application.

In less than a decade, the momentum has shifted to Web programming. Web programming emphasizes distributed thin-client programs, where the interface is the HTML displayed in a browser. In a Windows program, an application is a compiled or interpreted collection of graphical window interfaces. A Web application contains hyperlinks to Web pages. A Web page is a text document that primarily contains HTML. The database and any other code most likely runs somewhere else on the Web server. Web applications are called *thin-client applications* because the GUI, or presentation layer, resides consistently in the same client—a browser. Web applications are powerful and interesting for a variety of reasons. One of the most commonly mentioned reasons is that developers only have to update the server with new pages to give every end user immediate access to the updated application. Steve Balmer, President of Microsoft, predicts that, in the near future, all applications will emulate thin-client Web applications. Balmer's prediction is a pretty good bet for a self-fulfilling prophecy.

Microsoft Access 2002 supports thin-client Web development via Data Access Pages. *Data Access Pages* are Web pages that you can use to add, edit, and view data on the Internet or an intranet, and they can be sent by e-mail. Data Access Pages are developed in a way similar to Access forms, so you can leverage some of the skills you already have. The underlying code is HTML that can be generated by wizards and edited in Access 2002. In this hour, you will learn

- The difference between the Internet and an intranet
- How to create Data Access Pages using wizards
- How to use themes to enhance the appearance of your Data Access Pages
- How to customize Data Access Pages with Access 2002

Comparing Intranets to Internets

The *Internet* is a network of computers. Computers participate in the Internet by being connected to an online Internet service provider (ISP), using a common connectivity protocol (TCP/IP), and having an Internet Protocol (IP) address. IP addresses are comprised of four sets of numbers connected by periods. For example, my company's IP address is 198.109.162.177. An *intranet* is a private version of an Internet. Essentially, an intranet is a network of addressable computers that can be accessed by a limited group of users because the host computer is not connected or accessible to the Internet backbone.

NEW TERM *Hypertext* is text that contains embedded codes that are used as instructions to a hypertext reader. Web browsers, such as Internet Explorer and Netscape Navigator, are hypertext readers.

> PC browsers, such as Internet Explorer, generally display HTML text. Other
> Web-enabled devices such as cell phones use WML (the Wireless Markup
> Language). WML is a form of XML (the Extended Markup Language). Each
> of these markup languages is a kind of hypertext.

A medium for users on an intranet and the Internet is the browser. The main language
that makes Web data available to PC browsers is the *Hypertext Markup Language*
(HTML). HTML is a generic hypertext language that contains embedded text codes that
act as instructions to a hypertext reader. Internet Explorer and Netscape Navigator both
read and interpret hypertext. Microsoft's Word and Outlook programs are also capable of
interpreting hypertext.

Hypertext is more useful than plain text because you can embed commands that make
the text capable of displaying rich fonts, graphics, sound, video, data, and many other
kinds of information.

Installing and Running Internet Information Services

You can set up a basic intranet by installing the Personal Web Server (PWS) or Internet
Information Services (IIS) on Windows 2000. Using the Personal Web Server or IIS will
enable you to share information with other users if you are connected to a LAN or the
Internet. Although the Personal Web Server does not contain as many features as IIS, it is
capable of running an Internet or intranet site and makes an excellent test environment. If
you have a choice, using Windows 2000 and IIS is a great configuration for Web development and intranet hosting.

> Software Conceptions used Personal Web Server for its Web site in 1995. In
> 1996, we switched to the more robust IIS.
>
> Intranets are easy to implement. I generally make it a point to host an
> intranet site for every project I work on. I have found intranets to be an
> easy and convenient means of cutting down on paper clutter, and an
> intranet provides a good way to ensure that all your project information
> (that you want to be accessible) is accessible from one source.

20

To install Microsoft Internet Information Services on Windows 2000 Professional, follow
these steps:

1. Click Start, Settings, Control Panel.

2. In the Control Panel, click the Add/Remove Programs Applet.

3. In the Add/Remove Programs dialog, click the Add/Remove Windows Components button on the left side of the dialog.

4. The Windows Components Wizard will be displayed. Check the Internet Information Services box and click Next.

5. The wizard will install IIS and configure it to run as a service.

After you have installed IIS, you can manage the configuration from the Administrative Tools applet in the Control Panel. Select Internet Services Manager to open the Microsoft Management Console (MMC) containing the IIS configuration information. Refer to Figure 20.1 for a view of Internet Services Manager.

FIGURE 20.1

Internet Services Manager installed on Windows 2000 Professional.

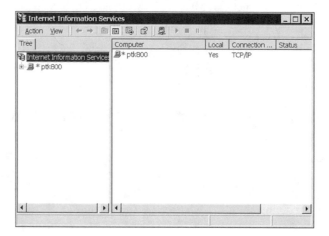

If everything appears to be configured correctly from the Internet Services Manager and you cannot browse to your computer, check with your network administrator to determine if you are running a proxy server. A *proxy server* is an application that helps multiple networked computers share access to the Internet.

If you have a proxy server, you need to tell Internet Explorer to bypass the proxy server for the local address. To do this, open IE and select Tools, Options, Connections. Click the LAN Settings button. If Use a Proxy Server is checked in the Proxy Server group box, select Bypass Proxy Server for Local Addresses.

If you are not real sure how you are connected to the Internet or messing with proxy servers and TCP/IP stuff makes you nervous, see your LAN administrator.

Figure 20.1 is the default view of the Internet Services Manager. From this view, it can be determined that the URL for IIS running on my workstation is the machine name, PTK800. By opening Internet Explorer and typing `http://PTK800`, if everything has been configured correctly, I should get some default pages created by Microsoft. Your machine name will differ, but you may use `http://127.0.0.1` or `http://localhost`. IP 127.0.0.1 is the loopback IP address, which refers back to the sending computer, and localhost is the URL for 127.0.0.1.

Adding custom pages to your intranet is as simple as adding HTML pages to `c:\inetpub\wwwroot`, which is the local directory and default web for IIS.

By saving the Data Access Pages to the root directory of your workstation's site, you can test the pages and make them available to users of your site. As already mentioned, the Personal Web Server and IIS make great testing environments. Tools such as FrontPage 2002 and Dreamweaver can significantly reduce the effort involved in creating advanced Web pages.

Establishing a Web Site

Using Personal Web Server or IIS is a good choice for a small-business intranet, and it makes an excellent test platform for developers. To build a Web site, you need to define a home page and add hyperlinks to any other pages containing data you want to make available to your users, including Data Access Pages.

> If you have serious security considerations or plan to participate in e-commerce on a large scale, you will need a commercial-quality platform, such as Windows NT or Windows 2000 Server and Internet Information Services.

Understanding Web Pages

20

A Web site can consist of as little as one page. Most Web sites contain many pages, however, and can become quite elaborate. The content displayed in your web site is only limited by your imagination. The Web is the logical connection between pages by references to hyperlinks. A hyperlink is a special HTML tag that contains a *uniform resource locator* (URL)—that is, the location of the linked Web page.

A good way to create a Web site is with Microsoft FrontPage 2002. Each Web page contains some required HTML tags. Listing 20.1 demonstrates the essential HTML code that must go into every text file with an `.HTM` or `.HTML` extension.

LISTING 20.1   An HTML File Stripped to Bare Bones

```
1:  <html>
2:  <head>
3:  </head>
4:  <body>
5:  </body>
6:  </html>
```

ANALYSIS   Lines 1–6 represent a complete (albeit blank) Web page. By adding additional HTML and text between the <body> and </body> tags, you can create the pages that will be visible on the Web. Tools such as FrontPage make creating Web pages easier. A Web site is established by creating one or more pages containing hyperlinks to pages in the site and pages at other sites. (Think of the hyperlinks as the threads of the Web.) A basic hyperlink has the following syntax:

```
<a href="http://Web/linked_page.htm>Link</a>
```

The a href tag contains the URL to the page you want to link to. Here, *Web* is replaced with the URL (or Web address). This is the dot-com address that is advertised for Internet sites and virtual directory names for intranet sites. For example, to add a link to Software Conceptions' Web site, replace *Web* with www.softconcepts.com. Use www.microsoft.com to link to Microsoft's Web site. The *linked_page* part of the syntax is the name of the actual page you want to link to at the site. A complete reference to a page looks like this:

```
<a href="http://www.softconcepts.com/index.htm">
➥Software Conceptions' Homepage</a>
```

The *Link* part of the syntax is the actual text you want to appear when someone views the Web page.

What Is a Data Access Page?

Data Access Page is the term used to describe a page in Access that contains HTML. It enables you to access data from a database on a Web page. The HTML to add controls and bind the pages to a database is much more advanced than basic text. Although you can write the HTML code from scratch, creating a Web page progresses much more quickly if you let the Access 2002 wizards create the initial page and then you customize it from there.

A good way to learn to write advanced HTML is to get a book on HTML and read HTML code that others have written, including the HTML generated by the Data Access Page wizards.

Advanced Web Page Topics

As mentioned earlier, Web programming is one of the fastest moving development topics today. There is more involved in advanced Web sites than simple HTML. An e-commerce site, such as Amazon's Web site, enables purchasing products online, offers advanced searches, and provides feedback. Pages such as those found at Amazon.com require many additional features.

Microsoft has created a standard referred to as *Active Server Pages*. Active Server Pages can contain both VBScript and JavaScript. Regular HTML pages can contain JavaScript. Advanced Web sites also have programs that run on the Web server. These are referred to as ISAPI, NSAPI, and CGI servers. These programs provide advanced capabilities to a Web site.

If you are interested in developing an e-commerce site, consider hiring a professional developer. At a minimum, consider purchasing a couple of books on Web server technologies, security administration, and ASP and HTML development. These topics are beyond the scope of this book.

Building the Database Used for the Demo

Even in a moderate-sized company, a good use for a company intranet is to create a company directory. If you are handing out internal phone lists on paper, you are paying for updating, printing, and operator services. If you keep the company directory on an intranet, distribution is eliminated, and maintenance can actually be delegated to one individual.

> Any internal information that must be maintained and published to support internal corporate operations can be managed handily on an intranet. This includes directories, company policy, training materials, requests for vacation days, and corporate news bulletins—or anything that might be important to the successful operation of the business.

20

Therefore, because it is practical and it fits into the time allowed, the examples in this hour are based on a company directory.

NEW TERM *Schema* is defined by Dictionary.com as a diagrammatic representation; an outline or a model. When applied to a table, *schema* refers to the field names, types, sizes, and keys. When applied to an Access database, *schema* refers to the definition of all the objects in the database, including tables, queries, Data Access Pages, stored procedures, modules, and the like.

The virtual company is *eSoft*, a company that specializes in custom software development. The personnel database for eSoft contains three tables: DEPARTMENT, EMPLOYEE, and ROLES. The schema for eSoft's directory is contained in Tables 20.1, 20.2, and 20.3.

TABLE 20.1   The DEPARTMENT Table Contains the Names of the Departments for eSoft

Field Name	Type	Size	Indexed
DEPARTMENT_ID	AutoNumber		Primary key
NAME	Text	50	

TABLE 20.2   The ROLE Table Contains the Job Descriptions for eSoft

Field Name	Type	Size	Indexed
ROLE_ID	AutoNumber		Primary key
NAME	Text	20	
DESCRIPTION	Text	50	

TABLE 20.3   The Main Table Is the EMPLOYEE Table, Which Contains Employee Data for eSoft

Field Name	Type	Size	Indexed
EMPLOYEE_ID	AutoNumber		Primary Key
FIRST_NAME	Text	20	
LAST_NAME	Text	20	
SSN	Text	11	
DEPARTMENT_ID	Number		Yes (Duplicates OK)
PHONE_NUMBER	Text	14	
EXTENSION	Text	6	
ROLE_ID	Number		Yes (Duplicates OK)

Logically, the main table is the EMPLOYEE table. The relationship between EMPLOYEE and DEPARTMENT is that for each department there are many employees, linked by the DEPARTMENT_ID. The relationship between the ROLES and EMPLOYEE tables is that for each role there are zero-to-many employees, linked by the ROLE_ID. (Everyone is assigned to a department, but not everyone has a defined role.) Take a look at Figure 20.2 for a visual representation, as depicted in Access's Relationships view.

Figure 20.2
The eSoft Access Relationships view.

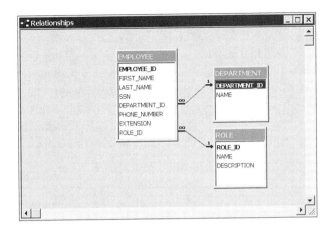

To complete the examples in the rest of this hour, you must create the eSoft database as described by the schema at the beginning of this section. I will continue by demonstrating how easy it is to use the wizards to create a Data Access Page.

Using Wizards to Generate Web Pages

Well-understood problems can be automated. Just as forms represent well-understood problems, likewise creating a basic Web page that contains data is quickly falling into the category of understood problems. As tools evolve, it is easier to express an understanding in the context of a tool. As with many other aspects of Access 2002 development, there are wizards that can help you create a Data Access Page. To view the list of wizards, open the eSoft database, click the Pages button in the Object View, and click New. The wizards are Design View, Existing Web Page, Page Wizard, and AutoPage: Columnar (see Figure 20.3).

Figure 20.3
The Data Access Page dialog listing the available wizards.

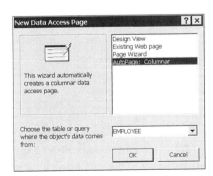

The Design View opens a blank page. This will require more work than customizing a wizard-generated page. The Existing Web Page Wizard opens the Locate Web Page Explorer; use the Explorer to find and open an existing page. Recall that Data Access Pages are stored outside the Access database, although Access stores a reference to the physical location of these pages. The AutoPage: Columnar Wizard requires the least work but offers the least amount of wizard customization. To use this wizard, simply click New, select the AutoPage Wizard and a table, and click OK. The Page Wizard balances ease of use with flexibility; therefore, I will go over the steps necessary to create a page using this wizard.

To demonstrate the Page Wizard, let's create a useful query that combines the lookup data from the DEPARTMENT and ROLES tables.

Defining a Multiple-Table Query

The query used in this section joins the EMPLOYEE, DEPARTMENT, and ROLES tables so that you can see the name of the department and role instead of the ID.

> Indexed fields that are used to logically join tables, such as DEPARTMENT_ID, ROLE_ID, and EMPLOYEE_ID, should never be displayed to users, except those who are administrators. Generally these fields exist to equate lookup data or associated data. It is the data in equated tables that you want to show.
>
> The previous paragraph defines the necessity for a join relationship. The SQL in this section demonstrates such a join.

Create the query in Listing 20.2 and save it as QUERY_EMPLOYEE_PHONELIST_BY_ DEPARTMENT.

LISTING 20.2   Defines a Multiple-Table Relationship That Contains Lookup Data

```
1:  SELECT DEPARTMENT.DEPARTMENT_ID, DEPARTMENT.NAME,
2:  EMPLOYEE.FIRST_NAME, EMPLOYEE.LAST_NAME,
3:  EMPLOYEE.PHONE_NUMBER, EMPLOYEE.EXTENSION, ROLE.NAME
4:  FROM ROLE RIGHT JOIN (DEPARTMENT RIGHT JOIN EMPLOYEE ON
5:  DEPARTMENT.DEPARTMENT_ID = EMPLOYEE.DEPARTMENT_ID) ON
6:  ROLE.ROLE_ID = EMPLOYEE.ROLE_ID;
```

ANALYSIS   The query returns the fields DEPARTMENT.DEPARTMENT_ID, DEPART-MENT.NAME, EMPLOYEE.FIRST_NAME, EMPLOYEE.LAST_NAME, EMPLOYEE.PHONE_NUMBER, EMPLOYEE.EXTENSION, and ROLE.NAME. The tables read are DEPARTMENT, EMPLOYEE, and ROLE. Because this query joins multiple tables, it will result in a read-only query. For an employee directory listing, this is exactly what you want.

Using the Page Wizard

Using the query from the preceding section, you can use the Page Wizard to complete the employee directory. Follow these steps to complete the Data Access Page:

1. With the eSoft database open, click the Pages button in the Object View.

2. In the New Data Access Page dialog, select Page Wizard and the query created in the last section, QUERY_EMPLOYEE_PHONE_LIST_BY_DEPARTMENT.

3. Click OK.

4. In the first step of the Page Wizard, select all the available fields except DEPARTMENT_ID.

5. Click Next.

6. Click Next. (If you want to group the result set on a particular column or columns, you can indicate the groupings of columns on this page.)

7. On the sort page of the wizard (the third page), add the LAST_NAME column as a sort field.

8. In the fourth page of the wizard, you can select the table you want to allow the user to update. However, because the page is based on a read-only query, the Data Access Page will be read-only. For an employee directory, that's exactly what we want. Click Next.

9. On the last page, change the title to Employee Directory. Click Finish.

> Because the directory listing is intended to be read-only, add test data to the tables in order to have data to browse in the completed Web page. You can open the tables and add data in the Table View.

A completely functional Web page results. Figure 20.4 depicts the Web page in Page View after the wizard completes. To test the page, click View, Page View. The navigation control (shown in Figure 20.4) can be used to navigate through each of the records in the result set.

20

FIGURE 20.4

The Employee Directory Data Access Page created by the Page Wizard.

Employee Directory

FIRST_NAME:	Lori
DEPARTMENT.NAME:	Parent
LAST_NAME:	Kimmel
PHONE_NUMBER:	
EXTENSION:	
ROLE.NAME:	Mom

QUERY EMPLOYEE PHONELIST BY DEPARTMENT 2 of 4

Using Web Page Design Tools

After you have a Web page, you can use Access 2002, the Toolbox, and germane menu items to visually customize the Data Access Page. It is important to note at this point that the page can be used as is.

Using the Data Access Page Designer

The Design View for Data Access Pages has been improved in Access 2002. New features are showcased in the subsections that follow.

Data Outline View and Server Filters

The Data Outline View shown in Figure 20.5 enables you to set page field properties, modify relationships between group levels, and define server filters.

FIGURE 20.5

The Data Outline View shown is a new feature in Access 2002.

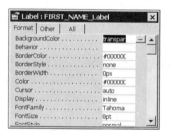

Server filters behave like additional SQL WHERE clauses on the data set. To define a server filter on the recordset defined in the data model, right-click the recordset (in our example, QUERY PHONELIST BY DEPARTMENT) and select the Properties context menu item. Add the server filter, shown in Figure 20.6, as you would a WHERE clause in SQL. Generally this is of the form *fieldname operator comparison_value*. In the example, LAST_NAME > "Kimmel" will be applied to the result set.

Visual Control Sizing and Snap-to-Grid

When you resize controls in Data Access Pages, Access 2002 offers better visual feedback and a refined snap-to-grid behavior that provides finer management of control size and placement.

Intuitive Drop Zones

Data Access Pages contain drop-zone menus during design time. Figure 20.7 shows the Group Level Properties menu item dropped from the Header band zone. These drop-zone menus make it easier to find capabilities related to specific aspects of the design-time page.

FIGURE 20.6

Add a server filter at design time in the Properties dialog for the recordset.

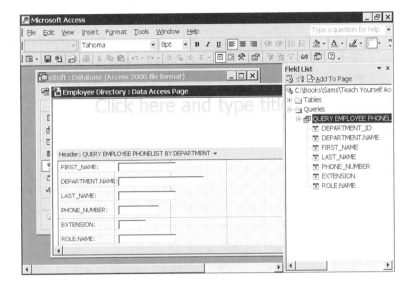

FIGURE 20.7

The figure shows the group header drop zone

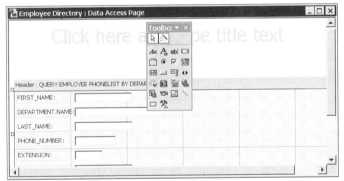

AutoSum Feature and Group Filtering

Access 2002 makes it easier than ever to add aggregate fields to your pages. Simply click the control containing the field for which you want to create an aggregate field and click AutoSum Σ on the toolbar. A footer section containing a label and text box will be added to your page containing an aggregate field.

The default aggregate field is Row Count, but you may click the drop-down list next to the AutoSum button and select from Sum, Average, Min, Max, Count, Standard Deviation, and Any.

20

Designer Inherits Extended Properties from the Database

The Data Access Page Designer inherits extended properties from the Jet and SQL Server 2000 databases. This means that if you define a field as a lookup field, the designer will add a lookup control when you create a Data Access Page.

Return to our sample employee database. The DEPARTMENT_ID and ROLE_ID fields are key fields. It is unwise and not very user friendly to require users to remember index fields when the underlying text value can and should be displayed. If we modify the table design such that DEPARTMENT_ID and ROLE_ID are lookup values that must exist in the related tables (ROLE and DEPARTMENT, respectively), then the user can select from a combo box containing the word values in a Datasheet View or view of the table. When that table is saved as a Data Access Page, the lookup capability will be supported in the Web page, too.

Here are the steps for defining the lookup value for EMPLOYEE.DEPARTMENT_ID and the subsequent steps for creating the Data Access Page based on the revised table:

1. In the Objects list of the Database View, select EMPLOYEE table and click the Design button.

2. In the Field Name column, select the DEPARTMENT_ID field.

3. At the bottom, where the field properties are defined, select the Lookup tab.

4. On the Lookup tab, change the Display Control value to Combo Box. Complete the lookup definition by filling in the remaining values as follows: Row Source Type = Table/Query, Row Source = DEPARTMENT, Bound Column = 1, Column Count = 2, Column Heads = Yes, Limit to List = Yes. Use the default values for any properties not mentioned.

5. Save the table. Double-click the EMPLOYEE table to verify that the EMPLOYEE.DEPARTMENT_ID field now allows you to select a value from a drop-down list.

6. In the Objects list of the Database View, select the Pages object. Click New.

7. Select the AutoPage: Columnar wizard and the EMPLOYEE table.

8. Click OK. (You are almost finished. Read the paragraph to use the inherited extended properties.)

9. Delete the DEPARTMENT_ID Label and Text Box from the Data Access Page.

10. Select View|Field List. Drag and drop the DEPARTMENT_ID from the Field List to the original position of the DEPARTMENT_ID field. (You should get a Combo Box control and label now.

11. With the DEPARTMENT_ID Combo Box still selected, open the Properties dialog by clicking View|Properties. On the Other tab change the TabIndex property to be the tab index immediately after the preceding control. (When I performed these steps the TabIndex was 1, right after the SSN field.)

A Data Access Page containing an editable version of the EMPLOYEE table with the inherited properties exists on the Data Access Page now.Customize the page as you would any other. For more on features available for customizing Data Access Pages, read the remaining sections of the hour.

Taking a Tour of Data Access Page Menus and Toolbars

Access 2002 displays makes menu items and context menus available based on what you are doing. This section covers the relevant menus, toolbars, and dialogs that will help you customize Data Access Pages.

When you have a Data Access Page opened and in focus in Design View, several menu items are useful. Table 20.4 lists the menus and menu items and provides descriptions of their uses.

TABLE 20.4 Relevant Data Access Page Menus

Menu Name	Item/Command	Description
File	Web Page Preview	Opens the page in the default Web browser.
View	Design View	Page design mode.
View	Page View	Enables you to browse or modify data.
View	Properties	Enables you to modify selected control properties at design time (see Figure 20.5).
View	Field List	Displays all the fields from all tables and queries. These are used to bind a data source to a control (see Figure 20.6).
View	HTML Source	Enables you to view and edit the HTML source code that defines the page.
View	Toolbox	Opens the Toolbox dialog. Drag and drop controls from the Toolbox onto the Data Access Page in design mode to customize the page (see Figure 20.7).
View	Toolbars, Data Outline	A hierarchical view of the recordset and fields displayed in the page.
Insert	Movie from File	Inserts a movie (.mov, .avi, .mpeg, or .asf) file into the page.

20

TABLE 20.4 continued

Menu Name	Item/Command	Description
Insert	Picture	Inserts a bitmap file (.gif, .jpg, .jpeg, .bmp, .xmp, or .png) formatted image into the page.
Insert	Office Chart	Inserts a graph (called a *chart*) into the page. You can bind the chart to a table to represent dynamic data.
Insert	Office Pivot Table	Inserts a pivot table into the page. A pivot table enables you to dynamically change the way in which data is presented.
Insert	Office Spreadsheet	Inserts a spreadsheet into the page. The spreadsheet can be dynamically bound to data from your database.
Insert	Hyperlink	Inserts a hyperlink tag into the page (see the previous section "Understanding Web Pages" for more information).
Insert	ActiveX Control	Inserts an external object, such as Microsoft NetShow Player, which enables you to incorporate streaming audio and video into your page.
Insert	Unbound Section	A part of a Data Access Page, such as a header, footer, or detail section.
Format	Theme	Enables you to apply a theme to a Web page. A theme contains background information, color schemes, and other information that describes the general appearance of a page.
Format	Background, Color	Specifies the background color of the page.
Format	Background, Picture	Specifies a background graphic for the page.
Format	Background, Sound	Adds a sound file containing music that is played when the page is opened.

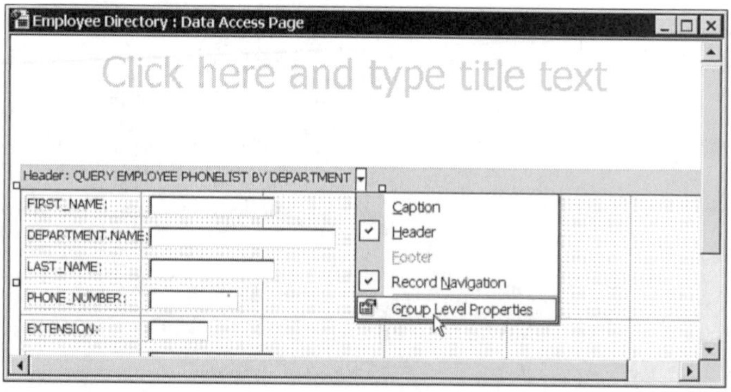

FIGURE 20.8

The Properties dialog enables you to modify object properties at design time (as well as with code at runtime).

FIGURE 20.9

The Field List dialog contains all the fields available from table and query data sources. These are used to associate data with controls.

FIGURE 20.10

The Toolbox contains controls that you can drag and drop onto your Data Access Page to customize the implementation of the page.

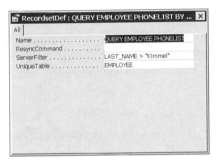

Access 2000 had a View, Sorting and Grouping menu. The sorting and grouping behavior has been relocated to a drop-zone menu in the header band. Click the triangle adjacent to the recordset name in the header to display the Group Level Properties. (The location of the menu is shown in Figure 20.8.)

The menus in Table 20.4 make it easier to create a Data Access Page. Menus generate the HTML code to accomplish the task indicated by the menu item. Using the menus is easier than writing the code. Of course, you can do either.

Adding a Control to a Data Access Page

The visual appearance of a Data Access Page is contrived by combining fonts, color, text, and graphics to create a visual effect. The utility of a Data Access Page is created by adding controls that can be bound (associated with) the Data Access Page. However, the process of adding a control is the same whether or not it contains data. To add a control to a page, follow these steps:

1. Click View, Toolbox to open the Toolbox dialog.

2. Click the control you want to add to the page.

20

3. Move the mouse pointer over the page where you want to paint the control and click the left mouse button.

Modify the properties to finish the appearance and utility of the control, depending on what you want to do with that control. (Read the section "Adding a Drop-Down List to a Page" for an example of adding a specific control and binding fields to that control.)

Using the Properties Dialog

The Properties dialog is a visual interface that effectively enables you to produce the same result as writing code to modify a property. The difference between using the Properties dialog and writing code is that changes made to properties at runtime are only visible at runtime. The Properties dialog, however, allows you to modify properties of controls without writing any code, at design time.

A visual design-time interface distinguishes a RAD development environment from a non-RAD development environment. To modify properties, when you have a Data Access Page open in Design View, click the control you want to modify and then follow these steps:

1. Click View, Properties.
2. In the Properties dialog, find the name of the property you want to modify.
3. Enter a new value for the property.

You see the result immediately. Try an example by following these steps:

1. Open the Employee Directory Data Access Page. You are going to modify the labels for the field names (currently in uppercase) so that they appear in a more readable format.
2. Click the LAST_NAME text on the page.
3. Click View, Properties.
4. Click the Other tab.
5. Find the property InnerText (property names are on the left and property values are on the right).
6. Change the property value to Last Name, which looks nicer than Last Name.

To practice changing text properties, repeat the process, changing all the uppercase field labels to a nicely formatted version for each label.

Binding a Field to a Control

Binding a field to a control means that, in the Properties dialog, you set the Control Source property on the Data tab to the name of the field from which data will be read and to which it will be written (if the page is writable). The recordset is established by placing the control on a bound section. The Record Source property of the bound section contains the Recordset value.

To add a text box to the Employee Directory page, open the Toolbox and paint a TextBox control to the right of the existing controls. Notice that a label (MSTheme-Label) is also painted. To bind this control to DEPARTMENT_ID, follow these steps:

1. Click the TextBox control, after it is painted on the form.
2. Click View, Properties.
3. Click the Data tab in the Properties dialog.
4. Click the drop-down list button for Control Source (which appears when you click the property) to drop down the list of fields.
5. Select the DEPARTMENT_ID field.
6. Click the adjacent text label and modify the text to Department ID.

This process is automated by the wizard, but you must know how to do it manually if you want to bind any controls other than the TextBox control—the default control added by the wizard.

A quicker way of adding a bound control to a Data Access Page is to drag and drop the field from the Field List into the bound section of the page. To add the DEPARTMENT_ID field and bound control to the Data Access Page, select the View, Field List menu item. The Field List dialog will open. Click and drag the EMPLOYEE DEPARTMENT_ID field onto the dotted grid section of the page in Design View. The rest is done for you. This visual drag-and-drop design is indicative of the term *rapid application design*.

Sorting and Grouping Data

The GroupLevel dialog, shown in Figure 20.11, enables you to customize the organization of data and indicate some specifics about how the page appears. The GroupLevel dialog is accessed from the header drop zone, as described in the section "Intuitive Drop Zones." The properties for sorting and grouping are described in Table 20.5.

20

FIGURE 20.11
The GroupLevel prop-
erties for grouping and
sorting data in Data
Access Pages.

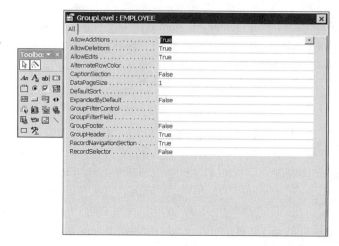

TABLE 20.5   GroupLevel Properties Define the Appearance of a Bound Section

Group Property Name	Description
AllowAdditions	A Boolean value that indicates whether a user can add a record. (Default is True.)
AllowDeletions	A Boolean value indicating whether a user can delete records. (Default is True.)
AllowEdits	A Boolean value indicating whether the user can modify records. (Default is True.)
AlternateRowColor	A selectable value for alternating the color of rows of data.
CaptionSection	A Boolean value indicating whether there is a section for a caption. (Default is False.)
DefaultPageSize	Specifies the number of records for a section. (The default is 1. Change it to All to show all records.)
DefaultSort	Indicates the name of the sorted field ordering. (For our example, a value of DEPARTMENT_ID would sort the recordset by DEPARTMENT_ID.)
ExpandedByDefault	A Boolean value indicating whether subgroups are expanded when the page is viewed. (Default is False.)
GroupFilterControl	A value used to indicate which records are returned in the recordset.
GroupFilterField	The filter field in the a recordset used to constrain records returned.
GroupFooter	A Boolean value that indicates whether a footer section is displayed on the page. (Default is False.)
GroupHeader	A Boolean value that indicates whether a header section is displayed. (Default is True.)

TABLE 20.5 Continued

Group Property Name	Description
RecordNavigationSection	A Boolean value that indicates whether a navigation control is displayed. (Default is True.)
RecordSelector	This property indicates whether a record selector indicator is displayed. (Default is False.)

There is a wide range of property settings that will provide you with precise control over your Data Access Page. For example, you can add a drop-down list control to filter on employee roles in the Employee Directory. Complete the following steps to try it out (this exercise assumes you created a lookup value for the EMPLOYEE.DEPARTMENT_ID field from the section titled "Designer Inherits Extended Properties from the Database"):

1. Create a Data Access Page based on the EMPLOYEE table.

2. Drag the DEPARTMENT_ID field from the EMPLOYEE Field List onto the Data Access Page you just created. (If you created the lookup on the EMPLOYEE table as described in "Designer Inherits Extended Properties from the Database," you will get a combo box value associated with the DEPARTMENT_ID.

3. The combo box should be named DEPARTMENT_ID1 by default. Verify the name by looking at the ID property for the combo box.

4. Open the GroupLevel properties. In GroupFilterControl, enter the ID value of the combo box.

5. In the GropupLevel properties, enter DEPARTMENT_ID for GroupFilterField.

6. View the page by selecting View, Page View.

Whatever value you select in the combo box will act as a group filter on the recordset. (In SQL, this is the role the HAVING clause has on SQL statements.)

Adding a PivotTable to Web Pages

The PivotTable is a component. As such, the behavior of the PivotTable will be identical in any context in which it is used. This means that the same outward behavior and attributes in the form of properties and methods are available to us to define the presentation and user interaction of the component.

Adding a PivotTable to a Data Access Page is identical to adding a PivotTable to a form. To use a PivotTable in a Data Access Page, open a Data Access Page in design mode and

20

select Insert, Office PivotTable from the menu. Everything else about the PivotTable is consistent with what you learned in Hour 19, "Creating Custom Forms and Reports," so I won't repeat that information here. Try the following steps to experiment with creating a Data Access Page with a PivotTable:

1. Open the eSoft Database from earlier in this hour.
2. Click the Pages button in the Objects View.
3. Select the Create Data Access Page in Design View option. Click New.
4. In the new Data Access Page, select the Design View option and click OK.
5. Select Insert, Office PivotTable from the menu (with the new Data Access Page in Design View).
6. If the Field List View is not displayed, select View, Field List.
7. Select the FIRST_NAME, LAST_NAME, PHONE_NUMBER, and EXTENSION fields from the EMPLOYEE table and drop them in the Drop Totals or Detail Fields Here section of the PivotTable.
8. Drag and drop the EMPLOYEE.DEPARTMENT_ID field to the Drop Filter Fields Here section of the PivotTable.
9. Select File, Web Page Preview to see how the PivotTable data will look in a browser.

There are two things you will want to do for a real Web page. First, you will want to adorn the page with HTML and other presentation data to make the page look consistent with the rest of your site. Second, you will need to deploy the Data Access Page to your Internet server.

If you are deploying your Data Access Page on your PC—your PC is the Internet server or you are hosting an intranet—then copy the Data Access Page to your Web site. Generally, the default Web site is c:\inetpub\wwwroot\. If you are deploying your Access database and Data Access Pages to another computer, make sure you update the Data Access Page connection string information. The Access Help file suggests you use a Universal Naming Convention (UNC) name or an Office Data Connection (ODC) file.

Uniform Naming Convention

Local drives and directories may be mapped drives and directories to shared physical locations. When you are defining the connection information, specify the physical location in the form \\computer\directory\database.mdb.

When you deploy your Data Access Pages, make sure you update the connection information and use the UNC name. Suppose your server name is SERVER, and your Web folder is MYWEB. To modify the connection for a page, using a UNC to point path described, the path value would be \\SERVER\MYWEB\eSoft.mdb.

To modify the connection properties for the page, open the page and select View, Field List. The DataLink component is at the top of the Fields List view. Right-click DataLink and select Connection from the context menu. The Data Link Properties dialog will be displayed, with focus set to the Connection tab. For "In item 1 Select or enter a database name", navigate to the eSoft.mdb file on your network, and click Open. If the database resides on a computer other than your own, a UNC path to the database along with the database name will be set. (Refer to Figure 20.12, which shows the Field List and DataLink selected on the right and the Connection tab of the Data Link Properties dialog with the UNC path to my eSoft.mdb database.)

FIGURE 20.12

The Data Link Properties dialog allows you to use UNC paths to your database to ensure you are not using a path that is unavailable to other users.

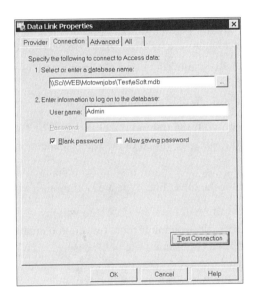

Before you close the Data Link Properties dialog, click the Test Connection button. If everything is okay, you should get a message box with "Test connection succeeded." Click OK. Now when you (or someone else) opens the Data Access Page, you will be looking at the right database.

Office Data Connection

The Office Data Connection (ODC) file is defined at the database level to ensure that you have properly specified configuration information for your Data Access Pages. (Keep in mind that Data Access Pages reside outside of your database and the connection information is stored as a script in the HTML file.)

20

To create an ODC connection file, select a page in Design View. Right-click the page to display the context menu. Select Page Properties from the menu. The page properties will be displayed; select the Data tab. Click the ConnectFile property and use the browse (...) button to open the Select Data Source Explorer. Follow these steps to finish creating the ODC file:

1. In the Select Data Source Explorer, select the item named "+Connect to New Data Source.odc".

2. Click OK. This will invoke the Data Connection Wizard.

3. For the kind of data source, select Other/Advanced. Click Next.

4. The DataLink Properties pages will be displayed (refer to Figure 20.12). On the Provider tab, select Microsoft.Jet.OLE DB Provider. Click Next.

5. The Next button will change tabs to the Connection tab of the DataLink Properties dialog.

6. Enter or browse to the UNC path to the database.

7. Click Test Connection. If the test passes, click OK. The DataLink Properties dialog will close, and you will be returned to the Data Connection Wizard dialog.

8. Click Next.

9. Enter a filename for the ODC file. Type a description, if you like, and click Finish.

The ConnectionFile property will have the ODC file you just created as a value. Once you have created the ODC file, you may reuse it when you create additional Data Access Pages. Using an Office Data Connection file helps ensure that all your Web pages are accessing the correct database.

XML's Role in Access

XML is a markup language like HTML. The Extended Markup Language (XML) is used as a means of sending data back and forth from Data Access Pages in Access 20002. (XML is also used to import and export data.)

Because XML is an industry standard, versus a Microsoft standard, many other types of applications and connectivity protocols know how to work with XML already. Using an industry standard means of moving data makes it easier for Microsoft to deploy distributed information across existing infrastructures, specifically the Web.

XML is just text, albeit specially formatted text; consequently, it can be sent back and forth across HTTP connections the same way Web pages are, without any special configuration requirements or supporting applications.

XML is used in three significant areas. First, XML is used as a means of transporting data from databases to Web pages. Second, XML is used to import and export data. Because XML is a standard, many vendors and applications already know how to work with XML, ultimately increasing the likelihood that other application vendors can integrate their applications with Microsoft's applications. And, finally, XML is used as the storage medium for working offline with Data Access Pages.

The best part about all this is that XML works quietly behind the scenes. When you create Data Access Pages, Access is sending XML back and forth; you don't need to do anything extra.

Summary

Think of a Data Access Page as a form. By adding text, graphics, and controls to a Data Access Page, you can define a rich interface for your end users. A Data Access Page differs from a form in that your users might be viewing the page on a Web site or in e-mail.

In this hour, you learned how to start a Data Access Page with a wizard and perform several kinds of customizations. When you create a form, you can write VBA code to support the behavior of the form. When you create a Data Access Page, the wizards create HTML code to support the page behaviors. You can write custom HTML, if necessary. However, there are several kinds of code that you can write to support a Web page, including HTML, JavaScript, and VBScript. Each of these is a programming language that a browser is capable of interpreting, but as independent languages, they require further independent study to master. VBScript is the most like VBA. Unfortunately, you cannot use VBScript in the Netscape Web browser. It allows you to use only Internet Explorer from Microsoft.

If you want to create a corporate intranet or use Web pages in your business solutions, Data Access Pages will help you get the job done quickly and easily. The "Q&A" and "Workshop" sections at the end of this hour will provide you with an opportunity to polish your skills.

20

Q&A

Q How do I know whether I need a more robust server than the Personal Web Server?

A You can always use the most powerful server available, but if you are offering e-commerce services, creating a public Web site, or if security is an issue, you want an industrial-strength server, such as Internet Information Services.

Q Can I run a Web site from a basic desktop computer?

A Yes. Personal Web Server was introduced in Windows 95. All you need is Personal Web Server, an IP address, an Internet service provider, and a registered URL with Network Solutions or some other registration service. Contact your ISP for any specific instructions or restrictions.

Q Do I have to have a Windows 2000 Server to create an intranet?

A No. PCs connected with network cards and CAT 5 cabling are capable of establishing a peer-to-peer network.

Q Can I use Data Access Pages in Access, too?

A Certainly. Although forms may provide faster response times and more programming control, you can use Data Access Pages in conjunction with or instead of forms.

Workshop

The Workshop includes quiz questions designed to help you test your understanding of the material covered and exercises to help put what you've learned to practice. You will find the answers to the quiz and exercises in Appendix A, "Answers."

Quiz

1. What is the Hypertext Markup Language used for?
2. Name one other language used to program Web pages.
3. What is a URL used for?
4. If you want to create a Web site for your employees only, do you want to create an intranet site or an Internet site?
5. You can use the same tables and queries for Data Access Pages as you do for your forms. True or false?
6. What does it mean to bind a control to a field?

Exercises

1. Apply a theme to the Employee Directory. (Use any theme you like.)
2. Add Department ID as the first control on the Employee Directory.
3. Change the background color of the Department ID text box to visually indicate that it is read-only.
4. Modify the Tab Index property of the Department ID control, ensuring that when a user tabs through the controls, the Department ID control is first.

PART VIII

Object-Oriented Programming in Access

Hour

HOUR **21**

Class Programming Basics

Until now, you have used classes that other programmers have written. A *class* is a user-defined type, and an instance of a class is called an *object*. You have probably heard a lot of hullabaloo about object-oriented programming. Classes are the primary idiom of object-oriented programming; without classes, there would be no *object* in *object-oriented programming*. However, understanding the mechanics of object-oriented programming is not that hard. After this hour, you will know how to write classes; in essence, you will know how to write object-oriented programs.

The hype behind objects is real. It is so real, in fact, that most mainstream languages now try to support object-oriented programming, including languages such as COBOL that were never meant to be object oriented. Object-oriented programming enables programmers to meet an increasing demand for complex software.

Object-oriented programming is not hard. It just takes some getting used to, partly because you have to unlearn older styles of programming. If you haven't programmed at all, objects will be easier for you because you have less to unlearn. In this hour, you will learn about

- The need for object-oriented programming
- Object-oriented terminology, which will help you continue learning after you finish this hour
- Writing new classes and extending existing classes to add new behaviors
- Debugging your object-oriented code in Access 2002

Understanding the Need for Classes

To explain why objects are considered so important, I will begin by describing what programming used to be like.

Before object-oriented programming, the prevalent style of programming was called *structured programming*. Structured programming was also invented as a means to manage complexity. Structured programming focuses on the process. When a programmer is using structure-oriented programming, the programmer focuses on defining all the processes and data that must be coordinated to solve a business problem.

The processes and data are not related in any significant way, other than that the processes involve manipulating the data at some point when the program is running. After all the processes and necessary data are identified, procedures are written to support all the processes. Then, code is written to call all of the procedures that complete each phase of the entire process. This is referred to as the *flow of control*.

Structured programming is supported by structured design. Structured design typically means that a mental or physical flowchart is created that depicts each process and the flow of all the processes. Mental flowcharting means the person has a conceptualization of the program flow; physical flowcharting uses specialized symbols that have specific meanings in the context of a flowchart, and the program flow is captured in a document referred to as a *flowchart*.

The difficulty with structured programming is that the digital world can become very complex. A large application can have thousands of procedures, and structured programming languages such as C and BASIC (pre–Visual Basic) did not support any mechanism for aggregating procedures. (Recall the earlier discussion of aggregation as a means to combat a limited supply of thinking memory.)

Before object-oriented programming languages, programmers had already defined a need to aggregate data to create user-defined data types. Aggregate data types enable programmers to collect many parts of data into one coherent compound type. Programmers had also established a need to aggregate lines of code into procedures to manage complexity related to lines of code. Aggregate data types and procedures enabled programmers to invent structured programming, but something was still missing.

As programs become more and more complex, they mimic the relative complexity of the physical world. In the physical world, "things" exist. These things have attributes that define their behavior and structure. A person is a thing. A person is capable of behaviors such as speech and movement. A person has attributes such as hair color, height, and weight. In the physical world, this is true of most things: They have capabilities and observable, measurable attributes.

However, separate procedures and data alone did not provide a convenient means of describing things. Further, what computer scientists decided was that the physical world (probably the most complex thing there is) is not made up of processes; rather, the physical world is made up of things interacting. Subsequently, computer scientists reasoned that programming languages should support a style of programming that enables programmers to create things that have capabilities and attributes and can interact with each other. This would enable programmers to write more powerful programs. Such programming languages are called *object oriented*.

What the software industry is finding out now is that the early computer scientists were right. Complex software can be much more manageable when written in object-oriented programming languages. However, bad object-oriented code is like any other bad thing— it's, well, bad.

Not all programmers are writing object-oriented programs, but a predominant amount of new code is being written in languages that support an object-oriented style of programming. However, individually, not all companies are reaping the promise of objects, even in 2001. They will, though. Object-oriented programming is here to stay. It might evolve further, but it isn't going away, and the industry will never go back to structured programming.

Invest the time to grasp the concepts in the rest of this hour, and you will be much better off. A couple words of warning are necessary before I continue. Avoid trying to create objects out of everything. Focus on solving the problem, regardless of the number and variety of classes you create or don't create. Also, keep in mind that good object-oriented code seldom comes out right the first time. Good object-oriented code evolves, sometimes slowly.

21

Creating Your First Class

When you are writing code in a class module, you write it just as you would in a regular module. The difference is that code in the regular module is treated by Access as disparate code, but code in a class module is treated by Access as code belonging to a class. To use code in a class, you need an instance of that class.

You already know how to create an instance of a class. Here's an example from Hour 13, "Storing Information in a Collection":

```
Dim Strings As New Collection
```

The preceding line of code declares an instance of a Collection named Strings. An object is exactly an instance of a class. When you write code in a class module, you are defining a class. Follow these numbered steps to define a simple class:

1. Create a new database or open an existing database.
2. In the Objects View, click Modules and click New.
3. In the module, add the code in Listing 21.1.
4. Save the module with the name Test.
5. With the editor open, click Insert, Class Module to add a new class module to your database.
6. In the class module, enter the code in Listing 21.2.
7. Save the module as FirstClass.
8. In the editor, click Window, Test to open the module with the test code.
9. Run the subroutine TestMyFirstClass. The code will display the message box with the text This is my first class!.

LISTING 21.1   Testing the Class You Will Write in Listing 21.2

```
1:  Option Compare Database
2:  Sub TestMyFirstClass()
3:      Dim MyFirstClass As New FirstClass
4:      MyFirstClass.Greetings
5:      Set MyFirstClass = Nothing
6:  End Sub
```

ANALYSIS   Listing 21.1 contains simple code that creates an object, MyFirstClass, from the class FirstClass on line 3. Line 4 calls the method Greetings, and line 5 releases the object. Notice that the object name, MyFirstClass, and the member-of operator (.) precede the call to the Greetings method. Look at Listing 21.2 for an implementation of FirstClass.

LISTING 21.2   Defining a Simple Class with One Method, `Greetings`

```
Option Compare Database
Sub Greetings()
    MsgBox "My first class!"
End Sub
```

 In VBA, code must be in a class module for it to be part of a class. You create a class module in the editor with the Insert, Class Module menu item.

ANALYSIS   Listing 21.2 defines the class `FirstClass`. Any code that you write in a class module becomes part of the class. `FirstClass` is simple; it contains only one method: `Greetings`.

Although not a very useful class, `FirstClass` is technically accurate, and all other classes are basically defined the same way. To define every class, open the editor and use the Insert, Class Module menu item to create the class module. After you have the class module, for the most part, the code you write in a class is the same as the code you write in a non–class module. The biggest difference is that when you put code in a class, you want to put code in the class module that is part of the definition of that class.

Before I elaborate on defining classes with more complex methods and data, I need to take a few minutes to talk about accessibility.

Hiding Information to Make Code Easier to Use

Have you ever used the phrase "too much information"? Well, sometimes too much information is a bad thing. Imagine for a moment if you had to think "Stomach, digest" and "Cells, grow" for these things to happen. It's better that we don't have to think about these things; it makes life easier. Or what about the brake master cylinder in your car? What if you had to squeeze a hand pump to build up pressure and then open a valve to apply that pressure to your brake calipers when you wanted to stop your car? There would be pileups all day long.

Information hiding (or complexity hiding) is a good thing. Life would be impossible if you and I had to think about every aspect of everything all the time. More than likely, everyone would go immediately insane.

21

Object-oriented programming has some precise facilities that enable programmers to conceal some of the complexity of objects. When you define a class, you have to write all of the class. That is, you have to define all the data and procedures that will make instances of that class capable of maintaining state information and exhibit the correct behaviors. What you don't have to do is require that all users of your class know how those behaviors are implemented. You can hide some of those details.

For example, when you wrote code in earlier chapters, you used the ADODB object, but you didn't know how all that code works. The best part is, you do not have to. All you needed to know was how to use the data and the methods that were made available. All you had to do to open a Recordset object was to call the Open method.

When you write classes, you want to keep this in mind: You will write a lot of code, but others who use your code, such as colleagues who want to customize one of your applications, will not need to know or even understand how that code works. If you hide some of the details, you make it easier for them to use your code and think about the code they want to write as they go beyond just using Access and become Access programmers themselves.

The *class* is the unit of encapsulation in the object-oriented world. In VBA, a class is a module just like a regular module. However, if you were to export it to an external file, a regular module would have a .bas extension, and a class module would have a .cls extension.

In a class, there are two kinds of accessibility. *Accessibility is the key to code management*. One kind of accessibility is called *public*, and the other is called *private*. Defining data and procedures as "private" means that users of the class don't have to worry about them. When you define data and procedures as "public," you are indicating that you intend for the users of your class to use the data and procedures.

In VBA, members of a class can be Public or Private. The keyword Public or Private is placed as the first word on the line of code that defines a method or data.

NEW TERM   A *member* is any procedure or data defined in a class.

The data and methods in a class are referred to as the *class interface*. If you use the word Public as the first word in a definition, the member is a Public member, or it is said that the member is *part of the public interface*. If you use the keyword Private as the first word in a definition, the member is considered a Private member, or it is said that the member is *part of the private interface*.

Things declared as `Public` are those things that you want users of your class to access. Things declared `Private` are those things that you do not want users to access. When you declare an instance of a class, even you cannot access the `Private` members of that class. You will get a compiler error—`Method or data member not found`—if you refer to a `Private` member outside the class module.

When a member is `Private`, it is considered an implementation detail of the class. That is, only the implementer/writer of the class has to be concerned with `Private` members. In fact, users of your classes don't even have to know that `Private` members exist.

Before objects, all code was accessible, and you had to concern yourself with all the code in a program. In object-oriented programs, you have to learn to use only the code in the `Public` interface when using classes. This can considerably reduce the amount of code you have to understand.

When you are authoring a class, you will, of course, have to write it all, but this has its advantages, too. When you are writing a class, it is important that an object be a complete and independent piece of code. This means that when you are authoring a class, all you have to think about is what goes in the class, what you want to make public, and what you want to make private. The human mind is a powerful tool when focused. Object-oriented programming enables you to focus on just the code in the class when writing classes and just the interface when using classes.

In coming sections, I will demonstrate how to use `Private` and `Public` access specifiers. Here are a couple of things to remember that will help you: You can define everything as `Public` in a class until you are comfortable with using `Private` access specifiers. Also, you can always change the access specifier later if you determine that this is necessary.

Defining Class Methods

Class methods are procedures. You can define subroutines and functions in a class module. The syntax is the same for procedures in class modules as for regular modules. Listing 21.3 demonstrates the technique.

LISTING 21.3   Examples of Methods Added to `FirstClass`

```
1:  Option Compare Database
2:  Option Base 0
3:  Option Explicit
4:  Enum LanguageType
5:      ltTechnoid
6:      ltEspanol
7:      ltDeutsch
```

21

LISTING 21.3 continued

```
8:  End Enum
9:  Public Sub GreetingsAufDeutsch()
10:     MsgBox GetGreetingsText(ltDeutsch)
11: End Sub
12: Public Sub GreetingsEspanol()
13:     MsgBox GetGreetingsText(ltEspanol)
14: End Sub
15: Public Sub GreetingsTechnoid()
16:     MsgBox GetGreetingsText(ltTechnoid)
17: End Sub
18: Private Function GetGreetingsText(ByVal Language As LanguageType) As String
19:     Select Case Language
20:     Case ltTechnoid
21:         GetGreetingsText = "Hello, World!"
22:     Case ltEspanol
23:         GetGreetingsText = "Buenos dias!"
24:     Case ltDeutsch
25:         GetGreetingsText = "Guten tag!"
26:     End Select
27: End Function
```

Group your methods by `Public` and `Private` access, and within each group, use alphabetical order. This will make it easy for you and others to find methods quickly.

ANALYSIS You can use the test code in Listing 21.1 to test the methods in the extended version of `FirstClass`. `FirstClass` now contains an enumerated type, `LanguageType`. `FirstClass` contains three `Public` methods in Listing 21.3: `GreetingsAufDeutsch`, `GreetingsEspanol`, and `GreetingsTechnoid`. I added a `Private` method, `GetGreetingsText`, to handle determining what the text will be, keeping all the greetings text in one place.

Users of objects of `FirstClass` cannot call the Private method `GetGReetingsText`. `GetGreetingsText` uses a `Select Case` statement to determine which text to get.

Because `Private` methods will not be used in any code other than the class module, you can freely change `Private` method names and implementations without adversely affecting other code.

For example, you could change the code in each of the three `Public` methods to call a new `Private` method, `GetFastGreetingsText`, and remove the `GetGreetingsText` method. The effect of this kind of change is limited to the class module. No other code outside the class module could have called the `Private` methods, so removing a `Private` method doesn't require you to change other modules. Listing 21.4 demonstrates the modified code.

LISTING 21.4   A Modified `Private` Method That Returns the Greetings Text

```
1:   Option Compare Database
2:   Option Base 0
3:   Option Explicit
4:   Enum LanguageType
5:       ltTechnoid
6:       ltEspanol
7:       ltDeutsch
8:   End Enum
9:   Public Sub GreetingsAufDeutsch()
10:       MsgBox GetFastGreetingsText(ltDeutsch)
11:  End Sub
12:  Public Sub GreetingsEspanol()
13:       MsgBox GetFastGreetingsText(ltEspanol)
14:  End Sub
15:  Public Sub GreetingsTechnoid()
16:       MsgBox GetFastGreetingsText(ltTechnoid)
17:  End Sub
18:  Private Function GetFastGreetingsText(ByVal Language As LanguageType)
➥As String
19:       GetFastGreetingsText = Array("Hello, World!", "Buenos dias!",
20:       ➥"Guten tag!")(Language)
21:  End Function
```

The code in 21.4 is identical to Listing 21.3 except for the new `Private` method named `GetFastGreetingsText`. The implementation of the new method uses the enumerated type, `LanguageType`, as an index into an array on line 19. Instead of several lines of code in a case statement, the greetings text is now derived from one line of code.

21

To recap, private members limit what users, or *consumers*, of your class have to grapple with and allow you to change the private members—referred to as *implementation details*—without affecting code written by consumers of your class.

When you are writing a class, you are the *producer*. When you are using the class, you are the *consumer*. Keep this tenet in mind when writing classes. Even if you are the only person writing or working with a given body of code, making classes easier to consume by using `Private` members makes your job easier. Remember, the mind you save may be your own.

In contrast, the `Public` interface is there to be used by other code. Therefore, any changes to `Public` interfaces might require you to change code outside the class module.

Defining Properties

Data stores the information about your program. If the data is wrong, the program cannot be right. For a long time, programmers have known that data must be validated. For example, any combination of numbers does not necessarily make a valid date, –1000 is not a valid age, and 1,000 shares of Microsoft is not a valid transaction if you don't own the shares (unless you are short selling). Each of these examples represents data. Not all data is valid in all circumstances; therefore, data must be validated.

GIGO (Garbage In, Garbage Out) is the acronym coined to describe what bad data does to your program. The strategy originally employed to validate data was to use a function to validate it. Unfortunately, validation procedures present problems of their own. Sometimes programmers got lazy and didn't write validation procedures. In other scenarios, programmers just didn't call the validation procedures even though they may have existed. Calling validation functions didn't work very well because it required extra, tedious code to be written and called every single time the data was used. Tedious, repetitive tasks and people do not go together very well. Tedious, repetitive tasks and computers, however, go together quite well.

The solution was to create a new idiom: the property. A *property* allows you to validate data with a function while still writing code as if you were using the data. A property is used to store data in classes. Properties also allow you to associate procedures with data in an unobtrusive manner to provide the validation automatically. (Refer to Figure 21.1 for a conceptual view of the relationship between properties and data.)

Property methods have their own unique syntax. There is one method for reading the property and one for writing the property. Listing 21.5 defines a new class that contains two properties: `Name` and `EmailAddress`.

FIGURE 21.1

The relationship between properties and data.

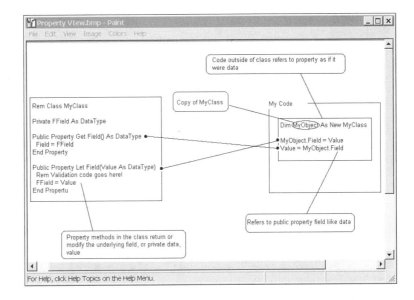

LISTING 21.5   Two Property Definitions in the Contact Class

```
1:  Option Compare Database
2:  Option Explicit
3:  Private FName As String
4:  Private FEmailAddress As String
5:  Property Get Name() As String
6:      Name = FName
7:  End Property
8:  Property Let Name(ByVal Value As String)
9:      FName = Value
10: End Property
11: Property Get EMailAddress() As String
12:     EMailAddress = FEmailAddress
13: End Property
14: Private Sub RaiseError(ByVal MESSAGE As String)
15:     Call Err.Raise(vbObjectError, "Contact", Message)
16: End Sub
17: Private Sub ValidateEmailAddress(ByVal Value As String)
18:     Const MESSAGE = "invalid email address "
19:     If (InStr(1, Value, "@") = 0) Then RaiseError (MESSAGE & EMailAddress)
20: End Sub
21: Property Let EMailAddress(ByVal Value As String)
22:     Call ValidateEmailAddress(Value)
23:     FEmailAddress = Value
24: End Property
```

21

ANALYSIS Remember, to create the `Contact` class, you open the Visual Basic editor and select Insert, Class Module. Lines 3 and 4 of Listing 21.5 contain the actual data. It is defined as `Private` because you do not want the data accessed directly; rather, you want it accessed through the `Property` methods. There are two pieces of data: `FName` and `FEmailAddress`. Both are strings. Line 5 defines the `Get` property method for `FName`. Given an instance of the `Contact` class, `MyContact`, you would use the `Name` property—for example, `MyContact.Name`. When `Name` is used as a right-side operand, the `Get Name()` property method is called, and the code on line 6 is run. Lines 8 through 10 define the `Let` property. `Let` properties are called when a property is used as a left-side operand. The next two lines of code demonstrate using `Name` as left-side and right-side operands, respectively:

```
MyContact.Name = "Noah Kimmel"

MsgBox MyContact.Name
```

The two lines of code look like code that is accessing data—that's what you want—but what really happens is that the `Property` methods are called. As I said, properties offer the convenience of data and the power of validation.

Lines 11–12 and 21–24 define the `Get` and `Let` properties for `EMailAddress`. (Note that the syntax is the same. `Get` property methods are defined like functions with a return type, and `Let` methods are defined like subroutines with arguments.) Line 22 of Listing 21.5 demonstrates how the data can be validated behind the scenes. To set an `EmailAddress` of the object `MyContact`, you would write

```
MyContact.EmailAddress = "pkimmel@softconcepts.com"
```

The code on lines 22 and 23 is run. Line 22 calls `ValidateEmailAddress`, passing the value `"pkimmel@softconcepts.com"` to the subroutine. (Notice that `ValidateEmailAddress` on line 17 is `Private`.) If the e-mail address is valid, the data passed as the argument `Value` on line 21 is assigned to the `Private` data, `FEmailAddress`.

Property methods give you more control over the data, but properties are as easy to use as plain data. The control over your data is obtained by embedding as much or as little validation code as necessary in the property method. All code that uses your property, by implication, has to use your validation code as well.

An additional benefit is that you can restrict what can be done with the data. For example, to make data read-only, don't define the `Set` or `Let` method. To make data write-only, don't define the `Get` method. When you define classes, make all your data `Private` and use properties to modify the data. Properties are a powerful idiom, and they are what make visual programming possible.

Using Object Properties

Classes can have data that are simple data types and objects. You use `Get` methods for reading property values of both simple and object types. To define write properties for simple types, you use the `Let` method, but to define write properties that are objects, you have to use `Set` property methods.

The `Set` keyword is used in place of `Let` in the property definition if the property refers to an object. For example, if you have a property that is a `Collection`, you would have to write `Get` and `Set` property methods. An integer property would use `Get` and `Let` property methods.

Using Static Properties

When you define a class, you are defining a user type. When you define an instance of that class, you are creating an object of that type. Every object gets its own copy of all the data and methods defined in the class. Therefore, given instances of `Contact`, `MyContact`, and `YourContact`, `MyContact.Name` and `YourContact.Name` refer to two different `Name` properties.

Think of the difference between classes and objects as the difference between DNA and clones. DNA describes the critter, and an actual critter from that DNA is a clone. Class is to DNA what object is to clone.

When the `Static` keyword is applied to a property method, it plays the same role as when it is applied to any method. A `Static` property declaration means that all variables declared in the property have local scope, but the values are maintained between successive calls to the property. Listing 21.6 demonstrates.

LISTING 21.6 A `Static` Property Maintains the Local Variable Values Between Successive Calls to the Property As Long As the Program Is Running

```
1:  Static Property Get UniqueID() As Integer
2:    Dim ID As Integer
3:    ID = ID + 1
4:    UniqueID = ID
5:  End Property
```

21

As long as the program containing this code is running, `ID` will increase by 1 each time `UniqueID` is accessed. The value of `ID` is maintained between calls to `UniqueID`. This is true for all variables in a `Static` property method.

The technique in Listing 21.6 might be useful to guarantee a unique identifier for database tables or instances of classes. You might add code to initialize ID to some stored value if ID is 0. For example, read the identifier from a table if ID is 0 and then begin accumulating from there.

Use Static at the property level when you want all variables in the property to be static.

Writing Initialization and Termination Code

Every class has two special subroutines available for you to define initialization and finalization code. The initialize subroutine is called when you create a new instance of an object, and any terminate code is called when you set an object equal to nothing. The subroutines are called only if you add code to them, and they are called implicitly. You do not call these two methods.

The initialize and terminate methods will always be named Class_Initialize and Class_Terminate. To add code to either of these methods, follow these steps:

1. Open the Visual Basic editor.
2. Select a class module or add a new class module.
3. Click the Object combo box on the left of the code window (it should have the word (General) in it), and select the word Class (see Figure 21.2).

FIGURE 21.2

The VBA editor showing the Object combo box focused on the General section and the Procedure combo box focused on TestFileStream.

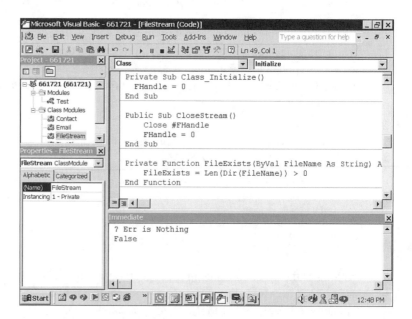

4. Click the Procedure window on the right (shown in Figure 21.2) at the top of the edit window, and select either Initialize or Terminate (whichever one you want to write code for).

The preceding steps will create an empty subroutine. All you have to do is add code to the subroutine. Class_Initialize is where you put code that you want run whenever a new object of that type is created, code that you want run first before any other code, and code that you want run only once. Class_Terminate is where you add code that you want to run last, just before the memory for the object is released. Termination code will be run only once, too.

Befitting their respective names, Class_Initialize is a good place to put initialization code, such as opening a database or other data file, and Class_Terminate is a good place to put finalization code, such as closing a database or data file. See Listing 21.7 in the next section for an example of an initialization subroutine.

Writing a New Class

This section demonstrates a whole class that I have found useful. This class defines a file-streaming mechanism. I call it FileStream. The class provides a consistent interface that makes it easy to open and close files, read and write text, and seek to a certain point in the file. Listing 21.7 contains the definition of the FileStream class.

LISTING 21.7   The FileStream Class, Which Makes Reading and Writing Text Files Easy

```
1:  Option Compare Database
2:  ' FileStream.bas - Defines a file-management streaming class
3:  ' Copyright (c) 1999. All Rights Reserved.
4:  ' By Software Conceptions, Inc
5:  ' Written By Paul Kimmel. Okemos, MI USA 800-471-5890
6:  Option Explicit
7:  Private FFileName As String
8:  Private FHandle As Double
9:  Private Type Buffer
10:    S As String * 1
11: End Type
12: Public Property Get Count() As Long
13:    Count = FileLen(FileName)
14: End Property
15: Public Property Get FileName() As String
16:    FileName = FFileName
17: End Property
18: Public Property Let FileName(ByVal Value As String)
19:    FFileName = Value
```

21

LISTING 21.7   continued

```
20:  End Property
21:  Public Property Get Handle() As Double
22:       Handle = FHandle
23:  End Property
24:  Public Property Get Position() As Long
25:       Position = Seek(FHandle)
26:  End Property
27:  Public Property Let Position(ByVal Value As Long)
28:       Call SeekStream(Value)
29:  End Property
30:  Private Sub CheckFile(ByVal FileName As String)
31:       If (FileExists(FileName) = False) Then
32:           Err.Raise 1, "FileStream.cls", "Invalid filename " & FileName
33:       End If
34:  End Sub
35:  Private Sub Class_Initialize()
36:    FHandle = 0
37:  End Sub
38:  Public Sub CloseStream()
39:       Close #FHandle
40:       FHandle = 0
41:  End Sub
42:  Private Function FileExists(ByVal FileName As String) As Boolean
43:       FileExists = Len(Dir(FileName)) > 0
44:  End Function
45:  Public Sub OpenStream(ByVal FileName As String)
46:       FFileName = FileName
47:       FHandle = FreeFile
48:       Open FileName For Random As #FHandle Len = 1
49:  End Sub
50:  Public Sub ReadStream(Str As String, ByVal Length As Long)
51:       Dim I As Integer
52:       Dim Buf As Buffer
53:       For I = 1 To Length
54:           Get #FHandle, , Buf
55:           Str = Str + Buf.S
56:       Next I
57:  End Sub
58:  Public Sub SeekStream(ByVal Length As Long)
59:       On Error GoTo EXCEPT
60:       Seek #FHandle, Length
61:       Exit Sub
62:  EXCEPT:
63:    If (Length = 0) Then Resume Next
64:    Err.Raise Err.Number, Err.Source, Err.Description, Err.HelpFile,
        ➥Err.HelpContext
65:  End Sub
66:  Public Sub WriteStream(ByVal Str As String)
67:       Dim I As Long
68:       Dim Buf As Buffer
```

LISTING 21.7 continued

```
69:    For I = 1 To Len(Str)
70:        Buf.S = Mid$(Str, I, 1)
71:        Put #FHandle, , Buf
72:    Next I
73: End Sub
```

ANALYSIS The FileStream class defines all the methods necessary to read and write text files. There are four properties: Count, FileName, Handle, and Position. Handle is a read-only property that stores the file handle. Count is a read-only property that returns the character count. FileName is the name of the file, and Position is the offset in the file where reading and writing will occur next. Using the Position property, you can read from or write to any position in the file.

There are eight methods in the FileStream class: CheckFile, Class_Initialize, CloseStream, FileExists, OpenStream, ReadStream, SeekStream, and WriteStream. CheckFile is a private validation procedure that raises an error if the file does not exist. Class_Initialize initializes the FHandle (a Double data type) to zero. CloseStream closes the file referred to by FHandle. FileExists provides a file-centric method for the statement on line 43 of Listing 21.7. The OpenStream method takes a file-name argument, stores the name, gets a file handle, and opens the file in Random file mode. Use ReadStream to read a specified number of characters from the current position in the open file. SeekStream moves the position to current position plus length. The WriteStream method writes data to the stream.

Used in concert, these eight methods enable you to completely manage a text file. Listing 21.8 demonstrates an example of using the FileStream class.

LISTING 21.8 Opening and Writing to a Text File with the FileStream Class

```
1: Sub TestFileStream()
2:     Dim Stream As New FileStream
3:     Call Stream.OpenStream("Test.txt")
4:     Call Stream.WriteStream("This is a test")
5:     Call Stream.CloseStream
6:     Set Stream = Nothing
7: End Sub
```

21

ANALYSIS Line 2 of Listing 21.8 creates a new FileStream object named Stream. Line 3 opens a file, Test.txt. Line 4 writes "This is a test" to the file, and line 5 closes the file. Line 6 releases the Stream object. The Class_Initialize procedure is called when line 2 runs. If there were a Class_Terminate procedure, it would be run when line 6 runs.

The ActiveX object `Scripting.FileSystemObject` provides some of the same services as those implemented in `FileStream`. To create an ActiveX object, you must define a `Variant` and use the `CreateObject` procedure or add a reference to the Microsoft Scripting Runtime Library and create an instance of `FileSystemObject` using the `New` keyword. For examples of using `Scripting.FileSystemObject`, search the VBA editor Help system for `OpenTextFile`.

The `FileStream` class in this section is easy to use, but `FileSystemObject` provides more power and flexibility. It is an alternative if your file-management tasks exceed the `FileStream` object's capabilities.

Object-oriented programming is powerful because it enables you to focus intently on a single problem at a time. The code is highly portable because it is in a distinct module and solves a complete problem. Object-oriented code is more maintainable for those reasons, too, and because you can modify the `Private` interface without adversely affecting class consumers.

Testing Classes

Classes you write should be tested. The scaffolding techniques discussed in Hour 17, "Removing Bugs," and the error-handling techniques discussed in Hour 18, "Adding Code to Handle Errors," are applicable to user-defined classes. When you create a class, write a simple test module that exercises all the properties and methods in the class.

If the class is complete, you should be able to create instances of the class and use it without errors.

Extending Existing Classes

A useful aspect of object-oriented programming in VBA is *class aggregation*. You can use a new class to extend the capabilities of an existing class. Aggregation, when used in conjunction with classes, refers to incorporating a class member as an attribute of a new class.

Hour 22, "Adding Capabilities to Your Data Types," demonstrates how to extend classes using code aggregation.

Creating an Instance of a Class

Creating an instance of a class is the same whether it is an existing class or one you have defined. The following statement defines an instance of the `FileStream` class:

```
Dim Stream As New FileStream
```

When you create an object by adding a reference and using the New keyword, this is referred to as *early binding*. When you call CreateObject and assign the return value of the CreateObject call to a Variant, this is referred to as *late binding*.

The Visual Basic editor can show you a list of properties and methods for early-bound objects because the editor knows the data type of the object at design time. This isn't so for late-bound objects.

ActiveX objects require that you add a reference to the library and use the New keyword, or use the CreateObject procedure, passing the class name as a string argument to CreateObject. Listing 21.9 creates a late-bound instance of Excel (see the note for more information on late versus early binding). In the VBA editor, select Tools, References to include the Microsoft Excel 10.0 Object Library in your project.

LISTING 21.9   Creating an Instance of Excel

```
1:  Sub CreateExcelInstance()
2:    Dim Excel As Object
3:    Set Excel = CreateObject("excel.application")
4:    Excel.Visible = True
5:    Excel.Quit
6:    Set Excel = Nothing
7:  End Sub
```

ANALYSIS Line 2 of Listing 21.9 defines an object named Excel. (The variable name seems fitting.) Line 2 uses the CreateObject procedure and passes excel.application as the argument. Line 3 uses the Visible property to show the running version of Excel, and lines 4 and 5 close Excel and release the object. You can create instances of Word, Outlook, Excel, Access, PowerPoint, and SourceSafe with this kind of code. CreateObject will create instances of any Automation servers.

The OLE Automation server is one of the facets of the Component Object Model (COM). An Automation server is a special kind of program that has part of its interface exposed to external applications. Automation servers can be used to provide services to other applications or as standalone applications. Access 2002 is an example of an Automation server.

21

Summary

Object-oriented programming is challenging because it offers a wealth of rich idioms that enable you to create useful data types. Without objects, there would be no ADODB and no components, creating graphical user interfaces would be much more complex, and there would be no VBA language. VBA, itself, is a product of object-oriented programming.

In previous hours, you learned how to use classes. In this hour, you learned how to "roll your own." A class is a user-defined data type. The class container is a class module. Classes contain properties and methods. Properties provide constrained access to data, and methods define the capabilities.

`Public` and `Private` access specifiers allow you to indicate accessibility. `Private` members of classes are only accessible to code in the class; `Public` members of classes are those properties and attributes that you want to make available to class consumers. Object-oriented programming is beneficial to programmers working alone because the class idiom enables them to concentrate on solving a whole piece of the problem independently of the rest of the problem. The mind is a powerful thing when focused on solving individuated problems. VBA classes afford you this opportunity.

Hour 22 demonstrates some advanced aspects of object-oriented programming that build on what you have learned in this hour. Complete the "Q&A" and "Workshop" sections at the end of this chapter to further hone your object-oriented programming ability.

Q&A

Q Why aren't subroutines and functions simply called that when they are part of classes?

A As meaning evolves, so must terminology. The new terminology captures the extended meaning. Methods are subroutines and functions, but they are something more, too. The same is true for properties: Properties are data, but something more, too. The new terms require additional learning, but they aid in communication.

Q Is it essential that I master object-oriented programming to use Access?

A Yes and no. Almost everything you do in Access will touch some aspect of object-oriented programming. However, you can use Access and use existing classes. If you don't create user-defined classes, you can still solve business problems. However, the full power of the tool can be achieved only if all its capabilities are available to you.

Q Are there idioms I must learn before I can create my own classes?

A No. This hour covers all the basic ones. Advanced idioms exist, but you can create useful classes without them. It is important to note that not all object-oriented languages are created equal. Other languages, such as Object Pascal and C++, have many more idioms and are therefore much harder to learn and use—but they are more powerful, too. Access VBA balances power and flexibility with ease of use.

Q How will I know when to create a class?

A That's a good question. All code does not have to be in a class. If you encounter a recurring problem that has associated procedures and data, that collective group of code might be a good candidate for "classdom." The good thing about classes is that you can eventually evolve structured code (code that is not in a class) into object-oriented code. An example is the `FileStream` class. Files require handles, and there are several operations you can perform on them; hence, collectively, the handle, the filename, and the operations you perform on files make good candidates to become part of the class.

Workshop

The Workshop includes quiz questions designed to help you test your understanding of the material covered and exercises to help put what you've learned to practice. You will find the answers to the quiz and exercises in Appendix A, "Answers."

Quiz

1. Type is to variable as class is to what?
2. A class can have data that is not a property. True or false?
3. What is the generic term that means a *class subroutine* or *function*?
4. What are the steps to create a new class module?
5. What is the keyword used to describe the read property method? What is the keyword for a write property method?

Exercises

1. Define a class that contains name and phone number properties.
2. Copy the `FileStream` class. Write a test procedure that writes a line of code to a text file, reposition the cursor at the beginning of the file, and read the same amount of text that you wrote, verifying that the class works.
3. Use `Scripting.FileSystemObject` to read from the text file you created in exercise 2.

21

Hour **22**

Adding Capabilities to Your Data Types

Analysis is the process of understanding a problem. *Design* is the process of choosing a solution. Analysis and design can be done formally. Formal analysis occurs when an analyst interviews a user of the solution-to-be to determine the nature of the problem. Informal analysis can take place when you, all alone, decide that you need some code to solve a problem. Informal analysis is commonly employed when the number of programmers is limited to just one or two people. For large-scale projects, the analyst might analyze only and do no programming. For our purposes, you will be the analyst, and analysis will be an informal process.

At first, it is easy to fall into the trap of becoming so excited about objects that you try to make everything an object. However, everything is not an object! (There are programming languages where everything is an object, but that does not apply to us or Access.) This hour is about identifying and building objects.

In this hour, you will learn how to identify the kinds of problems that generate good objects and how to build those objects when the need arises. In this hour, you will also learn how to identify problems that can generate good classes and learn how to build those classes by doing the following:

- Learning to identify a minimal set of circumstances that should exist before defining a class
- Applying basic principles of object-oriented design
- Extending an existing class through aggregation
- Using your new class

Defining the Objective

In this hour, the fictitious scenario driving the construction of a class is the need for an associative array. An *associative array* is an array that establishes an association between a name and a value. An associative array can be thought of as a kind of database. There are already real-world examples of computer problems that require this kind of class. For example, an INI file that stores configuration information is a kind of associative array. The Windows 95, 98, NT, and 2000 Registries are associative arrays. The Registry contains hundreds of key and value pairs. You can look at the Registry to get an example of these key and value pairs by clicking Start, Run and entering **REGEDIT**. However, don't make any changes to the Registry because this can adversely affect your computer's capability to run correctly.

A `Collection` is a kind of associative array because you can associate a key with each value you add to a `Collection`. A limitation exists on a `Collection` so that you cannot access the keys as values. You must know the keys beforehand to make use of them. Therefore, in this hour, I will demonstrate how to use a `Collection` in a new class to extend its capabilities. I will also add the `FileStream` class from Hour 21, "Class Programming Basics," to make it easy to read and write the associative array to and from a file.

Understanding When to Write a Class

You can write a class at any time. Technically, you can write a class containing a single data element; however, this is not the best use of a class. As a general guideline, the need for a class exists when you can identify approximately three or more pieces of data and three or more methods that can be applied to solve a discrete problem.

Keep in mind the distinction between classes and objects. A *class* defines the blueprint of what instances of the description will look and act like. *Object* is often used in speech when *class* is technically the correct word.

This was done at the opening of the chapter. What was meant at the chapter opening is that it is not necessary to define *classes* for all code in Access applications.

If you look in the help file and search on `Collection`, you will note that a `Collection` class contains a property and three methods. A `Collection` is a good and commonly used class. As a general guideline, a class should have fewer than a dozen public methods and properties. This is to inhibit the class from becoming too complex. As a rule, the number of private properties and methods isn't important because users of the class can't use these properties and methods anyway.

If you encounter code that occurs in more than one place, this is referred to as *divergent code*. Code should tend toward convergence; that is, programmers should strive to have only one occurrence of any block of code. If you find two or more lines that occur in a couple of places, try to find a home for that code in an existing class or create a new class. By converging code, you only have to modify one set of code that supports a given behavior.

Remember that these are only guiding principles. They provide you with a good starting point. To recap, the following guidelines determine when to define a class and how much to put in a class:

- When three or more properties or methods exist that together solve a discrete problem.
- When the number of methods and attributes in the public interface are limited to fewer than a dozen.
- When you encounter identical code occurring in two or more places.
- You can deviate from these guidelines if necessary and if it makes sense to do so.

If you create a class only when these conditions occur, you will end up with a better result.

Applied to our objective for this hour, I want to have a collection that can contain name and data pairs and that can be read from or written to a file. In essence, I have determined a need for an associative collection.

Applying Basic Principles of Object-Oriented Design

The first basic principles of object-oriented design (OOD) is that you name the classes that will implement a solution in the problem domain (*problem domain* refers everything that comprises the problem you are trying to solve). For our purposes, I am trying to solve the problem of storing data in name and data pairs to facilitate accessing data by name, data by index, or name by data.

Object-oriented design (OOD) and analysis (OOA) are actually aspects of object-oriented programming (OOP) that have tools, notational languages, and practices consigned to them. One such popular tool is Rational Rose, which employs the Unified Modeling Language (UML).

Modeling is the act of specifying a design, and the standardized modeling language is UML, which has its own notation that uses pictures and text to describe classes, use cases, actors, and interactions between objects and actors. For more information on UML, see *Sams Teach Yourself UML in 24 Hours* (0-672-31636-6).

Hence, object-oriented design can be a process distinct from programming. In single-programmer applications, however, basic designs can be captured with much less rigor and effort than more complex applications might require.

The basic principle of OOD is to define those properties and methods that capture the solution to a problem. You can use a list and a piece of paper to do this. I will list the basic requirements of the associative array in the text of this section.

Naming What the Class Must Do and Know

The associative array will hold data in name and data pairs as strings. Therefore, I will call the class Strings. The class must be capable of the following:

- Storing strings
- Accessing data values by name
- Accessing names by value
- Reading the strings from a file

- Writing the strings to a file
- Modifying the data

Now that I have named what the class must do or know, I have to pick names for these capabilities and decide whether the thing can be represented best as data or as a procedure.

I want to access the Strings class by index, so I can make this aspect an indexed property. Accessing data values by name is also a kind of indexing; therefore, I can make this an indexable property, too. The same is true for the names—names are a good property for the same reason data values are. After the data values are accessible by index, I want to be able to modify those values. Subsequently, I can affect data modification through the Value property. Picking the noun from each of the capabilities decided upon so far, I have properties called Strings, Names, and Values. (I choose to use the pluralized form because these are indexed properties, implying that there can be one or more values.)

The last two capabilities I want to support are reading and writing the data. I want to read from and write to a file; therefore, I can create good names for these capabilities by combining what I want to do and what I want to do it with. Hence, I have decided upon the method names ReadFromFile and WriteToFile. Table 22.1 contains the definition of the Strings class.

TABLE 22.1   The Definition of the *Strings* Class

Name	Member Type	Description
Names	Property	Indexable representation of the name values.
Values	Property	Indexable representation of the data values. It supports modification of the data values.
Strings	Property	Indexable representation of the entire string of data.
ReadFromFile	Method	Capability to read the data from a text file.
WriteToFile	Method	Capability to write the data to a text file.

Table 22.1 captures the design of the Strings associative array. The properties and methods in Table 22.1 will make up the public interface of the Strings class. How they are implemented is up to the individual programmer—in this instance, me.

Tips for Implementing Classes

A good means of implementing a new class is to keep the public interface as simple as possible. Another element of successful class implementation is the use of as much existing code as possible. Existing code is easiest to use because much of the work is already done—existing code will probably have been tested and used often. The end result is that your new class is easier to implement and cheaper to own.

In the following sections, I break down each aspect of the process of implementing the design as captured thus far. You can participate by writing the shell of the class. Based on the methods and properties listed in Table 22.1, Listing 22.1 shows the class's code.

LISTING 22.1   The Public Interface of the Strings Class

```
1:  Option Compare Database
2:  Option Explicit
3:  Public Property Get Names(ByVal Index As Integer) As String
4:
5:  End Property
6:
7:  Public Property Let Names(ByVal Index As Integer, ByVal Name As String)
8:
9:  End Property
10:
11: Public Property Get Strings(ByVal Index As Integer) As String
12:
13: End Property
14:
15: Public Property Let Strings(ByVal Index As Integer, ByVal Str As String)
16:
17: End Property
18:
19: Public Property Get Values(ByVal Name As String) As String
20:
21: End Property
22:
23: Public Property Let Values(ByVal Name As String, ByVal Value As String)
24:
25: End Property
26:
27: Public Sub ReadFromFile(ByVal FileName As String)
28:
29: End Sub
30:
31: Public Sub WriteToFile(ByVal FileName As String)
32:
33: End Sub
```

ANALYSIS   Lines 1–33 define the public interface. This simply means all the members of that are public. Notice that the implementation of the public members is as yet undefined, and there are no private members. I will define public and private members as I discuss each aspect of the Strings class.

Extending Existing Classes

A good way to build a new class is to extend existing classes. Applied to the `Strings` class, I have two aspects of a problem that need solving. The first aspect is that I need a place to store the actual data, and the second is that I need a way to read data from and write data to a text file. As it happens, I have code that will solve both these problems.

Using a Collection to Store the Associative Array Data

The `Collection` class already exists and is capable of storing string data. Therefore, it is a good candidate for storing the actual string data in the `Strings` class. All the properties are pieces of the name and data pairs of string values. After I have decided to use the `Collection` class, I can implement all the property methods. (Alternatively, I could have elected to use an array to store the string data, but the `Collection` class will require much less work. Avoiding unnecessary work remains a constant consideration throughout.)

Adding the `Collection` class to the `Strings` class is an example of aggregation. To use a `Collection`, the class needs a `Collection` variable and an instance of a `Collection`. Because the class is using the `Collection`, but the `Collection` is not part of the public interface, the `Collection` will be declared as private data. If you need initialized data, you initialize the data in the `Class_Initialize` method and release the data in the `Class_Terminate` method.

Modified to implement the properties in terms of the `Collection`, Listing 22.1 is extended in Listing 22.2.

LISTING 22.2   The `Strings` Class Evolving As It Is Implemented

```
 1:  Option Compare Database
 2:  Option Explicit
 3:  Option Base 1
 4:
 5:  Private FStrings As Collection
 6:
 7:  Public Property Get Names(ByVal Index As Integer) As String
 8:      On Error GoTo Except
 9:          Names = Mid$(Strings(Index), 1, InStr(1, Strings(Index), "=") - 1)
10:      Exit Property
11:  Except:
12:      Call RaiseError(Err.Description)
13:  End Property
14:
15:  Public Property Let Names(ByVal Index As Integer, ByVal Name As String)
16:      On Error GoTo Except
17:          Strings(Index) = Name & "=" & Values(Names(Index))
```

LISTING 22.2   continued

```
18:     Exit Property
19: Except:
20:     Call RaiseError(Err.Description)
21: End Property
22:
23: Public Property Get Strings() As Collection
24:     Set Strings = FStrings
25: End Property
26:
27: Public Property Get Values(ByVal Name As String) As String
28:     Dim Index As Integer
29:     Index = IndexOfName(Name)
30:     If (Index > -1) Then
31:         Values = Strings(Index)
32:         Values = Right$(Values, Len(Values) - InStr(1, Values, "="))
33:     Else
34:         Call RaiseError(Name & " not found")
35:     End If
36: End Property
37:
38: Public Property Let Values(ByVal Name As String, ByVal Value As String)
39:     On Error GoTo Except
40:     FStrings(IndexOfName(Name)) = Name & "=" & Value
41:     Exit Property
42: except:
43:     If (Err.Number = 5) Or (Err.Number = 9) Then
44:         Call FStrings.Add(Name & "=" & Value)
45:     Else
46:         Err.Raise Err.Number
47:     End If
48: End Property
49:
50: Public Function IndexOfName(ByVal Name As String) As Integer
51:
52:     Dim I As Integer
53:     For I = 1 To FStrings.Count
54:         If (InStr(1, Strings(I), Name) > 0) Then
55:             IndexOfName = I
56:             Exit Function
57:         End If
58:     Next I
59:
60:     IndexOfName = -1
61: End Function
62:
63: Public Sub ReadFromFile(ByVal FileName As String)
64:
65: End Sub
```

LISTING 22.2   continued

```
66:
67: Public Sub WriteToFile(ByVal FileName As String)
68:
69: End Sub
70:
71: Private Sub Class_Initialize()
72:     Set FStrings = New Collection
73: End Sub
74:
75: Private Sub Class_Terminate()
76:     Set FStrings = Nothing
77: End Sub
78:
79: Private Sub RaiseError(ByVal Msg As String)
80:     Err.Raise vbObjectError + 1000, "Strings.cls", Msg
81: End Sub
```

ANALYSIS   As you can see, the listing has grown substantially. Choosing to implement the class in terms of a Collection made the code easy to write. Line 5 declares the private FStrings variable as a Collection. The Class_Initialize and Class_Terminate procedures (on lines 71 and 75, respectively) initialize and clean up the Collection. The Class_Initialize procedure is run when you use the New keyword to create a Strings object. Class_Terminate is run automatically when you set a Strings object equal to Nothing.

NEW TERM   *rhs* is the term used to describe an operand that is used as the right-hand-side operand.

NEW TERM   *lhs* is the term used to describe an operand that is used as a left-hand-side value.

When the Names property is used as an rhs operand, the Get Names property method is called. Line 9 returns the string portion to the left of the equals (=) operator. The Let Names property method is called when Names is used as an lhs operand. Let Names overwrites the existing string with the new name and value pair on line 17 of Listing 22.2.

The implementation of the Strings property is modified. Table 22.1 describes an indexable property that returns the entire string. However, as I was implementing the class, I realized that there was no way to add or remove strings. Because the Collection supports these methods already, I chose to expose the underlying Collection as a read-only property as an interim solution. This supports adding and removing strings. You might think that I would modify the text of the chapter and refine my earlier definition.

However, mentioning the modification now, in the text, is illustrative of the way object-oriented programming is supposed to work. It is acceptable and, in fact, a desirable practice to iteratively improve a design and implementation as your understanding of the problem increases. When I implemented the Strings class, I identified a shortcoming and remedied it. This is exactly how object-oriented programming is supposed to unfold; it's an evolutionary process whereby classes are refined incrementally and iteratively. The Strings property is read-only because I do not want to accidentally assign a different Collection to the Strings object.

> Regarding exposing the underlying Collection object in the form of the Strings property, in a real application, I would further modify the design to implement the Add and Remove behavior as member methods of the Strings class and use the exposed Collection object as a temporary solution.
>
> The reason for this is precisely that by exposing the Collection object, I am allowing consumers of Strings to bypass the interface I have designed for the class.

Next, I established that a procedure, IndexOfName, would be useful; IndexOfName finds the index of a string by the name value. This procedure is implemented on lines 50–61. I used the IndexOfName function on lines 29 and 40.

The error handler on lines 43–45 handles a condition that occurs when you try to modify a name and value pair that does not exist. The behavior implemented adds the name and value pair. All other error handlers simply report the error by calling the RaiseError subroutine on lines 79–81.

Implementing the File Streaming Capabilities

The rest of the class can be implemented in terms of the FileStream class developed in Hour 21. Listing 22.3 demonstrates the implementation of the WriteToFile and ReadFromFile methods. When all the elements are added together, you have a class that is approximately 100 lines long, implements an associative array of names and values, and can be written to and read from a file.

LISTING 22.3   The Implementation of the ReadFromFile and WriteToFile Methods for the Strings Class

```
1:  Private Sub ParseStrings(ByVal Text As String)
2:      Dim P As Integer
3:      Do While (Len(Text) > 0)
4:          P = InStr(1, Text, vbNewLine)
```

LISTING 22.3   continued

```
 5:           ' If the last line is found then add the string and exit
 6:           If (P = 0) Then
 7:               Call Strings.Add(Text)
 8:               Exit Sub
 9:           Else
10:               ' Else if there is more data then add the string to the
11:               ' collection and remove the substring from the source string
12:               Call FStrings.Add(Left$(Text, P - 1))
13:               Text = Mid$(Text, P + Len(vbNewLine))
14:           End If
15:       Loop
16: End Sub
17:
18: Public Sub ReadFromFile(ByVal FileName As String)
19:       Clear
20:       Dim F As New FileStream
21;       Call F.OpenStream(FileName)
22:       Dim Text As String
23:       Call F.ReadStream(Text, F.Count)
24:       Call ParseStrings(Text)
25:       Call F.CloseStream
26:       Set F = Nothing
27: End Sub
28:
29: Public Sub WriteToFile(ByVal FileName As String)
30:       Dim I As Integer
31:       Dim F As New FileStream
32:       Call F.OpenStream(FileName)
33:       For I = 1 To FStrings.Count
34:           Call F.WriteStream(Strings(I) & vbNewLine)
35:       Next I
36:       Call F.CloseStream
37:       Set F = Nothing
38: End Sub
39:
40: Public Sub Clear()
41:     Do While (FStrings.Count > 0)
42:       Call FStrings.Remove(FStrings.Count)
43:     Loop
44: End Sub
```

ANALYSIS   Listing 22.3 implements the ReadFromFile and WriteToFile methods. Add the code in Listing 22.3 to Listing 22.2 for a complete implementation of the streamable string class. Lines 1 through 16 (the ParseStrings subroutine) were added to separate the strings in the text file. I chose the vbNewLine character as my string item delimiter (vbNewLine is a constant defined in VBA that has the value of a carriage return and linefeed pair). Both `ReadFromFile` and `WriteToFile` are implemented by using the `FileStream` class developed in Hour 21. A new `Clear` method was added to facilitate emptying existing strings. In Listing 22.3, `Clear` is used to ensure that only the contents of a read file are in the `Strings` collection.

To use a class that exists in another database, follow these steps:

1. Open the editor of the first database.
2. Select the file you want to export (`FileStream.cls`).
3. Click File, Export File.
4. Use the current name and the Export File dialog, shown in Figure 22.1, to select the file path. Then click Save.

FIGURE 22.1

Use the Visual Basic editor's Export File dialog item to save object-orient code in classes to external files.

The `Strings` class is easy to implement. That's because I use the `Collection` and the `FileStream` classes to do all the work. Aggregation of objects in this manner results in code that grows in capability over time. Although the code grows in capability very quickly, it grows in complexity much less quickly. The reason is that you are not writing new code; rather, you are using existing code, which is already written and tested. If you have the option of writing new code or using existing code, as a general rule, use the existing code. Existing code is cheaper to use and has probably already been tested and debugged.

Testing Your New Class

Like any new code, the `Strings` class must be tested. However, you do not need to test the `Collection` code (nor do you even have access to it). You also do not have to retest the `FileStream` code. You tested the `FileStream` code in Hour 21. When you reuse code, all you have to test is the new code and the interactions between the new code and the existing code.

The net effect of code reuse is faster implementation time, less testing, higher reliability, and greater capability. This is the promise that objects can deliver when implemented properly. It takes practice. Listing 22.4 contains some test code you can use to exercise the `Strings` class.

LISTING 22.4   Test Code for the `Strings` Class

```
1:  Sub TestStrings()
2:    Dim S As New Strings
3:    S.Values("Item1") = "Value1"
4:    S.Values("Item2") = "Value2"
5:    Call S.WriteToFile("Test.txt")
6:    Call S.ReadFromFile("Test.txt")
7:    MsgBox S.Strings(1)
8:  End Sub
```

ANALYSIS   Line 2 instantiates a new `Strings` object. Lines 3 and 4 test the `IndexOfName` function, the `Values` property, and error handling (because these statements request names that don't exist). In the implementation, this causes the name and value pairs to be inserted. Line 5 tests the write functionality, and line 6 tests the read functionality. Line 7 verifies that the data was read from the text file and displays the value at index 1. You can learn a lot about how code runs by creating test code and stepping through each line.

Using the `Strings` Class

I find the `Strings` class useful in storing data that must be equated by value. In Windows, an example is an INI file used to contain configuration data. I have also used associative name and data value string files to contain user configuration data for applications. An associative collection of strings is easy to use and provides a simple way to implement a collection of data that is indexable by number and an associated name tag.

From Hour 8, "Solving Problems a Piece at a Time," you learned how to use the Registry procedures `GetSetting` and `SaveSetting` to read and write Registry values. Reading and writing to the Registry is the preferred means of storing application information, rather than using an INI file.

The `Strings` class is useful for storing any associative data that your application needs to track. I would not, however, recommend the `Strings` class over the existing methods for reading from and writing to the Registry.

API procedures exist for reading and writing INI files. The procedures are named `GetPrivateProfileString` and `WritePrivateProfileString`. As noted, using the Registry is the preferred *modus operandi*; therefore, you will not need the API procedures.

Summary

In this hour, you learned how to create a class (`Strings`) that enables you to associate name and data value pairs. More importantly, you learned principles of object-oriented design and how to use existing code to create new capabilities. By extending existing classes in small ways, you can create tiers of solutions that enable you to grow simple classes into useful solutions.

This hour demonstrates that aggregation facilitates creating new solutions in terms of existing code. The `Strings` class demonstrates this technique by combining the `Collection` class (for storage) and the `FileStream` class from Hour 21 (for reading and writing data) into a new solution.

Uses for name and data pairs exist in many aspects of Windows. The Registry is a data file that contains application information in name and data pairs. The `WIN.INI` file and other INI files contain name and data pairs. You will likely find uses for the `Strings` class in your programs. Additionally, the techniques of evolving code will be useful when you have a new problem. Remember when you're writing code to keep your classes small and make changes in small ways. If you have an existing class and want to extend its capabilities, define a new class, but include the old class as part of the implementation. Don't just modify the existing class. In this way, you will have the old solution and the new one.

The "Q&A" and "Workshop" sections that follow are designed to help you perfect your understanding of the topics presented in this hour.

Q&A

Q Is it essential that I write classes?

A No. However, it is beneficial that you do so. You will gain the same kind of benefit from writing your own classes as you do when you use classes already existing in Access. You will create better solutions and ultimately write less code to solve problems when you use previously implemented solutions.

Q Can I share modules and classes in other databases.

A Yes. The Visual Basic editor has Import and Export menu items. This means that you can use VBA code from other databases as well as Visual Basic code written by other programmers.

Q Should I create classes from scratch or always use existing code?

A If code exists that solves part of the problem, use it. Even if the code contains extra code you don't need, you will benefit by using the existing code. Existing code does not have to be written or retested. By using existing code, you will not have to spend the time and effort to write, test, and debug new code.

22

Q How do I know I need to create a class?

A Experience will be your best guide. If you can identify a few methods and pieces of data that are used consistently to solve a problem, you should create a class. Practice will help you get better at creating classes and identifying code that makes good classes.

Workshop

The Workshop includes quiz questions designed to help you test your understanding of the material covered and exercises to help put what you've learned to practice. You will find the answers to the quiz and exercises in Appendix A, "Answers."

Quiz

1. What is a benefit of aggregation?
2. When designing a class, how many public methods and properties should you try to limit the class to?
3. What does it mean to evolve classes incrementally?
4. How can you determine the members that comprise the public interface of a class?
5. What are the two class methods that are called when an object is created and when it is destroyed?

Exercises

1. Add a `Text` property to the `Strings` class that returns all the indexed string elements as one string, separating each string by a `vbNewLine` character.
2. Add a `Let Text` property that assigns a single string containing line breaks to the `Strings` class. Each line break indicates a separation between string elements in the list.
3. Modify the `ReadFromFile` and `WriteToFile` methods to use the `Text` property.

Hour 23

Writing Access Add-Ins

A good test for a programming tool is whether the tool can be used to extend itself. When this test is applied to Access, the answer is a resounding yes. You can use Access databases and VBA code to extend Access and, ultimately, to make your job easier. That's what you will learn to do this hour.

NEW TERM   *Add-in* is a generic term used to describe code that extends or customizes the Access development environment. Specifically, in Access, an add-in refers to a COM object or an Access database that contains code that is created by the developers of Access. After you complete this hour, you will know the mechanics needed to create Access database add-ins, and you will create and test an add-in.

For the most part, add-ins are comprised of modules, classes, and supporting database code. In this hour, you will learn to create add-ins by setting up an automatic error-logging mechanism that will help you develop your applications and track user errors. When you complete the material presented in this hour, the task of debugging and testing will be easier, and assisting your users will be a snap. You will have a record of what went right and what went wrong.

In this hour, you will learn

- How to customize Access with add-ins
- How to create an error-tracking database
- How to define a viewer for the logged errors
- How to test add-in code
- How to install and uninstall add-ins

Introducing Add-Ins

As mentioned in the introduction, an Access add-in is an Access database or a COM object. In this hour, you will learn how to create add-ins with an Access database. You won't learn how to create COM (Component Object Model), ActiveX EXE, or DLL add-ins because doing so requires Visual Basic. Keep in mind, however, that using VB to create COM add-ins is an option.

A database add-in, by convention, is an Access database that has an `.mda` extension instead of an `.mdb` extension. Aside from the difference in database naming conventions, an add-in database can contain everything that a non-add-in database can contain. You can have modules with procedures, classes, macros, tables, queries, data access pages, reports, and forms in database add-ins.

The greatest advantage in creating add-ins is that add-ins—as the name suggests—are added to Access, effectively extending and customizing the behavior of Access. To create an add-in, you have to decide what capability you want to provide, create the database (replete with code, forms, and whatever else is needed), test the database, and then let Access know that you want to add the add-in to it. You know how to do most of these tasks—except, perhaps, how to let Access know you are adding an add-in.

Here is a brief summary of the skills you need to learn and apply to customize Access with the error-logging add-in:

- How to dynamically create an error-logging table
- How to append exception data automatically to the error database whenever an error occurs
- How to test the error-logging SQL, code, and database
- How to create a custom interface for managing the error-logging mechanism that allows you to turn the mechanism off and on in Access

- How to perform the necessary steps to use the solution as an add-in
- How to install and test the error-logging capability

When you are all done and the add-in is installed, you will get an opportunity to test the error-logging add-in. The net result is that you will understand the process and have an actual add-in to help you build solutions in the future and to offer more effective problem-resolution tools to your users.

Defining an Error-Logging Database

An *error-logging database* contains a table that makes it possible to reconstruct errors occurring in an application. Because Access is a database tool, you can keep the log close to the application. For practical reasons, I will define the error log to track the kind of error information that VBA code in Access is likely to have available. That information is defined by the `Err` object.

Before you begin any of the examples, create the `Log.mda` database. By convention, the `.mda` extension is used. To create the database, follow these steps:

1. Run Access.
2. Click File, New.
3. In the File New Database dialog, change the Save As Type field to `*.*`. If you leave the type as Microsoft Access Database (`*.mdb`), when you save the database as `Log.mda`, Access will add the `.mdb` extension. You will end up with `Log.mda.mdb` when you really want `Log.mda`.
4. In the File Name field, enter **Log.mda**, find the directory you want to save the database in, and click Create.

That's all there is to it. For now, just think of `Log.mda` as any Microsoft Access database. It is in `Log.mda` that all the add-in objects will be created.

From previous hours, you know that the `Err` object contains an error number, source, description, help file, and help context. Therefore, I will define the error log database to store that information. Also, I will include the date, time, and user information. With this data, you will be able to reconstruct what happened during an application run, even if the application crashes. In addition, because I know in advance that an error log will be created for each database that turns on error logging, I will use SQL to create the table that holds the logged data. Listing 23.1 contains the SQL to create the error-logging table.

LISTING 23.1   SQL to Create a Log Table on-the-Fly

```
 1:   CREATE TABLE LOG
 2:   ( ID AUTOINCREMENT PRIMARY KEY,
 3:     ERROR_ID NUMBER,
 4:     SOURCE TEXT(50),
 5:     DESCRIPTION TEXT(255),
 6:     HELPFILE TEXT(255),
 7:     HELPCONTEXT NUMBER,
 8:     WHEN DATETIME,
 9:     USER TEXT(25)
10:   );
```

ANALYSIS The CREATE TABLE statement in Listing 23.1 creates a table named LOG whenever it is run. Save the SQL as CREATE_LOG_TABLE. By using SQL, you can run the query as your program is running (when you actually need the error-logging table) to log an error, instead of creating the table manually.

Adding Code to Create the Table Dynamically

Each database that uses the Log.mda add-in will only need one copy of the LOG table. To ensure you get exactly one copy, create some code that checks to see whether the table exists. If the table doesn't exist, it must be created before the first log entry can be written. Listing 23.2 demonstrates dynamic table creation.

LISTING 23.2   One Example of Creating a Table Dynamically

```
 1:   Option Compare Database
 2:   Option Explicit
 3:
 4:   Private Function CreateLogQuery() As String
 5:     CreateLogQuery = _
 6:       "CREATE TABLE LOG " & _
 7:       "( ID AUTOINCREMENT PRIMARY KEY, ERROR_ID NUMBER, " & _
 8:       "SOURCE TEXT(50), DESCRIPTION TEXT(255), HELPFILE TEXT(255), " & _
 9:       "HELPCONTEXT NUMBER, WHEN DATETIME, User Text(25));"
10:   End Function
11:
12:   Private Sub CreateTable(ByVal QueryText As String)
13:     Call DoCmd.RunSQL(QueryText)
14:   End Sub
```

ANALYSIS Because Listing 23.2 is part of an add-in—a complete solution—create a new module in Log.mda and save it as LogUtilities. The SQL created in Listing 23.1 is incorporated in lines 1 through 4. Lines 12 to 14 use the DoCmd.RunSQL method to run the query, creating the table. CreateTable is one of the utility procedures that the Log.mda database will use to create the LOG table in each database that uses this add-in.

The entire utility is designed (as you will see) based on an assumption that the LOG table exists. If the table doesn't exist, an exception will occur. The exception-handling behavior creates the table and tries to add the entry again. The next section demonstrates writing to the error log and the code that calls CreateTable on the first write.

Logging Exceptions to the Database

Assume that the LOG table exists. The code that you will use simply logs the error data to the LOG table (see Listing 23.3). There are two public procedures for writing error data: WriteErrorEntry and WriteEntry. Ultimately, DoWriteEntry implements these two public procedures.

LISTING 23.3   The Code That Actually Logs Errors for the Add-In

```
1:  Public Sub WriteErrorEntry(ByVal Error As ErrObject, _
2:    Optional UserName As String = "Admin")
3:
4:    With Err
5:      Call WriteEntry(.Number, .Source, .Description, .HelpFile, _
6:        .HelpContext, UserName)
7:    End With
8:  End Sub
9:
10: Private Function TableExists(TableName As String) As Boolean
11:
12:   Dim Table As Variant
13:
14:   For Each Table In CurrentData.AllTables
15:     TableExists = Table.Name = TableName
16:     If (TableExists) Then Exit For
17:   Next Table
18:
19: End Function
20:
21: Public Sub WriteEntry(ByVal Number As Long, ByVal Source As String, _
22:   ByVal Description As String, ByVal HelpFile As String, _
23:   ByVal HelpContext As Long, Optional UserName As String)
24:
25:   On Error GoTo Except
26:   Call DoWriteEntry(Number, Source, Description, HelpFile, _
27:     HelpContext, UserName)
28:
29:   Exit Sub
30: Except:
```

LISTING 23.3   continued

```
31:    If (Not TableExists("Log")) Then
32:      Call CreateTable(CreateLogQuery)
33:      Resume
34:    Else
35:      Call Err.Raise(Err.Number, "LogUtilities.WriteEntry", _
36:        Err.Description)
37:    End If
38: End Sub
39:
40: Private Sub DoWriteEntry(ByVal Number As Long, _
41:    ByVal Source As String, ByVal Description As String, _
42:    ByVal HelpFile As String, ByVal HelpContext As Long, _
43:    Optional UserName As String)
44:
45:    Dim SQL As String
46:    SQL = "SELECT * FROM LOG"
47:    Dim Recordset As New ADODB.Recordset
48:    Call Recordset.Open(SQL, CurrentProject.Connection,
➥adOpenDynamic, adLockPessimistic)
49:    Recordset.AddNew
50:    Recordset("ERROR_ID") = Number
51:    Recordset("SOURCE") = Source
52:    Recordset("DESCRIPTION") = Description
53:    Recordset("HELPFILE") = HelpFile
54:    Recordset("HELPCONTEXT") = HelpContext
55:    Recordset("WHEN") = Now
56:    Recordset("USER") = UserName
57:    Recordset.Update
58:    Recordset.Close
59:    Set Recordset = Nothing
60:
61: End Sub
```

ANALYSIS   I created a module containing the preceding code, incorporated with the code in
Listing 23.2, and named it LogUtilities. Lines 1–8 accept an ErrObject and
implement the WriteErrorEntry procedure by calling WriteEntry. WriteErrorEntry is
implemented in terms of WriteEntry. This is a good strategy for saving work.
WriteEntry on lines 21–38 really just calls DoWriteEntry on line 14. The rest of the
code in WriteEntry is designed to catch errors, create the LOG table, and retry adding
the entry on lines 32 and 33. An exception is raised if the table doesn't exist, and the
error-handling block on lines 30 through 38 takes over. If the LOG table does not exist, it
is created. Lines 10 through 19 use the AllTables collection to determine whether the
LOG table exists. The real work is done in DoWriteEntry. By using a private procedure
(prefixed with Do), I am able to separate my error-handling code in WriteEntry from the

actual work in DoWriteEntry, keeping both procedures as simple as possible. DoWriteEntry appears in lines 40–61. Essentially, the code opens an ADO recordset, adds a new record, assigns the field data, and saves the changes.

You can devise a test for this code by creating a new module and writing code similar what's shown in Listing 23.4. As a rule, I generally try to separate test code from production code.

LISTING 23.4 A Test Procedure for the Error-Logging Add-In

```
1:  Sub Test()
2:    On Error GoTo Except
3:    Call Err.Raise(1, "LogUtilities", "Test", "No Help", 0)
4:    Exit Sub
5:  Except:
6:    Call WriteErrorEntry(Err)
7:  End Sub
```

ANALYSIS Test devises a scenario similar to using an error-logging database: It raises an error (simulating an error at runtime) and catches the error. Then, the error handler writes the error to the LOG table. By emulating the Test code in your code and combining the call to WriteErrorEntry or WriteEntry with error-handling code, you will get a robust program and an audit trail. If anything goes wrong, you can piece together what went wrong from the LOG table. The next section walks you through devising a user interface with logging capabilities. This user interface can enable and disable logging, and it lets you view the log data.

Defining a Viewer for the Error Log

The Add-In Manager is used to add external references to databases that you want to incorporate into the current database. You invoke the Add-In Manager from the Tools|Add-Ins menu. Adding references to external databases makes objects, like tables and code from external database accessible to the current database.

When you use the Add-in Manager to add the Log.mda code to a database, you have access to the capabilities it provides. By calling WriteEntry or WriteErrorEntry, you enable the logging mechanism. This section describes the code that enables you to view the error log.

When you install an add-in, a menu item is added to the Access Tools, Add-Ins menu. When you click the menu item, some code is run. For this demonstration, I chose to define a procedure that opens the LOG table for browsing. You can create more elaborate interfaces if you want. The code for browsing is shown in Listing 23.5.

LISTING 23.5   The Entry Point for the Log.mda Add-in Is the Code That Is Run When You Click the Add-Ins Menu Item

```
1:  Function EntryPoint()
2:    Call DoCmd.OpenTable("LOG", acViewNormal, acReadOnly)
3:  End Function
```

ANALYSIS   As you can see from this listing, the code is not very complex. Line 2 uses the DoCmd.OpenTable method to open the LOG table. If you haven't written any log entries, the table will not exist and this code will display an error. That's reasonable behavior. Listing 23.5 is also part of the LogUtilities module.

Testing the Error Logging Add-In Database

As with any code, you must test the add-in database. Because the Log.mda file is an Access database, you can test the code just as you would any other. Place your cursor on the procedure you want to test in VBE and press F5. You will find it easier to test the code before you add it to Access with the Add-in Manager.

An alternate way to test a database is add a reference to it in the Visual Basic Editor with the Tools|References menu. To add a reference to the Log.mda database—or any database for that matter—follow these instructions:

1. Open a new or existing database from which you want to test the Log.mda database.

2. Click Tools, Macro, Visual Basic Editor.

3. In VBE, click Tools, References.

4. In the References dialog, click the Browse button.

5. In the Add References dialog, change the Files of Type field to Add-Ins (*.mda) file types.

6. Find the Log.mda database and click Open. Click OK to close the References dialog.

7. The Log.mda modules will appear in the Project-Log dialog in VBE (as shown in Figure 23.1).

After the database is referenced, you can use the code in the referenced database to solve the problems in the referencing database. This provides you an alternative way to test add-ins and a means of reusing code without exporting or copying and pasting.

FIGURE 23.1

Reuse database code by adding a reference to a database in the Visual Basic editor.

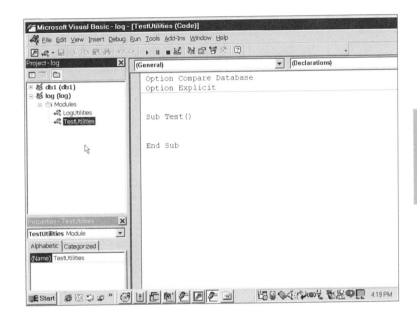

Installing and Uninstalling Add-ins

Having tested your add-in code, you are now ready to add it to the Access application. Use listing 23.6, showing the LogUtilities Module defined Log.mda, to verify that you have all the code and it is typed correctly.

LISTING 23.6   The Complete Listing for LogUtilities in Log.mda

```
1:  Option Compare Database
2:  Option Explicit
3:
4:  Function EntryPoint()
5:    Call DoCmd.OpenTable("LOG", acViewNormal, acReadOnly)
6:  End Function
7:
8:
9:  Property Get UserName() As String
10:   UserName = CurrentUser
11: End Property
12:
13: Private Function CreateLogQuery() As String
14:   CreateLogQuery = _
15:     "CREATE TABLE LOG " & _
16:     "( ID AUTOINCREMENT PRIMARY KEY, ERROR_ID NUMBER, " & _
17:     "SOURCE TEXT(50), DESCRIPTION TEXT(255), HELPFILE TEXT(255), " & _
```

LISTING 23.6 continued

```
18:      "HELPCONTEXT NUMBER, WHEN DATETIME, User Text(25));"
19: End Function
20:
21: Private Sub CreateTable()
22:    Call DoCmd.RunSQL(CreateLogQuery)
23: End Sub
24:
25: Public Sub WriteErrorEntry(ByVal Error As ErrObject, _
26:    Optional UserName As String = "Admin")
27:
28:    With Err
29:      Call WriteEntry(.Number, .Source, .Description, .HelpFile, _
30:        .HelpContext, UserName)
31:    End With
32: End Sub
33:
34: Private Function TableExists(TableName As String) As Boolean
35:
36:    Dim Table As Variant
37:
38:    For Each Table In CurrentData.AllTables
39:      TableExists = Table.Name = TableName
40:      If (TableExists) Then Exit For
41:    Next Table
42:
43: End Function
44:
45: Public Sub WriteEntry(ByVal Number As Long, ByVal Source As String, _
46:    ByVal Description As String, ByVal HelpFile As String, _
47:    ByVal HelpContext As Long, Optional UserName As String)
48:
49:    On Error GoTo Except
50:    Call DoWriteEntry(Number, Source, Description, HelpFile, _
51:      HelpContext, UserName)
52:
53:    Exit Sub
54: Except:
55:    If (Not TableExists("Log")) Then
56:      Call CreateTable
57:      Resume
58:    Else
59:      Call Err.Raise(Err.Number, "LogUtilities.WriteEntry", _
60:        Err.Description)
61:    End If
62: End Sub
63:
64: Private Sub DoWriteEntry(ByVal Number As Long, _
65:    ByVal Source As String, ByVal Description As String, _
66:    ByVal HelpFile As String, ByVal HelpContext As Long, _
67:    Optional UserName As String)
```

LISTING 23.6   continued

```
68:
69:    Dim SQL As String
70:    SQL = "SELECT * FROM LOG"
71:    Dim Recordset As New ADODB.Recordset
72:    Call Recordset.Open(SQL, CurrentProject.Connection,
 ➥adOpenDynamic, adLockPessimistic)
73:    Recordset.AddNew
74:    Recordset("ERROR_ID") = Number
75:    Recordset("SOURCE") = Source
76:    Recordset("DESCRIPTION") = Description
77:    Recordset("HELPFILE") = HelpFile
78:    Recordset("HELPCONTEXT") = HelpContext
79:    Recordset("WHEN") = Now
80:    Recordset("USER") = UserName
81:    Recordset.Update
82:    Recordset.Close
83:    Set Recordset = Nothing
84:
85: End Sub
```

ANALYSIS   Except for the UserName property, which calls the global Application.CurrentUser method, you have seen all this code in previous listings. Use Listing 23.6 to verify that you have all the code typed correctly.

To compile the code, make sure the Log.mda database is open. Start the Visual Basic editor and compile the module code with Debug, Compile. If you have syntax or compiler errors, this is your chance to fix them. Before you can add Log.mda to Access, you will need to complete one additional step, which is detailed in the next section.

Creating the Registry Information Table

Access add-ins require a table named UsysRegInfo. This table contains information that tells Access what to do with the add-in, and it is used to create Windows Registry entries. The USysRegInfo table can be created in the Log.mda database by running the SQL in Listing 23.7.

LISTING 23.7   The USysRegInfo Table, Defined by the Query in the Listing, Is Necessary for Access to Be Able to Load an Add-In

```
1:   CREATE TABLE USysRegInfo
2:   ( SubKey Text(255),
3:     Type Number,
4:     ValName Text(50),
5:     [Value] Text(50)
6:   );
```

ANALYSIS The SQL is self-explanatory, except for perhaps the brackets ([ ]) around the `Value` field. Because `Value` is a keyword, we must wrap brackets around it to indicate to Access that `Value` is a field name.

You must also add three rows to the table. The three rows describe the root key, the add-in's entry point and the location of the Access add-in directory. Table 23.1 contains each of the field values for the three rows of the USysRegInfo table.

 If you cannot see the USysRegInfo table, select Tools, Options. Find the View tab of the Options dialog and indicate in the Show group that you want to show the system objects.

TABLE 23.1   USysRegInfo Registry Data

SubKey	Type	ValName	Value
HKEY_CURRENT_ACCESS_PROFILE\ Menu Add-Ins\Log	0		
HKEY_CURRENT_ACCESS_PROFILE\ Menu Add-Ins\Log	1	Expression	=EntryPoint()
HKEY_CURRENT_ACCESS_PROFILE\ Menu Add-Ins\Log	1	Library	|ACCDIR\Log.mda

Row 1 of Table 23.1 is used to add a key to the Registry for the add-in. Row 2 defines the function that should be run when you click the add-in menu item that appears after you install the add-in; this the `EntryPoint` function, shown on lines 4 through 6 in Listing 23.6. Row 3 is used to store the location of the add-in on your computer. The `Value` cell of row 3 is `|ACCDIR\Log.mda`. The pipe character in `|ACCDIR` is automatically replaced by the Add-in Manager with the add-in directory for Access. This is usually `root\Windows\Application Data\Microsoft\AddIns`, where `root` is the drive that Windows is installed on, usually the C: drive. Regardless of where you create the add-in, it is important to remember that the Add-in Manager will copy the add-in database to the `AddIns` directory when you install the add-in.

Installing the Add-In

Add-ins are installed in Access via the Add-in Manager, shown in Figure 23.2. Follow the numbered steps to install the `Log.mda` add-in:

FIGURE 23.2

Use the Add-in Manager to add customizations to Access.

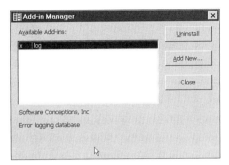

1. Open a new copy of Access. (Make sure you have closed the Log.mda database, and open a blank database. The Add-In Manager is not enabled unless a database is open.)

2. Click Tools, Add-Ins, Add-in Manager.

3. Click Add New in the Add-in Manager, locate the Log.mda Open dialog (Explorer), and click Open.

4. Verify that there is an X next to the add-in and that the Install button caption is changed to Uninstall. Then click OK to close the Add-in Manager.

If you install the Log.mda add-in and encounter problems, you will need to uninstall the add-in, close Access, and delete the copied Log.mda database from the add-in's directory. By default, this directory should be C:\Documents and Settings*user_profile*\Application Data\Microsoft\AddIns\Log.mda, where you would substitute *user_profile* with your Windows username.

Make modifications to the original database and reinstall the add-in once you have verified that everything works correctly.

You can tell whether the add-in was installed correctly by testing it. Click Tools, Add-Ins. The Log add-in will appear as a menu item below the Add-in Manager menu item. Click Log. If the add-in is installed correctly, you will get the following error:

```
Microsoft Can't Find the Object 'LOG'
```

This means the add-in is working—you just haven't logged any data yet.

Uninstalling and Modifying Add-Ins

Uninstalling add-ins is easy. In Access, click Tools, Add-Ins, Add-in Manager (refer to Figure 23.2) and then click Uninstall. To modify an add-in, close all copies of Access and delete the add-in from the AddIns directory.

After you have made modifications and tested the revisions to your add-in, repeat the numbered steps shown in the previous section, "Installing the Add-In." Now that you have a built-in debugging tool, you need to take it for a test drive.

Going for a Test Drive

Now every database can have built-in error logging. This is useful for you while developing and will be at least equally useful to the users of your database. Often, users will encounter an error, click OK, and continue without noting the error. The end result is that support personnel find out something is wrong only when the program crashes. With built-in error logging, you can find out exactly what went wrong.

Now that you have installed the add-in, one final round of testing should wrap things up. You can log entries anywhere in your code when you feel it is necessary. A natural place is in the error-handling blocks of procedures. Clearly, you will have an error object with the details. Simply add a line of code to log the entry right next to the code that handles the error. Listing 23.4 demonstrates how to use the code. When you want to view the errors, click the add-in Log menu item.

As a side note, you can easily enable or disable logging with conditional compiler directives. Add a module with two procedures that are identical to the `WriteEntry` and `WriteErrorEntry` procedures. Wrap a call to the Log versions of the function in a conditional compiler directive and use the value of the compiler directive to turn logging off and on. You learned about compiler directives in Hour 18, "Adding Code to Handle Errors."

Summarizing the Process

Because I took you on a roundabout trip to create and install an add-in, while developing the add-in, I have summarized the whole process for you in the steps that follow. These steps will work for any database add-in. It is important to remember that you don't have to create an add-in to reuse code and that you can create COM add-ins with Visual Basic. (Visual Basic is a separate programming language and a tool that comes with Microsoft's Visual Studio; when you complete the 24 hours in this book, you will be well on your way to being able to program in Visual Basic, too.) Here are the steps of the entire process:

1. Create the add-in database with an `.mda` extension.
2. Create the modules and classes in your add-in database; create any forms and other database objects that make up your add-in as well.

3. Create the UsysRegInfo table, making sure to define the add-in entry point. (You can use the query in Listing 23.7 each time and copy the data from Table 23.1 with very few changes. Remember to specify the actual entry-point function and the name of your add-in database in place of LOG. If you always use a function named EntryPoint as the starting point for your add-in, you won't have to change row 2 of Table 23.1.)

4. Test the add-in thoroughly before installing it.

5. Open a new copy of Access and use the Add-in Manager to install the add-in.

That's not so bad. Creating add-ins is a useful way to devise tools that help you work more efficiently. That's what Microsoft did with all the wizards. And, as with any coding endeavor, if your budget permits, you can buy the add-ins you need rather than creating them from scratch.

Summary

Add-ins give you the ultimate control in defining your productivity environment. By using the program skills you have already acquired, you can extend and customize Access in just about any way you can imagine. I encourage you to customize Access whenever you define a task that can be simplified or automated.

In this hour, you learned that Access add-ins are COM objects and other Access databases with .mda extensions. You can use Access to extend Access—the mark of a good tool—with Access databases. Write and test code and forms as you normally would, and when you have the code perfected, use the Add-in Manager to incorporate your solution into Access.

You can purchase third-party add-ins as an alternative to creating your own, and you can share your add-ins with other developers. To hone your craft, complete the "Q&A" and "Workshop" sections at the end of this hour.

Q&A

Q Can I use DAO and ADO in the same database?

A Yes. If you think of DAO and ADO as just objects, it makes sense to use both protocols. However, there is some potential for confusion because ADO and DAO have some of the same members.

Q Can I use classes from add-in databases?

A Yes, but indirectly. You need to define a function that returns the object instance. You cannot declare a variable of a class type for a class that is defined in the add-in.

Q Is the original MDA file deleted when the Add-in Manager places the database in the `AddIns` directory?

A No. You will have two copies; therefore, you will need to make sure you update the original database.

Q What do I do if an add-in procedure has the same name as an existing procedure?

A Use the name of the add-in as a prefix to the procedure, connecting the add-in name to the procedure with a period. For example, `Log.TableExists` clarifies that you mean exactly the Log add-in's `TableExists` function.

Workshop

The Workshop includes quiz questions designed to help you test your understanding of the material covered and exercises to help put what you've learned into practice. You will find the answers to the quiz and exercises in Appendix A, "Answers."

Quiz

1. Why do Access database add-ins have `.mda` extensions?
2. What is the name of the table you need to create for database add-ins?
3. You can define property procedures in nonclass modules. True or false?
4. You can use access specifiers (public and private) to encapsulate some of the implementation details of nonclass modules. True or false?
5. What does `|ACCDIR` refer to?

Exercises

1. Define a statement that checks whether the LOG table exists and calls the `CreateTable` procedure if it doesn't.
2. Write a statement that tests the `WriteEntry` procedure.
3. Create a blank database. Add a reference to the `Log.mda` database and trace it through the `WriteEntry` procedure. Does the call create the LOG table?

Hour **24**

Managing Outlook Contact Information

Outlook is an *Automation server application*. This means it can be run as a standalone program and can also be run by other applications. Outlook is used to manage contact, schedule, task-based, and journal entry information. This hour will demonstrate how to write VBA code in Access to use Outlook as a contact-management engine for your database applications.

The VBA code you will be creating in this hour is specifically designed to control Outlook contact information. After all, this is what Microsoft Office XP is really about: Using a powerful suite of interoperable office and desktop applications to automate office tasks, including managing contact and appointment information.

The skills you have learned in earlier hours will come in handy. For example, you already know how to create and use objects. When you create an instance of Outlook to extend Access capabilities, you will be using objects.

In this hour you will learn

- About the Outlook object model
- How to use Outlook folders
- How to view, update, and search for data in Outlook folders
- How to use Outlook to provide mailing services in your applications

Understanding Outlook 2002

Microsoft Outlook 2002 is an application. It is also an OLE Automation server. Microsoft Outlook 2002 was designed to enable you to manage contact, schedule, task, and journal entry information. These are all capabilities that help you manage your time.

Outlook is a great place to keep phone numbers and e-mail addresses for contacts. To create a list to organize and manage the tasks you want to accomplish, use Outlook. When you want to exchange e-mail with co-workers or external contacts, Outlook enables you to do this as well. The calendar helps you schedule appointments, and the Notes section provides you with a convenient place to create digital sticky pad notes.

NEW TERM   An *Automation controller* is an application that controls or uses an *Automation server*, such as Outlook.

Many kinds of applications need these same capabilities. Contact-management applications, such as ACT from Semantic and Gold Mine, require them. However, you don't want to re-create these capabilities from scratch; it takes too much time to duplicate what Outlook provides. If you need any or all these capabilities in the Access programs you create, just use Outlook itself. Think of Outlook as another object you can reuse. In this hour, you will learn how to do just that. Hour 24 demonstrates how to create an Automation controller for Outlook.

Introducing the Outlook Object Model

When thinking of Outlook as an object you can use in your programs, remember that this is not a simple object like the `Collection` object. Outlook is a massive object that contains many other objects, each of which contains capabilities, data, and other objects. Using Outlook is not unmanageable. You will, however, have to rely on documentation and a little patience.

You can get a bird's-eye view of the Outlook object model in Outlook. Because the object model is a programming aspect and not a usability aspect, follow these steps to find the graphical depiction of the top-level view of Outlook.

1. Open Outlook 2002.

2. Click Tools, Macro, Visual Basic Editor. (If you haven't already done so, you might have to install this component. Office XP doesn't install everything at the initial install.)

3. With the Visual Basic editor open (yes, it's the same editor used in Access 2002), press the F1 key.

4. On the Help Answer Wizard tab, type `Microsoft Outlook Objects` and click Search.

If the Office Assistance, Clippit, is displayed, you can hide it using the Office Assistant context menu. Simply right-click over the Office Assistant and from the context menu select Options. In the Office Assistant, Options View, deselect the Use the Office Assistant option. This will hide Clippit and allow you to use the Answer Wizard. (You can find out about Clippit's future adventures at www.officeclippy.com.)

Also, be forewarned that the link to the Outlook object model may not work correctly. When I entered "Microsoft Outlook Objects" in the Microsoft Visual Basic Help system, the object model was not returned. By mistyping Outlook as "Outloo," however, I was able to properly display the object model.

Steps 1 through 4 display a hierarchical view of the Outlook object model. Clicking any item in the model will take you to that item. As you can see from the model (if you are looking at it in Outlook), there are many objects involved. What is not immediately apparent is that the model does not show everything, and each of the objects shown has its own methods and properties, some of which are objects, too.

Although understanding the Outlook Object Model may appear to be a daunting task, I will point you in the right direction so that you can use Outlook to solve problems constructively right away.

Creating an Instance of Outlook

When you look at the Outlook model, you can see that the top-level object is the `Application` object. The same top-level object name is used for all the Office

Automation programs. Using the Application object is essentially how you get to everything else. Application is the top-level object, and everything else is a member of
Application. You create an instance of Outlook, just as you do for other objects. Follow
these steps, which, combined with the code in Listing 24.1, create an instance of Outlook
from Access and display the Office Assistant:

1. Create an Access database.

2. In the Objects View, click the Module button.

3. Click New to create a new module.

4. Type the code in Listing 24.1 and run it to create an instance of Outlook. (The code
   in Listing 24.1 creates an instance of Outlook and shows the Office Assistant.)

LISTING 24.1   Creating an Instance of Outlook and Using the Assistant Object

```
1:  Sub ShowOutlookAssistant()
2:      Const ClippitFile = "Rocky.acs"
3:      Dim Outlook As Object
4:      Set Outlook = CreateObject("Outlook.Application")
5:      Outlook.Application.Assistant.FileName = ClippitFile
6:      Outlook.Assistant.Visible = True
7:      Outlook.Assistant.Animation = 22 ' Relaxing Rocky
8:  End Sub
```

> You may need to install the rocky.acs animation file. It is not installed by
> default with Access.

ANALYSIS   Line 2 declares a constant for Rocky, the dog Office Assistant. Line 3 declares a
variable, Outlook, of type Object. Line 4 creates an instance of Outlook using
CreateObject. This style of object creation is referred to as late binding. *Late binding*
means that the object is associated with the variable when your code runs. An alternative
to late binding is *early binding*, which occurs when you declare a variable of a specific
type. To bind Outlook to a variable instance using early binding, add a reference to the
Microsoft Outlook 10.0 Object Library. An early binding example of line 2 would look
like this:

```
Dim Outlook As New Outlook.Application
```

You don't need line 4 of Listing 24.1 if you use early binding. Late binding is flexible; it
allows you to assign any object instance to a variable of type Object. Early binding

makes the properties and methods available at design time. Because the object is a specific type, the properties and methods of the object are displayed in the editor.

Line 5 sets the Office Assistant by changing the `FileName` property. Line 6 shows the assistant, and line 7 causes the assistant to perform its animation sequence.

Using Namespaces

Now you know how to get a reference to an instance of Outlook. (You can also use `GetObject` to get a reference to an instance already running.) The next thing you must know how to do is to get at objects representing mail, tasks, the calendar, and contacts. Unfortunately, this is not apparent from the object model.

Those objects in Outlook that represent where the data is stored are subordinate to the `NameSpace` object. You use `GetNameSpace("MAPI")` to get all the Outlook data; `GetNameSpace` returns a `NameSpace` object. After you have a `NameSpace` object, you can get to data stores, such as contact information, through the `Folders` collection. Listing 24.2 demonstrates how to get a `NameSpace` object.

LISTING 24.2 Getting an Instance of a `NameSpace` Object, the Location of All the Outlook Data

```
1:  Sub CreateNameSpace()
2:    Dim N As NameSpace
3:    Set N = GetNamespace("MAPI")
4:  End Sub
```

ANALYSIS Lines 1–4 declare a `NameSpace` variable and get an instance of the MAPI (Mail API) namespace. The MAPI namespace is the only one available in Access. The use of a function and a string name suggests that Microsoft can create other `NameSpace` objects in future revisions. To access Outlook data, you must get a `NameSpace` object every time. The code in the previous listing can accomplish this task.

After you have a `NameSpace` object, you can use the data in Outlook by folder. The next section describes how to use folders.

Using a Folder

The MAPI `NameSpace` object contains a `Folders` collection. Each of the items in the Outlook Folder List is a folder (see Figure 24.1). There is a `MAPIFolder` object representing each of the folders shown in Figure 24.1. Therefore, to use the data, you request a particular folder. Table 24.1 contains the list of constants that represent each of the default folders.

FIGURE 24.1

*When programming,
you use folder objects
that represent each of
the Outlook folders.*

TABLE 24.1   Default Folder Constants

Constant	Folder Description
olFolderCalendar	Contains calendar data; the `Items` collection contains `AppointmentItem` objects.
olFolderContacts	Contains contact information; the `Items` collection contains `ContactItem` objects.
olFolderDeletedItems	Contains deleted mail; the `Items` collection contains `MailItem` objects.
olFolderDrafts	Contains message drafts; the `Items` collection contains `MailItem` objects.
olFolderInbox	Contains incoming mail; the `Items` collection contains `MailItem` objects.
olFolderJournal	Contains journal entries; the `Items` collection contains `JournalItem` objects.
olFolderNotes	Contains notes; the `Items` collection contains `NoteItem` objects.
olFolderOutbox	Contains unsent messages; the `Items` collection contains `MailItem` objects.
olFolderSentMail	Contains sent messages; the `Items` collection contains `MailItem` objects.
olFolderTasks	Contains tasks; the `Items` collection contains `TaskItem` objects.

Each of the `MAPIFolder` objects contains objects of a specific type. Each `MAPIFolder` object type is listed in the folder description of Table 24.1. If you know the object type contained, you can use the Help documentation to find all the methods and properties for that type.

A `MAPIFolder` object contains an `Items` collection. You already know how to use collections. Each element of the `Items` collection is one of the types in Table 24.1. For example, the `MAPIFolder` object for contacts is returned when you call `GetDefaultFolder` (`olFolderContacts`). The `MAPIFolder` object has an `Items` collection, and each element of the `Items` collection for `oldFolderContacts` will be a `ContactItem` object. Listing 24.3 demonstrates how to get the first item in the default Contacts folder. (Additional examples are contained in the remaining sections of this hour.)

LISTING 24.3 Using Verbose Code to Return a Single Contact

```
 1: Sub PrintOneContact()
 2:    Dim Outlook As New Outlook.Application
 3:    Dim NameSpace As NameSpace
 4:    Set NameSpace = Outlook.GetNamespace("MAPI")
 5:    Dim Folder As MAPIFolder
 6:    Set Folder = NameSpace.GetDefaultFolder(olFolderContacts)
 7:    Dim Contact As ContactItem
 8:    Set Contact = Folder.Items("Lori Kimmel")
 9:    Debug.Print Contact.FullName
10: End Sub
```

ANALYSIS Listing 24.3 creates an instance of Outlook on line 2 using early binding. Line 3 declares a `NameSpace` variable. Line 4 gets the MAPI `NameSpace` object. Line 5 declares a variable named `Folder` as a `MAPIFolder` object. Line 6 sets `Folder` to the default Contact folder. Line 7 declares a variable, `Contact`, as a `ContactItem` object. Line 8 sets the `Contact` variable to the `ContactItem` object indexed by `"Lori Kimmel"`, the value of `FullName`. You can also use an integer less than or equal to the `Items.Count` property to index the `Items` collection. Line 9 prints the contact's full name to the Immediate window. A very brief version of this code is shown in Listing 24.4.

LISTING 24.4 A Brief Version of Listing 24.3, Showing You the Member Relationships of All the Outlook Objects

```
 1: Sub BriefPrintOneContact()
 2:    Dim Outlook As New Outlook.Application
 3:    Debug.Print _
 4:       Outlook.GetNamespace("MAPI"). _
 5:       GetDefaultFolder(olFolderContacts).Items("Lori Kimmel")
 6: End Sub
```

ANALYSIS Line 2 creates an instance of Outlook, assigning it to the variable `Outlook`, and line 3 demonstrates the membership hierarchy of the objects containing the data folders. Notice that the statement continuation character (_) can be used to break really long statements.

Viewing Outlook Contacts in Access

This section and the remaining sections contain some practical applications demonstrating how you might use Outlook. In this section, the sample code demonstrates how you can view all the contacts in your Contacts MAPIFolder object. Listing 24.5 shows the code. An analysis of this code follows the listing.

LISTING 24.5   Opening the Contacts Folder in Outlook, Enabling the User to Use the Outlook Interface

```
1:  Sub OpenContactsFolder()
2:    Dim Outlook As New Outlook.Application
3:    Dim NameSpace As NameSpace
4:    Set NameSpace = Outlook.GetNamespace("MAPI")
5:    Dim ContactFolder As MAPIFolder
6:    Set ContactFolder = NameSpace.GetDefaultFolder(olFolderContacts)
7:    ContactFolder.Display
8:  End Sub
```

ANALYSIS   Lines 1–6 create an instance of Outlook, a NameSpace object, and get a reference to the default Contacts folder. The Display method opens the instance of Outlook referenced by line 2 and sets the focus to the Contacts folder. Listing 24.5 demonstrates how you can use the Outlook interface to let users manage contacts.

Listing 24.6 demonstrates how you can get a reference to each ContactItem object. After you have a reference to a ContactItem object, you can do just about anything you want with the data.

LISTING 24.6   Iterating Through Each Contact in the Default Contacts Folder

```
1:  Sub IterateContacts()
2:    Dim Outlook As New Outlook.Application
3:    Dim NameSpace As NameSpace
4:    Set NameSpace = Outlook.GetNamespace("MAPI")
5:    Dim ContactFolder As MAPIFolder
6:    Set ContactFolder = NameSpace.GetDefaultFolder(olFolderContacts)
7:    Dim ContactItem As Variant
8:    For Each ContactItem In ContactFolder.Items
9:       Debug.Print ContactItem
10:   Next ContactItem
11: End Sub
```

ANALYSIS   You have seen code similar to this in lines 1–6 of prior listings. Line 6 gets a reference to the MAPIFolderContact object for the contacts. The Items collection in the MAPIFolder object is an instance of the same Collection class you already know how to use. For example, if you want to iterate through each ContactItem object using a For Each loop, you will need a Variant, as demonstrated in line 7. Alternatively, you could use the For Next loop and assign each element to a variable of the specific type ContactItem.

In Listing 24.6, the output is written to the Immediate window; however, after you have a ContactItem object, you can edit, format, or customize the data in any manner you wish. Additionally, you can add the data to lists or graphical user interface controls, output the data to reports, or send them via e-mail. The next section demonstrates some examples of modifying Outlook data.

Updating Outlook Information

Because of the growth in technology sectors, data is changing all the time. Phone companies add new prefixes to phone numbers to accommodate an increase in the number of phones. Companies and individuals are adding Web sites and e-mail addresses at astounding rates. People change jobs, companies change addresses, and information needs updating all the time.

You don't need to schlep through each of your dozens or hundreds of contacts to make routine changes. Write some VBA procedures and let Access update that data automatically. Listing 24.7 demonstrates an automatic update to a phone number area code, simulating a change in area codes. To extend this solution, you could add an interface and a dynamic prompt with an input box to verify that you want the change to occur, or you might check all phone numbers in the ContactItem object.

LISTING 24.7   Automatically Updating ContactItem Objects

```
1:  Sub UpdateAreaCodes()
2:     Dim Outlook As New Outlook.Application
3:
4:     Dim NameSpace As NameSpace
5:     Set NameSpace = Outlook.GetNamespace("MAPI")
6:
7:     Dim ContactFolder As MAPIFolder
8:     Set ContactFolder = NameSpace.GetDefaultFolder(olFolderContacts)
9:
10:    Dim I As Integer
11:
12:    For I = 1 To ContactFolder.Items.Count
13:      With ContactFolder.Items(I)
14:        If (InStr(1, .BusinessTelephoneNumber, "(313)") > 0) Then
```

LISTING 24.7   continued

```
15:        .BusinessTelephoneNumber = _
16:          Replace(.BusinessTelephoneNumber, "(313)", "(810)")
17:        .Save
18:      End If
19:    End With
20:  Next I
21: End Sub
```

ANALYSIS   Lines 1–8 acquire the `MAPIFolder` object for contacts. Line 10 introduces a loop control integer, `I`. The loop starts on line 12, and the `With` block on line 13 enables you to access members of the `Items` collection without repeating the `ContactFolder.Items(I)` prefix each time.

Members of the indexed `Items` object are indicated by the member-of operator (`.`) and by the fact that they are in the `With` block. (This is the first time you have seen the `With` keyword; refer to the note that follows for more information.) The `Instr` function is used to see whether the business telephone number contains the prefix; if it does, it is replaced with the new prefix (810) on line 16 using the `Replace` function defined in Access. Line 19 ends the `With` block, and line 20 ends the loop.

> I introduced the `With` keyword on line 13. The `With` keyword enables you to refer to an object in a block statement. By writing `With ContactFolder.Items(I)`, you eliminate the need to write that part of the statement each time. To indicate that a property or method is a member of the `With` item in the `Collection` object, you need to use the member-of operator. Lines 14, 15, and 16 demonstrate the `.BusinessTelephoneNumber` property.

Searching the Body of a Mail Item

Several folders contain `MailItem` objects. From Table 24.1, you know that `MailItem` objects are contained in the Outbox, Inbox, Sent Mail, Deleted Mail, and Drafts folders. `MailItem` objects contain sender, carbon copy, and recipient information as well as all the data in the body of the document. In this section, you will get an opportunity to manage mail-related folders.

There are several practical operations you may want to perform on MailItems. You might want to screen senders to filter junk mail. You can do that with code. You might want to use Outlook to send contacts an automated mailer. You can do that with code and

Outlook. The code in Listing 24.8 implements a search procedure and demonstrates how to use some of the capabilities of MailItem objects.

> The Body property contains the source text. Therefore, if the text is HTML, some of the source text might not appear when you are viewing the document.

LISTING 24.8   Searching a MailItem Object for Specific Data

```
 1:  Sub Test()
 2:     Dim Outlook As New Outlook.Application
 3:     Dim NameSpace As NameSpace
 4:     Set NameSpace = Outlook.GetNamespace("MAPI")
 5:     Dim DeletedItems As MAPIFolder
 6:     Set DeletedItems = NameSpace.GetDefaultFolder(olFolderDeletedItems)
 7:     Dim MailItem As MailItem
 8:
 9:     Dim I As Integer
10:
11:     Dim RefCount As Long
12:     Dim ItemRefCount As Long
13:     Dim Count As Long
14:
15:     RefCount = 0
16:     ItemRefCount = 0
17:
18:     For I = 1 To DeletedItems.Items.Count
19:
20:       If TypeOf DeletedItems.Items(I) Is MailItem Then
21:         Set MailItem = DeletedItems.Items(I)
22:         Count = CountWord("Microsoft", MailItem)
23:         If (Count > 0) Then
24:           ItemRefCount = ItemRefCount + 1
25:           RefCount = RefCount + Count
26:         End If
27:       End If
28:
29:     Next I
30:
31:     Debug.Print "Total Items: " & DeletedItems.Items.Count
32:     Debug.Print "Total References to Microsoft:" & RefCount
33:     Debug.Print "Percentage of Items Containing a Reference:" & _
34:       Round((ItemRefCount / DeletedItems.Items.Count) * 100, 2)
35:
36:  End Sub
37:
38:
```

24

LISTING 24.8   continued

```
39: Function CountWord(ByVal Word As String, ByRef MailItem _
40:    As MailItem) As Long
41:
42:    Dim P As Long
43:    P = 1
44:    Do While (1 = 1)
45:      P = InStr(P + 1, MailItem.Body, Word)
46:      If (P > 0) Then
47:        CountWord = CountWord + 1
48:      Else
49:        Exit Do
50:      End If
51:    Loop
52: End Function
```

ANALYSIS   The Test subroutine on lines 1–36 creates the Outlook object, gets a reference to the Deleted Items folder, and calls CountWord for each deleted item that is a MailItem object on line 22. The total number of deleted items, total number of references to Microsoft, and the ratio of deleted items containing Microsoft in the body is reported to the Immediate window. (On my PC, there are 912 items with 17 percent of those referring to Microsoft; time to compact my Outlook files.)

One thing you haven't seen before is the use of the TypeOf operator on line 22. TypeOf Object Is Class is used to dynamically determine whether a generic reference type is a specific type. Recall that collections can store data of any type. In Listing 24.8, we are sure that the DeletedItems.Items collection contains an Outlook folder object, but we only want to search MailItem objects. Using TypeOf DeletedItems.Items(I) Is MailItem allows us to examine each generic element of the Items collection to see whether it is a specific type, a MailItem. Only MailItem objects are processed; in the example, we do not want to process other deleted items such as NoteItem objects, which may be in the DeletedItems collection.

CountWord takes a Word and MailItem argument. The function on lines 39–52 uses a simple Do...While loop and the InStr function to count the occurrences of the word by searching the Body property (line 45). When no more occurrences are found, InStr returns 0 and the loop terminates.

Undeleting Mail Items

MAPIFolder items can be moved between folders. For example, you can archive mail items from the default Inbox to a new MAPIFolder object. An alternative example is that you can automatically undelete folders based on search criteria with the Move method.

Listing 24.9 demonstrates undeleting a `MailItem` object with the `Move` command, based on the sender's name.

LISTING 24.9   Creating an Undelete Behavior Using the `MAPIfolder` Object's Move Method

```
 1:  Sub TestUndelete()
 2:    Call UndeleteMailFrom("Tom Archer")
 3:  End Sub
 4:
 5:  Sub UndeleteMailFrom(ByVal SenderName As String)
 6:    Dim Outlook As New Outlook.Application
 7:    Dim Folder As MAPIFolder
 8:    Set Folder = _
 9:      Outlook.GetNamespace("MAPI").GetDefaultFolder(olFolderDeletedItems)
10:    Dim DeletedItem As Variant
11:
12:    For Each DeletedItem In Folder.Items
13:      If (TypeOf DeletedItem Is MailItem) Then
14:        If (DeletedItem.SenderName = SenderName) Then
15:          Call DeletedItem.Move( _
16:            GetNamespace("MAPI").GetDefaultFolder(olFolderInbox))
17:        End If
18:      End If
19:    Next
20:  End Sub
```

Don't be surprised if Outlook displays a dialog asking you to verify that you want another program—in the example, Access—to send mail on your behalf. This is part of the new security features in Outlook. Respond Yes to the message dialog to allow the VBA code to access the mailbox for a limited period of time.

If you are writing an Automation controller for Outlook, check with your administrator about turning the mail security features off.

ANALYSIS   Lines 1–3 test the `UndeleteMailFrom` subroutine. Lines 5–8 create an instance of Outlook and a `MAPIFolder` reference to `DeletedItems`. I used a `For Each` loop instead of a `For Next` loop on line 12, because when items are removed from a collection, `Count` is reduced. If you use an index when reducing `Count`, you will get an error because `Count` is reduced while in the loop. Using the `For Each` loop will avoid an out-of-bounds error. The `TypeOf` check on line 13 ensures that we are dealing with a `MailItem` item for each element, and the compare on line 14 tests `SenderName`. If `SenderName` is the value we are searching for, the `MAPIFolder` object's `Move` method moves the `MailItem` object to the Inbox folder.

You can use a For Next loop when iterating through a collection and removing elements. Simply write the loop to iterate from Count to 1 Step -1; that is, process the loop from the last element to the first. When you remove an element, the count will change, but the lower bound (1) is the controlling bound.

In Listing 24.9, a For Each loop was used because it saves the step of explicitly assigning the collection element to a temporary variable. (Refer to Hour 5, "Learning to Write Conditional Code," for more on writing conditional code and loops.)

As an alternative, you could pass in the name of the property to compare to, or you could use the StrComp function to compare the data case-sensitively or case-insensitively.

Sending Mail to Contacts Automatically

Automatic mail notification is a useful feature in many situations. One way I use this feature in an application is to send reminder notices for scheduled events. Instead of writing code to send mail in your applications, use Outlook to provide mail services. This can be an effective technique for small businesses that want to follow up on scheduled sales. Listing 24.10 demonstrates how easy this process is with Outlook.

I wouldn't recommend using automatic mail to send *spam*. Some Internet-savvy people have developed a special way of dealing with spam: They use a similar technique to flood your mail server with mail, usually resulting in your server crashing. Sending junk mail for the purposes of crashing a mail server is referred to as a denial-of-service attack.

New security features Outlook 2002 put speed bumps on VBA code that accesses your contacts or tries to send mail. A VBA application that reads your contacts list and mails everyone in your list the message and then repeats the process for each recipient is a kind of mail virus that has been cropping up in one form or another for a few years now.

LISTING 24.10   Using Outlook to Create an Automatic Mail Notification System, Sending Reminders to Qualified Customers

```
1:  Sub MailEveryone()
2:    Dim Outlook As New Outlook.Application
3:    Dim Folder As MAPIFolder
4:    Set Folder = _
5:      Outlook.GetNamespace("MAPI").GetDefaultFolder(olFolderContacts)
```

LISTING 24.10   continued

```
 6:    Dim Contact As Variant
 7:    Dim MailItem As MailItem
 8:    For Each Contact In Folder.Items
 9:      Set MailItem = Outlook.CreateItem(olMailItem)
10:      MailItem.To = Contact.Email1Adress
11:      MailItem.Subject = "Auto-notification test"
12:      MailItem.Body = "Auto-notification"
13:      MailItem.Send
14:    Next
15: End Sub
```

ANALYSIS   Listing 24.10 iterates through a list of contacts and sends each one an automatic mail notification. At a minimum, you need to create an `olMailItem`
object (line 9) and set the `MailItem.To` property. By iterating through the contacts
and using the `FullName` property for the `MailItem.To` property, you can send a blank
e-mail message (line 10). Adding subject content and a body, you get a complete mail
message. By assigning the contents of an HTML document, a data access page, or a
Word document, you can send detailed information automatically. Line 13 calls `Send`,
which sends the mail message using Outlook.

Summary

Congratulations! You have completed all 24 hours. You have gained insights and experience that would have taken considerably longer if you were hunting and pecking for
solutions.

In this hour, you got some insight into how powerful Access, VBA, and objects really
can be. In addition to being able to share data files between Microsoft Office applications, you can now share objects at the programming level. Outlook is a fully featured
application in its own right. It would be impossible to cover the entire Outlook object
model in one hour, so I elected to demonstrate several specific kinds of tasks.

If you need contact management in your applications, use Outlook instead of creating
tables from scratch. If you need mail capabilities in your business solutions, again,
Outlook is a practical choice.

After 24 hours, you know how to create and use objects. What it boils down to is that
whether you are using Access or Outlook objects, they are still just objects. Objects have
methods and properties; once you find out what the methods and properties of an object
are, you know how to use that object.

Thanks for taking the journey with me, and don't forget to complete the "Q&A" and
"Workshop" sections.

Q&A

Q Can I program VBA solutions in Outlook?

A Yes, definitely. Although that's not what this book is about, the same VBA that you use to program Access can be used to program Outlook, Word, Excel, PowerPoint, and FrontPage. You might want to get books that specifically cover programming in those tools because specific features will differ, and the object models will be different, too.

Q Can I create forms in Outlook?

A Yes, Outlook allows you to define a customized graphical user interface. Outlook has a rich development environment. This hour was designed to emphasize adding contact management and mail capabilities to Access applications.

Workshop

The Workshop includes quiz questions designed to help you test your understanding of the material covered and exercises to help put what you've learned into practice. You will find the answers to the quiz and exercises in Appendix A, "Answers."

Quiz

1. What is the name of the top-level object that provides you access to folders?
2. What is the name of the only (currently) available `NameSpace` type?
3. What is the type of all the folders that contain data?
4. What is the name of the method that allows you to relocate folder data?
5. What is the name of the object used to store mail data?

Exercises

1. Write a statement that creates a new `JournalItem` object.
2. Save the `JournalItem` object to Outlook.
3. Write code that displays the Journal browser/editor.

PART IX

Appendix

A   Answers

APPENDIX **A**

Hour 1

Quiz

1. What action does the More menu item perform?

   The More menu item displays additional menu items on each menu in Access 2002. Access only displays a subset of the total number of menu items available.

2. When you assign a hyperlink to an existing toolbar button or menu item, it circumvents the previously defined behavior for that button. True or false?

   True. The default behavior is overridden. It is probably best to create a new menu item or toolbar button for hyperlinked buttons and menu items.

3. The spelling checker will check spelling in SQL text and simple text data, such as abbreviations and non-words. True or false?

   False. The spelling checker checks only text data in fields and ignores non-word text data.

4. What is the name of the object that contains Procedure objects used for creating stored procedures?

   ActiveX Data Objects Extensions 2.7 for DDL and Security (ADOX).

5. Access 2002 contains wizards that will generate data-aware Web pages. True or false?

   True. The Data Pages Wizards will create an interface in a Web page that represents simple and complex database relationships, including connecting the Web controls to the database fields.

Exercises

1. Open the Online Meeting toolbar and anchor it to the top of the Access application.

   Click Tools, Customize.

   On the Toolbars tab, scroll down to the Online Meeting toolbar and click the toolbar item (making sure there is a check mark next to the option.)

   Click Close.

2. Add a new menu item to the main menu.

   Click Tools, Customize.

   On the Commands tab, scroll down to the New Menu item in the Categories column and drag the New Menu item from the Commands column to the end of the main menu bar.

3. Rename the menu, using the new name Contacts.

   With the Customize dialog open, right-click New Menu.

   In the pop-up menu, change the Name menu item to Contacts.

4. Add a command item containing a hyperlink to the publisher of this book (http://www.samspublishing.com).

   With the Customize dialog open, select the Commands tab.

   Find a menu item that is appropriate for what you want to do[md]in this case, you want to open a Web site. (I scrolled to Web in the Categories column.)

   Find a suitable Command item and drag and drop it to the new Contacts menu. (I used the Open command.)

   Change the name to &Open Sams Website.

   Assign a hyperlink from the pop-up menu (in this case, http://www.samspublishing.com) by right-clicking the Open Sams Web site command and clicking Assign Hyperlink: Open.

5. Establish a NetMeeting connection with another user on the Internet or your intranet.

   With Access 2002 open, click Tools, Online Collaboration, Meet Now.

Follow the steps in the wizard to set up NetMeeting for your computer.

After the connection is established, pick someone to connect to from the Find Someone dialog (the interface to the directory server).

If you do not have a microphone and speakers, choose Tools, Chat in NetMeeting to create a real-time chat session.

Hour 2

Quiz

1. Double

2. Numeric. The result is a floating-point number.

3. The ampersand (&) forces the concatenation of any data to a string. Plus (+) must have two string arguments to perform string concatenation.

4. Declaring variable introduces the name into the program. Initialziing a variable assigns the variable a value.

5. Const

Exercises

1. Dim D As Date : D = Date

2. Value * (1 + 0.05)

3. "You are " & 5 & " years old today!"

Hour 3

Quiz

1. Explicit variable declaration is when the variable is first introduced in code with a Dim statement. Implicit variable declaration is when a variable is introduced first without a Dim statement.

2. Add `Option Explicit` to the top of the module.

3. ReDim is used to change the number of elements in an array.

4. Global variables are defined outside of a function or subroutine at the top of a module.

5. A Variant data type can be assigned almost any value. Variants should not be widely used.

A

Exercises

1.

```
Const PI = 3.14159
Sub CalculateCircumference()
    Dim Circumference As Double, Radius As Double
' .. the other code minus the Const Pi statement
```

2.

```
Const PI = 3.14159

Sub CalculateCircumference()
    Dim Circumference As Double, Radius As Double
    Radius = 10
    Circumference = PI * Radius ^ 2
End Sub
```

3.

```
Dim MyDoubles(9) As Double
```

By default MyDoubles(0) is the first element and 9 would be the last, or tenth, element.

Hour 4

Quiz

1. What is one use of the + operator?

   Arithmetic

2. What are the four groups of operators?

   Arithmetic, Comparison, Logic, and Special Operators

3. What is the precedence order of operators?

   AddressOf, Arithmetic, Comparison, Logic

4. How do you redefine the natural precedence of operators?

   Group predicates with parentheses.

5. What group of operators has the highest precedence?

   Arithmetic operators have the highest precedence but the AddressOf oerator will be called first if it is present.

Exercises

1. Using the sample procedure `CalculateCircumference` from Hour 3 as a template for writing procedures, write a function that demonstrates all the possible tests of `True` and `False` with the `And` operator.

```
Sub TruthTable()
   Dim Test As Boolean
   Test = False And False
   Test = False And True
   Test = True And False
   Test = True And True
End Sub
```

2. In the Microsoft Visual Basic editor, use the Immediate window to evaluate the bitwise `Or` of the following number pairs: 2 or 3; 4 or 5; 6 or 7.

   <Task Only>

3. Use the Immediate window to calculate the remainder of the preceding number pairs.

   <Task Only>

Hour 5

Quiz

1. How would you define a loop to iterate through an array of 10 integers?

```
Dim I As Integer
For I = 1 To 10
Next I
```

2. If you wanted code in a loop to execute at least one time, which looping mechanism would you use?

   Either of the Do Loop While or Do Loop Until constructs would work.

3. How might you ensure that code in an `If` statement works correctly?

   Define a test for each branch of the `If` condition.

4. What is the `Exit For` statement used for?

   `Exit For` is used to branch out of a `For Next` statement.

5. What is a loop short circuit? Under what circumstances might you use one?

   Short circuiting a loop refers to branching out of a loop at any location other than the test condition. Use a short circuit when you cannot devise a test for the loop condition or more than one condition, one of which occurs in the middle of the loop, can create a program state requiring you to exit.

Exercises

1. Use the Microsoft Visual Basic Help system to look up the Switch function. Define a Switch statement to return a first name given a last name.

   Switch = (FirstName = "Paul", "Kimmel", FirstName = "Frank", "Arndt", FirstName = "Sharon", "Cox")

2. Use the Help system to look up the Iff function. Write a statement that demonstrates the use of the Iff function.

   Iff(Income > 50000, "Rich", "Not Rich")

3. Declare a collection object (you can write the code in the sample Fooo subroutine) and use the For Each construct to display each element of the collection in a message box.

```
Sub ForEachDemo()
  Dim C As New Collection
  Call C.Add("January")
  Call C.Add("February")

  Dim Elem As Variant

  For Each Elem In C
    MsgBox Elem
  Next Elem
```

Hour 6

Quiz

1. What besides a table can be used as a recordset?

   Queries can be used as recordsets.

2. How do you create a new module in Access?

   In the Objects list of the Database view select Modules and click the New button.

3. What are the steps for testing your code in a module?

   Open the Visual Basic Editor. Open the module you want to test. Place your cursor in the procedure you want to test and use the F8 key to step over each line of code. Ensure that branch statements like the if and else part of an if conditional are tested.

4. What does a catalog refer to?

   A catalog contains objects tables, views, users, and groups.

5. How can you position a recordset to the first record?

   Call the `Recordset.MoveFirst` method.

6. What kind of loop would you use to iterate through a defined number of items?

   A For Next loop exists for precisely this purpose.

Exercises

1. Modify the `CreateTable` code in Listing 6.2 to add address information to the CONTACTS table. Include the street address, city, state, and ZIP Code.

```
 1: Sub CreateTable()
 2:   Const DatabasePath =
 3:     "C:\Books\Sams\Teach Yourself Access 10 Programming in " + _
 4:     "24 Hours\Chapter 6\CONTACTS.mdb"
 5:   Const ProviderStr = _
 6:     "Provider=Microsoft.Jet.OLEDB.4.0;Data Source=" + DatabasePath
 7:   Dim Table As New Table
 8:   Dim Catalog As New ADOX.Catalog
 9:   Dim Key As New ADOX.Key
10:   Catalog.ActiveConnection = ProviderStr
11:   Table.Name = "CONTACTS"
12:   Table.ParentCatalog = Catalog
13:   Table.Columns.Append "ID", adInteger
14:   Table.Columns("ID").Properties("AutoIncrement") = True
15:   Table.Columns.Append "FIRST_NAME", adVarWChar, 20
16:   Table.Columns.Append "LAST_NAME", adVarWChar, 20
17:   Table.Columns.Append "PHONE_NUMBER", adVarWChar, 36
18:   Table.Columns.Append "EMAIL", adVarWChar, 50
19:   Table.Columns.Append "WWW", adVarWChar, 50
20:   Table.Columns.Append "ADDRESS", adVarWChar, 30
21:   Table.Columns.Append "CITY". adVarWChar, 20
22:   Table.Columns.Append "STATE", adVarWChar, 20
23:   Table.Columns.Append "ZIP", adVarWChar, 10
24:   Catalog.Tables.Append Table
25:   Key.Name = "ID"
26:   Key.Type = adKeyPrimary
27:   Key.Columns.Append "ID"
28:   Catalog.Tables("CONTACTS").Keys.Append Key, kyPrimary
29:   Set Catalog.ActiveConnection = Nothing
30: End Sub
```

   Lines 20 through 23 demonstrate the new code.

2. Define a query that displays all the columns in the CONTACTS table, ordered by the ZIP Code.

   The SQL Statement is "SELECT * FROM CONTACTS ORDER BY ZIP" (without the quotes).

A

3. Using Listing 6.5 as an example, use the query in exercise 2 to find a row by LAST_NAME and ZIP Code.

```
1:  Sub NewFindData()
2:
3:     Dim Connection As New ADODB.Connection
4:     Dim Catalog As New ADOX.Catalog
5:     Dim RecordSet As New ADODB.RecordSet
6:     Dim Field As Field
7:     Const DatabasePath = _
8:       "C:\Books\Sams\Teach Yourself Access 10 Programming in " & _
9:       "24 Hours \Chapter 6\CONTACTS.mdb"
10:
11:    Connection.Open "Provider=Microsoft.Jet.OLEDB.4.0;" & _
12:      "Data Source=" & DatabasePath
13:
14:    Set Catalog.ActiveConnection = Connection
15:
16:    Dim LastName As String
17:    Dim ZipCode As String
18:
19:    LastName = InputBox("Enter Last Name to Search for", "Last Name
➥Search String")
20:    ZipCode = InputBox("Enter Zip Code to Search for", "Zip Code Search
➥String")
21:
22:    Dim SQL As String
23:    SQL = "SELECT * FROM CONTACTS WHERE LAST_NAME = '" & _
24:      LastName & "' AND ZIP = '" & ZipCode & "'"
25:    RecordSet.Open SQL, Catalog.ActiveConnection, adOpenDynamic,
➥adLockOptimistic
26:
27:    MsgBox "Found: " & RecordSet("FIRST_NAME") & " " & 
➥RecordSet("LAST_NAME")
28:
29:    RecordSet.Close
30:    Set RecordSet = Nothing
31:    Set Catalog = Nothing
32:    Connection.Close
33:    Set Connection = Nothing
34:
35: End Sub
```

Hour 7

Quiz

1. To how many records does a recordset refer at one time?

   One

2. Which contains the `Tables` collection, a `Catalog` or a `Connection` object?

   Catalog

3. What objects does a `Catalog` object contain?

   Catalog contains tables, stored procedures, views, users, and groups.

4. What two kinds of services does a `Catalog` object offer?

   Catalogs manage schema information and database security.

5. What methods are available for iterating over each record in a table?

   MoveNExt, MoveFirst, MovePrevious, MoveLast, EOF, and BOF

Exercises

1. Create a query in your database. Open the query with code using the `Recordset` object.

   Dim RS As New ADODB.Recordset

   Rs.Open "LIBRARY Query", CurrentProject.Connection

2. Write code that iterates over every key in a `Catalog` object.

   Modify lines 5, 6, and 7 in Listing 7.5 to refer to the Keys collection as follows:

```
5:     For I = 0 To Catalog.Keys.Count - 1
6:         Debug.Print Catalog.Keys(I).Name
7:     Next I
```

3. Write code that begins at the end of a `Recordset` object and iterates over every record backward.

```
Sub QueryAll()
  Dim Rs As New ADODB.Recordset
  Rs.Open "LIBRARY Query" CurrentProject.Connection, adOpenKeySet
  Rs.MoveLast
  Do While( Rs.BOF = False )
    Rs.MovePrevious
  Loop
  Rs.Close
End Sub
```

Hour 8

Quiz

1. What is a good average length for a function?

   Subroutines and functions should be singular in nature and short in length. Generally a few lines (3 to 5) is best.

2. If you want to define a function with an Optional argument, in what position should the argument be placed between the parentheses?

All Optional arguments should be last after non-Optional arguments.

3. What would be one possible good name for a function that reads an e-mail address from a database?

Function ReadEmailAddress() As String

4. What is the name of the object that refers to the current, open database?

CurrentProject in ADODB.

5. What's the name of the application property containing many useful capabilities?

DoCmd contains many general kinds of capabilities.

Exercise

1. In the section "Defining Argument Types," you created a subroutine that calculates sales. Implement this subroutine as a function.

```
Function CalculateTotalSales(ByVal SaleAmount As Double, _
  ByVal SalesTax As Double ) As Double
  CalculateTotalSales = SaleAmount * (1 + SalesTax)
End Function
```

2. In the section "Creating a Table with Code," you created a table in a demo database. Write a function that deletes or drops a table.

```
Sub DropTable(ByVal TableName As String)
  Call DoCmd.DeleteObject(acTable, TableName)
End Sub
```

3. In the section "Importing a Comma-Delimited Text File," you imported a text file. Use the Access Help to rewrite the function to import an Excel spreadsheet.

Provide arguments for the following functional syntax:

DoCmd.TransferSpreadsheet [transfertype] [, spreadsheettype], tablename, filename[, hasfieldnames][, range]

Hour 9

Quiz

1. What command can I use to transfer data from an Excel spreadsheet?

TransferSpreadsheet

2. How is an import specification created?

By using the import wizard to import a file. Click the Advanced button, define the specification, then click Save As.

3. What command uses import specifications?

TransferText

4. What is the name of the object you can use to program macro commands in code?

DoCmd

5. Can commands such as DoCmd be used in other Office applications too?

Yes. You can use DoCmd in any application that supports VBA or that can use OLE Automation objects, such as Visual Basic or Delphi.

Exercise

1. Write a macro to back up all tables to a database.

```
Sub Backup(ByVal Table As TableDef)

    On Error Resume Next
    DoCmd.DeleteObject acTable, Table.Name & " Backup"
    DoCmd.CopyObject , Table.Name & " Backup", acTable, Table.Name

End Sub

Sub BackupAllTables()

    Dim I As Integer
    Dim Table As TableDef

    For Each Table In CurrentDb.TableDefs
        Call Backup(Table)
    Next

End Sub
```

2. Write code to get the input filename from a user for transferring text.

```
FileName = InputBox("Enter file name to import:, "Import File",
"default.txt")
```

3. Write the code equivalent of a backup macro that uses DeleteObject and CopyObject.

See the Backup subroutine in exercise 1.

A

Hour 10

Quiz

1. What is the function for finding a substring?

   ```
   Instr
   ```

2. What is the difference between a modal and modeless dialog?

   A modal dialog must be closed before any other forms can be used. Other forms may be used while a modeless dialog is open.

3. What is the statement for opening a text file for reading purposes?

   ```
   Open filename.ext for input as #handle
   ```

4. What function can you use to get input dynamically from a user?

   The InputBox function.

Exercises

1. Write a statement that formats a nine-digit postal code.

   ```
   Format( PostalCodeVar, "@@@@@-@@@@")
   ```

2. Write a subroutine to add a line of text to a named file. Pass the line of text and the filename to the subroutine.

   ```
   Sub WriteToFile(ByVal FileName As String, ByVal Text As String)
       Dim Handle As Double
       Handle = FreeFile
       Open FileName For Append As #Handle
       Print #Handle, Text
       Close #Handle
   End Sub
   ```

3. Write a subroutine that searches a binary file for a specific name. Use the email type and assume that more than one record exists.

   ```
   Sub FindByName(ByVal Name As String)

       Dim Handle As Double
       Handle = FreeFile

       On Error GoTo Finally
       Open "A:\10\test.bin" For Binary Access Read As #Handle

       Dim Mail As Email

       Do While Not EOF(Handle)
   ```

```
        Get #Handle, , Mail
        If (Mail.Name = Name) Then
            MsgBox "Found: " & Mail.Name & ", " & Mail.Email
            Exit Do
        End If
    Loop


Finally:
    Close #Handle

End Sub
```

Hour 11

Quiz

1. Can a user type contain an enumerated variable?

   Yes. User types defined with the keyword Type can contain nested types and enumerated types.

2. What is the difference between the uses for Type and Enum?

   Types are used to define and aggregation of many subtypes of data that describe a whole new data type. Enumerations are used to define a range of related, integral values.

3. Can types contain functions and procedures?

   No. However, you can define classes and classes can contain methods.

4. Can types contain constant members?

   No. User types cannot contain constant members.

5. Can types contain references to variables?

   Yes. A user type can contain object references, although this is not a common practice.

Exercises

1. Define a type that contains a name, address, and phone number.

```
Type Contact
  Name As String
  Address1 As String
  Address2 As String
  City As String
  State As String
  PostalCode As String
End Type
```

2. Define a user type that aggregates the user type in exercise 1. Why might you want to create a new type and not just modify the old type to include the new data?

```
Type WebContact
    Who As Contact
    Email As String
End Type
```

By extending contact through aggregation, existing code that used the old contact type would not have to be modified to accommodate the new piece of information—the email address.

3. Define an enumeration that describes flavors of ice creams.

```
Enum Flavors
    Vanilla
    Strawberry
    Chocolate
    ButterPecan
    Boisenberry
End Enum
```

Hour 12

Quiz

1. What is the name of the function that returns an array?

Array()

2. What function initializes the memory of an array to the data type's equivalent to null?

Erase

3. Does Erase perform exactly the same operation on all arrays?

No. It performs slightly different operations on different data types; for example, objects are set to nothing and a variant array is set to Empty.

4. How do you resize an array dynamically (that is, when your program is running)?

Use the ReDim command.

5. Which sort type is faster: Bubble, Selection, or Quick?

Generally, the Quick sort is faster comma unless the data is mostly sorted period. Then you might get better performance from a selection sort.

Exercises

1. Write the statement for a sort that tests string data.

```
If (StrComp(Data(I), Data(J)) > 0) Then
```

2. Modify the dump subroutine to write to an output file. Why is it better to use a function instead of writing code, such as the Dump code, directly where you need that behavior?

```
Sub Dump(ByVal Data() As Long)
  Dim Handle As Double
  Handle = FreeFile
  Open "dump.txt" For Output As #Handle
  Dim Elem As Variant
  For Each Elem in Data
    Print #Handle, Elem
  Next Elem
  Close #Handle
End Sub
```

3. Modify the Bubble sort to sort in descending order. (Hint: Listing 12.9 sorts in ascending order.)

```
Sub BubbleSort(ByRef Data() As Long)
  Dim I As Long, J As Long
    For I = LBound(Data) To UBound(Data) - 1
      For J = I + 1 To UBound(Data)
        If (Data(J) > Data(I)) Then
          Call Swap(Data, I, J)
        End If
      Next J
    Next I
End Sub
```

(Swap the J and I on the line that performs the comparison.)

Hour 13

Quiz

1. What is the difference between a method and a function or subroutine?

   Methods can be either function or subroutine, but the term method implies membership in a class.

2. What is the name of the method that appends items to a collection?

   Appending items to a collection is the default behavior of the Add method.

3. What effect does Nothing have on objects?

   Assigning an object variable, called a *reference*, to Nothing returns the memory allocated to the reference to the memory pool.

4. Do you have to remove items from a collection before assigning the collection variable to Nothing?

   No. Even if the references in the collection are objects themselves, the garbage collection built in to the VBA language will clean up memory.

A

5. What is one of two ways to iterate over the items in a collection?

Use either a `For...Each` or `for...Next` loop and the `Count` property.

Exercises

1. Create an instance of a collection and add 10 integers to it.
```
Sub AddTenIntegers()
  Dim Integers As New Collection
  Dim I As Integer
  For I = 1 To 10
    Call Integers.Add(Int(Rnd * 10))
  Next I
  Set Integers = Nothing
End Sub
```

2. Write a subroutine that writes all the collection items in exercise 1 to the Immediate window.

Add the following statement to the code in exercise 1.
```
For I = 1 To Integers.Count
  Debug.Print Integers.Item(I)
Next I
```

3. Modify the Bubble sort algorithm from Hour 12 to sort elements in a collection.
```
Sub Swap(ByVal ACollection As Collection, ByVal I As Integer, _
  ByVal J As Integer)
  Dim Temp As Integer
  Temp = ACollection(J)
  Call ACollection.Add(ACollection(I), , J)
  Call ACollection.Remove(J + 1)
  Call ACollection.Add(Temp, , I)
  Call ACollection.Remove(I + 1)
End Sub

Sub BubbleSortCollection(ByVal Integers As Collection)
  Dim I As Integer, J As Integer
  For I = 1 To Integers.Count - 1
    For J = I + 1 To Integers.Count
      If (Integers(I) > Integers(J)) Then
        Call Swap(Integers, I, J)
      End If
    Next J
  Next I
End Sub
```

The sort is basically the same as that for an array. However, you will have to write the swap differently based on the data type of the data you store in the collection. (In this solution I used `Add` and `Remove` to implement the `Swap`.)

Hour 14

Quiz

1. What is a good way to derive procedure names?

   Use a verb and noun pair that describes the action the procedure implements and what it acts upon.

2. What is one benefit of code reuse?

   Existing code has already been tested.

3. Hungarian notation refers to a prefix notation based on the abbreviation of variable types. True or false?

   True.

4. *Procedure* is a generic term for both functions and subroutines. True or false?

   True.

5. What is a good generalization to describe the amount of code contained in a procedure?

   Stated as a rule, add just enough code to a procedure to implement the behavior described by the procedure name.

Exercises

1. Define a name for a function that sums a principal and interest amount.

   `SumPrincipalAndInterest`

2. Define names for function pairs that close a file, verifying that the handle is greater than zero.

   `CloseFile` and `DoCloseFile`

3. Define a name for data that stores a file handle, calculates the interest amount (given the principal and interest rate), and stores a constant for a bad file handle.

   `FileHandle`, `GetInterestAmount` (one possible choice), and `BAD_FILE_HANDLE`.

Hour 15

Quiz

1. To what does the term *provider* equate?

   A provider is roughly equivalent to a data source. A provider can be streamed recordsets, too.

A

2. What clause filters data in a SQL query?

   The WHERE clause filters the resultset.

3. What property limits the data available in a recordset?

   The Filter property of a recordset performs an operation equivalent to the WHERE clause in SQL.

4. What is the name of the property that contains the data in a field? To what object does it belong?

   The Value property contains field data. The Value property belongs to a Field object.

5. What is the name of the collection in a recordset that holds the data?

   Fields.

Exercises

1. Modify the query in Listing 15.6 to order the query in ascending order by SearchFieldName. (Hint: Use the ORDER BY clause).

   SQL = "SELECT * FROM MUSIC WHERE " & SearchFieldName & "='" & FindValue & "' ORDER BY " & SearchFieldName

2. Explain how you might make the code in Listing 15.7 more generic—that is, more generally useful.

   A good way is to pass the collection as an argument to the function. This makes the code useful for copying to any collection.

3. Demonstrate how you could associate the elements in an arbitrary collection to the rows in the recordset. (Hint: Use the Key property inherent in collections.)

   When you add the item to the collection, add the Primary Index (a unique value) as the key parameter as follows:

   Call Target.Add(Recordset("ARTIST").Value, Str(Recordset("ID").Value))

   The key argument has to be a string; remember to convert it to a string when storing the key and convert it back to a long integer when using it to find the original record.

Hour 16

Quiz

1. What is a subquery?

   A *subquery* is a query that provides a value for a predicate in a WHERE clause—it's a query within a query.

2. What does the `ALL` keyword do in a `UNION` statement?

   The `ALL` keyword in a `UNION` statement returns redundant data. The default is that redundant data is dropped from a `UNION` result set.

3. Can you use a nested subquery in a `DELETE` query? If so, why might you?

   Yes, in the `WHERE` clause. You might use a nested subquery in a `DELETE` query to refine the data deleted based on data that might exist in a second table.

4. Are stored procedures limited to `SELECT` statements?

   No. Any SQL you can write can be written as a stored procedure. However, not all databases or database drivers support stored procedures.

Exercises

1. Write a `WHERE` clause containing an `IN` predicate that returns all Elektra and Empire music publishers

   ```
   WHERE PUBLISHER IN ("Elektra", "Empire")
   ```

2. Modify the update query in Listing 16.6, line 2, to capitalize the first letter of the first and last name data in the MUSIC table.

   ```
   UPDATE MUSIC SET FIRST_NAME = ICap([FIRST_NAME]), LAST_NAME =
   ICap(LAST_NAME);
   ```

3. Write the text of a stored procedure that would delete a specific artist from your music collection.

   ```
   PARAMETER [THE_ARTIST] Text; DELETE FROM MUSIC WHERE ARTIST = [THE_ARTIST]
   ```

Hour 17

Quiz

1. What is the name of the object that contains basic debugging capabilities?

   `Debug`

2. What two methods does the object from question 1 offer in support of debugging?

   `Print` and `Assert`

3. What is a good security use for tracing?

   Code auditing

4. Should debug code be removed with the editor or the compiler before you ship your program?

   Always use the compiler, leaving the code in place for debugging revisions and new code.

Exercises

1. Implement a function that returns `True` or `False` based on whether a file exists.

```
Sub FileExists( ByVal FileName As String ) As Boolean
        FileExists = Len(Dir(FileName)) > 0
End Sub
```

2. Create a scaffold to test the implementation of the function you write in exercise 1.

```
Sub ScaffoldFileExists()
        MsgBox FileExists("C:\AUTOEXEC.BAT")
        MsgBox FileExists( 123 )
        MsgBox( "" )
End Sub
```

3. Write a version of `Trace` that writes output to a text file.

```
Private Function GetTraceOutput(ByVal FileName As String,
➡ByVal TraceMessage As String, ByVal TraceNumber As Long) As String
    GetTraceOutput = "Traced: " & FileName & "(" & TraceNumber & ") on " &
➡Now & vbCrLf & _
        TraceMessage & vbCrLf
End Function
Private Sub DoTraceFile(ByVal FileName As String,
➡ByVal TraceMessage As String, ByVal TraceNumber As Long)
    Dim Handle As Double
    Handle = FreeFile
    On Error GoTo FINALLY
    Open FileName & ".log" For Append As #Handle
    Print #Handle, GetTraceOutput(FileName, TraceMessage, TraceNumber)
FINALLY:
    Close #Handle
End Sub
Sub TraceFile(ByVal FileName As String, ByVal TraceMessage As String,
➡ByVal TraceNumber As Long)
    #If DebuggingOn Then
        Call DoTraceFile(FileName, TraceMessage, TraceNumber)
    #End If
End Sub
Sub TestTraceFile()
    Call TraceFile("Module1", "Test", 1)
End Sub
```

This code contains a complete implementation, including a scaffold. (Notice that I moved the output-formatting function to a separate function. This way, it is easy to ensure that `DoTrace` and `DoTraceFile` write identical output.)

Hour 18

Quiz

1. What two arguments must you provide to associate Help information with an error?

   HelpContext and HelpFile.

2. What is the name of the object that sends output to the Immediate window while you're testing your code?

   The Debug object, with the Print method.

3. What is the difference between a resource-protection block and error-handling block?

   A error-handling block is run only when an error occurs. A resource-protection block is always run.

4. Can you raise errors? If so, when should you do so?

   Yes. You should raise errors when an error condition occurs in your functions or subroutines. This is preferable to returning an arbitrary error code as the function's return value.

Exercises

1. Write a resource-protection block to setting a Recordset variable, Rs, to Nothing.

```
FINALLY
Set Rs = Nothing
End Sub (Or End Function)
```

2. Write code for Listing 18.3 that prompts the user to delete a file set to read-only.

```
Sub DeleteFile(ByVal FileName As String)
  On Error GoTo Except
  Kill FileName
  Exit Sub

Except:
  Const FILE_NOT_FOUND = 53
  Const ACCESS_ERROR = 75

  Select Case Err.Number
  Case FILE_NOT_FOUND:
    If (MsgBox(Err.Description & "(" & FileName & ") try again?", _
      vbRetryCancel) = vbRetry) Then
      FileName = InputBox("Enter file path:", "File Name", "")

      If (FileExists(FileName)) Then Resume
    End If
```

A

```
Case ACCESS_ERROR:
  If (MsgBox(Err.Description & "(" & FileName & ") delete anyway?", _
     vbYesNo) = vbYes) Then
     Call SetAttr(FileName, vbNormal)

     Resume
  End If

Case Else
  Call RaiseError(Err)
End Select

End Sub
```

The code uses a Case statement, which is neater for multiple conditions. To avoid making the code more confusing, the error-handling code was left in the DeleteFile subroutine. As a rule, move the actual error-handling code into a separate procedure. For example, you could make the error-handling block a separate procedure and then make each case a separate procedure. Continuing the example, you might add HandleError, RetryDelete, and ChangeAttribute. Once you have adjusted the response, you can retry the DeleteFile procedure.

3. Write a line of code that handles a case where a file does not exist. The line of code should raise a user error with error number 100 from Module1.

```
Call Err.Raise( vbObjectError + 100, "Module1", "File not found")
```

Hour 19

Quiz

1. What is object-oriented term used to describe data belonging to a class?

   Property.

2. Methods require an object prefix. True or false?

   True.

3. What are events?

   Events are properties that keep track of procedures. The procedures are referred to as event handlers. The code in the event handlers defines the response behavior to a particular event.

4. What are event handlers?

   Event handlers are procedures that handle events.

5. How do you add controls to a form?

   Click View, Toolbox and select the control you want to add to your form. Paint the control on the form and modify its properties to suit your needs.

Exercises

1. Create a relationship between the MUSIC and TRACKS tables from Hour 15 in Access 2002.

    1. Open the MUSIC database.

    2. Click Tools, Relationships.

    3. Add both the MUSIC and TRACKS tables to the Relationships View.

    4. Close the Table dialog.

    5. Click the ID field from MUSIC and drag and drop it onto the TRACKS table's MUSIC_ID field. A line connecting the two tables at those fields will be drawn.

    6. You have created a join relationship. To modify the join, right-click the line and click Edit Relationships from the context menu.

2. Use the new relationship to define a master detail form from the wizard.

    1. Click the Objects View, Forms, New button.

    2. Select the Form Wizard and the MUSIC table.

    3. In step 1 of the wizard, add all the fields from the MUSIC table.

    4. Also in step 1, select the TRACKS table and add all the fields from it.

    5. Click Finish.

    6. Save the form as MAIN with the File, Save As menu.

3. Save the new master detail form. Modify the startup properties so that the new master detail form is the startup form.

    1. Click Tools, Startup.

    2. In the Display Form/Page combo box, select the name of the new form, MAIN.

    3. Click OK.

Hour 20

Quiz

1. What is the Hypertext Markup Language used for?

    The Hypertext Markup Language (HTML) was the first language for programming Web pages.

2. Name one other language used to program Web pages.

    JavaScript or VBScript.

3. What is a URL used for?

    URL, or *Uniform Resource Locator*, is the term used to refer to an internetworking path.

4. If you want to create a Web site for your employees only, do you want to create an intranet site or an Internet site?

More than likely you want to create an intranet site.

5. You can use the same tables and queries for Data Access Pages as you do for your forms. True or false?

True. The same queries and tables can be used for Data Access Pages as those for forms.

6. What does it mean to bind a control to a field?

You are specifying a control source that is the field name indicating where the control's data comes from.

Exercises

1. Apply a theme to the Employee Directory. (Use any theme you like.)

Click Format, Theme. Choose an available theme and click OK.

2. Add Department ID as the first control on the Employee Directory.

Click View, Toolbox. Paint a TextBox control onto the page, moving the other controls down to make room. Open the Properties dialog and set the control source to DEPARTMENT_ID. Change the label to read Department ID.

3. Change the background color of the Department ID text box to visually indicate that it is read-only.

On the Format tab of the Properties dialog (with the Department ID text box selected), change the BackgroundColor property to silver.

4. Modify the Tab Index property of the Department ID control, ensuring that when a user tabs through the controls, the Department ID control is first.

The Tab Index property is on the Other tab in the Properties dialog. Enter a digit to indicate the tab order for the selected control. Department ID is 1, Department Name is 2, and so on.

Hour 21

Quiz

1. Type is to variable as class is to what?

Object

2. A class can have data that is not a property. True or false?

True. A general rule of object-oriented programming is to make all data Private and use properties to provide access to only the data you want consumers to modify.

3. What is the generic term that means a *class subroutine* or *function*?

Method.

4. What are the steps to create a new class module?

Open the VBA editor and click Insert, Class Module.

5. What is the keyword used to describe the read property method? What is the keyword for a write property method?

Get is used for reading, Let is used for writing simple types, and Set is used for write object types.

Exercises

1. Define a class that contains name and phone number properties.

Insert a class module into a database and add the following code:

```
Private FName As String
Private FPhoneNumber As String
Property Get PhoneNumber() As String
    PhoneNumber = FPhoneNumber
End Property
Property Let PhoneNumber( ByVal Value As String )
    FPhoneNumber = Value
End Property
Property Get Name() As String
    Name = FName
End Property
Property Let Name( ByVal Value As String )
    FName = Value
End Property
```

2. Copy the FileStream class. Write a test procedure that writes a line of code to a text file, reposition the cursor at the beginning of the file, and read the same amount of text that you wrote, verifying that that class works.

```
Sub TestFileStream()
    Const TEXT = "This is a test"
    Dim Stream As New FileStream
    Call Stream.OpenStream("Test.txt")
    Call Stream.WriteStream(TEXT)
    Stream.Position = Stream.Position - Len(TEXT)
    Dim V As String
    Call Stream.ReadStream(V, Len(TEXT))
    MsgBox V
    Call Stream.CloseStream
    Set Stream = Nothing
End Sub
```

A

3. Use `Scripting.FileSystemObject` to read from the text file you created in exercise 2.

   Add the Microsoft Scripting Runtime Library. The following code works:

```
Sub TestScriptingObject()
    Dim FileSystemObject As New Scripting.FileSystemObject
    Dim File As Scripting.TextStream
    Set File = FileSystemObject.OpenTextFile("Test.txt", ForReading, True)
    MsgBox File.ReadLine
    File.Close
    Set File = Nothing
    Set FileSystemObject = Nothing
End Sub
```

Hour 22

Quiz

1. What is a benefit of aggregation?

   You can implement new code by using existing code.

2. When designing a class, how many public methods and properties should you try to limit the class to?

   A class should most likely have fewer than a dozen public methods and properties. Too many members will make the class prohibitively hard to use and make it less likely that the class can be reused in other classes.

3. What does it mean to evolve classes incrementally?

   Additions and subtractions of members to and from the class change it slowly, as more about the class is understood.

4. How can you determine the members that comprise the public interface of a class?

   They will be preceded with the keyword `Public`.

5. What are the two class methods that are called when an object is created and when it is destroyed?

   `Class_Initialize` and `Class_Terminate`, respectively.

Exercises

1. Add a `Text` property to the `Strings` class that returns all the indexed string elements as one string, separating each string by a `vbNewLine` character.

```
Public Property Get Text() As String
    Dim I As Integer
    For I = 1 To FStrings.Count
        Text = Text & FStrings(I) & vbNewLine
    Next I
End Property
```

2. Add a Text Let property that assigns a single string, separated by vbNewLine characters, to several elements in the Strings class.

```
Public Property Let Text(ByVal Value As String)
    Clear
    Call ParseStrings(Value)
End Property
```

3. Modify the ReadFromFile and WriteToFile methods to use the Text property.

```
Public Sub ReadFromFile(ByVal FileName As String)
    Clear
    Dim F As New FileStream
    Call F.OpenStream(FileName)
    Dim S As String
    Call F.ReadStream(S, F.Count)
    Text = S
    Call F.CloseStream
    Set F = Nothing
End Sub

Public Sub WriteToFile(ByVal FileName As String)
    Dim F As New FileStream
    Call F.OpenStream(FileName)
    Call F.WriteStream(Text)
    Call F.CloseStream
    Set F = Nothing
End Sub
```

Hour 23

Quiz

1. Why do Access database add-ins have .mda extensions?

   This is a convention to distinguish them from regular, non-add-in databases.

2. What is the name of the table that you need to create for database add-ins?

   USysRegInfo

3. You can define property procedures in nonclass modules. True or false?

   True

4. You can use access specifiers (public and private) to encapsulate some of the implementation details of nonclass modules. True or false?

   True

5. What does |ACCDIR refer to?

   It refers to the Access AddIns directory. For example, if you install Windows in the default directory, the AddIns path is C:\Windows\Application Data\Microsoft\AddIns.

Exercises

1. Define a statement that checks whether the LOG table exists and calls the
   CreateTable procedure if it doesn't.

   ```
   If( TableExists("LOG") = False ) Then
      Call CreateTable(LOG_QUERY)
   End If
   ```

2. Write a statement that tests the WriteEntry procedure.

   ```
   Call WriteEntry(0, "Module", "Test", Helpfile.hlp", 0, "admin")
   ```

3. Create a blank database. Add a reference to the Log.mda database and trace it
   through the WriteEntry procedure. Does the call create the LOG table?

   Yes. Line 20 of Listing 23.3 will call the CreateTable method.

Hour 24

Quiz

1. What is the name of the top-level object that provides you access to folders?

   ```
   NameSpace
   ```

2. What is the name of the only (currently) available NameSpace type?

   ```
   MAPI
   ```

3. What is the type of all the folders that contain data?

   ```
   MAPIFolder
   ```

4. What is the name of the method that allows you to relocate folder data?

   ```
   Move
   ```

5. What is the name of the object used to store mail data?

   ```
   MailItem
   ```

Exercises

1. Write a statement that creates a new JournalItem object.

   ```
   Dim Journal As JournalItem
   Set Journal = Outlook.CreateItem(olJournalItem)
   ```

2. Save the JournalItem object to Outlook.

   ```
   Journal.Save
   ```

3. Write code that displays the Journal browser/editor.

   ```
   Journal.Display
   ```

INDEX